G. Gunby Jordan
Columbus, Georgia

The Money Crowd

The
Money Crowd

by DANA L. THOMAS

G. P. Putnam's Sons, New York

TO MELBA AND PETER
with love and admiration

Contents

7

8 / Contents

The Money Crowd

Preface

This work deals with a select group of men and women who are members of what may loosely be called the international Money Crowd—the inheritors of huge global fortunes amassed over many generations together with self-made multimillionaires who have accumulated their wealth since World War II. It describes what they are doing to protect and multiply their capital in a world shaken by economic uncertainty and the impact of a rapidly escalating technology, one undergoing convulsive changes in moral and social values, caught in a relentless inflation that is dangerously debasing the currency and threatening to turn the worth of all material possessions topsy-turvy.

Much of the material in this book is the result of the author's own experiences during his sixteen years as a financial journalist in the course of which he has met a number of the people he writes about and has had personal knowledge of many of the events he describes. In addition to the stories of success, there are many examples of misjudgment, miscalculation and folly. The mistakes, as well as the achievements, are magnified beyond the scale of the ordinary, since they have taken place in a larger arena.

Thanks to a substantial rise in living standards in the industrialized Western world and the emergence of an increasing number of people into a condition of material well-being, the conservation of capital has for the first time become a major concern not only of a handful of the Very Rich but of the masses of middle and lower middle classes. But the irony is that amidst the unprecedented redistribution of wealth, the recipi-

11

ents of this largess are threatened with being cheated of its substance. Government economists and politicians, while they have been successful so far in preventing a major 1930's-style depression, have not yet learned how to control a runaway inflation with consequences that may yet become painfully apparent to us all.

Keynesian economists will perhaps look askance at the author's emphasis on the deteriorating worth of money. In today's era of sophisticated debt financing, the currency managers are displaying a most uncanny mastery of the old shell game. If the author presumes to point a skeptical finger at the shell and inquire whether there is really anything under it, that is because the history of managed money up to now has been a dreary one of blunders, crookedness and catastrophe. While the government's policies affect everyone's pocketbook, on no subject is the citizenry more poorly informed or, to put it more accurately, more deliberately misinformed.

This book makes no attempt to undertake a comprehensive discussion of all the intricacies of the subject. But in surveying the strategy the Money Crowd is employing to protect its wealth from the depredations of an eroding currency, the author trusts he has placed the issue in a perspective to which those below the ranks of the wealthy can also relate, since inflation threatens them even more severely. He hopes the reader is persuaded that the problem of controlling inflation is far too serious to be left to the judgment of the politicians, any more than the waging of war should be left solely to the generals. An informed citizenry whose life savings are at stake must be continually on the alert to protect itself against the irresponsibility of those politicians whose chief occupation is to buy votes—with cheap money.

The author is indebted to a number of people who have made this book possible. A bibliography indicates the more noteworthy sources. Special mention must be made of William Targ, editor in chief of Putnam's, who first suggested this book and who has been a most invaluable adviser and friend, and also my wife, Melba, who aided so industriously in the editing of the manuscript.

DANA L. THOMAS

New York City, 1972

Part I

THE BACKGROUND

Knowledge makes one laugh, but wealth makes one dance.

—G. Herbert

1

The First Families: Dynastic Wealth from Banking to Brothels

"Beauty," observed a philosopher, "is potent, but wealth is omnipotent." Throughout the ages money has served as the power behind the throne of emperors, the subsidizer of military heroes and victorious armies, the salvation of artists, composers and dowagers. But for all its seminal role, historians surprisingly have had relatively little to say about money per se. Countless volumes have trumpeted the exploits of kings, generals, diplomats dangling on the strings of financial handouts. But the history of money, its evolution and growth, its twists and turns, its advances and setbacks, its convolutions of prosperity and collapse, awaits the pen of a modern Gibbon or Taine to do it full justice.

Money, like war and philosophy, has its own brand of heroes —the regal manipulators of the tools of credit, the *Übermenschen* grown abnormally wealthy through their ability to stake out a claim to a strategic natural resource, capture the monopoly of a universally needed commodity, ferret out the critical fulcrum of a financial deal and leverage their assets into tomorrow.

Volumes could be written about this untouted hagiology— about Jacob Fugger, the first modern banker and wealthiest man of the Middle Ages, who launched history's first consortium capitalized along the lines of modern finance to extract copper and silver from the mines of Hungary; of Ouvrard, the French minister who financed Napoleon's military campaigns by coming up with a scheme for grabbing gold from the mines of Mexico and smuggling it through the British naval blockade into France; of the nineteenth-century British textile barons, the first businessmen to be referred to as captains of industry, a phrase coined by Thomas Carlyle in 1843; of the imperialist Sir William Lever, who in 1911 signed a private treaty with a sovereign government, Belgium, to obtain valuable mining concessions in the Congo; of the astute Jewish merchant-bankers of Frankfurt who virtually single-handedly developed the concepts of modern investment finance.

Even more fascinating than the personalities of these money accumulators is the story of the currency they and all of us deal in, how it evolved and grew, what it means in psychological as well as materialistic terms. For the behavior of man throughout history has been to a large extent influenced by the behavior of his money, and the histology of one is linked to the other.

This book deals with a segment of that story—the present. It is rooted in the assumption that money acts as if it has a life force of its own, a biological drive, if you will, that causes it to grow, prosper and deteriorate precisely like all other forms of existence on this planet and that the men and women discussed in these pages are controlled in their behavior by a realization, either consciously or subsconsciously, of this eerie dynamism. It is the rise and fall of money, its inflation, deflation and collapse —indeed, its inevitable *mortal instability*—that we use as the framework of our story.

Because capital—large quantities of it—is the gateway to the accumulation of even more capital, it is not surprising that the big money today in America and elsewhere is, by and large, old, mellowed money, husbanded through generations of tender loving care.

Despite all the brouhaha about the chance the United States, especially, provides for becoming a multimillionaire on a shoestring, statistics demonstrate that the overwhelming bulk of America's riches is in the hands of the inheritors of fortunes amassed in the halcyon days prior to the New Deal and high taxes—when capitalism was freewheeling and completely uninhibited.

Today's SuperRich, for the most part, are members of the first families of wealth, with money derived from the formation of railroad empires, real-estate dynasties—from retailing and banking and manufacturing all stemming from the nineteenth century or earlier.

However, while family wealth is on the increase, paradoxically the influence of dynastic families on the management of industry and finance has been diminishing sharply.

As recently as twenty-five years ago one could point to a healthy number of blue-chip corporations run by the offspring of those who launched them. But today major corporations handed down from father to son are becoming as rare as the buggy whip. True, the grandson of old Henry is still guiding the helm at Ford, Bob Sarnoff, the son of the founder, is chairman of RCA, Edgar Kaiser, the offspring of the flamboyant Henry, rules the roost at Kaiser Industries and Edgar Bronfman is carrying on at Distiller's Corp.-Seagram's which his father, Sam, founded. The newspaper industry is still liberally larded with family ownership. But most of the major family fiefs have vanished. Outside management has taken over at DuPont, the big steel producers and the auto industry (with the exception of Ford). Harvard Business School graduates and their brethren in and out of the Ivy League have moved en masse into the executive suites of the financial, capital goods and service industries. Some businesses still functioning as an arena for family ambitions have turned into bitter battlegrounds between the father-founder and his heir apparent. "Unconsciously," points out Harry Levinson, Harvard Business School professor, "the father does not want his son to win, take away his combination baby and mistress, and displace him from his summit position. . . . The son resents being kept in an infantile role, always the little boy in his father's eyes—with the accompanying contempt, condescension and lack of confidence that . . . frequently characterizes the father's attitude."

Two particularly bitter quarrels with conceivably Freudian overtones have broken into the open recently. One involved Twentieth Century-Fox, where Darryl F. Zanuck, the sixty-eight-year-old chairman, became embroiled with his forty-two-year-old son, Richard, who was appointed to the presidency of the moviemaker in 1969 on a contract that had five years to run at $300,000 a year. When a series of costly picture flops thrust Fox into the red to the tune of $25,000,000 in 1969, followed by a whopping $77,000,000 loss in 1970, a committee was appointed to analyze the problem, and it urged that son Richard be fired.

The father reluctantly yielded. At a highly emotional board meeting in December, 1970, Richard stormed out of the room and resigned. He and his mother, Virginia, who had separated from the senior Zanuck after a marital dispute, joined a group of insurgent shareholders who launched a proxy battle to unseat the old man and his associates. The day after announcing that he and his mother had joined the dissidents, a story broke in the press that an attorney for the embattled Fox management tried to induce Richard to swing his support to his father's side by offering an immediate $1,000,000 settlement of his contract which, as noted, still had five years to run. Commenting on the story, Richard retorted, "I couldn't live with myself if I went along with their offer, inasmuch as I sincerely felt the insurgent slate offered a better hope for the future of the company."

The senior Zanuck fought off the attack, resigned as chairman, but held on as director. Son Richard wasn't exactly consigned to skid row. He found employment as senior vice-president of Warner Brothers at a handsome salary. During the annual meeting which took place at the height of the quarrel, one Fox shareholder took the floor and summed up matters tartly. He recommended that Fox make a motion picture of the Zanuck family employing the theme of "father against son for the love of the mother—and call it Oedipus Rex." Subsequently, Richard filed a $14,000,000 suit against his father and the film company.

Another father-son imbroglio that has raised eyebrows involves Midas International, a manufacturer of automotive parts including the well-known Midas muffler. Nate Sherman, the seventy-two-year-old chairman, had for years been at loggerheads with his son, Gordon, the president, over the course the company should take.

In the fall of 1970 the father forced Gordon out of the presidency and the son, joined by his mother and his two sisters, launched a proxy fight to oust Nate Sherman from the business. Bitter charges and countercharges were hurled via some sizzling proxy material. Gordon accused his father of having driven highly valuable executives from the firm and alienating most of the key people. The father denied this and warned he would "act vigorously" to defeat his son and "protect the best interest of the company and the stockholders." The company meeting at which the proxies were voted was tense. The father turned down his son's request to address the stockholders. While Sherman senior presided over the meeting, junior, flanked by his mother and two sisters, sat with the insurgent block out to get the old man. As in the Zanuck case, the father retained control. Afterward he told the press he would not receive his son back into the firm under any conditions. "He has chosen his course and I have chosen mine."

In short, there are often strains to a father-son relationship.

And yet there are even more powerful forces at work keeping the family in tandem. Throughout the history of the accumulation of great fortunes the instinct of the clan to protect and perpetuate its holdings has been far stronger than the rifts that periodically develop within it. The monied tribe from the genesis of free private enterprise has acquired great adroitness in protecting its holdings. It has been an industrious student of a lesson those with much less to protect never seem able to learn.

This lesson is illustrated by the Irish playwright Lady Gregory, who once wrote how a famished farmer during a severe famine in Ireland was left with a supply of only forty-four potatoes. He figured he would be getting a new supply in forty-five days and that by going without eating the first day he would have a potato a day to tide him over; but he made a minor miscalculation. That first day he died of hunger. The strategy of the Money Crowd has been to make certain it and its descendants will enjoy an ample share of potatoes—and caviar—come what may.

The rich have developed an artful strategy to keep their wealth from dissipating over generations of social change. Although United States law prohibits the outright entailment of large estates through the instrument of primogeniture—that is, passing the estate intact to the oldest son—the wealthy have been able to circumvent this through astute devices. The old Boston families have been especially successful in transmitting their fortunes through trusts that in some cases are untouched for three or more generations, allowing the founder to exercise his command for a century after his death.

The grip of the founder on his money has been perpetuated not only in Boston but elsewhere. When William Rockefeller, John D., Sr.'s brother, died in 1922 in his eighties, he left almost $200,000,000 via the largest will to be probated in the United States up to that time. It was entailed through trusts to remain intact through the fourth generation. Both the Thomas Fortune Ryan and Payne Whitney estates, amounting to $135,000,000 and $178,000,000 respectively, were entailed through the third generation.

The campaign to keep one's assets intact has taken on an increased urgency in recent years thanks to the deterioration of the American dollar. One aging inheritor summed it up this way: "In the good old days they passed money from generation to generation like a good after-dinner liqueur. Now, it's more like a hot potato. A lot of people have it, sure, in oil and in stocks, and in tankers and Black Angus. . . . But it's not the uncommon denominator it once was." Today a man would need several billion dollars to buy the goods and services William Vanderbilt obtained for a mere $100,000,000.

Faced with today's steep taxes, inheritors have been keeping their lawyers hopping to conjure up new ways to keep what they have. Remarks Ferdinand Lundberg in *The Rich and the Super Rich*, "One of the surer ways of spotting truly big wealth is that it shows itself in huge public transfers of assets during the lifetime of the owner. . . . Many of the rich . . . die stripped of assets." According to currently accepted doctrine, the man of wealth hands over as a gift to family members during his lifetime at minimum tax rates his assets which are often substantially underappraised, consisting of undeveloped lands, mineral resources and highly depreciated real estate.

Experts have studied with fascination the transference of the Rockefeller fortune from John D., Sr., to his heirs, noting that John D. died a relatively poor man. The probate of his will revealed that he had in his possession only $25,000,000, half of which went to state and federal tax agents. Before his death he had transferred the major portion of his huge fortune to his son and various foundations. Similarly, by the time John D., Jr., died in 1960 half of his fortune had been left to his wife. (In 1948 Congress had conveniently amended the law to provide that half of an estate inherited by a widow would henceforth be exempt from taxes.) The other half was left, in the good old Rockefeller tradition, to family foundations. As a result Rockefeller senior and junior paid a piddling inheritance tax.

An even more intriguing example of synthetic impoverishment is Henry Ford. Indeed, the Ford heirs would be even wealthier than they are today if Henry, Sr., who lived to be an octogenarian, had been a little more foresighted. Holding onto the direction of the auto business virtually until his death, he refused to make the normal preparations engaged in by the prudent rich—that is, hand over his fortune during his lifetime to escape prohibitive taxes. Thanks to the measures conceived by the New Deal to carve up big inheritances, Henry was confronted with a whopping 90-percent death tax on a fortune estimated to be over $600,000,000. He had held on to the bitter end to almost 60 percent of the Ford Company's voting stock, and he was caught with his breeches down.

A catastrophe was averted by Sidney Weinberg, the nimbleminded chairman of Goldman, Sachs, who worked out an eleventh-hour scheme to set up a Ford Foundation for Human Advancement. Edsel, Henry's son, before he died prematurely at forty-nine was able to transfer the bulk of his holdings to the foundation, and Henry, Sr., followed suit. As a result of this shotgun arrangement, almost 90 percent of the stock of the Ford Company passed into the hands of the foundation. (It was nonvoting but received an equal share in dividends, with the remaining 10 percent of the stock left in the hands of the family with full voting power.) Thanks to Sidney Weinberg, Henry Ford's federal tax was a paltry $21,000,000 on a taxable estate of $70,000,000. The rest of his fortune—over $500,000,000 —was sluiced tax free into the foundation. It is an irony that the Ford Foundation, a leading subsidizer today of black people's civil rights and welfare, was set up in an emergency to spare the archconservative Henry having to hand over his money to the hated New Deal "Socialists."

The Fords, Rockefellers and the other members of the firstfamily brotherhood through one device or another are yeomanly withstanding the rigors of the welfare state, with its Keynesian strategy of taking a swipe at capital savings and the commitment of its social engineers and deficit spenders to redistributing the wealth.

Today, despite the far-reaching social and economic changes taking place under the "greening of America," as one social commentator characterizes it, the first families, for the most part, remain staunchly blue, rooted in a strong tradition of aristocracy which, while lacking the ceremonious trappings of European nobility, is as fully conscious of its prerogatives. And this was true from the earliest days of the Republic. The founding fathers were for the most part inveterate snobs. In the view of the overwhelming majority of the delegates to the Constitutional Convention, the American Revolution had been a palace revolt—an uprising of the aristocracy against the king—and the Constitution was being forged as a new Magna Carta for the upper classes. Points out the historian James Truslow Adams:

> There was not, and never had been, a single one of the Revolutionary leaders, not even the most radical of all, Sam Adams himself, who believed in the people. What they believed in, with varying degrees . . . was the people who had money, talents or social position.

After the framing of the Constitution, the founding fathers plunged into a lively discussion of what sort of aristocratic title George Washington should be given as chief executive. Rufus Griswold, the historian, recalls how during a political dinner held in Philadelphia the Chief Justice of the Supreme Court asked the gathering for ideas. Thomas McKean, a Senator, reported, "I have been examining all the titles of the princes of Europe to discover one that has not been appropriated; 'Most Serene Highness' is used, but 'Serene Highness' without the word 'Most' is not; and I think it proper that our Chief Magistrate should be known as 'His Serene Highness the President of the United States.' "

Washington himself toyed with the title "High Mightiness" used by the Stadtholder of Holland; the Senate in May, 1789, made an attempt to bestow on him "High Highness the President of the United States of America and Protector of Their Liberties," only to be rebuffed by the more democratically spirited House. Not only the aristocrats but a large portion of the American masses were snobs. When Congress finally settled for simply "President," the title caused Washington acute embarrassment. Once while he was traveling in New England, an innkeeper refused to give him a room for the night under the impression he was only the president of the local college. Despite the development of egalitarianism, there remained embedded in the American psyche of ensuing generations awe for the mystique of the gentleman. J. P. Morgan II, the banker, defined what a gentleman was: "You can do business with anyone, but you can only sail a boat with a gentleman."

One of the notorious trappings of a gentleman, of course, is his family tree. This has been as true in the United States as in the Old World. As Cleveland Amory, a historian of American society, points out, family coats were officially recognized in a Colonial America ruled by the British monarchy. And even though they ceased to be accepted officially by the United States government after the Declaration of Independence, this didn't prevent America's first families from continuing to pursue the prize of heraldry with the zeal of a cat chasing a squirrel up a tree. Coats of arms became so fashionable after the Civil War that Tiffany in New York opened a special department to help eager inheritors work up a genteel lineage, whether or not they were entitled to one. Vast sums were offered genealogists who would conjure up an impressive escutcheon for milady and her husband, the pork baron. Two imaginative linealogists co-authored a book spiced with provocative tidbits. They insisted they had incontrovertible evidence that John D. Rockefeller, Sr., Abraham Lincoln and Grover Cleveland sprang from the royal line of Henry I of France and that William Shakespeare and Calvin Coolidge were descended from the loins of Charlemagne.

Even today, in an age of computers and jet airplanes, members of the American elite boast of escutcheons that would do justice to the lordliest Old World seigneur. Cleveland Amory indicates that experts in heraldry, an esoteric set who assume a mystique reminiscent of students of Cabala, have certified that the DuPont family, for instance, owns a coat of arms of indisputable quality linking them to Old World nobility, that the Chryslers of the automobile fortune have a bona fide coat of German aristocracy, but that the coat of the Dodges is spurious. Oddly, the prestigious Kennedy family has never been able to come up with a respectable coat of arms. Indeed, the middle name of the former President, "Fitzgerald," has a curious origin, etymologists point out. Irish names beginning with "Fitz" historically denote the bastard son of a royal prince. "Beware of Fitzsimmonses or Fitzgeralds," an elderly dowager once warned her granddaughter. "They're all illegitimate, you know."

For all its layers of snobbishness, American society, in contrast to the European breed, has been distinguished by a lively class mobility. The Irish Catholic Kennedys broke through the nation's Wasp barriers late in the day, it is true, but the Jews have played a notable role in the hierarchy of American aristocracy from pre-Civil War times. Several founded fortunes and laid their social roots in the antebellum South. The Lehman family emigrated from Bavaria to Montgomery, Alabama, making its first millions as cotton merchants during the Civil War. The Ochs family, founder of the New York *Times*, launched its newspaper career in Chattanooga, Tennessee. The Strauses of Macy's started in the crockery business in Georgia and were fervently loyal to the Confederacy. Jewish blood has crept into the veins of some of the most prestigious Gentile families. The DuPonts, who are French Huguenots, have a Jewish strain in one branch of descent. One of the daughters of Henry Ford II is married to a Rothschild. The socialite Douglas Dillon, ex-Secretary of the Treasury and a partner of Dillon, Reed, descends from a paternal grandfather, Sam Lapowski, who was the son of a French Catholic mother and a Polish Jewish father. Irish blood runs in the veins of a number of the elite. Indeed, the Irish have contributed some of the wittiest chapters to the memorabilia of American society.

There is the case of Jack Kelly, who started out as a bricklayer and lived to see his daughter Grace married to Prince Rainier of Monaco. Long before this triumph occurred, Kelly had become a multimillionaire contractor, responsible for building three-quarters of the office buildings in Philadelphia and playing a major role in the United Nations building, the Coliseum and Radio City in New York.

The Irish are masters at calling a spade a spade. When Kelly learned of his daughter's plans to marry Prince Rainier, he snapped, "I'm not impressed with royalty." He asked the emissary who brought the news how much the prince was worth.

"When he got to one million dollars," Kelly recalls, "I stopped investigating." The Irishman refused to provide the prince with a penny's worth of dowry. "I don't want to give the impression I am against sons-in-law. If they are the right type, they will provide for themselves and their families."

Kelly had a sense of humor touched by the leprechauns. He left one of the strangest wills on record. "For years," he wrote, "I have been reading last wills and testaments, and I have never been unable to understand any one of them at one reading. Therefore, I will attempt to write my own will with the hope that it will be understandable and legal. Kids will be called 'kids' and not 'issue' and it will not be cluttered up with 'parties of the first part'. . . . As for me, just shed a respectful tear if you think I merit it, but I am sure that you are all intelligent enough not to weep all over the place. I have watched a few emotional acts at graves, such as trying to jump into them . . . but the thoroughbred grieves in the heart. . . . So just remember, when I shove off for greener pastures or whatever it is on the other side of the curtain, that I do it unafraid and, if you must know, a little curious."

The healthy regard for lineage plus cold cash has been endemic to the *Homo americanus* (despite all disclaimers to the contrary). No blood lines have been more boastful of their heritage than New Englanders, and no people have more zealously extolled wealth. In Boston, the tough old merchant princes who founded New England's first families were looked upon by their contemporaries with an awe bordering on veneration.

Cleveland Amory relates how one Sunday Father Taylor, a popular preacher of the early nineteenth century, was delivering a sermon when he noticed a new face in his congregation— that of Colonel Thomas Handasyd Perkins, a shipowner and Boston's wealthiest citizen. Father Taylor broke off from his meditations on the Lord to exclaim, "Boston's merchant princes! Do you want to see one of them, boys? There he sits, look at him!" Then, as the congregation craned its necks, he murmured, "God bless you, sir! When you die angels will fight for the honor of carrying you to heaven on their shoulders."

Colonel Perkins would have been an exceedingly heavy burden for the angels if he had taken along his property. When President Washington invited him to become the first Secretary of the Navy, Perkins declined, explaining he owned more ships than the government and could better serve Uncle Sam by looking after his own interests.

Perkins was by J. P. Morgan's definition "a gentleman." And in the New, as well as the Old, World, wealth was a basic criterion, although in Europe it had a few more centuries of mellowing.

In addition to the fact it has been around much longer, Old World aristocracy has other characteristics differentiating it from the New World's. A greater proportion of European wealth is inherited compared with that of the United States. Moreover, while class-consciousness is more pervasive abroad, Europeans have never worshiped moneymaking per se as part of their culture or been so obsessed with it as their American counterparts. Legions of American novelists and historians have written books analyzing the phenomenon of the American businessman. The British businessman, on the other hand, as an English historian points out, "has not inspired a comparable outburst, although [we] have an ample supply of philosophers of government and . . . imperialism."

One of the reasons is that there has been less opportunity for scholars (and satirists) to dig up material. European businessmen operate in much greater privacy than their American colleagues. Remarks one observer of Europe's rich, "They seem to respect the maxim of the Prussian officer caste: 'A Prussian general dies—but he leaves behind no memoirs.' "

Apart from a phobia for publicity, Europe's wealthy are completely at home with the pace of modern living. Many Old World fortunes date back to landed estates created centuries before the Industrial Revolution. Yet a goodly number of inheritors, rooted though they are in historical traditions, are psychologically quite comfortable in this era of the Common Market and space flights to the moon.

One of Italy's top magnates, Count Edoardo Visconti di Modrone Erba, who heads the nation's second-largest pharmaceutical business, possesses wealth that goes back to the Middle Ages, when his ancestors were *condottieri* involved in the plottings of feuding ducal states. During World War II the family business was seized by the Fascists; Count de Erba parachuted into Italy with a British squadron, landed in Milan behind the German lines and charged with a machine gun into the headquarters of his family concern, forcing the Mussolini-installed management to flee.

A leader of the fashion industry is a descendent of another of Italy's oldest families—Marchese Emilio Pucci. He comes from a Florentine clan which was embroiled in a power struggle with the Medicis five centuries ago. In his fifties, Pucci lives and designs his world-famous clothes in a thick-walled, twenty-five-room Florentine *palazzo* which was built in the thirteenth century and to which successive generations of Puccis have added architectural innovations. The current *marchese* is a controversial fellow. He was a bomber pilot in Mussolini's air force. After the dictator was murdered by partisans, Pucci helped his daughter, Edda Ciano, escape to Switzerland.

Some of Europe's inheritors have played key roles in the economic rehabilitation of the postwar Continent. Baron Jean Charles A. Soppouers, whose ancestors were cronies of Louis XV's, has served in Belgium's Ministry of Economic Affairs, contributing to the negotiations that led to the European Common Market. Today he is managing partner of Banque Lambert, one of Belgium's top banks.

An inheritor who continues to participate in the family's business is Carson Johannes Price Berreleburg, chief of West Germany's nonferrous metal industry. He received his fortune through ancestors going back to the eighteenth century, when the Holy Roman Emperor raised his family to nobility. In Spain, Don Alfonso Güell y Martos fourth Marqués de Comillas, is a young man in his thirties who runs the nation's biggest passenger and cargo steamship line, in addition to managing a dynastic fortune. Manfred von Mautner Markof, Austria's wealthiest citizen, operates the family brewing business begun a century ago, which he has expanded tenfold. In Britain, Arthur Francis Benjamin Guinness, in his thirties, manages the family business that makes the celebrated stout.

The ranks of the Very Rich have not been immune to the turbulent *Zeitgeist* of the youth rebellion. In Europe, as elsewhere, the generation gap which has split the young from their parents is most piquantly illustrated in the tribes of the wealthy. Indeed, sons and daughters of the aristocracy are displaying a fervor for the antihero that has no counterpart among prior generations. And some of the most vigorous apostates are not all that young. For instance, Louisa Isabel Alvarez de Toledo y Maura, the twenty-first Duchess of Medina-Sidonia, is in her early thirties. A small, graceful woman who rides horses and dances the flamenco expertly, she has been dubbed the "Red Duchess" because she has sponsored marches by dispossessed farmers and bankrupt workers against the regime of Generalissimo Franco. Isabel descends from one of Spain's oldest families; an ancestor led the Spanish Armada against Queen Elizabeth. The duchess' title goes back to 1442, and she looks scornfully on her fellow aristocrats, most of whom date only from the eighteenth century. She has been clapped into jail and has thoroughly scandalized her relatives. One uncle lodged a complaint with the authorities that led to her imprisonment for writing a novel of social protest.

Isabel, who frequently slips into the coarse argot of the peasant, told an American reporter, "I do not understand how people can respond to a painting, to music, to an idea and yet go into the street and ignore the first beggar who comes up to them." The duchess has a highly developed talent for self-dramatization. She is well aware of the shock value of appearing in the panoply of her rank for sentencing in a shabby police court. Once while being shipped to a prison in Almería, a city forty miles distant, she insisted on stopping for refreshments at every inn on the way, shouting, "I am the Duchess of Medina-Sidonia. Feed me well for I am off to jail." When the embarrassed police pleaded with her to be quiet, she snorted, "Do you imagine I want people to think I am travelling with you because I like you?" Upon arriving at the prison, the duchess overwhelmed the jailer with her demands. "I insist on daily delivery of newspapers and a plug for my record player. The food must be improved. The exercise is inadequate. I demand the use of the lending library."

Another aristocrat who has staged a rebellion, albeit in a more quiet way, is Alexander Plunket Greene, who descends on his mother's side from the Duke of Bedford and who is a cousin of Lord Bertrand Russell, the philosopher who was himself a gadfly of the Establishment. Plunket Greene married Mary Quant, a designer who set the fashion world on its ears when she introduced the mini-skirt. Working as a team in Chelsea, the Bohemian section of London, Greene and his wife have shattered the traditions of Old World elegance and class distinction.

Marylin Bender, the fashion writer, who interviewed the couple, reports, "Mary and Alexander are a husband and wife team who not only live and work together but talk together. To converse with them is like playing a piano, with her responses coming from the treble, his from the bass."

Declares Alexander Plunket Greene, "Before the war there was this great, gracious living bit. I used to loathe things like *Vogue* with their titled boredom in a 40-room house." "Fashion leaders were duchesses," chimes in Mary. "Fashion was not democratic. Now it has become realistic and available. None of the really rich girls, the millionairesses in their own right . . . would be caught dead in a mink coat." In this mod world where all the right people are perennially young, Mary Quant describes the woman of fashion as one who is "sexy, witty and dry-cleaned."

In America, as in Europe, the inheritors have rebelled with varying degrees of severity. There is the mild reaction of the blue-blood liberal reformist; there is the Maoist eruption. (The leadership of the militant Weathermen is heavily represented with sons and daughters of fathers making $100,000 a year and over.)

But, despite the dissent, the bastions of vast, pervasive American wealth endure, a wealth far outdwarfing the European variety. In the art of moneymaking the pupils have exceeded their masters. The family founders of America, having had less of a time span in which to accumulate their riches, were even more redoubtable than the picaroons who hoisted themselves into the dukedoms of Europe.

Some of the first big American fortunes were made in privateering, which in many cases differed from piracy only in semantics. Roaming the high seas and looting enemy vessels under the cover of serving the American flag during the Revolutionary War generated enough money to turn George Cabot from a peasant into a gentleman and send him to Congress as the first Senator from Massachusetts. Other canny New Englanders lined their purses shipping goods over the seven seas, in some cases doing a lucrative trade with czarist Russia as well as Western nations. Despite the hazards of their occupation, they lived for the most part to be octogenarians, proving that plenty of money in the bank is the best medicine for long life.

After the Colonies won their freedom, the shippers and privateers multiplied their wealth by investing it in turnpikes, canals and factories, as the young nation burst its seams with growth. However, the biggest source of riches after the shipping boom tapered off was the ownership of land in America's rapidly growing cities.

Big money was made especially in Manhattan when the Astors, Stuyvesants and Van Cortlandts received from city politicians grants of land underwater at bargain basement prices. In those days the banks of the Hudson and East rivers extended much farther inland than now, and the downtown area was pocked with streams and marshland. The winner of a grant got land under very shallow water, and he filled it in with solid ground to build wharves and warehouses. The land, handed over for a pittance, yielded during succeeding generations hundreds of millions of dollars.

Among the shrewdest exploiters of these grants were Jacob Astor and his heirs, who followed the strategy of stubbornly holding onto their land without putting a penny in for improvements, waiting for the needs of the city to grow and then sell out at fabulously high prices. Old Jacob was adept at buying hundreds of corner lots for a song and letting them rot while the rest of the land was developed into fashionable neighborhoods. Astor held out to the bitter end until, thoroughly frustrated by the unsightly corner lots and the depressing effect it had on their property values, the owners of center properties yielded, accepting his stupendous prices.

Chicago, like Manhattan, was an epicenter of opportunity for adroit operators. In 1830 a farsighted investor could have bought a quarter of an acre in the center of what later became the chief metropolis of Midwest America for $20. In ten years he would have had to pay $1,500 for the same lot. Ten years afterward the property went for $17,500. By 1870 the price was $120,000. By 1890 it had mounted to $900,000 and four years later to an eye-popping $1,250,000.

In addition to real estate, some of the major fortunes in nineteenth-century America were made in Wall Street during the thriving days before the Securities Exchange Commission, capital gains tax and restrictions on cornering the market. Yet the bushveld of stock manipulation was a treacherous one, and fortunes were lost as rapidly as they were won.

Some of the most astute traders ended as victims of their own tactics turned on them by even cleverer pupils. Jacob Little, a pioneer of the technique of short selling, was a notable case. He made a financial killing by going short during the panic of 1837 triggered by President Andrew Jackson's attack on the United States Bank. Little was a highly suspicious fellow, insisting on personally delivering every bit of stock he sold instead of trusting his office boy to carry it to the buyer. In his final years, he was hoisted with his own petard. He got caught in a squeeze by the bulls and was wiped out. Before he died, he was reduced to buying and selling five shares at a time from handouts by old cronies. He passed away in a poorhouse, imagining himself in his final delirium to be a blue-chip stock, raving, "I'm going up. Who will come with me?"

Another gifted eccentric ambushed by his own audacity was Anthony Wellman Morse, who made a financial killing when, through a battlefield spy, he learned of the Confederate victory at Chancellorsville and took a long position in gold before the news became public. When prices rose sharply, he covered and raked in over $200,000. He became an expert in market corners, making millions squeezing railroad stocks. Then his luck turned. Hit by the countercoup of an adversary money pool, he went broke and died in a boardinghouse. The landlady refused to release his corpse to his family because he hadn't paid his rent for months. But several friends got up the cash and redeemed the body.

Before the days of federal income taxes, when the dollar was really worth a dollar, America's wealthy sachems had plenty to spend, and they dispatched it with panache. As time went on, the carriage yielded to the limousine and the grand waltz gave way to the fox trot at social levees. But the basic motivation for the display of bon ton remained. Flaunting its cornucopia was the chief protection the upper-class ego had against the encroachment of American egalitarianism.

Sometimes the Money Crowd carried its life-style to bizarre

lengths. There were the *soi-disant* Newport hostesses—Mesdames Astor, Stuyvesant, Fish, Goelet—who entertained with the lavishness of the Bourbon queens of France. Inspiring overpowering awe from their contemporaries, they remind one of the remark attributed to W. C. Fields, the earthy philosopher: "Woman are like elephants to me. I like to look at 'em but I wouldn't want to own one."

The distaff side was not the only branch given to extravagances. There was that incomparable example of first-family morality run mad in the person of Ned McLean, the husband of Evelyn Walsh McLean, who owned the celebrated "Hope" diamond. McLean's capers would have broken par even in the yeasty days of King Charles and the Restoration. Indeed, his life was a glowing litany to the gospel of Omar Khayyam. Once when he was especially euphoric, he purchased a locomotive and drove it in the wee hours of the morning all the way from Washington to New York, blowing the whistle and routing the inhabitants out of bed in every town he roared through. He made the rounds of saloons, waving his cane and knocking the derbies off the barflies' heads, ordering his manservant to buy new hats for them. He gave parties at which he hired prostitutes to stand like nudes on pedestals, and one New Year's Eve he led his guests stark naked down Fifth Avenue to welcome in the year. He kept in his gardens a pet seal he called Colonel George Harvey and had his valet daily deliver a bottle of burgundy to whet the colonel's pipes. During a diplomatic reception at the White House when Warren Harding was President, McLean urinated in the fireplace of the East Room and then repeated his performance down the leg of the Belgian ambassador. In the final stages of a drinking bout, when his hands shook uncontrollably with delirium tremens, he would insert his head in a pulley rope, tie a towel around his wrist and jack his hand up to his mouth for still another drink.

McLean admittedly was an extreme example of uninhibited roistering, but the Very Rich as a group lived with the inimitable impudence that only money can buy. Into the 1920's, before the New Deal put a crimp on expense accounts, high living meant lavish giving.

Atwater Kent, who amassed millions making the first radios, once called his wife into his study. "You aren't spending enough money, Mabel!" he scolded. This euphoric state of affairs lasted up to the stock market crash of 1929, and in some instances beyond.

Cleveland Amory tells how in the 1940's Gerard Lambert, the Listerine heir, quarreled with his wife over building a home in Palm Beach. Lambert wanted the house to face a lake; his spouse insisted it face the ocean. The couple resolved the matter by selecting for their site a peninsula narrow enough to straddle the issue. The house was built in such a fashion as to permit Mrs. Lambert to live in one half, on the oceanside, and her husband to occupy the half facing the lake. The mansion had duplicate kitchens, dining rooms, bedrooms, libraries—one for each mate. And the couple moved in with two staffs of servants; those serving on the lakefront were black; those on the ocean side were white. On Christmas, Mrs. Lambert, with her retinue of maids, visited her husband's quarters with the ceremoniousness of a queen attending another royal head.

The edifice of high society has locked away in its recesses the spiders of many a scandalum magnatum.

Frank Costello, the gambler, once told friends he hoped someday to set up a research foundation to probe the origins of the Astors, Vanderbilts and company to prove they had sprung from predatory ancestors who were no better than he was. Costello felt he was definitely entitled to a place in high society's pantheon.

Even the circumstances that one's ancestors came over *before* the *Mayflower* is no proof of "unimpeachable" pedigree. One haughty Philadelphia clan traces its ancestry back to the French Huguenots who settled in St. Croix in the Virgin Islands, from whence a branch emigrated to America before the Revolutionary War. Recently a dowager of the clan took a trip to the islands to find out how her cousins were doing. She discovered that in the course of ten generations of intermarriage they had all become black.

There are rumors a prominent socialite is living like an Edwardian marchioness on a Midwest fortune that sprang from the most *déclassé* origins. The millions that support her so stylishly were amassed by her two great-aunts in a most curious way.

These aunts, Minna and Ada Everleigh, were sisters, the

daughters of a well-to-do lawyer and born in Louisville, Kentucky, in the last century. Educated by private tutors, gowned in the choicest fashions, they made a charming duo, the toast of Dixie's most eligible young bloods. Voracious readers of philosophy, they were steeped in Flaubert, Shakespeare and Verlaine and connoisseurs of art and chamber music. The sisters both married early and left their husbands after a period of unhappiness. On their wedding day, each received a $40,000 inheritance from their father, and they looked for a way to invest it for maximum return.

Keen students of life as well as literature, Ada and Minna noticed that big money was being made by madams running brothels catering to the Very Rich. The young ladies, who were twenty-three and twenty-one at the time, proved to be adroit entrepreneurs. After trying out a house in Omaha to get a feel for the game, they moved to Chicago, where they had heard that Effie Hankins, the madam of a downtown establishment, was eager to sell out. The sisters bought the lease and Effie's stable of girls for around $60,000 and launched a lavish face-lifting of the property, turning Effie's middling establishment into America's most elegant sporting house—and, according to connoisseurs, one of the world's finest bagnios.

It was as difficult to get into the Everleigh Club as Buckingham Palace. The applicant needed a letter of recommendation for a formal introduction just to stick his nose inside. But once he was in, it was well worth the effort. The visitor was confronted with two mahogany staircases that swept grandly upward from the entrance, flanked by palm trees and busts of Greek goddesses peeking coquettishly through the shrubbery. There were fourteen parlors on the first floor alone and a library crammed with the writings of Plato, Montaigne, Lamartine. There was an art gallery at one end featuring exquisite oil canvases by great masters. Upstairs there were Japanese, Moorish, and Egyptian rooms each fitted with marble inlaid beds and mirrors on the ceiling. Nothing was overlooked to beguile the guests. String musicians stationed at strategic intervals softly played Mozart and Haydn quartets. A $15,000 gold piano stood ready to yield its dulcet tones at the wish of a patron, and Buddhist censers suffused the air with ravishing Oriental perfumes. Summed up one irreverent young news reporter as he made a tour of the club on opening night, "Minna and Ada Everleigh are to pleasure what Christ is to Christianity."

The proprietors had a peculiar social outlook. They opened their doors freely to missionaries who sought to convert the girls to clean living. If the salvationists succeeded in rescuing a lass, the sisters felt, they were entitled to their conquest. One zealous temperance crusader, Lucy Page Gaston, became a close friend of the Everleighs and constantly darted about the whorehouse exhorting the girls to read her pamphlets. Once Miss Gaston took Minna Everleigh aside. "The girls are headed for certain damnation. . . . There is one thing you can do to prevent this."

"What?"

"Make them stop smoking cigarettes!"

In the early 1900's the club was heavily patronized by the Wall Street crowd. Indeed, the Street conducted a virtual New York-to-Chicago shuttle service. "Betcha Million" Gates frequently led a contingent of fellow plungers to the club, and he gave his son the most elaborate education money could buy there.

The fame of the club spread overseas. In 1902 when Kaiser Wilhelm sent his brother Prince Henry of Prussia on a goodwill tour of the United States, one of the first things he asked for when he stepped from the boat was the whereabouts of the Everleigh Club. The prince visited Chicago, and there is a rumor that persists in Windy City folklore that, after laying a wreath on Abraham Lincoln's monument in Springfield, Illinois, he slipped his escort and spent a festive evening at the brothel. To hear old-timers tell it, the jollity broke all records. The Everleigh girls, decked in faun-colored tights, launched bacchanalian dances on the tables, the prince drank a toast to the kaiser and the President of the United States and sipped champagne from the slipper of one of the terpsichorean nymphs who had caught his fancy.

Long after it closed, the Everleigh Club hovered invidiously in the background of America's wealthiest families. When Marshall Field, Jr., II was found shot to death in his home in 1905, rumors swept Chicago that the young millionaire had spent the hours before his demise in the arms of an Everleigh girl. In

1910, Ford Moore, the twenty-six-year-old son of the multimillionaire owner of the Rock Island Railroad, died of a heart attack brought on by a prolonged orgy. He had been to the Everleigh Club and topped this off with a visit to a rival brothel. When the senior Moore learned of the circumstances of his son's death, he refused to attend the funeral. The Chicago newspapers had a field day with stories of how the unfeeling tycoon declined to look upon his son in his coffin. The Everleigh Club continued to crop up in embarrassing disclosures. In 1923, when the courtly Wall Streeter W. E. D. Stokes brought divorce action against his wife, a prominent society hostess, he disclosed she had been a former *fille de joie* in the Everleigh stable, a revelation that provoked a gale of titters around many a Park Avenue table.

The Everleigh sisters plied their trade from 1900 to 1910, when the mayor of Chicago, yielding to a crusade by the city's moral elements subsidized by rival madams who were out to eliminate competition, sent his police in to shut the club down.

The sisters accepted the closing philosophically. They were rich and quite prepared to retire and take whatever place in high society their money could buy. They purchased a home on Chicago's fashionable West Side but were compelled to sell when their respectable neighbors set up a howl. They came to New York and lived there in quiet anonymity into the 1920's. None of the community suspected who they were.

A news reporter, Charlie Washburn, who had known them in the old days when he was a cub writer in Chicago, visited them during the 1920's and found they were still living in the turn-of-the-century style with furnishings they had carted from the club. The ladies still slept in their marble inlaid beds, hung their walls with oil paintings from their art gallery. The stairway that swept up from the hall was a replica of the grand old stairway of the club. The $15,000 gold piano stood in the parlor surrounded by portraits of the *filles de joie* who had been the sisters' favorites.

The sisters left behind a fortune, earned in the best traditions of free private enterprise, which for all one knows is currently invested in some of America's choicest real-estate properties and a variety of blue-chip businesses.

"Money," observed Bernard Shaw, "is the most important

thing in the world. It represents health, strength, honor, generosity and beauty as conspicuously and undeniably as the want of it represents illness, weakness, disgrace, meanness and ugliness. . . . The first duty of every citizen is to insist on having money on reasonable terms."

And this has been the credo of America's first families to this day.

2

The Day Money Ends: The Apocalypse of the U.S. Dollar

Today the Money Crowd is living in a substantially different environment from the halcyon climate of yesterday. Its style of existence, lavish as it is, cannot compare with the days before income and heavy inheritance taxes and President Roosevelt's New Deal. Gone are the times when first families traveled in private railroad cars that were princely palaces on wheels, when Wall Street paladins built Fifth Avenue mansions glittering with Florentine terrazzo floors and terraces patterned after the gardens at Versailles. In that paradise for plutocracy, money was worth much more and social guilt was virtually nonexistent.

Until the 1929 market crash and the Depression, business was relatively uninhibited by government controls. Wall Street was the stately fulcrum on which the economy turned. Today the center has shifted to Washington; heavy taxes have redistributed large amounts of wealth from the few into the hands of the many.* The rich are trapped in the paradoxes of a world that is considerably different from the oligarch-oriented, property-structured one in which they played so influential a role.

America is the center of an agonizing dichotomy. Thanks to its mighty industrial and technological muscle, it is providing unprecedented material wealth along with piling up the prob-

* It has become fashionable for the new radical left to deny this; but one need only compare the workingman's standard of living today with what it was fifty years ago.

lems of Job. Our factories pour out more and more autos and hair sprays, and our air, lakes and rivers become increasingly poisoned by our chemicals. We grow wealthier in our possessions—and we become increasingly poorer in our capacity to enjoy them. As John Gardner, the former Secretary of the Department of Health and Welfare and currently head of Common Cause, predicts, if things continue this way we'll grow "richer and richer in filthier communities until we reach a final state of affluent misery—Croesus on a garbage heap."

There is a terribly irony to what modern man considers "progress." A team of American art historians recently touring Europe observed that Venice, a queen city of art and culture that has survived the ravages of a thousand years, has aged a century in the last ten and is threatened with extinction. In the last five years the traffic of oil tankers and coal barges has become so dense in the city canals that vibrations from the noise and pollution have begun to peel the walls and damage the frescoes of princely homes built during the Renaissance. A museum curator pointed out a celebrated marble angel, the jewel of his collection. In the three centuries since it was sculptured it had lost only a finger. In the last three years smog and pollution from newly erected chemical factories have caused half the face and one hand to disintegrate.

In Paris, parking lots jammed with autos and trucks have invaded the charming historic approaches to the Champs Élysées. In London, beautiful Georgian structures dating from Queen Anne have been torn down to make way for glossy steel skyscrapers. The massive vibrations of 747 jumbo jet airliners have shattered the medieval stained-glass windows of French Gothic cathedrals. In Ferrara, the historic Church of San Michele has been turned into a garage. In Athens, air pollution is eroding the venerable Parthenon and the authorities have been considering closing it to the public and spraying it with a plastic film to protect it awhile longer.

But the deterioration of the physical and aesthetic quality of life is only one aspect of the problem. The impact is more far-reaching. Today's revolution in social standards, sexual mores and youth-parent relations is creating overwhelming disorientation. "It is as if modern man were fighting to get out of a set of Chinese boxes," writes John Le Carré, the novelist. "After setting up one's life in one frame of reference, one finds it expanded and altered into another." "Change is proceeding so rapidly," points out another commentator, "trying to make sense of change [may] come to be our basic industry."

In its feverish hunt for new values, our age has made a fetish of appearances. Not long ago the *Wall Street Journal* wrote about one swinger in his twenties who during the daytime is a clean-shaven salesman for a copy machine manufacturer. At night he becomes a playboy, gluing on a beard and mustache. "I don't care to be governed in my private life by the conservative style of a businessman," he explained. Part-time Bohemians, reports the *Journal*, have set off a business boom in fake facial shrubbery. Ersatz mustaches, sideburns, beards are being donned by playboys of all ages who don't care to imperil their jobs by wearing the genuine article. Embarrassing things can happen, like to a playboy who lost his mustache while sipping a martini with his girl at the Ritz. The glue dissolved in the vermouth.

We live in an age in which a fashionable Italian princess, Luciana Pignatelli, advises that "Every woman over thirty needs a homosexual in her life. Husbands and lovers are too busy to give advice, or are just not interested." The redoubtable princess discloses she has employed the latest tools of technology to make herself more beautiful. When she wished to have her nose changed, she was handed a chart of famous noses to choose her style from, and she selected one that was a cross between Vivien Leigh's and Consuelo Crespi, her sister-in-law's; a Manhattan doctor injected her with silicone to give her a fuller face; she took cell implants to puff out her breasts; and she plans to visit a doctor in Paris who specializes in permanent eyelash transplants.

The notion that fun is innocent has long since vanished from America. When the Pittsburgh Pirates won the 1971 World Series, the citizens of the smokeless city reacted in a fashion hardly reminiscent of the days when Casey went to bat. Amidst the festivities, one citizen was shot to death, over thirty were injured. A young lady stripped herself to the waist and danced atop an auto. The police reported three rapes. In one case, a woman was dragged from her car by six youths and attacked in the middle of the street while a crowd looked on impassively.

This is an age that has scaled the heights of technological achievement. Banks have been opened in Minnesota and New York where, for a fee, a man may have his sperm put into cold storage at 321 degrees below zero and decades later artificially procreate a child with his wife or any other woman he selects. One nationally prominent politician has had his semen stored for posterity since his only son is feared to be sterile and dad figures he may want to use the sperm to impregnate his son's wife to continue the distinguished family line. Artificial insemination of humans has already resulted in almost 400 births. The first person conceived this way is a boy, now eighteen, who enjoys splendid health and has won top honors as a student.

But oddly, while this is an era that has advanced the frontiers of technology spectacularly, millions of people continue to live in the pervasive ignorance of the Middle Ages. The Knight newspapers have discovered in a survey that large numbers of Americans refuse to believe the United States has landed men on the moon. One slum woman interviewed in a West Philadelphia supermarket snorted derisively, "I'll never believe they [the astronauts] walked on the moon I see shining in the sky at night." In Boone, North Carolina, a manager of a dime store retorted, "If you got in an airplane and flew over that mountain there [pointing at the peak towering over the town] and you disappeared and then came back and said you'd been to Asheville, how do I know you've been to Asheville?" Others confided that the television networks had staged a phony moon landing "out west in a desert." Two skeptical Southerners assured a Knight reporter that the walk on the moon actually took place in a crater "somewhere on Earth."

In short, bewildered by the dehumanization brought on by a ravaging technology, racial unrest, the revolution in social standards, America is undergoing severe pressures. And nowhere are they more evident than in the sphere of the economy.

Overhanging the future is one stubborn, intractable fact. To the well-known saying "Nothing is certain but death and taxes," Americans might well add a third phrase, "and that the United States is relentlessly trapped in an endless spiral of inflation under its present system of values."

The U.S. dollar that was issued at the turn of the century is worth a little over 20 cents today. The 1950 dollar has shrunk by almost 40 cents. Nine years from now it will buy only 46 cents' worth of goods and services if inflation were to remain at the rate of only 3 percent annually—a pace which is below the current one and which most economists believe is the maximum practical extent inflation can be slowed down to if government price-wage stabilization actions are successful.

Inflation is ineradicable because of the values the nation lives by. It has decided that full employment is a more desirable goal than keeping prices stable. It is permitting the collective bargaining process to operate with virtually no restraints, enabling labor leaders to exact whatever they want under the threat of paralyzing the life of the economy and depriving millions of Americans of vitally needed goods and services.

A concomitant force exerting an inflationary push is that many business firms, abetted by computers and sophisticated inventory controls, have learned how to keep their prices at the highest practical level, even if this means substantially limiting their production. Gone are the days when businessmen naively sought profits through pell-mell volume production, as Henry Ford did with the Model T auto. Today it is the profit *per sales unit* that counts with management and investors alike.

Adding to the inflationary thrust is the nature of the economy, which has been transformed from a basically production-into a service-oriented one. More people are employed in providing services than in turning out goods, and the service dollar, which is higher in labor quotient, is deteriorating more rapidly than the production dollar.

The seriousness of the inflation virus is underscored by the fact that a Republican administration, elected on the promise to maintain a balanced budget, has engaged in the biggest deficit-spending spree of any administration in peacetime America. In its four years in office, the Nixon people will have run up a deficit of close to $90 billion—that is, if the government manages to stay within the $25.5 billion deficit limits it has imposed on itself for fiscal 1973. Since the spending for fiscal 1972 was $38.8 billion on a budget projected for $11.6 billion, one may well be skeptical about the government's ability to stay within the currently announced limits.

To grease the skids with even more debt accumulation, the administration has asked Congress to increase the statutory ceiling on the public debt from $430 to $480 billion—in other words, to give the Federal Reserve the right to print another $50 billion worth of IOU's. And this request might still not be large enough to see the administration through beyond February, 1973.

This or any other administration will continue to pile debt upon debt, in the view of pessimistic economists, because of the very nature of the disease. Like cancer cells that follow their own inevitable momentum toward metastasis, the Federal Reserve has to continue a relentless expansion of credit, they are convinced, precisely because America is already so heavily in debt. It has to enlarge the money supply to let Americans continue to pay off installments on the massive bill they have already run up. If the Fed were to stop priming the pump, there would be a collapse of the economy. Against this somber background, the aura of optimism exuded by government officials reminds one of a remark by Disraeli: "Confidence is suspicion asleep."

The problem admittedly is a highly vexatious one. Obviously governments need money to expand the economy to meet today's rising social demands. But where and how does one draw the line? Throughout history a massive, unrestrained printing of currency has ended up in wiping out the value of money, forcing governments into becoming dictatorships to compel their citizens to accept what remained of it.

The problem of an enormous government debt has ominous implications for everybody. Until Roosevelt took America off the gold standard, U.S. citizens could convert their paper money into its equivalent in gold. This meant that the supply of available money was limited by the amount of gold in the Treasury's reserves and it could not be increased endlessly to meet the needs of politically inspired spending.

By abandoning this controvertibility, the government took the lid, at least theoretically, off the amount of paper that could be issued to suit its whims, and if the government became an irresponsible spender, the value of the currency faced the threat of a deterioration virtually without limit. When a private family spends more than it earns, it faces bankruptcy if it doesn't put limits on its spending. So, too, did the government when its money supply was limited to its gold reserves. But once this restriction was lifted, it no longer had to suffer punishment for spending beyond its means. Today, instead of going into bankruptcy, it simply issues more money, creating it at the stroke of the pen. This money is nothing but debt, but Uncle Sam has the sovereign power to force Americans to accept this debt as money.

The nation's founding fathers were so suspicious of fiat money—currency created by governmental decree—and its tendency to cheat the people that they specifically wrote into the Constitution in 1787 a clause prohibiting the states from permitting transactions to take place in anything but gold and silver coin as legal tender. Article I, Section 10 of the Constitution declares: "No State shall enter into any Treaty, Alliance or Confederation; grant Letters of Marque and Reprisal; coin Money; emit Bills of Credit; *make any Thing but gold and silver Coin a Tender in Payment of Debts;* pass any Bill of Attainder, ex post facto Law, or Law impairing the Obligation of Contracts, or grant any Title of Nobility." (The italics are the author's.)

Over the last century, the U.S. government, pressed by expediency, has steadily watered down its interpretation of this clause, first by issuing paper money convertible into gold or silver and finally by printing paper money convertible into nothing whatever. But the sentiments of the constitutional fathers remain clear. They believed that an unchecked flood of fiat paper money, by threatening to wipe out a people's savings, was as much an infringement of freedom as censorship of speech, the prevention of free assembly and free religious worship. (Incidentally, no test has ever been made in the Supreme Court of the government's arbitrary prohibition of citizens' owning gold. People can own gold virtually everywhere but in the United States and Great Britain.)

It is within this historical context of government behavior that the current threat of inflation must be seen. Most people in considering inflation see only the tip of the iceberg—the phenomenon of rising prices. A more realistic—and frightening—approach is to ponder the disintegrating worth of paper money per se and the factors at work that have made the face value the government prints on its currency a lie. For when a government lies, its people are in trouble.

Throughout history governments, free to manipulate the value of paper currency by printing as much of it as they need to serve their political schemes, have time and again wiped out the savings of their people and plunged them into misery. Inflation and the debasement of the currency under the emperors was a major factor leading to the collapse of ancient Rome. During the French Revolution the rapidly deteriorating paper money issued by the Revolutionary Tribunal, which the people were forced to accept under the threat of being put to death on the guillotine, resulted in a wholesale swindle and was a major cause of the failure of the revolution and the advent of Napoleon, the dictator. The runaway inflation in Germany during the early 1920's, which pauperized millions of Germans —at one stage it was cheaper to light a cigarette with a paper mark than to use a match—helped trigger the rise of Nazism and the eventual coming to power of Adolf Hitler. And modern governments, plunging into uncontrollable debt which they try to cover by printing a flood of paper currency that has no intrinsic assets and depends essentially on political promises, threatens to hurl their citizens into a catastrophe as terrible as those of the past.

The practice of issuing money without restraint is being excoriated today by a growing number of hard-money advocates. C. Vern Myers, a leading Canadian financial analyst, puts it this way:

> The millions in the cities who buy eggs, and the excited traders on the commodity exchanges who sell and buy hundreds of millions of eggs, probably never thought of the chicken. Certainly the commodity guys buy and sell more eggs than have been laid by all of the chickens in history. They also buy and sell more silver than has ever been mined or probably ever will be mined. They have forgotten that an egg is more than a figure in a book. It would be sensible if the commodity dealers would appoint a committee to scour the farmyards of the nation and count the chickens. They might report: "Many millions of eggs which we have bought or sold

don't exist and can't exist. We are not really buying or selling anything. We are matching wits with one another."

Similarly with money. Presumably money means convertibility into SOMETHING. For instance, a dollar will buy a certain number of eggs, or a certain amount of beef, or wheat, etc. But if you go out and count up all the goods in the world, and then compare it with money, you will see that there is not nearly enough goods to match the amount of money. It follows that some of these goods are being bought up with some NOTHINGS.

In short, Myers and other custodians of a sound-currency philosophy claim, the money Americans fold into their wallets is not really money at all in the traditional sense, but debt. Uncle Sam's incontrovertible dollar represents no tangible physical asset. The nation's banking system is being utilized to create exchangeable paper, which through a series of sophisticated maneuverings the banks are accepting in place of real physical assets. The recipient of a dollar may be under the illusion he has a legal claim on a tangible asset. But he hasn't, for the Fed's expansion of fiat money has created a situation where the outstanding claims far outweigh the tangible physical assets. Today's dollar is a government IOU which Uncle Sam hopefully will pay off—through the medium of going still deeper into debt. And this process of servicing debt by issuing more debt will continue—in the way a compulsive spender, heavily in hock, continues to hand out IOU's all over the place—until the roof falls in.

While the Federal Reserve creates its money through sophisticated and elaborately obfuscating techniques—*i.e.*, buying U.S. Treasury bills, etc.—creating fiat money is hardly a new phenomenon. The Germans, as already noted, did it, albeit more crudely, in the early 1920's simply by pouring money from the printing presses, running down the mark until it was worth one-trillionth of its former value. At one point, it took a wheelbarrow full of marks to buy a cigarette. Since World War II, the governments of the Western world, committed to ambitious social programs, have been printing a rising flood of fiat paper money behind the façade of various deficit financing techniques. Every government has paid lip service to the need for stopping inflation. But nothing has been done to eradicate its basic causes.

The vanishing worth of money represents more than a loss on paper. Measured in human terms, the dollar, points out Illinois Congressman Philip M. Crane, a member of the House Banking and Currency Committee, "is minted human energy. You can calculate how precious it is . . . by figuring out how many of these you earn in the course of an hour. Then, you simply divide the number of human heartbeats into that and you can get an idea of just what portion of your life this piece of paper represents." A government that can decree just how much this piece of paper is worth by manipulating the supply for political ends, Crane contends, "is directly laying claim to a portion of your life."

The great irony is that never did the masses of ordinary people seem to have it so good from a material standpoint. The age-old dream of the social philosopher to redistribute wealth from the rich into the pockets of the average man has been taking place at a dramatic pace.

However, as some irreverent folk point out, there is a built-in joker to the workingman's march toward utopia. As he demands and gets more of the world's goods, the money he receives is drastically shrinking in value. The end result could be a cruel jest. For if the masses ever managed to get their hands on the whole of the world's wealth, they could find it had turned into ashes.

The threat of money turning into nothing is not an idle one. A serious erosion of money is a major herald of social collapse. As noted, an ominous sign of the decline of Ancient Rome, that colossus of industrial resourcefulness and military might, was the inability of its government to work out a viable economic system that would prevent ruinous inflation. As the upper classes plunged into luxurious living, the poor flocked to welfare programs and a huge military establishment spread over the world to protect Rome's imperialist interests, inflation got out of hand; to cope with rising prices, the emperors progressively debased the currency, reducing the content of the precious metal in the coins so that it took more and more money to buy the same amount of goods.

The emperor Diocletian made a desperate effort to prevent a

collapse of the currency by issuing an edict in 301 A.D. setting maximum price ceilings for goods. But the decree was ignored by the merchants, and the nation rushed on toward ruin.

Since Rome, governments have learned how to use the more subtle device of issuing paper as money in place of scarce metal and hide from the people for long periods of time the steady deterioration of the currency until it is too late for them to extricate themselves.

During the French Revolution, the government of Robespierre issued paper money, *assignats,* and gave it a value based on the security of the landed estates of the nobility confiscated by the government. Despite vigorous efforts to keep prices stable, the *assignats* depreciated in worth and prices rose dangerously. The people were reluctant to take the paper money and hoarded gold and silver coins instead. The government huffed and puffed and issued a greater and greater amount of the paper to cope with rising prices. Finally it passed a decree ordering that "any person selling gold or silver coins . . . should be imprisoned in irons for six years." Anybody caught refusing to accept paper money was to be sentenced to the guillotine.

But even the death penalty could not keep the *assignats* from skidding toward zero. Smart people—financiers, merchants and others who foresaw what would happen—plunged heavily into debt, using the paper money to buy up real goods or foreign currencies. They were right in their prognosis.

Within six years, the pockets of the loyal citizenry were filled to overflowing with virtually worthless paper. Expressed in terms of the American dollar, a bushel of flour that had cost a Frenchman 40 cents in 1790 when the *assignats* were introduced couldn't be bought for under $45 by 1796. A cartload of wood that cost the farmer $4 in 1790 sold for $250 six years later. Eggs, which had been priced at 24 cents, now cost $5. The price of a pound of soap had soared from 18 cents to $8.

And a very natural thing occurred. The people, realizing how they had been cheated by the government of "Liberty, Equality, Fraternity," pounced furiously upon its paper money. On February 18, 1796, a mob broke into government offices, seized the plates and machinery that had printed the *assignats,* along with a carload of currency, and hauled them to the Place

Vendôme. There, at nine in the morning, before the clenched fists and curses of 300,000 people, the machinery was smashed to pieces and, together with the money, was made into a blazing bonfire. But the witch of worthless paper money was by no means exorcised in the flames of the Place Vendôme. It lives on under various guises today.

In the last 60 years through inflation, "the biggest cheat of all time," the British pound sterling, that one-time proud symbol of sound money, has shrunk over 80 percent in its purchasing power. Since World War II, there have been over 300 devaluations of national currencies, either on a full or partial basis. The U.S. dollar has deteriorated to one-third of its worth since 1939, confiscating from the American people over $600 billion in savings and life insurance.

As the Federal Reserve pumps an increasing flow of money into the economy, raising the paper wages of blue-collar workers to unprecedented levels, Americans are receiving more and more of less and less. Unpalatable though the fact may be to current sociologists and other socially minded schoolmen, the only thing that has given money its value through the ages has been its scarcity. What W. S. Gilbert, the British satirist, wrote eighty years ago was never truer than today: "When everybody is *somebody* then nobody is *anybody*."

Those who stubbornly insist on remaining *somebody*, who refuse to accept the fate of those simple souls who fell into the molten pot of Ibsen's peddler to be turned into buttons adorning the coats of other men, have been anxiously searching for a way out.

While the morality of government deficit spending can be debated endlessly, the harsh economic facts of a galloping inflation are here. And sophisticated people are trying to cope with it pragmatically. Today's Money Crowd, those inheritors and accumulators of wealth, the money managers, the panjandrums of finance—and all the affluent members of the middle class who are tagging along, striving to emulate their tactics—are doing what the sophisticated have always done during periods of dangerous inflation. They are embarked on an intricate gamesmanship to save the purchasing power of their dollars. Admittedly some are gambling for even bigger stakes, gaming with the wheel of time in the hope of building and passing onto their successors something that will outlast their own brief selves and stand as a testament to eternity. They want remembrance of them to persist as, in the phrase of Horace, the poet, *"Labitur et labetur in omne volubis aevum."*

Whatever else may be said of it, the Money Crowd is putting on a rattling good show. True, as noted, in today's egalitarian era its style of living is not quite on the scale of the *belle époque* of the last century. The regal railroad cars have been replaced by functionally slick business planes; the leisure lunch of Maryland terrapin, *filet de boeuf Mirabeau,* washed down with a vintage Madeira, has given way to a the hasty snack grabbed at the office desk and sandwiched in between a busy day of board meetings. Instead of acquiring a son-in-law with the title of marquess or count, today's nabob more often than not is likely to find his daughter married to a bearded young radical whose beau ideal of achievement is growing vegetables in a modern version of Stony Brook Farm.

Things have certainly changed amidst the current shift in social attitudes. Yet when it comes to high drama and a nice display of the *beau geste,* the modern tribe needn't take off its hats to anyone.

Today's gamesters are pitting their wits against the gyrations of currencies, scalping profits in a variety of global enterprises, playing the cold, logical forces of the marketplace against the social planners, and they are succeeding or succumbing in this contest according to the code of the modern commercial samurai—the blood-letting of free competition which punishes the wrong guess, the ill-timed move ruthlessly and rewards the right judgment abundantly. Indeed, these panjandrums are the last vestigial practitioners of a rapidly fading art, one that is almost painfully incongruous in an era that worships security above all else. They are society's final remaining risk takers, the cavaliers who dare to fail in the campaign to win it all.

They must be noted, if nothing else, for their bravura and their audacity. For they come from a lineage, as the poet Byron wrote:

> Whose game was empires and whose stakes were thrones.
> Whose table earth—whose dice were human bones.

Part II

ODD ADVENTURES IN THE MODERN WORLD OF MONEY

They well deserve to have
That know the strong'st and surest way to get.

—SHAKESPEARE

3

Swiss Banks and Nervous American Cash:
A $40,000,000 Gamble in Cocoa

On the morning of September 10, 1970, the Swiss police swooped down and arrested Dr. Paul Erdman, an American businessman, the head of a rapidly growing bank in Basel. The genial son of a missionary with a folksy air and a bubbling extrovertive concern for folks, Dr. Erdman was clapped unceremoniously, along with six of his top associates, into an ancient, dingy dungeon that had been built in the seventeenth century to house common criminals, spies and other enemies of the state. Erdman and his associates were suspected of particularly heinous dealings by Swiss standards—misusing some $40,000,000 of its depositors' money.

America makes similar arrests with more grace. There one is innocent until proven guilty. A man under indictment is rarely treated as a common criminal as long as he wears a clean white collar. First, evidence is presented to a grand jury; then the indictment is handed down, followed often by a lengthy trial at which the defendant is represented by clever lawyers. Then, if a jury finds him guilty, there is a series of appeals, during which he is free to live the easy life to which the fruits of his financial peccadilloes—if in fact he has committed them—have accustomed him. But in blunt, austere Switzerland, a man can be clapped into a dungeon simply on allegations while the prosecuting attorney proceeds with an investigation to determine whether the state has a case against him. The more intricately the records have been fouled up, the longer it takes to unravel the evidence and the longer the accused is kept sweating in a cell. The Bank of Basel's records were so scrambled, it was evident its officials would be kept jailed for many months before they were tried by a jury of their peers.

The dilemma of Dr. Erdman and Company is a striking result of the ailing condition of modern finance; for this is an age of monetary uncertainty that is giving rising emphasis to Swiss banking as a haven for nervous money from all quarters of the globe. Since the end of World War II, Europeans, worried about the instability of their economies, have been sneaking their savings into Switzerland. Money has been smuggled through the customs by passengers carrying lunch boxes in trains, sewn into the lining of suits, or hidden in the trunks of autos crossing borders. In 1969 when a leftist government took office in Italy, nationalizing the electric power industry and levying a substantial tax on dividends, Italian capital took flight in a tidal wave. In Lugano, close to the Swiss border, two dozen banks sprang up. The majority were owned by Italians who snatched billions of lire's worth of business smuggled in by their countrymen. As West Germany began recovering its industrial muscle after World War II, a similar flight of capital erupted; wealthy businessmen bought land for summer homes in Ticino, Switzerland, and stashed away millions in Swiss banks.

The Swiss reputation as a haven for jittery money dates to 1635, the year of the revocation of the Edict of Nantes by the Catholic French government, which forced many French Protestants to flee with their savings into Switzerland. Complete banking secrecy, achieved by keeping the identity of clients anonymous, has been in existence since 1934 when Hitler's Gestapo moved into Switzerland, attempting to trace the money of Jewish refugees. Since the government will not probe into a depositor's account for political offenses (only for criminal ones), numerous dictators and kings have placed their personal fortunes in Swiss banks to provide insurance against their overthrowal and exile. These include ex-King Farouk, Peron, Trujillo, and, more recently, South Vietnamese politicians who, while rallying the peasants to fight the Vietcong, have whisked their fortunes into Swiss banks, just in case.

The lengths to which the Swiss go to preserve secrecy from the pryings of foreign tax collectors (the Swiss don't consider tax dodging a criminal offense) has been reported by Paul Feriss, a journalist, who wrote about a visit he paid a bank in Basel where he noticed near the porter's desk a paper-shredding machine. Nightly the contents of all the bank's wastebaskets were emptied into it and ground up so not a scrap was left for even the cleaning woman to read.

While Europeans traditionally have been the ones to duck under the Swiss umbrella when it rained, in recent years Americans, jittery over inflation and the overall malaise of a battered, baffled society, have been squirreling Yankee dollars into Swiss numbered accounts at an accelerated pace. Nervous old ladies in tennis shoes, stalwart Texas oil tycoons, wealthy right-wingers who loathe a government-managed economy with an ideological frenzy, as well as astute, cool-headed investors who are gloomy about the future, have been channeling their money into Swiss banks to protect themselves, as one aging inheritor has put it, "against the cockeyed policies of American politicians which are plunging the country deeper and deeper into the red."

Banking cash in Switzerland is a way to convert shaky American dollars into native francs, one of the world's most stable currencies. Feriss tells how he met two Swiss in successive days who picked from their loose pocket change franc pieces dating back to the 1800's.

Uncle Sam, to curb the flight of American capital, recently passed legislation requiring U.S. banks and individuals to report on money exported from these shores, but the outflow continues as inexorably as the inflow of whiskey during Prohibition days.

There is nothing so potent, it has been said, as an idea whose time has come. With the invasion of American money into Switzerland, it was inevitable that Americans would bob up to greet the cash with all the enthusiasm reserved for a grand homecoming.

In the 1960's when a passenger stepped from the plane on arriving at the Basel airport, one advertisement that thrust its way into his range of vision was a big, gaudy sign proclaiming, in English: WE KNOW HOW TO DO IT. UNITED CALIFORNIA BANK IN BASEL, A.G.

Behind this message lies the story of Dr. Paul Erdman, a

genial, bespectacled man of forty who gives the appearance of a hard-working professor of economics. An American, the son of a missionary, Erdman received an education at Georgetown University in Washington and a doctorate of economics at the University of Basel, scoring one of the most distinguished records ever attained there.

His outstanding scholarship enabled Dr. Erdman to get employment with the European Coal and Steel Community headquarters of the Common Market, located in Luxembourg, and here he made a close-at-hand study of the complexities of international finance.

For years, he had been impressed with the inviolability of the Swiss banking system and its allurement for troubled investors. But the privacy and clannishness with which the Swiss operated had one drawback: It inhibited them from tapping the virtually inexhaustible wealth of the world's most prosperous society —upper- and middle-class America—which, with the exception of a few wealthy sophisticates, was unaware of these investment advantages. Erdman was struck with the notion that if an American with a knowledge of Yankee psychology and the gift for hard-hitting American-style merchandising were to open a bank in Switzerland, offering high-powered global investments for American money, the patronage could be boundless.

There was one major difficulty. Swiss bankers are, as noted, extremely clannish. It would not be easy for an outsider to break into the fraternity and establish a bank in the land of the *eidelweiss*. A few patrician banking families, going back to the times of Calvin, dominated the financial community, and they shied away from the spotlight like the plague. The aristocratic banks in Geneva even eschewed nameplates and addresses to mark their location. The clients they did business with didn't have to be told where to find them. The bankers lived in the genteel past. One notable firm owned by the Pictet family still used the furniture of its eighteenth-century ancestors and would have blanched at the notion of employing a computer to keep its records. Each Pictet patron received a bank statement handwritten on personal stationery. To send out an impersonal ledger would have been unthinkable.

It was into such a circle that Dr. Erdman presumed to enter

with Yankee-style promotion. His debut certainly was not hampered by the fact that he had a wife who came from a fine Basel family. Erdman had no money of his own to start a bank, but he got backing through a friendship he had developed with Charles Salik, a California financier for whom he had done consultant work. Erdman so impressed Salik with his brilliance that the latter raised $600,000 to put him in business.

In 1965, Erdman opened the Salik Bank in Basel, a simple two-room office whose most important piece of furniture was a four-foot safe. Introducing himself as an investment adviser, Erdman offered a tasty package of services. Swiss bankers, unlike their American counterparts, are permitted to wear a second hat as brokers. Erdman had the power of attorney in many cases to put portions of his clients' money into a variety of investments—*i.e.*, gold or silver, the buying of currencies for speculation during monetary upheavals, German, Japanese, South African stocks, real estate, or whatever seemed attractive at the moment.

Under his ministrations, the assets of the Salik Bank swelled. At the end of 1966, the first year of operations, they were $3,000,000, the following year they had climbed to $9,000,000, and within twelve months they had shot up to $49,000,000. To win customers, Erdman traveled all over the world, holding seminars explaining the blessings of the Swiss banking system.

In the course of his travels, Erdman joined forces with other financial counselors, notably zealous advocates of hard money who were pessimistic about the future of the American economy and its paper currency. Prominent among these was a highly popular investment analyst, Harry Schultz, who, while of modest height and girth, exuded a bravura beyond his physical stature. Schultz has written books on how to make money in the bear market and how to defend oneself in financial panics and in recent years has been publishing a market letter in which he evokes the flavor of a financial Samuel Pepys as he roams around the world interviewing leading bankers, finance ministers and industrial nabobs to wrest tips, provide anecdotal tidbits and report to his readers on the latest inside developments in the gold and silver markets, the international stock exchanges, and so forth. So formidable has his reputation become that Schultz currently charges $700 an hour to give personal advice to the Very Rich on how to protect their fortunes from Uncle Sam's monetary depredations.

Once a year this financial counselor has been holding an International Monetary Seminar—or Think-In, as he likes to call it—at various spots around the world. And the band of faithful readers of the *International Harry Schultz Letter* fly in to listen to speeches, attend workshops and receive the latest warnings from the lips of the doctor and his colleagues. A Schultz seminar audience is a spectrum of conservative investment bankers and newspaper publishers, British Tory leaders, French Gaullist economists, South African politicos, owners of gold mines in Canada and Latin America, and the inevitable white-haired dowagers from America, inheritors of superannuated fortunes who have much to lose if Uncle Sam spends himself into bankruptcy.

A featured speaker at the Schultz seminars was Paul Erdman, whose views on hard money coincided with Harry Schultz's and who was not at all shy about extolling the advantages of putting one's dollars into a Swiss bank to build a protective ark against the coming flood.

The present writer first met Dr. Erdman in November, 1967, when as a financial reporter he covered the first international seminar that Harry Schultz hosted at the New York Hilton Hotel. Under the massed flags of nine nations represented by the featured speakers, the conclave included over 100 noteworthy guests. Former British Minister J. Enoch Powell was there to speak his piece for right-wing Toryism. Also present were Lord Grantchester, a top monetary expert in the House of Lords; Dr. A. M. A. McLean, a leading member of the Canadian Parliament; Herbert S. Mabin, financial adviser to South Africa's Prime Minister; Nobutane Kiuchi, one of Japan's foremost economists; urbane, sardonic Professor Michael Heilperin, internationally known U.S. monetary expert; Gustave R. Velasco, a notable Latin American banker and adviser to the Mexican government; Raoul Audouin, a prominent disciple of De Gaulle's monetary adviser, Jacques Rueff, who represented top-echelon French conservatism.

The setting was resplendent. The guests dined in groups at a number of festively decorative tables. Before each setting a place card featured a ringing quotation from Bernard Baruch, the elder statesman of U.S. finance, reminding the eaters that "the fiscal strength of a nation lies not in what the government owns, but in what its people own." This sterling conservatism was further underscored by the keynote address delivered by the Right Honorable Enoch Powell, the baffling British politician who is a brilliant Greek scholar, as well as a rabid spokesman for right-wing Toryism and the banning of colored immigration into Britain. Powell delivered a speech peppered with Greek ironies and Latin witticisms as he drove home the message: "You ultimately surrender your freedom to whom you surrender your common sense."

It was at this seminar that Dr. Erdman materialized to speak persuasively about the perils threatening the British pound. He predicted that it would shortly be devalued (something Her Majesty's government was vigorously denying), and he explained to his eager listeners—all those Texas oil tycoons and adoring dowagers overloaded with jewels and anxieties—how they could make a killing if they left their money with him. In predicting the pound's devaluation, Erdman told his audience that for an investment of $2,500, he would offer them the opportunity to sell the pound short, technically by short-selling a six months' futures contract for $10,000 in pound sterling at a price of around $2.77. And he hit it right on the head.

On Saturday, November 18, after a three-year losing battle with inflation and a galloping deficit in Britain's balance of payments, Harold Wilson's government announced the devaluation of the pound. In the wake of the news which sent the House of Commons into an uproar and plunged chancelleries and stock exchanges around the world into consternation, over twenty nations in the sterling area and outside devalued their own currency.

This development shocked most Americans. But not Dr. Erdman. He had correctly foreseen the event. The pound had been devalued from $2.77 to $2.40, and clients who had invested with him made a $3,000 profit for every $2,500 they wagered. One customer cleaned up $80,000 selling the pound short.

This spectacular coup enormously enhanced Erdman's reputation. Henceforth his fortunes, which had been climbing modestly, took a quantum leap forward. For one thing, the Salik

Bank got a big injection of capital. Erdman's record caught the attention of the top people of the United States' number-one multibank holding company, the Western Bancorporation of California, which has twenty-three subsidiaries with over $10 billion in assets.

The Western high command tabbed Erdman as one of the coming stars in the financial firmament, and to get him on the team, in the spring of 1969, Western bought the Salik Bank, lock, stock and barrel, for $12,000,000. The parent hovered over its protégé like a proud father watching his son win one school honor after another.

This brisk infusion of capital served as a heady hypo for Erdman. He became a one-man global doorbell ringer for Salik, traveling 100,000 miles a year to drum up clients. It was said jestingly that his patronage alone kept Swiss airlines in business. The Swiss banking community, reportedly embarrassed by Erdman's courtship of the press—it was unthinkable for a Swiss banker to solicit publicity—begged him to quit seeking it. But Erdman pursued his appointed rounds. He continued to emphasize American patronage. In the sixteen months after Salik was founded, the number of his countrymen who were induced to put their funds in his bank doubled, comprising 25 percent of his clients.

The present writer met the exuberant doctor again at Harry Schultz's monetary seminar held in London in 1968. The meeting was packed with the usual assortment of Americans flown by chartered plane to hear Schultz and his associates expatiate on current conditions. Once more Erdman was a smash success. Elderly retired millionaires, opulent dowagers, active young mining executives and veteran Wall Street plungers ate up his advice and roared their approval.

Several months later this writer lunched with Erdman in the Wall Street area during one of the doctor's money-raising trips to the United States. As usual he was brimming with optimism. The weakening of the dollar made it imperative that Americans put their money into high-yield investments, he observed. The real risk taker was the "cautious" man who had salted his money away in a U.S. bank in the 1940's only to discover in the 1960's it would buy only a fraction of the goods and services he had counted on. Erdman, thanks to his power of attorney, could take a client's money and invest it anywhere on earth where the appreciation promised to be the greatest—West German stocks, Tokyo real estate, Mideastern oil, or whatever. As the writer sat listening, the notion occurred to him that if Erdman hadn't existed, the anxieties engendered by the relentless deterioration of money would have made it necessary to invent him.

That was the last the writer saw of the doctor. Suddenly his fortunes took a somersault, and eighteen months after the luncheon he was clapped into jail.

Dr. Erdman at this writing is still awaiting possible trial. It is not known to what extent, if any, he was personally involved since his story is not a matter of public record and a jury has not yet passed verdict on his innocence or guilt. Nevertheless, there have been reports emanating from Basel, together with records relating to the folding of the bank, that throw a certain light on matters.

The bank had developed a fast track record, and it was difficult to maintain the pace. The 30 percent rise in its portfolio assets achieved in a single year, the harvest reaped from the devaluation of the pound—these were achievements for which there was really no encore. The bank got involved in some adverse investments, reportedly trading in silver and in attempting to recoup its losses and regain its previous touch, it looked around for other investments and allegedly decided to try its luck trading commodities, notably cocoa.

Cocoa has been a fool's gold that has peopled many an investment graveyard. For instance, Ghana, where the bulk of the world's output is produced, in its brief period as a nation has been rent by civil war, political assassinations, guerrilla violence. The weather is unpredictable; torrential rains can kill the cocoa crop; and an unexpected outbreak of a disease called black pod can destroy the trees and ruin one's investment. Moreover, there is the notorious unreliability of the production figures put out by the Ghana government. Even at best, it is difficult to estimate how much cocoa has been stored by the native tribes who grow the crop in the hinterlands.

Moreover, it has been charged by foreign experts that the government has a penchant for issuing misleading figures to get a better price for its crop on the world market. When it wants to sell, it passes hints around that there is a shortage and the current output is the last available. Then, when buyers have taken it, they are hit with waves of additional cocoa that had been withheld from the market, plunging prices downward. As one professional trader, saddened by experience, observes, "You gotta be crazy to gamble in cocoa."

Even such an expert as Hershey, the world's largest chocolate maker whose livelihood depends on its expertise in the cocoa market, has, according to trade rumors, been badly burned. In January, 1967, it made the wrong guess in the futures market and was taken to the cleaners. That year Ghana reported figures indicating that its crop output wouldn't be as small as speculators had figured. A raft of traders unloaded, and as margin calls mounted, cocoa prices continued to plunge. During one session, contracts dropped below the Cocoa Exchange's 1-cent limit for execution of trades, and at the close over 1,600 panicky sell orders couldn't be negotiated.

At this point, all eyes turned toward Hershey, the powerhouse, whose volume of hedge trading normally had a fundamental impact on prices. Everybody wondered what J.H., the firm's veteran trader, would do. J.H. had become a fixture of the exchange over the years while pacing up and down and finally taking a stance a few steps away from the pit on a strip of piles that became known as J.H.'s tiles. In this fateful January, as prices tumbled, the old pro for a few anxious sessions made no move, standing silent, with his hands thrust into the pockets of the trenchcoat he habitually wore on the exchange floor, his hat thrust over his eyes. Then, when he went into action, it was calamitous. Believing that cocoa futures would continue to dive, Hershey heavily increased its short lines. At this juncture, another big buyer, reportedly Nestlé, moved in to buy. A gaggle of speculators rallied behind it and futures started to zoom. In forty-eight hours, the market completely got away from Hershey, and it had to cover its short sales at heavy losses, all because it had missed the right moment to enter the buying pool.

Into this rat's nest, according to reports emanating from Swiss financial circles, the Basel Bank stumbled. It dispatched an expert armed with the latest research of high-powered computers and all the other sophisticated regalia of twentieth-century technology to stalk the primitive wilds of Ghana and "explore" the situation. Looking into the recondite mysteries of cocoa growing, the bank became enthusiastic about the prospects of a shortage in the Ghana crop. Demand, it was pontificated, had soared above supply for the last three years. Heavy rains, the black pod, a whole mess of troubles had hit the crop, and prospects were overwhelming that the shortage would continue, resulting in rising prices for some time to come.

So the bank plunged. It wasn't a cautious little splash; not at all. The waters really parted with this dive. In two months, the bank reportedly (as the rumors went) bought up futures contracts amounting to no less than *half the entire world's supply of cocoa*. Obviously, it had no intention of accepting this gargantuan stockpile for delivery; it was dealing in contracts involving only a technical ownership. The idea was to unload them on other buyers at a profit.

In its wild plunge into tomorrow, the Basel Bank bought, according to some estimates, 17,000 cocoa contracts at around $9,000 per contract for delivery during the next year. The worth of these contracts amounted to about $150,000,000, for which the bank put down the equivalent of $25,000,000 in Swiss francs, buying the rest on margin. That $25,000,000 represented three times the total net assets the bank showed on its books.

It had committed itself with such bravura at a time when cocoa prices were approaching their peak. Shortly afterward, they began slipping off. It turned out that once again rumors, abetted by government spokesmen that the crop was in short supply, were misleading. There was considerably more cocoa available, and speculators were unloading fast. Prices skidded, turned up momentarily and then fell sharply. Growing increasingly queasy, the Salik Bank tried to narrow its losses, according to reports, by straddling the market—that is, for contracts it sold for delivery one month, it bought equal amounts for delivery another month to take advantage of fluctuating prices. But the tactic failed, for the prices kept plunging without any reactions to profit by.

Before the bank got out of the cocoa jungle and wound up its titanic fantasy, it had dropped an awesome bundle of $40,000,000.

The denouement was not long in coming. The big loss

showed up when a team of Swiss auditors, making a routine check of the bank's books, noticed what seemed to be a discrepancy in its accounting. Immediately the authorities launched an investigation.

On the morning of September 10, 1970, the authorities arrested Dr. Erdman, together with his top associates, and bundled them off to jail. While the question of officially apportioning guilt—or innocence—among them was to be hammered out in a court of law, Erdman and his confreres languished for months in an ancient dungeon deprived of all the accouterments of the gracious life.

The predicament of Erdman and his bank was more than a private one. The Swiss authorities referred to the $40,000,000 loss as the greatest scandal in the nation's banking history. Financial observers calculated it could have serious repercussions on both sides of the Atlantic. Indeed, the Salik Bank suspended its operations and folded. Subsequently its parent, the Western Bancorporation, which, through an affiliate, owned Salik and which had transferred funds to its prodigal offspring to meet its creditors, showed a whopping $19,000,000,000 write-off of its Basel operations.

The writer heard no more about the Basel case or the bank that gambled for the lion's share of the world's cocoa until October, 1971, when he flew to Bermuda to soak in the sunshine and cover the Fourth Annual International Monetary Seminar run by the industrious Harry Schultz. The usual international galaxy of speakers was present with the exception of two stellar ones—the Right Honorable J. Enoch Powell, the maverick Tory, and Dr. Nicolaas Diederichs, the Finance Minister of South Africa. Mr. Powell's racial utterances and the apartheid policy of Dr. Diederichs' government had so embittered the native blacks of Bermuda, who comprise 85 percent of the island's population, that under threat of riots and bombings their trips had to be canceled at the last moment.

But Harry Schultz, who figured that a visit of white militants couldn't possibly shatter the morale of an island that permitted black militants from the United States to visit and practice their oratory, was nothing if not resourceful. He had prepared for the emergency by arranging for Powell and Diederichs to record their speeches beforehand on tape, and he had these quietly flown into Bermuda. The second day of the conference, with a masterstroke of dramaturgy, Schultz wheeled two television consoles into the plushly accoutered hotel nightclub that had been turned into an auditorium for the meeting and introduced the controversial gentlemen bigger and more colorful than life thanks to the electronic tubes. Because feeling was running high—black militants had threatened to burn down the hotel where the conference was held if Powell and Diederichs showed up—Schultz placed a tight security guard around the auditorium to prevent, he assured the conclave of 250 millionaires, the slightest possibility they would be blown into the hereafter.

After the seminar ended, over coffee on the terrace of the elegant Princess Hotel, overlooking yachts cruising through the harbor, Schultz brought the writer up to date on the latest developments in the Basel case. Like everyone else, Schultz had been flabbergasted by Dr. Erdman's sudden arrest. However, he reported, Erdman, after nine months' imprisonment, had been released from jail on $100,000 bail and was living quietly in London while the Swiss police, in association with Scotland Yard, were investigating new evidence that could conceivably reduce Erdman's personal share of responsibility partially, or entirely absolve him or possibly mitigate the charges. Indications are, however, that the final verdict will be determined in court.

In any event, the $40,000,000 Basel fiasco has by no means demolished the allure of Swiss banks in the minds of rising numbers of insatiable investors who are continuing to squirrel money into them, not primarily because of the secrecy they provide—after all, this extends only to political and tax matters, not criminal acts, which the Swiss prosecute as vigorously as anyone—but because Swiss investment channels provide an attractive hedge for those who no longer have faith in their government's will or ability to protect the savings of their citizens.

Indeed, Americans are just beginning to wake up to something Europeans have known all along: A runaway inflation can be as ruinous as a depression. Most Europeans in their fifties and sixties have experienced crises of shattering inflation—the collapse of the German mark in the 1920's and the virtual wiping out of Hungarian currency after World War

II, for example. Americans have had no such experience from which to contract a phobia for paper money.

The American psyche, on the contrary, is scarred by the experience of the Depression of the 1930's, and the chief concern of the politicians is to avoid a repetition at any cost. Accordingly, they have been willing to force-feed the economy into "growth" and full employment, even if this means endlessly printing money and priming the pump.

Just as doctors would go broke without diseases to contend with, rampant global inflation is keeping Harry Schultz and other hard-money advocates busy around the clock, holding seminars, gaining converts, pronouncing jeremiads on the economic blunders of man.

True, taking one's dollars and investing them in cocoa grown by a heathen government that refuses to oblige the prognosis of Westernized computers can wipe out one's savings quicker than the machinations of welfare planners and deficit-spending politicians can. But Swiss banks, like psychotherapists, remain irresistible to the anxiety-ridden. Insecurity is the albatross flung around man's neck in his contemporary doldrums.

Before leaving Bermuda, the writer asked the peripatetic market analyst where he planned to hold next year's monetary conclave (assuming the dollar is still strong enough to buy a plane trip). Schultz, who has an inimitable flair for the debonair and who likes to give his congregation a rattling good time whether Valhalla burns or not, said with a twinkle, "Who knows? Maybe we'll schedule three days of sessions on a steamboat up the Rhine."

4

Guggenheims, "La Peregrina" and Andy Warhol: Financial Killings and Spillings in the Art World

In 1969 an anonymous purchaser bought at an auction at the Parke-Bernet Galleries the world's most famous pearl. Found over four centuries ago in the Gulf of Panama by an African slave and worn by a succession of queens, the pearl has traveled through so many lands it has become known as "La Peregrina," "the Wanderer." The pear-shaped bauble, an inch and a half long, weighing just under half an ounce, was owned by King Philip II of Spain, then passed into the possession of Bloody Mary Tudor; it was inherited by Louis Napoleon, the French emperor, who in 1848 sold it to an English family that kept it until six years ago.

The newest buyer of the pearl turned out to be a mystery bidder who had sent an agent to Parke-Bernet to represent him in the negotiations. A rival for the gem, Prince Alfonso de Bourbon Asturias, who lost it when his offer was topped by the secret purchaser, told reporters afterward, "I had telephoned in a bid of up to $20,000. I didn't think it was going to reach the $37,000 price it went at. I wanted to make a gift of the pearl to Queen Victoria Eugenia of Spain"—an eighty-year-old queen-in-exile who had been engaged in an argument with Parke-Bernet over the jewel. Although the gallery had insisted it owned the genuine "La Peregrina," Queen Victoria claimed that she had the real jewel locked in a safe deposit box in Lausanne, Switzerland. Prince Alfonso had hoped to resolve the dispute by buying the Parke-Bernet version for the queen so that she would own both specimens. But his plan was thwarted when the anonymous bidder snatched the gem from him.

Several days after the auction, the identity of the purchaser was revealed. It was Richard Burton, the actor, who bought "La Peregrina" for Elizabeth Taylor, his wife. Burton had worked through an agent to keep down the price. But he was exposed by a reporter who recalled that the actor had used the same ruse previously to snap up the 33.19-carat Krupp diamond for $305,000, outwitting Harry Winston, the jeweler, who had dropped out at the $300,000 level.

Several months after purchasing "La Peregrina," Burton presented his insatiable wife with a diamond costing over $1,000,000. Lines of people queued up at Cartier's in New York to get a glimpse of the bauble before it was delivered to the actress. One wag, fascinated by the sight of the "peasants gawking" at the diamond, quipped that it "would have been nice for Marie Antoinette to have worn in the tumbril on the way to the guillotine." Next day, the New York Times sternly editorialized:

> . . . the inch-long, inch-thick Cartier diamond is a smart buy because it goes with everything. It won't clash with the smaller Krupp diamond costing over $300,000 already given by Mr. Burton as a modest gift to his wife. It won't seem out of place on the yachts parked in the Bahamas or in the Mediterranean where the Beautiful People spend much of their time, not to mention money, impressing each other. In this age of Vulgarity marked by such minor matters as war and poverty, it gets harder every day to scale the heights of true vulgarity. But given some loose millions, it can be done. . . .

Despite the New York *Times'* wounded sensibilities, the very rich have been stepping up their purchases of fancy jewelry and costly works of art, not merely, or even primarily, for reasons of conspicuous consumption but for highly practical motives. Investing in *objets d'art* has been an exceedingly profitable venture, especially since World War II. The Money Crowd has always realized that great paintings are one of the few gilt-edged securities available in times of social and political upheaval. With the worth of money depreciating, the masterpieces of painting, sculpture and antique jewelry have been serving as a highly negotiable currency in New York, London and Paris. Indeed, over the last thirty years, master paintings especially have appreciated considerably more than the Dow Jones Industrial Averages.

Among old masters, the prices of Rembrandts have been climbing on each successive sale. In 1950, Rembrandt's portrait of a boy believed to be his son Titus was sold for over $160,000. Fifteen years later, Norton Simon, the West Coast industrialist, shelled out $2,200,000 for it. In the 1950's, etchings by Goya fetched about $5,000; in the early 1960's, an aquatint by this artist went, in a London auction, for $58,000. In the early 1950's, a work by Jackson Pollock could be bought for under $1,000. In another ten years, his paintings were netting $100,000 and over.

Stimulated by skyrocketing prices, a number of art investment funds, similar to closed-end funds, have mushroomed up around the world. One prestigious vehicle has been launched by two of Europe's leading financiers, Baron Leon Lambert, a senior partner in Belgium's second biggest bank, and his cousin by marriage Baron Elie de Rothschild. Named Artemis, after the Greek goddess of hunting, the fund has not had to scrounge for capital. It has been bombarded by eager investors.

What is a painting or sculpture actually worth? Anything anybody will plunk down for it. Confronted with the rapidly changing worth of money, painters have, with exquisite irony, seized upon the very nub of value. Reports *Life* magazine: "Money is generating a new kind of interest in the art world. Always glad to make money out of art, some enterprising artists are now trying to make art out of money."

Not long ago, a Manhattan bank staged an exhibition of "monetary art." The feature display was a sculpture made entirely of $1 bills, totalling a quarter of a million. The sculptor had to borrow the cash to execute his "sculptural daydreams." The bank stationed security guards around the work and placed it in a vault each night. During the five-day display, the artist ran up a bill of $300 for the interest charged on the money.

Another stellar contributor to "monetary art," Edward Kienholz, has produced a series of "watercolors" consisting of only one thing: his asking price—in effect handing out, like the U.S. Treasury, his own currency. "All I am doing is creating a situation to allow for human greed," explains the painter. "I'm really the loser anyway, since [the money] I get in return will depreciate while the value of the work goes up."

Another painter who has tried to exploit this strange behavior of value is Andy Warhol. In 1962 he painted a work, "Dollar Bills," which was grabbed by an art collector for $200—the face amount painted on the bills. But Warhol was short-changed; he had been under the impression he was making money by exchanging his painted dollars for Uncle Sam's currency. He soon learned how naïve he was. Today his painting is worth $20,000, representing a 10,000-percent gain to the collector who bought it as an investment. The $200 Warhol received has depreciated to about $140.

Investing in art can be risky as well as profitable, since tastes change arbitrarily. Once-fashionable paintings have plummeted in price under the altered critical appraisal of subsequent generations. A drop in the stock market and poor business conditions can also have an adverse impact. (During the 1969-70 bear market, the market for higher-priced paintings peaked somewhat; but prices for etchings, prints and engravings continued to prosper.)

Moreover, art trading in auctions and private sales is replete with questionable practices. It is a field only for an expert or an investor who is represented by an expert. Greedy amateurs need not apply.

London is the capital of the auction world, and here the game takes deftness and guts. All sorts of tricks are used to beat down prices. Reports one insider familiar with the stratagems at Sotheby's (it and Christie's are the two major auctioneers):

> . . . bids are made by a finger lifted an inch. A New York dealer buys the diaries of Sir Arthur Sullivan at 11,000 pounds ($30,800) by rhythmically raising his eyebrows. Another dealer appears to be whispering to someone behind him, meanwhile signalling the auctioneer with his thumb. Such tactics are calculated to disconcert rivals, who it is presumed, will be disadvantaged if they don't know where the other bids are coming from.

Top man at Sotheby's during much of the postwar period and a blue-chip member of the Money Crowd has been a remarkable fellow by the name of Peter Wilson. In his late fifties, Wilson springs from one of England's great families. His grandfather on his mother's side was Lord Ribblesdale, a crony of King Edward VII's; Peter's father, Sir Mathew Wilson, was a close friend of the Duke of Windsor's. Wilson went to the best schools, Eton and Oxford. During World War II, he joined the British Intelligence. Before working for Sotheby's, he served for a brief period as a Reuter's reporter; then he joined the business staff of an art magazine.

In 1936 Wilson was invited by one of Sotheby's directors to join the firm. He started in modestly, cataloging furniture. His creativity and promotional flair propelled him up the ladder. In the early 1950's he brought off a deal that won him kudos in the art world. Farouk, the dissolute King of Egypt, had just been toppled from his throne and had fled to Rome, abandoning a valuable collection of watches, coins and snuffboxes, together with some highly spiced pornography. Wilson rushed to Cairo, hoping to get his hands on the collection. Threading his way through a maze of legal complexities, he organized an auction and sold for almost $2,000,000 all but the pornography, which he discreetly refused to touch.

Wilson continues to be a zestful, hard-driving promoter who is convinced that art will assume an increasingly important role, serving as an international currency as affluent people come to rely more on aesthetic values than money exchanges.

Several years ago, Sotheby's moved into America, taking over Parke-Bernet, the blue-chip New York gallery. A million and a half dollars was offered to Parke shareholders, and the merger turned Sotheby's into the biggest auctioneer in the business. Wilson's strategy is to search every nook and cranny of Britain for old masters, coaxing them from owners plagued by taxes. Thanks to masterly publicity, he has been getting customers to shell out more money for his paintings than experts ever thought possible. Before his regime, the top bid for a painting at Sotheby's was $86,000. Wilson has cracked this ceiling, soaring into the stratosphere. He has packed the auction room with record crowds by turning it into superb theater.

There are other members of the Money Crowd whose investments in art are paying off in spades. Calouste Gulbenkian, the Armenian who made an oil fortune and was known as "Mr. Five Percent" because of his lifetime percentage of royalties from his Middle East investments, put together a collection of traditional art that is unrivaled outside of museums. It passed into the hands of his son, Nubar, and was valued for probate in 1968 at 4,500,000 pounds. (If the pieces were put up separately, experts believe, they would fetch two or three times that amount.)

Another collector who has amassed a substantial investment is the American J. Paul Getty. Finding himself loaded with cash thanks to a series of profitable oil deals during the Depression, when virtually everyone else was broke, Getty laid the foundations of his collection by acquiring masterpieces at bargain prices. Among other things, he purchased from the Viennese Rothschilds the world's greatest collection of eighteenth-century French furniture just before Hitler marched into Austria. But there are limits even to the resources of Getty, a billionaire and one of the world's two or three richest men. Once he visited the British Museum and asked an official what the frieze from the Greek Parthenon would cost; he was told, "More money than you've got, Mr. Getty."

Still another scion of wealth and a leading patron of modern art is Marguerite "Peggy" Guggenheim of the mining family. Inheriting $900,000 from her parents, she parlayed a relatively shoestring investment—$250,000—into a collection of modern art that is worth up to $12,000,000 by some estimates.

Peggy has learned from bitter experience just how much of a gamble art investments can be. She was the first to champion Jackson Pollock, considered by some to be the greatest painter after Picasso. She discovered Pollock when he was a struggling artist earning a living as a carpenter. Pollock had a drinking problem and Lee, his wife, persuaded Peggy to lend him $2,000 as a down payment for a house on Long Island. She felt if she could get her husband out of Manhattan he could cut down on his drinking. Intrigued with Pollock's potential and desiring to ease his problems, Peggy offered him a contract providing $150 a month and an additional settlement at the end of the year if she was able to sell $2,700 worth of his paintings.

She couldn't peddle Pollock, and no gallery would take the

contract off her hands. She wound up giving away his pictures to various museums, keeping only two. Ten years later Pollock's work caught on. The artist's use of his whole body to rub paint onto the canvas with psychic frenzy became the rage of the art world. Pollock died, worn out by illness, just as he hit the jackpot; but his wife became a millionaire. And Peggy Guggenheim, who had given away twenty-nine of his paintings for nothing, had made the biggest miscalculation of her career.

Peggy has been a black sheep of the Guggenheims, one of America's wealthiest dynasties that sprang from humble enough origins. Meyer Guggenheim, a Swiss Jew, came to America in 1847, sold shoe polish in the streets of Philadelphia, entered the mining business and wound up in control of the American Smelter and Refining Company, dying a multimillionaire. His son Daniel took over the enterprise, and although he went no further than high school, he expanded the family wealth worldwide, opening tin mines in Bolivia, diamond fields in South Africa, gold mines in Alaska, rubber plantations in the Belgian Congo. One of Daniel's brothers, Benjamin, was Peggy's father. Her mother's family—the Seligmans—sprang from equally paltry origins and also acquired substantial wealth.

Recalls Peggy in her autobiography, "I come from two of the best Jewish families, one of my grandfathers was born in a stable like Jesus Christ . . . and my other grandfather was a peddler." Actually, the Guggenheims had more than their share of eccentrics. One of Peggy's aunts was an "incurable" soprano who, while walking in the street, or waiting for a bus, opened her mouth wide and belted out the scale, urging everybody within hearing distance to do the same. She wore her hat hanging from the back of her head, with long hatpins emerging dangerously. She was a compulsive gambler, had a phobia for germs and went about constantly bathing her furniture in Lysol. Her husband fought bitterly with her and tried to murder her with a golf club. Not succeeding, he hurried off to a reservoir, tied weights to his feet and drowned himself.

An uncle of Peggy's lived on a diet of charcoal until his teeth were black as soot. He went around with pieces of cracked ice in his pockets, continually sucking on them. He drank heavily before breakfast, gambled the day away, locked his mistresses in his bedroom to keep them faithful. Finally he put a bullet through his head; whereupon his father appeared at the funeral squiring one of his dead son's mistresses. Another of Peggy's uncles was fond of acting like a snake. He strung a number of chairs together and wiggled along on them sending the children into paroxysms of terror. The other two uncles were nearly normal. One spent the entire day washing himself in his bathtub, the other writing plays which never got produced.

Peggy's father, Benjamin, was also an oddball. Two of his brothers entered the family business; Benjamin refused. He abandoned his wife and three daughters and went to Paris to lead a gypsy life. In the spring of 1912, he booked passage to the United States. The trip was canceled by a strike of the stokers. He took the next ship, the *Titanic,* and was drowned when it sank in mid-ocean. Benjamin had kept a lavish stable of mistresses, and he set up trust funds for them, decreeing that upon the death of each, the money should revert to his daughters. For years, Peggy inherited dribbles of money from her father's assorted concubines. Her last benefactor lived to be over one hundred.

Despite his footlooseness, Peggy adored her father. She was in her teens when the *Titanic* sank, and she suffered a nervous breakdown. She worried about matches falling to the floor and stayed awake nights fearful the house would catch fire because she had neglected to pick up a match. "I wandered about evolving in my brain all the problems of Raskolnikov, thinking how much I resembled this hero of Dostoyevsky's *Crime and Punishment.* Little by little I became normal again."

Even after she came into her inheritance and was independently wealthy, she had a severe inferiority complex. She was distressed over the ugliness of her nose and went to a family surgeon to have it changed. He asked her to choose a plastic model of the nose she preferred, but he never was able to give her what she desired. "I want a nose tilted like a flower; something I had read about in Tennyson." During the operation, performed under a local anesthetic, while suffering the "tortures of the damned," she told the surgeon to stop and leave things as they were. Her nose remained painfully swollen for a long time and she hid from her friends until it shrank to normal. "Every time it rained, I knew it beforehand because my nose was a barometer that would swell up in bad weather."

Lonely and bored, she went abroad, had a fling in Paris, throwing herself into the radical life of postwar Bohemia, going through a succession of liaisons. Her romantic attachments were stormy. Her first marriage, with Lawrence Vail, the painter, was punctuated by bitter quarrels. An affair with John Holmes, an Englishman, ended with his death in an auto accident. Her marriage to Max Ernst, the modernist painter, broke up. "I have been lucky with everything in life, but love," Peggy reminisces.

She was highly fortunate in her career as collector of modern art. Yet her introduction to it was quite unpromising. She visited Alfred Stieglitz, one of the pioneer promoters of twentieth-century painting, who put the first abstract work she had ever seen into her hands. It was painted by Georgia O'Keeffe, the sister of the wife of Robert Young, the railroad tycoon. She turned it around four times before she decided which way it should be hung.

She wasn't the only one who was bewildered in those days by the effusions of modern painters. When Picasso met Igor Stravinsky for the first time, in Italy, he painted the composer's portrait as a farewell gift. Upon Stravinsky's return to Paris, the customs officials refused to let him through. They took one look at the painting, which was done in the Cubist style breaking the face down into geometrical essences, and accused Stravinsky of being a spy who was trying to smuggle in a military map of secret defense fortifications. The Russian narrowly avoided having it confiscated by sending the portrait to a friend who worked at the British embassy in Rome and who transmitted it to Paris via a diplomatic pouch.

But Peggy rapidly overcame the hurdles to understanding Picasso and his colleagues. Upon her mother's death she received an inheritance which, added to her father's, gave her ample means to indulge as a collector. She opened a gallery first in London, then in Paris, and launched a crusade to sponsor struggling young painters and sculptors—a campaign she has pursued indefatigably to this day. By the time World War II broke out, she had acquired an extensive collection of Cubist, Dadaist and Impressionist works and was celebrated as a patron of the avant-garde.

In the course of collecting, she hobnobbed with the leading artists and intellectuals of Europe between the wars. The Paris in which she made her home was considerably different from the nineteenth-century city of Toulouse-Lautrec. In the 1920's, the colony of Bohemian artists and writers had migrated from the Montmartre to Montparnasse. The vaudeville halls that had echoed to the can-can of La Goulue gave way to the sophisticated new musical shows of Maurice Chevalier and Mistinguette. Until World War I, virtually the only black people seen in Paris were North African colonials sporting crimson fezzes. But with the signing of the Armistice, blacks arrived with trombones from Chicago and New Orleans to plunge the city into a bacchanalia of jazz. Josephine Baker, blessed with a husky voice and a flaming ostrich feather that waved saucily over her rump, danced into the hearts of the Gallic world.

In the glass-enclosed bistros of the Boulevard Montparnasse, Ernest Hemingway planned *The Sun Also Rises*; cub reporters swapped dreams of becoming internationally celebrated correspondents; American heiresses unwound over drinks after a torrid weekend with a bullfighter in Spain.

Yet in some respects this Paris was unchanged from the day of Henri Murger. If one walked up a certain back alley, he would come upon the café where Voltaire and Diderot debated the rights of man; workingmen and their families still danced to the tunes of a barrel organ in a *bal musette* of the streets; and young lovers stretched out, as of old, in a *fête champêtre* on the banks of the Seine while the pinnacles of Notre Dame sparkled in the sunlight.

With the outbreak of World War II, this Paris came abruptly to an end—and with it Peggy Guggenheim's career as an impresario of the arts. When the German armies broke into France, she was suddenly confronted with the problem of how to save her valuable and extensive collection from the Nazis. She looked around for a suitable hiding place. An official of the Louvre, which planned to ship its own treasures out of Paris and hide them in an underground vault, offered Peggy a cubic meter of space next to its masterpieces. Peggy took her paintings out of their frames and packed them for shipment.

Then several officials objected. She learned to her astonishment that the Louvre had decided her collection was not worthwhile enough to be given a refuge. "The art the Louvre considered not worth saving," she recalls, "included a Kandinsky, several Klees, Cubist studies by Braque and Léger; among the surrealist paintings were those of Miró, Max Ernst, Tanguy, Dali, and sculpture by Brancusi, Lipchitz, Giacometti, Arp, Henry Moore!"

Fortunately a friend who had rented a château near Vichy to use as a schoolroom for evacuated children offered Peggy a barn in which to conceal her works. Two days before the Germans entered Paris, she shipped her collection there. Eventually she got it out of France, hiding it under sheets, pots and pans and shipping it to New York as "household goods." And through her contacts, she managed to smuggle a number of European artists into the United States.

For the duration of the war she ran a gallery in Manhattan. But after V-J Day, she gave it up to return to Europe. Fulfilling a lifelong hankering, she bought on Venice's Grand Canal a *palazzo* built in the eighteenth century by an illustrious Venetian family which had given two doges to the republic. The palace had a floor below water level, and this became Peggy's art gallery. Built in white stone and covered with vines, the *palazzo* possessed a splendid courtyard with stairs going down to the canal and one of the largest gardens in Venice bearing trees dating back to the Middle Ages. Peggy turned the *palazzo* into a mecca of art that drew *aficionados* from around the world. She cut a picturesque figure in this city of lagoons, sallying forth in her private gondola with the air of a Renaissance duchess; her gondoliers wore the colors of her *palazzo*—armbands and sashes of turquoise blue—and the poles at her palace landing were striped in the same color.

Peggy startled the Venetian establishment with her badinage. One one occasion, she bought a sculpture representing a horse and rider, the latter with his arms spread out rapturously; and to underscore this, the artist had added an erect phallus. But he had made it separately so it could be removed. The artist placed the horse and rider in Peggy's courtyard directly opposite the headquarters of the prefect (mayor) of Venice. Peggy's best view of the sculpture was from her sitting room; from here she could observe the reactions of visitors who came upon the horseman unexpectedly. When the nuns on their way to a blessing by the Patriarch of Venice passed the palace in their motorboat, Peggy discreetly unscrewed the organ and hid it. She also did this when she received straitlaced visitors, but occasionally she forgot and suffered embarrassment.

For years Peggy's unconventional life, to say nothing of the autobiography she had written trumpeting it, had been frowned upon by the less heteroclite members of the Guggenheim family. But as time passed and she emerged as an acknowledged panjandrum of the art world, the complaints subsided. A reconciliation was effected in 1969 when Peggy, in her seventies, announced to the press that her valuable collection of 263 works would go at her death to the Guggenheim Museum in Manhattan, built by her uncle and run by her cousin Harry, the present head of the family.

The breach was sealed by a glittering party given Peggy at the Guggenheim Museum during a visit to the United States. The New York *Times* reported the next morning:

> 1000 denizens of the art and social worlds turned out to greet her. . . . There, in Peggy Guggenheim's honor, the fountain had been painted a deep blue and stocked with goldfish, and the golden lion of Venice reigned on his red banner. . . . "The best show is on the floor rather than on the walls," remarked Jackie Rogers, the boutique owner. . . . "I've never seen anything like it," exclaimed Joan Van de Maele [Harry Guggenheim's daughter]. "Why there's a girl wearing nothing under her dress." "That girl," who turned out to be Andy Warhol's new superstar, Ultra Violet, wore a dark green lace dress with a red velvet band strategically covering her from the navel down. . . . About half of the women came in pants. Joanna Barnes, the actress, wore hers with an embroidered violet tunic. Marisol, the sculptress, topped hers with gold embroidered black sweater.

Marguerite "Peggy" Guggenheim has made money and derived much satisfaction from her jousts in the art world. At the same time, other investors are continuing to place money into paintings and sculptures at a rising pace, considering them a better currency than the green stuff put out by Doctor Nixon. Accordingly, proven works are continuing to appreciate in value. At a recent Parke-Bernet auction, "A Landscape by a River," attributed to the school of Hercules Seghers, a seventeenth-century minor Dutch artist, and expected to bring in about $2,000, sold for an eye-popping $110,000. The auction as a whole grossed three times more than the gallery had estimated.

This year American art in particular is "in." Not only has Parke-Bernet been briskly peddling a plethora of U.S. paintings and sculpture by illustrious Yankee Caucasians, but the folk art of their Indian brothers is going well. Americana is booming in Europe, especially in Germany, where pop paintings are having a field day. President Nixon, in devaluing the dollar, has given a heady assist to the native muse, since foreign collectors can buy American art for less money than before.

The *Zeitgeist* is infectious. Staid Parke-Bernet, making obeisance to the electronics age, has installed a computerized system through which it is compiling an intelligence dossier on well-known collections and their owners to map out promising areas of future auction business, much as an enterprising supermarket manager monitors its inventory to locate the dead spots on its shelves and keep the sales dollar spinning.

There is unquestionably a growing efflorescence of art appreciation by the American consumer. And this is by no means confined to works on canvas. According to press reports, a rising number of women—stenographers, show people, flower children—in their zest for complete equality with the male have been flocking to tattoo shops to have themselves decorated, not with the barroom designs traditionally burned into hirsute sailors, but dainty little hearts and flowers—"permanent body jewelry," as one tattooer advertises his wares—daubed across milady's shoulders, her breasts and less mentionable places.

Apart from the tattoo needle wielders, there are, of course, the more conventional peddlers who are hawking the latest models of paintings like slick new Fords to Americans needing to decorate their homes with something that fits in nicely with beer cans. One West Coast merchandiser, who got his training selling paintings through a grocery chain, now has a force of busily employed artists turning out piecework, some specializing on trees, others on houses, still others on women's noses. Retorts one art dealer, criticized for the assembly-line techniques he demands from his artists, "Rembrandt could knock out a sketch in ten minutes. I want to supply artists with the aggressive techniques they need to be as wealthy as they deserve to be."

If any further evidence were needed that big money is being made today not only from kitsch art but the high-toned variety provided *soi-disant* collectors of Park Avenue and Mayfair—and not only by the collectors but painters too—the case of Mark Rothko, an abstract impressionist artist can be adduced. Rothko, an artist of solid reputation but no Picasso when he committed suicide in 1970 at the age of sixty-six, left an estate worth over $5,000,000 from his forays with pigment. Recently the guardian of Rothko's two children (their mother is deceased) filed suit claiming that the executors, in collaboration with a leading Manhattan art gallery, had entered a conspiracy to "defraud" the children and "waste the assets of" the estate.

In short, modern art has assumed all the trappings of big business, including the ultimate accolade of inheritors battling through high-powered legal attorneys over the proceeds of an ancestral fortune. This is something that Picasso, when he handed out that subversive Cubist painting to Stravinsky in Rome, scarcely could have foreseen.

5

Mr. Goldfinger's World of Yellow Metal: The Gold Crowd Bets Against the American Eagle

For years, as one drove along the main highway below Louisville, one passed a series of road directions warning DANGER, KEEP OUT, ARMED GUARD. The signs pointed the way to Fort Knox. If a curious traveler ever wanted to get past the elaborate labyrinth of radar, pill boxes, signal devices, he would come upon an impressive sight. For here, packed neatly into stacks worth billions of dollars, lies half the nation's gold supply.

While fiction writers have dreamed up all sorts of ways of robbing the gold from Fort Knox, the likelihood is nil. The protective devices developed over the years have been ingenious and meticulous. Each time a gate swings open, an electronic instrument records the entrance of an individual. Each attendant's report is slipped into a vault which locks automatically so the message cannot be withdrawn by unauthorized hands. The slightest whisper is picked up by high-powered microphones. All employees handling the precious metal have to shower and discard their work clothes, which are examined for the tiniest speck of gold dust adhering to them. So dismal, so chillingly aloof is this fortress, it has been called a cemetery of gold. And the treasure so painstakingly stored there does not serve any obviously practical use.

The gold, points out Joseph Joachim, a journalist who visited Fort Knox, "does not light a single gleam in a pretty woman's eyes. It does not herald the glory of a mighty king. It is not wrought . . . to delight the eyes of an art lover. . . . It does not pass from hand to hand in fair payment of goods delivered and services rendered." For years, the sole purpose of the gold stored in this gloomy citadel has been that *it was there and people believed it was there.*

True, things have changed recently. The United States government, savaged by a rising trade deficit and a drastic slumping in its gold reserves brought on by Europeans' flight from the dollar, ended the convertibility of the dollar into gold for foreigners in August, 1971, and no longer will pay $35 an ounce or any price for it.

Despite this severance of the umbilical cord, millions of people around the world still remain psychologically attached to the precious metal as the ultimate haven of security.

In this century of wars, dictatorships and depressions, the ownership of gold at critical times by Europeans and Asians has made the difference between eating and starving. Whenever governments have fallen and economies collapsed, the yellow metal has been honored throughout the world as the most acceptable medium of exchange. Unlike paper money, which as a commodity is worthless, gold has an intrinsic value as jewelry and for a myriad of other artistic and industrial uses.

Throughout history, gold has exerted a strange witchery over people. In Russia, the favorite jewelry of the czarinas was Easter eggs fabricated from gold. Even Communist Russia has succumbed to the spell of the yellow metal. When Lenin came to power, he lashed out savagely at what he called "capitalism's metal" and said that gold was fit only to line public toilets. But subsequently, the Soviets, needing foreign exchange, began exploiting their huge gold mines in the Urals, and today they have become the world's second-largest producer of the aureate metal.

Hoarding gold in Asia is a veritable style of life. Most people cannot buy autos or TV sets or refrigerators (there aren't enough produced), so they hoard gold. A tourist strolling through the twisting, fetid streets of Bombay will find amidst the cow dung and the beggars, goldsmith shops laden with golden bracelets, necklaces, religious amulets for the Hindu masses, who collect them as Americans collect insurance policies.

So great is the lure of gold among Asians that smugglers daily dare to sneak it past customs into countries where the penalty for being caught is prison or death. Slivers of the yellow metal are concealed in cans of powdered milk or under bicycle seats, in the folds of robes of Buddhist priests or gurus. Runners bring in contraband gold under tiny strips of adhesive plaster glued to their bodies.

The precious metal exerts an equally strong attraction for many Westerners. While Americans are prohibited from owning gold as a result of a law passed thirty-seven years ago by the Roosevelt administration, this has not prevented adventurous individuals from buying it illegally. The nation is plagued with chronic inflation and the historical-minded cannot forget that the United States is one of a handful of nations that have repudiated their debts to the people in modern times. (Chief among them was the Bolshevik government of Russia, which upon seizing power in 1917 welshed on the debts of the czarist regime; another was the Confederacy, which after the Civil War repudiated its obligations.)

In recent years, a growing number of Americans (precise figures for obvious reasons are unknown) have crossed the Canadian border to buy gold in Toronto, where the price of kilo bars is quoted on the stock exchange, and salted it away against hard times.

While gold cannot be owned by Americans for monetary purposes, it can be bought by licensed fabricators for industrial uses. Modern technology is making ingenious employment of gold's unique properties—its extreme hardness and resistance to corrosion, its superb stability under high temperatures—for electronic systems, integrated circuitry and atomic reactors, as well as jewelry and dental equipment.

For industrial users in the United States, as well as individuals who can legally own gold (everywhere in the Western world but the United States and Britain), the market price of the precious metal is arrived at in a quaint fashion. Every morning at precisely 10:30, five men, representing the five major gold-trading houses in Britain, mount the stairs leading into the Bank of Rothschild in London's St. Swithins Lane, entering a room furnished with an ancient grandfather clock, a faded green carpet, green chairs, from whose walls hang the portraits of the last czar of Russia and Frederick William III of

Prussia. Each man sits down at a small desk which has a calculating machine, a telephone with an open line to his firm's trading room and a tiny British flag. The men, placing their Union Jacks downward, launch into a brisk exchange of bidding. But the moment a member calls "Flag up" and raises his Union Jack, all trading stops. The trader is given the opportunity to think things over, perhaps put in a quick phone call to his home office before making another bid. Once he has reached a decision, he lowers his flag and the spirited trading resumes.

Such is the quaint ritual by which the price of gold is fixed at the Bank of Rothschild, and on this price is based virtually every transaction that takes place around the world. This ceremony has been going on for half a century, ever since the British Rothschilds were appointed official gold brokers to the Bank of England.

The London market operates under a cloak of secrecy. Although the prices at which the gold is fixed are publicized, the amount of gold bought and sold is not disclosed. However, the London financial press has, to the embarrassment of the brokers, come up with figures of daily turnover that are thought to be highly accurate. According to it, trading ranges from 2½ to 8 tons on a normal day; during periods of speculative activity, it has risen to 50 and 100 tons, as in 1967 when the pound was devalued. There is a second market, of lesser importance, in Zurich, and this is run differently. Zurich's three main banks—Credit Suisse, the Union Bank of Switzerland and Swiss Bank Corporation—function as a trading pool to set the price spread, normally 5 cents an ounce higher than the London quote. A third market of peripheral importance exists in Paris, but it reflects basically national supply and demand.

In 1968 a vital change took place in the gold business. Ever since 1934, when the Roosevelt administration first fixed the price of gold, the U.S. Treasury had been selling it at $35 an ounce to America's dental and jewelry firms and electronics manufacturers, as well as to foreign traders. But the U.S. government, jittery over the raids on its gold reserves by overseas holders, in March, 1968, after an especially sharp wave of speculation had pushed these reserves to a dangerously low level, arranged with central banks around the free world to set up a new system under which all monetary gold would be frozen and supplies of the yellow metal, desired for industrial use domestically and trading abroad, would be determined by the natural forces of supply and demand.

This launching of a free market triggered a chain reaction around the world. With gold freed from the $35-an-ounce ceiling price and rising $8 over the official Treasury quote within the first year of operations, a number of Americans were seized with exuberant visions. People around the nation cast a quizzical eye on their property, wondering whether they owned a hidden vein of gold which could be licensed to industrial users. The classified sections of newspapers blossomed forth with a profusion of ads peddling gold mines that were for sale to anybody willing to restore them and work the veins.

Then in August, 1971, the United States government took the even more extreme step of eliminating the convertibility of the dollar into gold altogether and freeing the metal from its monetary function, or so it hoped. But the trust of millions of people in the metal remains pervasive.

A kingpin of the gold and precious metals market, which has been operating a massive worldwide hedge against inflation, is Engelhard Minerals and Chemicals Corporation. Its head, Charles W. Engelhard, died suddenly in 1971 at the age of fifty-four after an active career of over thirty years running the family business. To fully understand the role of Engelhard Minerals and Chemicals in today's world of precious metals and to provide a meaningful background for the policies his successors have instituted, it is well to examine the career and personality of Charles Engelhard, a stalwart member of the Money Crowd.

A huge, stout individual with heavy jowls and a balding dome, who bore a remarkable resemblance to the actor Sidney Greenstreet, Engelhard walked with an ebony cane favoring an arthritic hip. Although he was only in his fifties when he died, his stooped gait, the lines in his face, his fringes of snowy hair made him look twenty years older.

A business colleague and personal friend of Sir Harry Oppenheimer's, the South African gold and diamond magnate, Engelhard operated a precious metals complex whose influence reached around the world. He had inherited his father's business and turned it into a colossus, expanding a $20,000,000 inherited fortune more than ten-fold.

The fortune was founded by his father, a gruff, ascetic German who came to America in the 1890's to represent a line of precious metals for jewelers and dentists. He went into gold processing for himself, running his operation with Teutonic thoroughness. At his death in 1950 he had put together a fair-sized business, which his son expanded into a mammoth complex. The keystone was Engelhard Hanovia, a $100,000,000 family holding company operating out of Newark. The younger Engelhard also became chairman of American-South African, an investment trust dealing in South African gold-mining stocks. Also he was the biggest stockholder of International Silver, the number-one silverware maker, and additionally he was the leading shareholder in Eurofund, Inc., a specialist in European securities.

In 1949 Engelhard junior traveled to London to open a precious metals development firm. The legal work was done by a relative of Ian Fleming's, the creator of James Bond. Fleming met Engelhard socially and was fascinated by his far-flung business dealings. Later, when Fleming wrote *Goldfinger* he reportedly patterned his fictional operator on the real-life gold tycoon. Engelhard is said to have been amused by the resemblance. Upon the publication of the book, he nicknamed a stewardess on his personal plane "Pussy Galore" after James Bond's curvaceous sweetheart.

Among other things, Engelhard proved to be a bulwark to the South African economy. His involvement in it began after World War II, during which he flew a bomber in South Africa. At the war's end, he returned to Africa to buy gold for his father and became so entranced with the country's potential, he launched his own business venture. "I wanted to do something different from what my father had done," he recalled.

South Africa was an intriguing experiment. In the early postwar years there was no free world market for monetary gold, and newly mined metal was banned from international trade except for use in jewelry and industrial markets. To overcome this hurdle, a group of bullion dealers launched manufacturing ventures in South Africa, turning out bracelets, amulets, necklaces, most of which were sold in the Orient, where they were reduced by hoarders into bullion again.

In supplying capital to expand South Africa's position as a gold producer, Engelhard became a major financial power. He brought capital into South Africa in the nick of time. When he came on the scene, the nation's economy was sagging. Its gold reserves had slumped to a dangerously low level, but Engelhard brought in funds from abroad to shore up the rand (the nation's basic currency unit). Although Engelhard publicly spoke out against South Africa's apartheid as being morally and economically shortsighted, he became so vital a part of the nation's financial life that South Africans tended to forget he was a foreigner. One news reporter, writing a story about him, inadvertently called him Englebricht, which is a good old Afrikaner name.

The American magnate resided in splendor. Once he flew Charles Baskerville, a prominent portrait painter, in from New York in his private plane to paint a mural for his residence. Johannesburg, where it is located, is surrounded by pyramids of gold slag gleaming with brilliant colors, and the artist was enthralled. Engelhard took him on a six-hour tour of the forests of eucalyptus trees he owned. The pines were pruned up to a twenty-foot level and stood like soldiers on review. Upon returning to New York, Baskerville showed friends a sketch of the mural he had created. It was an abstract representation of Engelhard's South African business enterprises, featuring a stylized gold mine linked to a geometric pattern reflecting the eucalyptus forests. Near the center was a glowering black sphere. Explained the artist, "This is the sun of Africa. Or possibly the race problem. It's my first abstraction and so I'm not quite sure."

Engelhard in his personal life-style (like other scions of second-generation wealth) broke sharply from his father, who was a man with simple tastes and a limited outlook. Engelhard moved easily with the international jet set, had his own private air fleet, maintained baronial estates in New Jersey and Boca Grande, Florida (as well as Johannesburg), a suite at the Waldorf in Manhattan, a fishing lodge on the Gaspé Peninsula.

Breeding champion horses was his special passion. He owned a string of over 100 thoroughbreds which he raced in America, Britain and South Africa.

In 1947 he married a patrician blonde, Jane Mannheimer, the widow of a Dutch banker. She is a fashion leader and a stellar member of the Beautiful People, written up extensively in *Vogue* and photographed wherever high society capers. She has five children, all daughters, manages five houses, raises golden retrievers. (One morning, she woke up to find a baby hippo in her swimming pool.)

With plenty of money and drive to spare, Engelhard tried his hand at politics, becoming a big financial backer of Democratic Presidents. When Kennedy ran for office in 1960, Engelhard organized the National Committee of Business and Professional Men and Women for him. After the election, there were rumors that Engelhard was headed for a high post with the administration or the Democratic nomination for governor of New Jersey. But he crossed everyone up by running for the House of Representatives and getting beaten. During the Johnson regime, he was a confidant of the President and carried out several important economic missions for him. The Johnsons were his house guests at his Boca Grande residence a week before he died.

Engelhard has attributed his business success to his sense of timing. "The people of the world today are demanding a period of controlled inflation, and you wouldn't say you were merely playing a hunch if you invested your money in companies likely to cash in on that controlled inflation." Over the last decade, Engelhard's precious metals inventories have been sharply increasing in value. Before he died, he summed up the opportunities presented by the eroding worth of money:

> . . . the profit potential in gold and silver [is] enhancing our earnings picture to a more significant degree than has hitherto been the case. Obviously these holdings are at least as liquid as cash [and] represent an important although unstated part of shareholders' equity and are of particular value as long as we must live in a world economy that is basically inflationary in nature.

Although Engelhard left no sons—five daughters and his wife survive him—his mammoth empire is being carried on by capable outside management which is continuing his strategy for expanding the firm's position in the world of gold. "Mr. Goldfinger's" judgments and prophecies are looking better every day now as the world stumbles in a deepening money crisis, inflation spreads, with mounting unemployment, and investors grow more frustrated as they seek ways to protect their capital. Some of the more uncompromising critics of Keynesian economics, which has held the industrial West so long in its spell, suspect that the holders of gold, who for years have been ridiculed by the bulls for predicting the paper credit economy was going to smash, could be entering their day of vindication.

The case for gold, as presented by hard-money advocates, is highly persuasive today. By abolishing gold's convertibility, they argue, the United States has plunged the world into a period of grave uncertainty. Threatened by a decline in international trade, they argue, Uncle Sam will have no alternative but ultimately to put the dollar back on the gold standard and raise the price of gold. The first devaluation of the dollar has already occurred—a moderate one, to be sure, of 8 percent—but this will not be sufficient to salvage the situation, predicts the hard-money crowd, and within two or three years there could be a second massive boost of up to $100 an ounce.

These proponents point to the discrepancy between the public statements of Washington officials belittling the role of gold and their private actions regarding it. While the Nixon administration has publicly downgraded gold's role, claiming it is no longer necessary in international trading, Uncle Sam has been fiercely holding onto every ounce he possesses and has shut off payments to central banks to keep his reserves from dwindling further. Another significant sign is that since the United States divorced itself from gold, the free gold market, which many expected to fall apart, has on the contrary strengthened considerably. Less than five months after the U.S. severance, the gold price had zoomed to over $65.

The reason gold is such an excellent bargain for investors, say hard-money apostles, is that in the face of a galloping inflation during which the prices of virtually everything else have tripled and quadrupled since World War II, the price of gold alone had been kept for thirty-seven years at the artificially low ceiling of $35 an ounce. Because of this, production from mines has remained depressed, while demand has been rising, not only for gold as a monetary metal but in industrial markets, which have quadrupled over the last ten years.

Recently, the harassed international monetary authorities have come up with a new expedient for paying off debt and staving off a worldwide credit bust—issuing more debt through gold-backed SDR's (Special Drawing Rights), which members of the International Monetary Fund decreed in 1969 to be a new kind of global money used to supplement gold and the dollar in international payments. But the idea that the world will actually (as some avid Keynesians hope) adopt this "paper gold" as its sole or main reserve currency is believed to be extremely farfetched, says the hard-money tribe.

For one thing, no one has yet come up with a commonly accepted plan for converting the dollar holdings of central banks into SDR's if the United States continues to refuse to resume dollar convertibility. Moreover, the SDR's are reserve assets created and administered by an international institution on the basis of international agreements and understandings. If nations accept SDR's as their main reserve asset, they will be placing themselves at the mercy of that international body. What assurance is there that SDR's would be able to withstand the test of possible future military conflict between nations or even of heightened political tension? How many nations will be willing to place their gold reserves in the custody of this international organization in return for SDR's? Declares one skeptical investment counselor, "I'll believe in SDR's when my wife asks me for a bracelet made out of them."

In short, any way one looks at it, conclude the precious metals promoters, gold today is a great buy, either from the short- or the long-range view. In relation to other prices that have soared as the result of paper money inflation, the exchange value of gold until Nixon unhitched it had dropped to the lowest level since records have been kept. Observes one hard-money economist, "If you believe that governments can control the exchange value of anything in the long run, you perhaps will accept the viewpoint that they can, by edict, control the exchange value of gold indefinitely, but the historical record suggests otherwise."

The gold gang has one basic question for its opponents: If gold is really nothing more than a "barbarous relic," a hopelessly obsolete standard of monetary value, as Washington continues to state publicly, why does Uncle Sam insist on hoarding his own gold supply and refusing to yield a sliver? The hypocrisy of the situation is prodigious, they argue. Although the right to own gold has been snatched from Americans, Congressman Philip M. Crane of Illinois, a member of the House Banking and Currency Committee and a former history teacher, introduced a bill last year to return it to them. He believes there is a good chance of Congress sooner or later passing the legislation, since the Nixon administration has detached the dollar from gold. An administration that has officially decreed that gold is of no importance in government monetary transaction, Crane argued to this writer during a meeting on the subject, cannot logically have any objection to Americans owning this "unimportant little commodity." * In the meantime, a National Committee to Legalize Gold has been launched to challenge in the courts the constitutionality of the government's gold ban. In 1933 Uncle Sam forced U.S. citizens to turn in their gold at the then price of $20.67 an ounce. A year later the Roosevelt administration raised the price to $35 an ounce for foreign sales.

Observes Milton Friedman, the economist:

> This was an act of expropriation of private property in no way different in principle from Castro's nationalization of U.S.-owned factories and other properties without compensation, or from Allende's nationalization of U.S.-owned copper mines in Chile at a price well below market value. As a

* Charles Stahl, a leading precious-metals analyst, points out that in 1971 two men were tried in Toronto for possession of counterfeit U.S. gold coins. U.S. Treasury representatives called by the prosecution indicated in the Canadian court that gold coins are considered legal tender in the United States. The defense accused these witnesses of prevarication in their zeal to help convict the defendants, since the U.S. government had been telling Americans for thirty-seven years that gold coins are *not* money in the generally accepted sense. This inclination to maintain one thing in a Canadian court and the exact opposite for domestic consumption indicates at the very least an attitude of ambiguity on the part of U.S. officials. (*Green's Commodity Market Comments,* February 9, 1972.)

nation, we do not have a leg to stand on when we object to these acts of expropriation. We did precisely the same thing to the residents of the United States.

If Americans regain the right to own gold the price could soar through the roof, some hard-money boys believe, although others disagree. Even if only a small part of the population bought the yellow metal, demand, say the proponents, could get way out of balance with supplies and the economics of the game would be revolutionized. Henry Hazlitt, the economist, is convinced that even if the U.S. government never returns to the gold standard, the growing possession of gold by the peoples of the world, plus increasing economic uncertainty, could restore gold as the *de facto* international money. National paper currencies will sooner or later be quoted in gold by international businessmen in the world's exchanges with or without any formal international agreements, and paper money in nation after nation will return in effect to the gold standard.

In short, the message emerging from the long-ridiculed gold crowd contrasts sharply with the public statements pouring forth from the paper-money sectarians in Washington and all the suave, articulate economists who have been teaching Keynesian gospel to a generation of university students. Whether or not the gold crowd proves to be right, their argument is taking on an increasingly ominous plausibility— ominous to all the millions upon millions of people committed to the side of the paper economy bull. For the first time since the Bretton Woods Agreement at the end of World War II, the mighty American dollar has been tumbled from its perch. Is an era of new economics about to arrive to befuddle the Keynesians?

6

The Big Wheel: High Rollers at Monte Carlo— London and Las Vegas Gambling Clubs— Will the Real Howard Hughes Stand Up?

Not long ago a newspaper wrote about a casino in San Francisco "where all the losers can laugh." It's a place where a fellow can be $50,000 behind in a crap game and still wear a great big smile. For he is playing in a den known as The Wheel located on the verge of the financial district, a casino that provides all the games found at Las Vegas—roulette, craps, blackjack. There is only one difference. With every $1.25 worth of drinks, this casino hands out $25 worth of chips in make-believe money.

"There are many attractions," explains Harry Haneman, the owner, who used to operate in Las Vegas. Some of his patrons come to learn the games, going through dry runs before taking off for the real thing in Las Vegas or Lake Tahoe. Others bring along pencils and notepaper to test systems they've dreamed up for beating the house. Still others come to free themselves of the furies within them in a nondestructive way.

During one lively session at the tables, Haneman introduced a visiting reporter to his clientele. "This sure beats everything," chortled a senior citizen. "I lost $150,000 tonight and I don't feel a thing."

"I get one hell of a kick out of this," said an aging female whose hand shook as she drank a martini.

"Some folks are suspicious about the deal," confided Haneman. "They insist my customers are secretly playing with real money. But I wouldn't get mixed up in anything as phony as that."

Harry Haneman didn't say—and perhaps didn't realize—that real money is also getting phonier all the time.

The growth of worldly affluence, the ease of jet plane travel, the flood of cheap paper money from the printing presses have increased the ease as well as the appetite for gambling. And like the mescaline addict who needs increasingly larger shots for kicks, the gambler is playing for higher and higher stakes.

The managers of European casinos, eager to attract the patronage of well-heeled Americans, have in recent years added to the age-old roulette table one of the major enticements of Las Vegas, the lively American game of craps. From the plush gambling clubs off London's Piccadilly Circus to the gaudy, neon-lit clubs in Yugoslavia (where the first gambling dens in a Communist country were opened), the halls are reverberating with the cries of "get hot, baby" and the clatter of slot machines. All the electronic gimmickry conjured up at Las Vegas—the alarm bells that scream when phony dice hit the table, the hidden TV eyes monitoring the crowds, the cleverly concealed mirrors that pick up the crooked sleight of hand—have been imported into the casinos of San Remo, Deauville, Monte Carlo.

The American game of craps was imported into Monte Carlo shortly after World War II when Edward G. Robinson, the actor, spent an evening playing roulette in the casino salon and got so bored with the genteel game that he said to a friend, "God damn, I'd give my shirt for a good crap game."

Monte Carlo officials were intrigued with this wish of Little Caesar. They sent their chief croupier, Louis Delmere, to the United States to study the possibility of introducing the game. Delmere visited Las Vegas, was impressed with the incredible rapidity with which money can be lost in craps and recommended that Monte Carlo break from its patrician past and turn one of its salons over exclusively to dice. The game made its debut in the Salle Schmidt, whose heavy mahogany walls conveniently deadened the prayers and curses that rent the air when nervous players rolled the cubes. It took a little while for aristocratic Continentals to get used to grown men murmuring "baby needs a new dress" before rolling for sevens. But Europeans took the plunge and survived. Monte Carlo boldly added slot machines to give visiting firemen the feeling they had never left home.

To protect itself against American-style banditry, Monte Carlo took the precaution of hiring the U.S. firm that made the dice for Vegas casinos and commissioned it to develop a special tamperproof die, made of red and see-through-green plastic of a secretly specified weight, stamped MONTE CARLO.

Despite the invasion of Yankees on the "economy plan," the old-style European aristocrat who is prepared to stake $150,000 on the turn of a card in baccarat is by no means extinct. Baccarat and roulette still survive in chic dens on the Continent. These games, which can involve huge stakes, have been the hobby of exiled kings like Farouk, who absconded with enough of Egypt's treasury when he quit the throne to support his gambling appetite for life.

Meanwhile, kings and parvenus, heiresses and chippies continue to seek, as they have done for centuries, the absolutely foolproof system for "breaking the bank." Some students have grown bitterly skeptical. Two generations ago Hiram Maxim, inventor of the one-man machine gun, visited Monte Carlo to evaluate the chances of beating the house. At the first session he spent at the tables black came up twenty times in a row. A man next to him was so sure it wouldn't turn up again that he bet heavily on red; for the next six spins the wheel continued to stop at black, and the man was wiped out. Maxim reported his findings to the press. "All roulette systems are worthless. If red comes out 20 times there is no reason why the ball should not fall on red 40 or 70 times. . . . Each round offers a fifty-fifty chance, neither more nor less."

Actually there's one strategy, experts claim, that will guarantee a player to come out at least even in the long run; but the catch is he must have barrels of money to begin with. According to this system, the Martingale, a player each time he loses must continue to double his bet until he wins. In this way he will, theoretically, at least recover his costs. Since there are people obviously rich enough to stay with this system, the Monte Carlo directors years ago adopted a rule prohibiting anybody from doubling his stake twelve successive times. J. P. Morgan III, irritated at this limit, strode angrily from the casino and never returned. The house would have been happy to let J.P. win to his heart's desire for the publicity generated, but to have made an exception in this case would have opened a Pandora's box.

All this was before the age of computers. Today the wonders of high technology have enabled at least one talented gamester to provide what journalists call hot copy. In 1969 a thirty-seven-year-old professor of medicine at the University of Heidelberg, Dr. Richard Jarecki, emerged as a sensation at roulette, picking numbers by using a computer. He was so successful, the management of the casino at San Remo, Italy, begged him to stay away from its tables for two weeks. In forty-eight hours it had lost 120,000,000 lire ($190,000) to Dr. Jarecki and his electronic brain.

Dr. Luigi Bartolini, the casino director, explained to newsmen, "Dr. Jarecki is a very nice man with a very clear mind and strong nerves, but he wins too much." It wasn't only the doctor's ability to break the bank that bothered him, the director complained, but the crowds of people he attracted to watch him play; they were too big a problem for the security police. In a telephone interview, Dr. Jarecki attacked the casino's ban. He was a scientific not a compulsive gambler, he explained. He had played in Las Vegas but preferred the roulette wheels on the Riviera which had only one zero space to win, instead of the two at Las Vegas. He had made a comprehensive study of which numbers had the strongest attraction for the roulette ball, he said, fed them into a computer and programmed the black box to come up with a mathematical strategy for winning. "If casino managers don't like to lose they should sell vegetables." Asked whether computer-devised systems could spell the end of gambling, Dr. Jarecki retorted, "No, because as soon as you develop a successful method, they throw you out."

Whether the doctor's computer is really capable of permanently ending the house's advantage or whether it merely exploited a freakish one-time streak is anybody's guess. In any event, a number of notable contemporaries, while not as scientifically minded as the doctor, have displayed as keen an appetite for the game.

One celebrated plunger and a colorful member of today's Money Crowd is the septuagenarian Hollywood movie executive Jack Warner, who is one of the world's most skillful baccarat players. In two weeks of gambling, he parted ex-King Farouk from $250,000. Warner's most frequent partners have been the Shah of Iran and fellow movie moguls Sam Spiegel and Darryl Zanuck, Sr., as well as Frederick Loewe, the Broadway composer.

Warner's biggest coup took place in the summer of 1967 when he won over 30,000,000 francs in a single evening's play. Age hasn't dulled the thrill. Shortly after his sixty-sixth birthday, Warner won $40,000 during a party given by a friend. Driving home, he was nearly killed in a crash and lay in a coma for a week; but he recovered and went on gambling. Twelve months later, he won over $100,000 in a friendly affair with a Saudi Arabian prince.

Monte Carlo has been the scene of some of the Money Crowd's most gaudy high jinks, and it is only appropriate that the family reigning over the Duchy of Monaco, where Monte Carlo is situated, should be equally picturesque. The consort rulers are the well-known international couple Princess Grace, an Irish-American, and Prince Rainier, of French-Italian lineage. The princess comes from a family of Philadelphia bricklayers who became "royalty" the hard way—*i.e.*, by making a lot of money. Grace reached the throne of Monaco through the unlikely route of a Hollywood movie studio. She met the prince while filming on the Riviera. Alfred Hitchcock, one of her directors, couldn't have thought up a more surprising twist.

Monte Carlo was promoted into a world-renowned gambling resort in the mid-nineteenth century by François Blanc, a French waiter who, with money made in the stock market, came to the "Rock" and organized a corporation with the queer name of Société de Bains de Mer et Cercle des Étrangers (the Sea-Bathing Society and Circle of Foreigners) to run the casino which, until then, had been doing only a small-time local business. One charter investor who put money into the gaming resort was Cardinal Pecci, an astute businessman who later became Pope Leo XIII. Through adroit showmanship, Blanc enticed the rich and fashionable the world over to stake their money at his tables. The place swirled in controversy; while the wealthy frolicked, the clergy denounced it as a reincarnation of Sodom and Gomorrah.

The prudish Queen Victoria was so revolted that whenever

her train passed through Monte Carlo en route to a vacation on the Riviera, she had the blinds of the royal car drawn tightly. Her *bon vivant* son, the Prince of Wales, had no such inhibitions. He visited Monte Carlo frequently in disguise, calling himself Baron Renfrew; and even after he became King Edward VII, he slipped in incognito to play baccarat. Another royal gambler was Kaiser Wilhelm II who, learning of a system for "breaking the bank" dreamed up by a German mathematics professor, rushed to Monte Carlo to try it out. He lost 100,000 francs in a single evening, left in a fury and never returned.

During the nineteenth century the grand dukes of czarist Russia participated sumptuously in the high life of Monte Carlo. They were gargantuan imbibers of alcohol, and they displayed their prowess with bravura during a summer sojourn at the principality. A self-respecting duke thought nothing of starting the day with a dozen glasses of champagne and ending it by tossing his empty wine bottles at the mirrors and chandeliers in his hotel suite, smashing them to smithereens and cheerfully paying up with a seemingly inexhaustible supply of rubles. So thirsty were these gourmandizers they kept their carriages loaded with racks of vodka so that after making the rounds of the bars, they could tipple on their way from the casino to their hotel.

The Russian Revolution put an end to such sybaritic living. Two-thirds of the nobility that had patronized Monte Carlo were murdered by the Bolsheviks. Several of the czar's relatives managed to escape to the Riviera; and the casino management, remembering the sums they had lost to the casino in happier days, allowed these bankrupts to live rent free and sip a few last glasses on the house as they faded into the shadows.

During the 1920's and '30's, Monte Carlo was the choice resort of tycoons, politicians and stage and screen celebrities. One rambunctious patron was the aforementioned Farouk of Egypt, while he was king and afterward. Rivaling his appetite for gambling was his passion for food. He stayed up till dawn wagering prodigious sums while consuming can after can of caviar along with half a dozen chickens. Farouk was one of the world's most knowledgeable baccarat players. One evening he played against a Britisher, hit an unlucky streak and lost $12,000, maintaining his usual poker face. His opponent sat equally emotionless, so much so that Farouk summoned an attendant, who upon examining him, found him dead. He had suffered a heart attack from the excitement of winning the jackpot.

During World War II, although Europe was in ruins, Monte Carlo did a thriving business at the gaming tables. Wealthy Nazi collaborators, German and Spanish businessmen gambled away their war profits at the casino. It wasn't until after the Armistice that business receded sharply. War plunder ended; the exhausted nations imposed strict controls on export of capital in an effort to rebuild their economies; and the appetite for gambling waned. The casino piled up heavy losses, and since it provided the major revenues for the principality, Monaco's 16,000 residents were threatened for the first time with the prospect of having to pay income taxes.

The problem defied any but the wiliest of solutions and, appropriately, this was provided by the wiliest of men, Aristotle Onassis, the Greek shipping magnate who entered the scene and turned the economy around.

In the winter of 1951, Jackie Kennedy's future husband showed up on the Riviera for a vacation. While strolling through Monte Carlo, he noticed a vacant building near the casino and got the notion that it would make excellent headquarters for his shipping operations, since Monaco was strategically located between the major ports of Marseilles and Genoa. Onassis asked the directors of the Société de Bains de Mer et Cercle des Étrangers, which owned the property, if he could rent it for his offices, and they turned him down summarily without even bothering to discuss a price.

They could not have made a worse blunder. A proud man, Onassis made a thorough investigation of the society's financial affairs and found they were in a mess. The society had a million shares of stock outstanding, but the price had tumbled badly because of the deficit operations of the casino. Onassis learned that the largest stockholder was Prince Rainier, the ruler of Monaco, but he owned only 20 percent of the shares. Through a cleverly masked operation, Onassis quietly bought up stock in the open market. By the time the directors awoke to the fact that unusual activity was taking place, it was too late; Onassis had accumulated over 300,000 shares and owned the society lock, stock and barrel.

Ownership provided Onassis not only with the office building he wanted but also the casino, Monaco's three hotels, a theater next to the casino, a spacious park in front, a pigeon shoot and a sporting club. "For a million dollars," Onassis recalls, "I got control of a property worth twenty million dollars in real estate alone."

With characteristic verve, Onassis launched a program to rehabilitate the resort and get it prospering again. He refurbished the theater and hotels, had the casino redecorated, established a helicopter service along the Côte d'Azur to fly in customers via a regular shuttle service. He drained the harbor, turfed the filled-in land, built a race track. And he brought in a legion of friends and business associates to spend their money there. Oddly, Onassis has no appetite for gambling. "People ask me why I never play at the casino," he told reporters. "I don't oppose it. I understand it. But to sit there for three hours kidding myself that I care about losing a few dollars just doesn't interest me."

In recasting Monte Carlo to fit his aesthetic tastes, Onassis ran into opposition from Prince Rainier. The conflict was over differing concepts of the role Monte Carlo should play. Rainier felt that the casino could no longer exist on its former glory as a watering place for the *haut monde* but must cater to the less wealthy middle classes—the kind who enjoyed the crap games and girlie shows at Las Vegas. Onassis, a patrician to the fingertips, insisted on recapturing the legendary days when Monte Carlo was a center of grand opera as well as roulette, when the Russian Imperial Ballet danced for the grand dukes, Saint-Saëns and Massenet conducted in the casino theater and Monte Carlo epitomized all that was aristocratic in the arts. The quarrel was heated, and no attempt was made to conceal it from the public. The press openly referred to Onassis as Rainier's Rankle and the prince was reported to have said contemptuously that Monte Carlo under Onassis' regime was turning into "Monte Greco [the Greek]."

The dispute was settled ultimately when Onassis grew tired of his plaything and sold Monaco back to Rainier and the society.

Regaining control, Rainier has been doing, it is generally agreed, a competent job administering the duchy's economy.

To create more space for hotels and tourist housing in a country comprising only 390 acres the prince has launched an ambitious real-estate program. To provide more room for tourists he has uprooted the railroad that ran through Monaco on the way from France to Italy, rerouting it through a tunnel dug into the mountains. With the rock salvaged from the excavation a French-Italian real-estate construction syndicate has been at work filling in half a mile of the sea and building a community of hotels, artificial beaches and boat basins set in a surrounding of parkland. There will be a huge underground parking area, and no autos will be permitted above ground. When completed in several years, the development will add 20 percent to Monaco's usable land.

The Tisch Brothers, Larry and Preston, who took over the Loew's movie theater chain and revamped it into a far-ranging hotel, theater and real-estate imperium, have announced they are bringing an American touch to Monte Carlo. They have entered a partnership with French and German interests to build a $35,000,000 hotel-casino-convention complex in Rainier's fun resort.

Monte Carlo, a legendary playground for the Very Rich, is a logical outcropping of the Bohemian spirit, but few could have predicted that the motherland of Queen Victoria, the little old lady who was so scandalized by the capers at the Rock, would plunge in recent years into gambling with a gusto that has turned London into one of the world's leading centers for roulette, blackjack and dice to beguile the Money Crowd.

The Reverend Gordon Moody, general secretary of Great Britain's Churches' Council, who has made a study of Britain's current wave of gambling among the not-so-rich as well as the opulent, believes his countrymen are wagering because society is failing to satisfy their needs. The poorer classes have gone heavily into racetrack betting, lotteries and numbers games, he is convinced, because they observe that money is being distributed unfairly among the classes. "You can absolutely see that wealth is being distributed by chance. It is a function of health, I.Q., education, parents." So why shouldn't one woo Lady Luck to reshape the pattern of distribution in his favor?

As spending needs grow and money itself becomes less valuable in the relentless inflationary crunch, governments have abandoned their puritanical strictures and have legalized gambling to exact taxes from it. In 1960, the British Parliament abolished the gambling laws and allowed millions to do publicly what they had been engaged in *sub rosa*.

Today gambling is Britain's largest single industry in terms of gross revenues and is a source of burgeoning profits for a mushrooming class of entrepreneurs. It employs 100,000 people and annually brings in over $4 billion income (stated in American dollars). No less than 48 percent of the British population —twice the number of Americans—gambles regularly.

The Brobdingnagian boom has been accompanied by widespread violations of the law passed in 1960 which expressly stipulated that gambling houses could not exercise an advantage over the players but must give them an equal chance to win. The big, sophisticated houses got around this via a series of cynical devices. They developed magnetic dice that took funny bounces; they inserted an extra piece of felt between the most popular slots on the roulette table, narrowing them so that it was more difficult for the ball to fall into them. Moreover, the police were lax about enforcing the law, since they considered gambling illegalities to be of the lowest priorities of violations worthy of their attention.

Spurred by this permissiveness, gambling financed by big business has spread rapidly. By the mid-sixties there were 1,000 casinos in Britain. One-fifth of the players were foreigners, mostly Americans, who flew to London by chartered plane for a fast weekend at dice and blackjack. Among the clubs were prestigious ones like the Pair of Shoes, which, housed in an elegant Mayfair mansion, included among its membership twenty-five lords, seven maharajahs, a dozen movie stars. (Its membership was chauvinistically male; only two women were admitted— Sophia Loren and Ursula Andress.) The club was owned by a former Swedish merchant marine, Eric Steiner, who challenged Vic Lownes, host of the rival Playboy Club, to a well-publicized crap game. It was a costly experience for Lownes, who lost $1,200 in fifteen minutes.

There were also gambling clubs catering to the lower end of the spectrum—the Victoria Sporting Club, for instance, where, according to one reporter, "the blackjack dealers are big-breasted women who deal fast and sloppy. Everything goes fast.

There are no dramatic pauses after big bets—something you still see in Monte Carlo or at the Palm Beach in Cannes."

By the mid-sixties gambling violations were so widespread the authorities became seriously worried. There were rumors that American gangsters had muscled into the London gambling industry, threatening to take it over. In 1968 the politicians put their heads together to tighten up loopholes in the law. The number of licensed casinos was sharply cut; and the ax fell on some mighty big pooh-bahs. Crockford's of London, which traced its history back to 1828 and whose clientele included British peers and multimillionaires, had its license revoked. (No reason was given publicly, but there was gossip that the background of the ownership was questionable.)

Altogether fifty London clubs were refused licenses. Taxes were raised on gambling revenues. To cut the number of foreigners—many of whom had shadowy backgrounds—who flew over for a weekend's quick flirtation with Lady Luck, the law required that new members had to wait forty-eight hours after signing up with a club before being allowed to play. Tipping was banned. No credit was given gamblers. If a player signed a check to buy chips, his bank had to honor it whether he won or lost; previously the check would be handed back to him unbanked if he won.

In Britain casino gambling is largely the pastime of the wealthy and upper middle classes. But in an inflation-ridden, permissive society, others are increasingly joining the fun. Distinctions between the upper and the lower middle classes are steadily becoming obliterated. The blue-collar masses prefer horse betting and numbers games. When the British government legalized casinos, it made a concession to horse betting for the masses, permitting bookies for the first time to accept cash for bets. Bookmaking had been legal since 1926, but the government with *noblesse oblige* had required that bookies accept only credit for bets. The supposition was that only the rich had good enough credentials to obtain credit and the poor would be effectively excluded—a desirable situation, for as Anglican churchmen preached, it was immoral for the poor to gamble away what little they had.

Now under the new law the worker's cash was as good as the lord's credit, and blue-collar England, taking the cue, plunged into gambling zestfully. One survey concluded, "The new [gambling] act has made the largest revolution in the habits of the British working class since the war." According to government statistics, two-thirds of blue-collar families regularly gamble. The typical player wagers about $250 a year (measured in U.S. dollars); and since he loses only a fraction of this—$25 on the average—he gets a big run for his money. On the other hand, many Britishers must be losing considerably more than the average, since embezzlement and bad debts have been on the rise.

Striking evidence of the horse-betting boom is the success of Ladbroke's, which is Britain's largest bookmaking chain. The bookie, which is publicly owned, began business in 1966 with 31 betting shops. By 1970 the network had mushroomed to over 550. Profits before taxes in 1970 were up a scintillating 54 percent over the previous year. Ladbroke's and other bookies will bet on anything at the drop of a hat. And they get burned too. One bookie, William Hill, in 1964 gave odds of 1,000 to 1 that no man would land on the moon by January 1, 1971. As the American space program got into high gear, Hill lowered its odds to 33 to 1. When the first man landed, in 1969, it lost a substantial sum. Ladbroke's got clipped when Goldie, a popular eagle, escaped from the London Zoo. It bet that Goldie wouldn't return to her cage within twenty-four hours. Twelve thousand pounds were wagered by the public that Goldie *would* come back; and sure enough, the weather was so bad she did, the next day. Ladbroke's has offered 10 to 1 that the Lochness monster doesn't exist. It has offered odds of 100 to 1 against the existence of manned flying saucers. It has bet with the public on such esoterica as who would be appointed president of the Bank of England, win the Miss Universe title and, of all things, be named the next professor of poetry at Oxford.

The mass urge to bet is by no means confined to rabid Britishers. The numbers game, as every child knows, is a smash hit in the United States. Not long ago, the *Wall Street Journal* reported that numbers operators in a Cleveland ghetto were using a highly intriguing combination—the last digit of the number of stocks advancing, declining or closing unchanged each day on the Big Board. Cynics may wonder why the stock market wasn't recognized much sooner as prime material for a numbers racket.

One curious American lottery is a big success in the frozen Alaskan tundra. In fact, it is the hottest thing up north since the discovery of gold in the Yukon. Betting pools have been formed to guess when the ice will break up each year on the Tanana River that runs through Nenana, Alaska. In this region where temperatures drop to 60 degrees below zero, the forty-inch-thick slab of ice usually breaks up sometime between April 20 and May 20, heralding the approach of spring. The state runs a lottery awarding up to $105,000 to the player or players who come closest to guessing the exact day, hour and minute of the crack-up. At $1 a chance, every minute between mid-April and mid-May is covered by at least one guess, and many Alaskans form pools, paying as much as $1,000 per entrant to blanket as many minutes as possible. The exact moment of the breakup is calculated by anchoring into the ice a four-legged contraption wired to a timing device on shore. When the ice has moved ten feet, this triggers a wire, setting off a siren that informs everyone the crack-up is imminent. Out comes the whiskey, and a new winner is feted.

The Alaskan lottery is heady stuff for the descendants of the old sourdoughs, but the number-one gambling lure for most Americans is several thousand miles to the south.

Las Vegas, Nevada's largest town, is unquestionably the Holy City for American high rollers. It is carnal and carnival: America blown up to a bigger-than-life cartoon. Observes *Time* magazine, "There is a depth of corruption here that would leave even the Vietnamese breathless."

Compared with nine cities of comparable size, Las Vegas ranks second in murder and rape, third in armed assaults. In suicides it is far ahead of the field. Writes Fletcher Knebel, the journalist, "Name another city of 130,000 people that can boast 120 beauty salons . . . 125 cocktail lounges, 15 detective agencies, 14 dog-grooming shops, and almost daily listings in the classified ads for three 'anonymous' groups—Suicides, Gamblers and Alcoholics."

Las Vegas has a coloration of pietism. Mormons, who comprise one-fourth of the population, will finance a gambling den but refuse to play at its tables. From money that pours from its slot machines, dice and roulette wheels Nevada, which levies no income taxes, spends virtually as much per capita on its school system as does New York.

At the peak of its prosperity in the late 1960's, before the tumble of the stock market and the tight-money squeeze applied by the Nixon administration put a damper on high rolling, Vegas catered to over 12,000,000 tourists a year who staked almost three-quarters of a billion dollars on craps, roulette, blackjack and the slot machines.

The quintessential attraction of the city is not its marriages, divorces or suicides but the Strip—that great white way of nightclubs, hotels and casinos that spends over $1,000,000 a week on entertainment and features gargantuan display signs containing thousands of electric lights that blink, wink and cartwheel twenty-four hours a day.

A wide spectrum of patronage converges on the Strip. There is the high-rolling industrial tycoon, the weathy inheritor, the international screen star who wagers $20,000 and up during a weekend at the casino tables and receives $10,000 worth of credit from the pitman merely by nodding his head. Patrons can pick for the night an assortment of call girls, some of whom earned high academic degrees in universities before detouring into hustling in which they make up to $100,000 a year.

There are the salesgirls and stenographers who come to Vegas for a weekend fling, staking $50 on the tables and tightly budgeting their expenses so they won't run short of cash. Vegas makes the bulk of its money from the average Americans who arrive for a few inexpensive thrills.

Paradoxically, most of this money is wagered in the one form of gambling where the house enjoys the biggest advantage—the slot machine. These are set to hold up to 80 percent of the take, although those located in the lobbies of the downtown casinos keep as little as 20 percent to attract the crowds and lure them to the gaming tables. Sometimes a machine with a 20-percent hold will be placed alongside one with an 80-percent take, but most plungers—80 percent of whom are women—haven't any notion that the odds vary so widely.

Other forms of gambling offer the players much better odds. In roulette, the Las Vegas house has a favorable advantage, averaging, according to insiders, about 5.3 percent. One retired hotel captain, who has seen oceans of money lost by the unwary, warns the novice gambler not to stay too long at any one roulette table, also not to gamble in any game that offers odds as poor as 10 to 1. "Most amateurs," he observes, "freeze up when they hit a winning streak. They can't stand to win." In blackjack, another popular game, the house enjoys a 2.5-percent advantage—half that of roulette. As the number of players increases, so does the dealer's advantage, while the player's percentage remains unchanged. The game in which the house enjoys by far the smallest edge—only 1.4 percent—is craps. That is why it appeals to the most sophisticated players. But even here the ego displays a peculiar quirk. Because the advantage to it is so slim, a Las Vegas house will generally permit a gambler to play with it against the other players. However, such wagering is infrequent because of the gambler's perennial urge to beat the house. Consequently, players insist on betting against the casino in the mood of lemmings going to their destruction.

Despite all the credit handed out to high rollers, bad debts in Las Vegas average out to an amazingly low 1 percent of the take. The invincible advantage the house enjoys is essentially the honesty and reliability of the overwhelming number of people.

With such a setup, it was inevitable that sooner or later the benefits of owning a Las Vegas casino would come to the attention of the nation's money managers—the corporate entrepreneurs and bankers who are accustomed to moving into enterprises where the odds are solidly in their favor.

Historically, much of the Las Vegas gambling industry, according to the FBI and other government investigators, has been controlled by the underworld. In the mid-sixties industrialists and Wall Street financiers began taking a hard look at the profits in gambling and decided to legitimize through the structure of American free enterprise what the Mafia had been accomplishing in its own unorthodox fashion.

Del E. Webb, the real-estate and construction outfit, was the earliest of the respectable interests to buy up a Las Vegas casino. Lum, Inc., the hot-dog chain, dangled $60,000,000 before management and snapped up Caesar's Palace, a hotel casino that looked like the set of a De Mille technicolor spectacular. Stock market buyers rallied behind the corporate invasion of

Vegas, sending the shares of favorite entrants to price earnings ratios of 60-80 to 1.

In those heady years, in addition to professional management teams, dynamic individual heads of empires also moved into Vegas. Chief among them was the notoriety-prone Howard Hughes. There are gamblers and gamblers: the plunger who stakes $100,000 on the turn of a card, and the high-roller who gambles not with cards or chips but with hunks of corporate assets and real estate in a gambit to expand an empire. Such a plunger is Hughes.

Thanks to a barrage of press coverage, remarkable and ironic for a man who professes a desire for seclusion, Hughes' personality has been analyzed, atomized, debated over, lampooned and commercialized virtually ad infinitum.

When all the layers of gossip and myth have been stripped away, the fact remains Hughes is unquestionably one of the world's great eccentrics. With him odd behavior is not an occasional avocation. It is something he has mastered after long, hard years of devotion. In his younger days, he was substantially more conventional. Associates trace the beginnings of an obsession for furtiveness to the crash he suffered flying an FX-11, a plane he had designed in 1947. He walked away from the plane wreckage in Beverly Hills alive but wracked with ailments. His face was scarred. A tendency to deafness became more pronounced. He developed bladder difficulty resulting in frequent trips to the toilet. All this intensified his shyness.

Outsiders can only guess the approximate extent of Hughes' wealth. (See the table on individual and family wealth elsewhere in this book.) The bulk of his fortune resides in the Hughes Tool Company, a private concern. Hughes' father laid the foundation for the fortune by inventing a drill that slices through the toughest oil shale. A key equipment for the oil industry, it still supplies 60 percent of the market around the world. Hughes' father left an estate of about $1,000,000. The son has increased this 4,000 percent.

In an economy gripped by escalating inflation, Hughes has expanded his net worth with skill and luck. While he has made his share of business blunders, he has emerged from them largely unscathed. He moved into the motion-picture industry, took over RKO, lost over $20,000,000 in five years, yet sold out at a handsome profit. He lost control of Trans World Airlines and was ejected; in retaliation he sold his stock at $86 a share. This turned out to be its high. Had he waited it would have dropped to 12⅛. Instead of being pushed by adversity into taking a profit, he could have remained at the helm of TWA and absorbed heavy losses.

It was with his TWA winnings, amounting to $546,000,000, that Hughes came to Las Vegas in 1966 and made the nerviest high roller look like a piker. Spending over $200,000,000, he snapped up four hotels, seven gambling casinos, the municipal airport, a regional airline and mining properties throughout the state. He sparred and haggled with Kirk Kerkorian, a tycoon from Texas who moved into Nevada and bought up hotels and casinos to challenge his hegemony. All this scheming and dickering emanated from the penthouse of the Desert Inn Hotel, one of those Hughes purchased and where he lived apparently in self-imposed seclusion, served by a handful of intimates, sending his commands via handwritten memos to the satraps running his empire.

For a recluse shut up in a hotel suite, Hughes stirred quite a fuss in Nevada's civic life. He launched a campaign to build a mammoth airport and turn Las Vegas into the major Western port of entry for the giant supersonic jets expected to spearhead the travel of the 1970's. But the idea of bringing the world's jets directly to Las Vegas when the neighboring state of California was studying the possibility of building its own port of entry seemed impractical even to the egocentric villagers of Las Vegas, and the project fell through.

One issue triggered a vigorous reaction from Hughes. The Atomic Energy Commission selected the Nevada desert to conduct a series of hydrogen bomb tests, and Hughes became highly upset, especially after the impact of the first underground bomb set off at Pahute Mesa sent office buildings careening on their foundations. While Hughes claimed, through his press agents, that his motives for wanting the tests halted involved lofty social and environmental considerations, irreverent Hughes-watchers believed that at least part of his ire sprang from a more mundane source. This man, they speculated, who was widely publicized as a superhypochondriac, must have hit the ceiling of his Desert Inn retreat when he learned he had taken up residence within a stone's throw of a testing center for hydrogen bombs. Moreover, there was the matter of the $200,000,000 he had sunk into Nevada hotels, ranchland and mineral properties; he wasn't about to expose these to a nuclear fallout.

Hughes launched a campaign, bristling with money and intensive lobbying, to get the government to stop the tests. He was embarrassed somewhat by the fact that his position coincided with the demands of left-wing antiwar demonstrators, campus radicals and other vocal proponents of America's getting out of Vietnam. Hughes was a staunch conservative who, through the Hughes Tool Company had been a longtime supplier of war weaponry and technology to the Defense Department. Nevertheless, since his was the most prominent name associated with the ban-the-bomb protest, he was used uninhibitedly by the Women's International League for Peace and Freedom, the American Federation of Scientists and other promoters of war dissent.

The attack by the Hughes crowd was launched initially against the Johnson administration, which had instituted the Nevada testing. They concentrated their efforts on urging Hubert Humphrey, the Vice President, to use his influence with President Johnson. But Humphrey, deep in his new role of being more royalist than the king, shrugged off these overtures.

Hughes had better luck when Nixon assumed office. In 1960, in a complicated financial transaction while Richard Nixon was running for the Presidency, Hughes is reported to have provided a $205,000 loan to Nixon's brother and later to have furnished financing for Nixon's Presidential drive in 1968. Whatever the facts of the case, Washington, after insisting for two years that the tests in Nevada were absolutely essential for national security, quietly pulled up its stakes and moved all further testing to the Aleutian Islands, where (some irreverent folk aver) no heavy Republican campaign contributor was likely to take up even a temporary residence.

In short, the hermit at the Desert Inn retreat was kicking up quite a rumpus around the nation when, in the beginning of 1969, things commenced to sour for him and for the city he had chosen as his residence. The stock market, that cornucopia of money in good times, began to tumble, and the high rollers no longer gambled as uninhibitedly as before. Along with the Dow Averages, stocks of corporate-owned casinos sharply plummeted, and several of the businesses that had moved into Vegas with such bravura got burned in questionable dealings. Parvin-Dohrmann, a furniture and food equipment merchandiser which had snapped up a string of Las Vegas hotel casinos, was charged by the SEC with stock manipulation. Continental Connector, Lum's and Levin-Townsend, which had also moved into casino operations, were pounced on for alleged violations of security laws.

Hughes' own fortunes began to sag. His casinos showed skimpy profits, and his nerves grew frazzled. He reportedly accused Robert Mahue, the lieutenant in charge of his gambling operations, of inefficient management. Several top officials of the Hughes imperium who were critical of Mahue's stewardship moved into Las Vegas, produced a letter purportedly signed by Hughes which ordered the firing of Mahue and took over the gambling operations in the name of their chief. In the meantime, Hughes vanished from Las Vegas amidst a rash of rumors that he was seriously ill, had suffered a mental breakdown, was threatened by personal harm.

On the night of November 25, 1970, he left his Desert Inn suite, according to subsequent reports, walking down a fire escape with the help of assistants, boarded his own plane at McCarran Airport and was flown to Nassau, where he landed after midnight and was whisked through dark, deserted streets to the Britannia Hotel. He slipped in through a back entrance, was lifted by elevator to a suite on the top floor and retired once more into seclusion.

An intriguing question is why is Howard Hughes continually on the run? In a phone call made from Paradise Island in January, 1972, to a group of newsmen in the United States in an effort to discredit the authenticity of an about-to-be-published book that was claimed to be his autobiography, the billionaire implied that a major reason for leaving the United States—indeed, for living the life of a recluse—was to avoid personal harassment from court litigation still continuing after eleven years in the TWA case and from a more recent suit instituted by Robert Mahue for having been fired by Hughes' aids with slurs on his competency. Declared the sixty-six-year-old Hughes, "I don't want to spend the rest of my life sitting in some court-room." He had work to do before he died, he added, that could not stand interruption.

A month after the phone interview, Hughes was on the move again. Embroiled in a quarrel with the Bahamian government for ousting several of his staff because they had no work permits, Hughes pulled up stakes and flew off to Managua, Nicaragua, where presumably the smell of all that Hughes money induced the government to provide a welcome climate. Hughes didn't get very much of that Central American sun, however, for he shortly enplaned for Vancouver, British Columbia, and holed himself up in still another luxury hotel.

Whatever the hugger-mugger of Hughes' personal life— Clifford Irving's attempt to peddle the mogul's "exclusive" autobiography is merely the latest example—the undisputed facts of his business career continue to chart a highly visible, intelligent course, and in no area is this truer than in Hughes' financial investments. His strategy in the face of today's economy makes capital good sense.

For instance, Hughes is retaining key properties in Nevada that could appreciate considerably in the years ahead. During his Las Vegas years he sent his agents crisscrossing the state to buy up gold and silver mining claims. He acquired over 700 such claims in the Sierra Nevada mountains and elsewhere at bargain prices from prospectors and mine owners who despaired of being able to bring the precious metals out of the ground profitably. The U.S. mining industry had been going through rough times. Silver prices slumped. The government had been deemphasizing gold as a monetary metal.

But Hughes, like other investors with a huge fortune to protect, appreciates that whatever political or economic situation arises, gold and silver have a basic and enduring value that speaks as eloquently to Russian Marxists and Chinese Maoists as to stalwart Occidental capitalists.

Moreover, according to reports circulating from the Hughes' camp, a team of expert mineralogists and technologists working for Hughes have developed a revolutionary new method using computers, laser beams and atomic energy for finding bodies of ore and digging them out of the ground at a sensationally low cost. Hughes' research experts estimate there could be over $1 billion worth of gold in his Sierra Nevada properties, waiting to be extracted profitably by modern mining methods. One of Hughes' acquisitions is a portion of the celebrated old Comstock Lode Mine, whose initial strike a century ago made fortunes for a lucky team of Americans. One writer, Omar Garrison, on Hughes' Nevada operations quotes a prospector as saying, "There's more gold left there [in Nevada] than they have at Fort Knox. If Mr. Hughes finds an economical way of getting it out, he'll be twenty times as rich as he is now." As noted, the technology has been developed, awaiting only the go-ahead signal from the enigmatic boss.

As far as Hughes' silver holdings are concerned, prices of the metal have been erratic and the government's actions uncertain; and it is perhaps no coincidence that Hughes has not begun mining his properties. He can afford to wait for prices to settle and the government's attitude to become clearer; and if the crisis in U.S. currency should worsen and the political and social situation of the country become dangerously unstable, he can bring the silver up and use the bullion to negotiate the purchase of other assets when most people will have nothing left to negotiate with.

In addition to his mining interests, Hughes emphatically has been holding onto his Vegas casino properties. Indeed, the gambling industry not only continues to claim his interest but that of other extremely well-placed tycoons. One of Hughes' major business competitors during his years in Las Vegas, not quite as rich or flamboyant as the billionaire but a worthy second to him, is Kirk Kerkorian. The son of an Armenian fruit dealer and worth some $200,000,000, the bulk of it accumulated in recent years, Kerkorian is a former boxer who ferried planes for the British Air Force during World War II. Subsequently he got into the business of selling surplus aircraft and launched a Los Angeles-based airline to fly, among other routes, chartered gambling parties to Las Vegas. In 1968 Transamerica Corporation, the big financial conglomerate, puchased Kerkorian's interest in the airline, and the latter sold his Transamerican stock for over $100,000,000. Following this he acquired control of

Western Airlines, bought Metro-Goldwyn-Mayer, the movie producer, and International Leisure Corporation, owner of two Las Vegas casinos.

In the course of his rapid expansion, Kerkorian went heavily into debt. The Bank of America gave him a $73,000,000 unsecured loan, the bulk of which was used to buy control of Western Airlines. When the Fed tightened up on money, Kerkorian dodged the domestic squeeze by borrowing another $72,000,000 from a European banking consortium and the Eurodollar market.

However, the steady deterioration of capital markets, highlighted by the 1969-70 drop of the U.S. stock market, continued to pinch him, and by 1970 rumors spread that he was in serious financial trouble.

Kerkorian, like other men who have made money rapidly, has left a carload of critics along the way. Adversaries have charged him with having had business dealings with the gambling underworld; Kerkorian emphatically denies the charge, and no one has proved it.

Still criticism persists. Plagued by financial reverse, Kerkorian was compelled to close one of his Las Vegas hotel-casinos, the Bonanza, and in the fall of 1970 the management of Metro-Goldwyn-Mayer, a corporation he controls with 39 percent of the stock, came up with a proposal to buy it from him for $5,000,000, most of the money to be employed to pay off hotel debts on the verge of being called. The meeting at which the proposal was put was stormy. An irate stockholder charged that the proposal was "outrageous—a deal to rescue Kerkorian from bankruptcy." However, the measure was passed, and the big moviemaker has entered the gambling industry—a business some argue is not nearly as hazardous as making big-budgeted films.

In any event, the alliance of big gambling with big business is attracting zealous new converts. While Hughes is perched in Vancouver and Kerkorian is licking his wounds in Las Vegas, a third nawab has supposedly recently bobbed up in the field— Henry Ford II, who in the fall of 1970 reportedly joined a syndicate of investors to build a casino resort and vacation complex on the island of St. Martin in the Netherlands Antilles. The group apparently believes it has gotten hold of a good thing.

Dice and blackjack games, set in the sunny Caribbean, should attract hordes of footloose tourists so long as they are able to rub two dimes together.

However, this syndicate could be quite disappointed in its hopes, like many other entrepreneurs who found the vagaries of the business more than they could handle. The gambling industry is loaded with booby traps. As the croupiers say, *"Dans le jeu, tout arrive."* It may be that the shrewdest ones after all are those who play with phony money in Harry Haneman's 'Frisco casino, where all the losers can laugh as long as the drinks hold out.

7

"Buy on Bad News; Don't Sell on Yom Kippur": The Revolution in the Stock Market

During one whimsical occasion, this writer lunched with David Williams, a former engineer with Con Edison. Over coffee, Williams spoke of how he had been applying astrology to forecasting the stock market. Digging back into 200 years of American history, he found that periods of financial crisis have erupted every twenty years with astonishing regularity—and have been marked by major changes in the solar system, involving the conjunction of the planets Jupiter and Saturn. Indeed, Williams says he uncovered a remarkable correlation between these heavenly bodies and business cycles. Jupiter and Saturn, depending on their momentary relationship to each other and to the sun, exert either a stabilizing or an unsettling influence on magnetic fields, Williams avers, which in turn makes large masses of people euphoric or depressed in their investment behavior. When the planets are grouped around old Sol in a triangle, people are optimistic, but when they move in a straight line with the sun, folks are plunged into the deepest gloom. It was the wrong grouping of the planets, Williams is convinced, that brought about the 1929 market crash. "There was trouble in the fifth house of the Zodiac for three years leading up to the disaster."

Williams' charts warned him in March, 1969, that another bull market was finished (and sure enough, it ended). The major astrological sign that predicted stormy weather was the "Jupiter-Uranus conjunction which became exact on April 4,

1969, at 182 degrees 8 minutes of heliocentric longitude. This
. . . has occurred 15 times since 1761 and has correctly indicated a low spot in the business cycle on 13 occasions," which
represents for Williams a batting average of 867.

Wall Street, like the psalmist's conception of heaven, is a
house of many mansions.

At the opposite pole from Williams and his following is a
band equally dedicated to a mystique, but one whose credo
involves not a reading of the sun and stars but probability statistics, regression series and distribution curves. In line with
the stepped-up trading of institutional managers and the mushrooming of conglomerate operators, a new kind of gamester has
arisen, armed with the quintessential equipment of the age of
technology—the computer. The black box that makes millions
of calculations in seconds and instantly retrieves information
too complex to be filed in the cells of the human memory is
being used not only by traders of stocks but a variety of other
investments.

For instance, Dr. Henry Jarecki, a jovial, bespectacled associate professor of psychiatry at the Yale Medical School who is in
his mid-thirties, has good reason to be enthusiastic about computers. A clinical behaviorist generally skeptical about Freudian
psychoanalysis who believes in using drugs to change human behavior, Dr. Jarecki first adopted the computer to massage
statistics in his diagnostic work. Then several years later, the
professor began looking into a business far removed from the
practice of psychiatry—trading in gold and silver bullion. And
he was struck with a notion.

Dealing in precious metals is essentially a giant arbitrage operation in which the trader has to figure out the fine deviations
in rates in order to harvest profits. The computer, which makes
millions of calculations each second, Dr. Jarecki reasoned,
could outwit the brains of the shrewdest trader armed only
with a pencil or calculating machine. Since the bulk of bullion
traders and dealers were conservative old fellows who played
the game by instinct and wanted nothing to do with new-
fangled technology, the doctor figured he had a definite edge.
In 1969 he formed a company to make a market in bullion,
using a strategy programmed into a computer. This firm became affiliated with J. L. Mocatta in England, one of the hand-

ful of firms making the gold market in London and a fine old concern dating back to 1687. Mocatta was already a well-established business when a struggling little bank came to it hat in hand, asking it to become its bullion dealer. The infant bank grew to become the Bank of England, the majestic Old Lady of Threadneedle Street.

When Dr. Jarecki entered the bullion business, the price of gold converted into the U.S. dollar and the ratio of other world currency conversions had been fixed for twenty-five years by the Bretton Woods Agreement signed by the international community after World War II. But Jarecki, watching the erosion of the dollar, had a hunch that the world's money system was headed toward a crisis. He had his black box programmed to shift ground and institute a new trading strategy in the event the dollar was devalued or detached from gold, and he went on the alert.

On August 15, 1971, the crisis which he had anticipated erupted. President Nixon took to the air to announce he was abolishing the convertibility of the dollar and setting it afloat in the constellation of currencies. The morning after the speech, the British silver market was shut down. The Bank of England ordered British silver dealers to accept only sterling silver in payment, not U.S. dollars, whose status had become highly unpredictable.

At this juncture, Dr. Jarecki snatched his opportunity. For a solid week his firm was virtually the only dealer in the world having the courage to make a market in silver bullion and accept payment in shaky dollars. Thanks to its computer, it was able to measure the market with unusual accuracy and protect itself against unpredictable dollar fluctuations. Mocatta Metals Corporation has not disclosed what earnings it harvested, but there are some very happy faces around.

As a psychiatrist, Dr. Jarecki is obviously fascinated with the behavior of human beings as well as electronic brains. Indeed, it was the crowd response of the genus *Homo,* he told the writer, that first attracted his attention to the silver market. In the thirty-seven years since President Roosevelt took the United States off the gold standard, one segment of U.S. currency has until recently remained convertible into a precious metal. Thanks to successful lobbying by populist politicians in the

1930's, a law was passed committing Uncle Sam to hand over the equivalent in silver to the bearer of all dollars carrying the inscription of silver certificates. By the 1950's, there were over $2 billion of these certificates in circulation.

As the 1960's drew to a close, a serious situation developed. The ability of Uncle Sam to redeem silver dollars was jeopardized because the mushrooming demand for silver for photography and other industrial uses was placing a strain on the Treasury's silver reserves. As need for the precious metal climbed, its price on the commodity exchange skyrocketed, until an embarrassing discrepancy arose between the worth of the silver dollar and the metal itself. While Uncle Sam stood ready to turn over a dollar's worth of silver for every certificate dollar, the price silver commanded on the commodity exchange had risen to almost two dollars. By hurrying over to the U.S. Assay Office, cashing in silver dollars and selling the metal on the exchange, an enterprising citizen could turn a profit of almost 100 percent. Uncle Sam was as aware of this as any gimlet-eyed citizen. Fearful of the run on its already depleted reserves, the U.S. Treasury announced a deadline after which it would no longer redeem silver dollars for silver.

The result was predictably tumultuous. People scurried into New York from as far away as Texas, queuing up at the government Assay Office to cash in their silver dollars before the window was slammed shut. Some speculators, impatient at waiting in line, sold their dollars at premium prices to currency traders.

One of the most interested observers was the Yale psychiatrist Dr. Jarecki. Duly taking note of the profits to be harvested by the alert, the doctor has become a highly sophisticated student of silver movements. Studies embarked on by his computer indicated something he could never have detected with pencil and paper—namely, that a bagful of silver coins has had the habit over the years of commanding a premium price over silver bullion and that frequently it rises in price while silver bullion declines. Accordingly, the doctor has set up a highly effective strategy for hedging as a trader—that is, going long on bags of silver coin while simultaneously short selling silver bullion, thereby profiting when the bullion plunges sharply (as it did in 1971) by covering his shorts, and at the same time protecting himself against a rise in bullion by cashing in on a long position in bags of coin. This, Jarecki points out, is roughly analogous to the way some traders hedge by playing with a stock and its convertible debenture. Short selling the stock, they profit on its decline. If on the other hand the stock rises, they crash in by turning their convertible debenture into common shares of the stock.

Jarecki is a firm believer in holding precious metals as a protection against economic uncertainties. He is fond of telling how, during his researches, he unearthed a fascinating story about the august Bank of England when it was first launched in 1697. To raise money for its capitalization, the bank sold notes to the public. The interest on money in England at the time was 6 percent, so the bank's notes bore this rate. Within a few years, the interest rates on money slid to 3 percent and the bank was worried about having a large debt outstanding at 6 percent. It called in an attorney to determine how it could legally squirm out of its plight. The lawyer said that nothing could be done. People were lawfully entitled to receive 6-percent interest as long as they held their notes. The bank then called in a second attorney who studied the matter and declared that, while he did not like to disagree with his learned colleague who was *technically* correct, he had found in his own experience and a reading of history that when a governmental or quasi-governmental institution announces it will call in its notes by a certain date and not honor them afterward, people invariably rush in to turn in their notes, without bothering to question the legality of the decree.

And this is exactly what happened. People flocked to the Bank of England surrendering their 6-percent notes and docilely accepting in return notes carrying a 3-percent interest. No one bothered to find out whether his legal rights had been violated or whether the arbitrary decision of the bank could be successfully challenged in the courts.

The same thing held true when the U.S. government suddenly announced it was going to stop redeeming its silver certificates. The basic law requiring the Treasury to hand over silver for certificates was written into the Silver Purchase Act of 1934. There was nothing in the law that gave the Treasury the right to stop paying silver on its own whim. Nevertheless, human nature remains unchanged. When Uncle Sam announced he would quit paying out silver, people unquestioningly rushed to turn in their certificates. Anyone stuck after the deadline with silver certificates was out of luck. Because most citizens made a profit from the transaction, they didn't bother to question the legality of it.

There is a definite lesson to be learned, Dr. Jarecki and other precious metal experts argue. If Uncle Sam can repudiate his gold and silver payments, *he can arbitrarily repudiate his paper debts, too, if times get rough enough.* For the basic principle of all governments (and the politicians who run them) is that they act first of all to protect their own interests, not those of their citizens.

Dr. Jarecki took the writer into the basement of an aging building in the Wall Street area where his firm keeps a licensed inventory for distribution to industrial markets of gold and silver bars buried in a vault. Entering through a door barred like a prison cell, checked by security guards and monitored by television cameras every step of the way, we entered the repository where a hundred or so bricks of gold were piled neatly against the wall. Dr. Jarecki estimated we were looking at $15,000,000 worth of the yellow metal. He picked up one jagged shaving from the floor that alone was worth about $17,000. The doctor believes he is storing one of the largest amounts of gold existing in the United States outside of the government's deposits in Fort Knox.

"The day may yet come when we could be the only bank in the country open for business," mused the Yale psychiatrist, with a twinkle.

So much for precious metals and Dr. Jarecki's resourceful gamesmanship with the computer. There are clever users of the black box in other areas of investment. A case is the volatile field of commodities trading. The writer has come across Mr. Robert Arata, former engineer with Texas Instruments Corporation, who has been using the black box since the beginning of 1970 to manage the accounts of a group of gung-ho Texas investors dealing in wheat, corn, cocoa. From his engineering experience, Mr. Arata has devised a mathematical method which, by analyzing previous trading trends in a commodity, estimates the probability of the trend's continuing. The computer has worked out for Arata a market reversal point (MRP)—that is, the point at which the odds favor that the futures price will reverse its trend in an up or down direction. Arata is in the market 90 percent of the time either long or short. If, say, he is long in cattle and the trend reaches the MRP point, he promptly sells out and goes short. If he is short at this point, he covers and goes long—until the trend reaches the next MRP point, at which he will sell and go short, and so on.

Using this system, Arata stays away from the pandemonium of the trading pit and doesn't deal emotionally. The computer provides another benefit. Without it, a trader can intelligently handle only one or two commodities at a time. Equipped with his electronic brain, Arata is able to deal in fifteen or more commodities simultaneously, and such widespread diversification substantially decreases his risks.

His results have been impressive. In 1970 he was able to register a return of 260 percent on his invested money. His computer, he claims, has given him most timely clues on moves about to occur. For instance, he went heavily short on silver on August 23, 1971, when the price was $1.60 and rode it down as it plummeted to $1.32, reaping a neat profit. He has also been especially successful trading in copper and cocoa—although the latter is the riskiest of commodities to speculate in.

Arata is one of a handful of traders using the black box to outwit other commodity gamesters. However, it is in the stock market that the computer has really come into its own, for here it is being used in widespread fashion.

The most astute investor cannot begin to match the computer when it comes to evaluating stock performance statistically. The black box figures out millions of variables in seconds and recalls instantaneously hundreds of thousands of details stored on its magnetic tapes, relieving the hard-pressed security analyst of endless, dreary statistical labor. Also, by pouring out earnings-and-trends reliability studies, comparing the price behavior of a stock to the market averages in a variety of situations, the electronic brain can zero in on those securities which statistically deserve further investigation. One student of the new arcanum who has used the computer for investment counseling work explains, "Years ago fishermen went where they had a hunch the fish would be biting. Today, using electronic sounding devices, they go where they *know* the fish are biting.

This knowledge doesn't assure they'll hook the most desirable fish—or any at all. But it makes the odds a hell of a lot better."

Together with the enthronement of the computer in Wall Street, there has occurred an influx of a new kind of personnel —engineers and higher mathematicians—who are bobbing up in positions of influence in banks and broker houses, vying for power with old-line security analysts and other financial pundits who once had the field to themselves. The students of exponential curves, differential calculus (speaking in the new computer languages of Fortran, Cobol and Agol), who have turned Wall Street into a laboratory of monumentally complex statistics, are a far cry in psychology and training from the traditional Wall Street breed. Under their programming efforts, computers are putting out market analysis studies which are fed to individual traders through the medium of investment counselors and offered by the computer research departments of banks and broker houses to money managers of mutual and pension funds. The computer has opend up vast new horizons, along with a labyrinth of problems. It has expanded the magnitude and speeded up the tempo of stock market trading and in so doing, has pushed to the straining point the mechanism of Wall Street as an auction market.

Since the electronic brain has been a key abettor of current market complications, a few words of background are in order.

During the postwar decades, with the breakup of wealthy estates on the death of the founder, rising sums of money have been passing from private families into the hands of institutional money managers—mutual, pension funds, bank trusts, insurance houses. Institutional money, guided by computer-based analysis, today dominates stock market trading. It is responsible for over half the shares traded on the Big Board and provides most of the swing action in prices. Discontent with having to pay the standard commissions originally devised by the Wall Street exchange and broker fraternity to handle the much smaller retail trade, the big-volume fund traders are threatening to get seats on the floor of the nation's exchanges and trade directly with one another.

During the mid-sixties, when institutional trading began assuming big-league proportions, there emerged a new breed of *wunderkind*, the portfolio managers of "go-go" performance

funds. These Wall Street glamor boys, products of the computerized market and swaggering as if they owned the earth, got
rich so fast, they hadn't the time in many cases to adjust psychologically to the fact. One manager of a well-known fund,
who made several million dollars in a couple of years, continued to buy bargain suits at Barney's and bring his lunch to
work in a paper bag. Another noted gunslinger was so busy
trying to outperform the market, he installed a ticker quote
screen in his bathroom so he could watch the latest fluctuations
of stock prices while sitting on the toilet. He still hasn't found
the time to drive his brace of Porsches or use his new beach
house at Malibu.

They were an assorted crew, sprung from diverse backgrounds, displaying heterogeneous talents. Fred Mates, the
founder of the Mates Fund, which scored a 150-percent growth
in assets during a single wondrous year, started out with a work
force consisting of his wife and himself doing all the typing and
mailing until an inundation of orders vaulted him into the
big-money class. Mates was interviewed by a writer of the *Institutional Investor*, who reported he "seems like a cross between
a highway used-car salesman and an aging [he is thirty-six]
member of the Hell's Angels. His face is a mixture of watchful
craftiness and karate-chop-at-the-ready toughness." Mates' career before his thrust into stardom was a waiting for Godot. He
went from one odd job to another, dabbling in playwriting,
selling foreign cars and motor scooters. Even after he got into
the financial business, he wasn't above playing a practical joke.

As a security analyst working for a broker house, Mates, according to one anecdote which, apocryphal or not, is making
the rounds, got interested in a mining firm in Canada; but before putting funds into its stock, he decided to visit the company. He was convinced its reputedly closed-mouth management might be induced to give him more information if he
brought along a mineral technologist. He didn't have one on
his staff, but that was no deterrent. While riding the subway, he
picked up a heavily bearded hippie and offered him several
bucks to accompany him to the Old Dominion. The hippie
kicked off his sandals, got into shoes, put on a neatly pressed
suit, and so greatly impressed the corporation management
with his authoritative mutterings as he examined the mine and

its ore samples, it gave Mates all the information he wanted, and then some.

Mates reached top billing with a handful of other virtuoso performers. There was Fred Alger, who as a kid loved to build model airplanes and who discovered that Wall Street offered an opportunity for creative analysis not unlike that used for inventing gadgets. As consultant for Security Equity Fund, Alger boosted his clients' assets over 250 percent in four madcap years. Then there was Fred Carr, who started as a broker's assistant searching for "emerging growth" companies and boosted the Enterprise Fund from nowhere to assets approaching a billion dollars in the space of a couple of years. A shy, retiring fellow with a balding head and a gentle, winning smile, Carr to his competitors functioned as a wolf in lamb's attire.

In addition to the younger, brash swingers, there was a coterie of older fund managers, more mellow, more cognizant that the stock market was a two-way street and that people had taken some mighty hard lumps in that little old affair in October, 1929. While not caught up quite so devotedly in the existentialist fever of the youth movement, they had to sail in the same investment seas, and they tacked as deftly as possible to outmaneuver their younger rivals.

Several came to the Wall Street stage from Broadway. Arnold Bernhard, the founder of one of the nation's most popular advisory services, the Value Line, and manager of the Value Line Mutual Fund, started out as a frustrated playwright, wrote an unproduced play about Wall Street, served a stint as a drama and music critic and lost money as a Broadway angel before he found a permanent home with the investment community.

Howard Stein, manager of the prestigious Dreyfus Fund, also flirted with the arts, studying to be a violinist, earning money while going to Juilliard by peddling librettos at the Metropolitan Opera House, and producing several off-Broadway plays before gravitating to the Wall Street arena.

Some of the more rambunctious younger portfolio managers seized upon a new philosophy of economics as avidly as the turn-of-the-century physicists embraced the theory of relativity. This new dictum decreed that investing money in the nation's corporations no longer required putting it to work to produce goods and services. All that was needed was to push the stock of a company up and collect its market profits. As Ralph Saul, the former president of the American Stock Exchange, put it, ". . . the basic alteration in corporate enterprise and in the securities markets during the 1960's has been a change from industrial capitalism to finance capitalism, from concentration on producing goods and services to an increasing concern with earnings—per-share, price-earnings ratios, and financial results almost independent of the process of production and consumption of industrial products and services."

And, as noted, a major factor making possible such a surrealistic investment strategy has been the emergence of computers tempting technical traders in particular to try to "turn on a dime."

Harnessing the brains of the black box, the portfolio managers have been engaging in trades of increasingly bigger blocks of stock and have split open the traditional procedures of market trading at the seams. The New York Stock Exchange was not organized to cope with this sort of thing. It had been set up long before the days of fund managers and computers to serve as a central trading place for thousands of individual traders who bought and sold anywhere from a few hundred to a few thousand shares of stock. The auction exchange never envisaged the mass wholesaling of securities; it never dreamed the day would come when mammoth institutions would be capable of unloading $5,000,000 worth of a stock at a throw. For their part, institutional managers, chafing at having to pay the same commissions for their volume patronage that the individual paid for his trades, got together and began trading off the floor of the exchange through block houses. (Recently the schedule has been changed to allow the institutions to negotiate commissions on their volume dealings.)

In this age of computer trading, several of today's leading block houses, acting as market makers for institutional investors, have evolved from old-time bond houses, adding equities as a service to their clients. The ascendancy of the block houses has been sudden and overwhelming. Since 1966, the percentage volume of block trades—10,000 shares and over—negotiated on the Big Board has skyrocketed from 5 percent of the total shares traded to over 19 percent in 1971.

In short, the "feel" of today's stock market has shifted from the floor of the exchange to the upstairs office of the block houses. These are not so much bargaining rooms as pits of pandemonium. Plunging $5,000,000 and up in a single transaction, the block trader lives in an atmosphere of perpetual crisis. Only a fellow who has the nerves of a Russian roulette player can endure the pace.

A spectacularly successful example of the new breed is Jay Perry, the head trader for Salomon and Hutzler, Wall Street's leading block house. Perry is a dark, wiry, intense man in his thirties. After a frenzied day of trading, he ambles into a side room, wipes away the sweat and sips a bottle of Coca-Cola as he slowly unwinds, playing over in his mind each deal he made to see how he could have improved it.

The writer visited Perry one afternoon in May, 1970, to watch him operate. It was during the worst of the stock market decline when issues were plunging like a runaway elevator. A few days previously Perry had been through the bleakest session the market had experienced since President Kennedy's assassination.

Perry filled the writer in on a typical trade he had negotiated during that Armageddon on May 4, when the DJI Averages sank 19 points. At 2:55 in the afternoon when the averages were already down 16 points, a big fund phoned him saying it wished to unload—before the close of the market, only thirty-five minutes away—250,000 shares of Sperry Rand. Just like that. Sperry was selling at 62½. There were no takers. Immediately, Perry launched a reconnaissance through an intelligence network almost as complex as the CIA's. He flashed the news of the offer to Salomon's network of branch offices, pushed buttons and got in touch by direct wire with managers of institutional funds across the nation. The network located one potential buyer—a state fund that was willing to take 25,000 shares of Sperry at 24. Then Perry's bird dogs flushed out another possible seller waiting in the wings prepared to unload 30,000 shares at 29. At the moment he appeared to be safely out of the action, but there was no guarantee that once Perry committed himself to a position, the potential seller wouldn't lower the boom, releasing his own holdings and driving down prices.

Perry had to think quickly. He phoned a trader on the floor of the Big Board asking him to sound out the Sperry specialist regarding his inventory of stock. The specialist had orders to buy amounting to 15,000 shares at prices down to 24. He hinted he might be willing to acquire another 10,000 for his own account. Meanwhile, a Salomon branch office flashed a message that a second fund had been found agreeable to buying 100,000 shares at 24½. That meant two institutions were prepared to take 125,000 shares off Perry's hands, and the only other known seller remained at a price significantly above the market—at 29. Perry decided to gamble going long on the 125,000 remaining shares. At 24½ he bought them, putting over $3,000,000 on the line. He completed the trade at 3:12, seventeen minutes after the original seller had phoned him with his offer. When news of the trade crossed the tape and it became clear that most of the overhanging stock had been mopped up at a firm price, a dozen institutional managers, all of whom only minutes before had turned down Perry's overtures to be buyers, suddenly jumped in to purchase Sperry, leaving him, at the close of trading, with only 22,400 shares to unload. He got rid of this bundle over the next few days on price up-ticks, getting back the firm's $3,000,000 investment and garnering for it profitable customer commissions that were the original incentive for the deal.

With fellows like Perry around and computerized research enormously speeding up gamesmanship, condensing into weeks and even days trends that formerly took months to unfold, the penalty for wrong guesses is severe. This holds true not only for the big-block trader but for the smaller investor who buys or sells a few hundred or thousand shares for his own account.

Indeed, today's stock market has become an arena in which elite factions, armed with electronic brains (or the research derived from electronic brains), are being pitted against one another in a high-powered, highly sophisticated struggle. Since it takes two parties to trade, computers are being used not only to sharpen the investor's own strategy but to track the footsteps of those on the other end of the buy or sell position. The computer is being used as an anticomputer, the way an antiballistic missile is geared to screen out the decoys in a fleet of incoming enemy missiles and shoot down the real thing.

Increasingly the stock market has been plunged into the kind of tactics pro football quarterbacks employ. A quarterback, upon bringing his teammates up to the line of scrimmage, will frequently notice that his opponents have suddenly shifted their defense pattern, and he will instantly change the play that had been decided on in the huddle, calling an "automatic." The defensive captain may retaliate with another tactical switch before the ball is snapped and so on.

Electronic brains, using highly ingenious formulations, are being trained to determine not only what a genuine stock is worth but what other people are planning to do about it. "In the old days," points out one insider, "J. P. Morgan and his friends would get inside information about a company and quietly begin to accumulate its stock. Their buying wouldn't be visible to outsiders until the price had been put up to where the 'smart money' wanted it. By then it was often too costly to get in."

Today computers, programmed to spot unusual trading volume, can frequently pick up at the earliest stage the first faint traces of accumulation by "smart money." Thanks to complex mathematical analyses of price-volume movements, computers can analyze the behavior of traders with large blocks of stock who try to sell in stages on rising prices. The unloaders by their action usually slow down the pace of acceleration in the buying power of a security, even though the price may continue to rise. By the same token, big traders, beginning their accumulation of a stock in a declining market, often have the impact of slowing down the pace of decline even though the price itself may continue to slide.

Since the beginning of Wall Street, this has been the pattern of "smart money" trading. But before the age of the computer, the precise stage at which such patterns shifted usually was undetectable to outsiders. Before the price-volume studies by electronic brains, the outsider was like a bystander watching an auto speed by. He could only *estimate* its velocity. Now, he is in the driver's seat, and he can *feel* when acceleration or deceleration begins, as well as how rapidly the vehicle is gaining or losing momentum.

Just how effectively a computer can pick up a "sleeper" stock was brought home to the writer by a friend, John Hammerslough, who at the time was director of computer research at Shields, the broker house. The stock was Natco, a maker of ceramic tile. The firm had unimpressive earnings in an unglamorous industry. There was little trading and the price was stranded at 14, substantially below its net asset value. Then, out of the blue, Hammerslough's computer detected unusual trading activity and signaled Natco as a buy. His clients had a windfall. The stock, whose name was subsequently changed to Fuqua Industries, continued zooming until it hit 74, to become one of the Street's star performers.

What had happened was that an aggressive Atlanta businessman, J. B. Fuqua, had taken control of the company and was diversifying it into television broadcasting and other more profitable businesses. Mr. Fuqua's friends, aware of his plans and his reputation as an achiever, bought heavily into Fuqua stock. And they were right. A year after Mr. Fuqua took over, he increased the company's profits 700 percent.

Obviously Hammerslough's computer had no way of knowing the story behind the rejuvenation of Fuqua's firm. But it picked up the first traces of insider buying before they showed up in the price behavior and signaled outsiders to get in on the kill.

J. B. Fuqua, the man who achieved this turnaround, in addition to being a successful entrepreneur has been a powerhouse in Southern politics. Some time after the breakout of the Fuqua stock, he visited the writer to fill him in on his future corporate plans. He brought along a companion who was so shy he barely uttered a word during the conversation, which lasted an hour. Only as he got up to leave did the talkative, absent-minded Mr. Fuqua introduce his friend. "This is Mr. Sanders, my corporation attorney. He is also a former governor of Georgia."

Another avid user of the computer who has been reaping profits for his clients through studies of money flows in and out of stocks is Leslie Barnett, who runs an investment advisory service in New Jersey.

Barnett in 1939, before the computer era, joined Du Bois Chemicals as a salesman. In 1955 he bought $400 worth of Du Bois stock for $6\frac{2}{3}$ cents a share. In 1962, when Du Bois was acquired by W. R. Grace, the big chemical combine, Barnett managed to sell his stocks for an average $53 a share, reaping a handsome profit.

Looking for a way to multiply his winnings, Barnett developed a strategy of trading which he programmed into a computer. He tried it out on the stock of Leasco, the equipment-leasing firm, taking an initial position in 1965 at less than $2 a share (on adjusted basis). He stuck to this system in this highly volatile stock, weathering some severe sell-offs and refusing to be shaken out. At one point Leasco dove from 146 to 90, but Barnett held fast. His computer indicated to him that beneath the façade of this heavy tumble there was steady, if unobtrusive, insider buying. Barnett held on. The stock rebounded, and he was able to sell it in December, 1968, and January, 1969, at prices of about $244 a share, or for almost twenty times his investment. During the week of August 9, 1971, Barnett's computer scored a coup. The market was gloomy; it had been declining steadily and had penetrated the 840 area on the DJIA, which many pundits considered to be a critical support level. Amidst this pervasive pessimism, Barnett suffered a private woe. He was rushed to the hospital with pneumonia. His secretary visited him daily with the latest statistics poured from his computer.

By midweek Barnett noticed from his sickbed a fascinating trend. In a weak stock market that was drifting downward as the nation grew increasingly skeptical about the Nixon administration's ability to roll back inflation, Barnett's black box indicated the stepped-up buying of stocks by powerful blocks of money that had quietly moved into the market. On Thursday, he had his secretary flash a report to his clients predicting there would be a "strong market for at least a week. This pattern reflects a mini-rally." The prediction turned out to be overly modest. That weekend President Nixon made his speech in which he surprised the nation by instituting a wage-price freeze. The next day, Monday, the stock market skyrocketed 33 points, comprising the greatest one-day rise in the history of the Big Board.

Reports have floated around Washington that a week before the President's speech, Secretary of the Treasury John Connally held a highly secret confab with top executives of major U.S. corporations at a retreat owned by Alcoa, Incorporated, high in the Smoky Mountains, during which he briefed the magnates on what Nixon was going to announce. Whether Connally disclosed information that could be turned to profit—and Treasury spokesmen vigorously deny this leakage—the fact is, as Barnett's computer and undoubtedly those of other observers reported, there was unusual buying activity before the speech. For those shrewd or lucky enough to have gotten into the market just before that record-breaking Monday, the financial rewards were handsome.

Computers are being unveiled in a number of other applications. In February, 1971, the electronic brain made what is probably its most dramatic appearance to date when it emerged as a mechanism for automating the quotation system of the vast, amorphous market for over-the-counter stocks. Tucked away in the hills outside the sleepy village of Trumbull, Connecticut, 60 miles from Wall Street, a complex of buildings has sprung up to house two giant Univac computers, which flash and receive messages over 30,000 miles of high-speed transmission lines. The building operates under the tightest security measures. To get into the computer room one has to place a card, issued by a guard, under an electromagnetic eye, which alone will swing the door open. The windows are transparent only from the inside so that, while people can look out, outsiders can't peer in. The building is loaded with sensor devices that detect the slightest change in heat. If a person so much as lights a cigarette in a forbidden spot, this sends alarm bells ringing all over the place. When an alarm is set off by a fire, guards rush to the spot with extinguishers that exude a cloud of carbon dioxide snow. (They are used instead of sprinklers since water is damaging to the multimillion-dollar computer equipment.) A person who happens to be in a room where a fire starts has exactly ten seconds to get out or he will be smothered by the carbon dioxide fumes.

This curious complex is the headquarters of Nasdaq. Operating by remote control, "Fortress Nasdaq," as one financial writer has nicknamed it, has automated the market for over-the-counter stocks, bringing it with a leap into the twentieth century and dissipating the miasma of secrecy in which it had been wrapped for generations. The computers are enabling market makers to exchange bids and offers with other market dealers, flashing them onto televisionlike desk screens that are continuously updated as the trading proceeds.

There are still bugs to be ironed out of the system. Surveillance and disciplinary measures must be instituted to force dealers to stand by quotes they put into the system and not back away when actual negotiations are begun. However, the implications for tomorrow are clear, for the Nasdaq system is potentially capable of executing actual trading and processing orders. As one exchange official points out, "The market no longer has to be in Wall Street; it can function wherever there is a trader's terminal hooked into a computer."

The black box is unquestionably playing a major role in the revolution of the stock market.

Donald Stott, whose father, Robert, started out working for Jesse Livermore on the old curb exchange and wound up becoming one of the Big Board's most famous stock specialists—the son is now a partner of Wagner Stott—pointed out to this writer that the price action of stocks the firm handles—and it makes a market in the biggest and most active ones on the New York Stock Exchange—has changed significantly in the computerized-block trading age. Formerly, stock prices had the tendency to move up and down in a series of steps, reflecting profit taking and buying on reactions. But since the institutionalization of the market, there has been case after case of prices shooting straight up or down virtually in a vertical line. Stott attributes this to the fact that when a major institution buys or unloads a stock, other institutions, technically monitoring the action, rush in herdlike to follow and push the price up or down beyond the range of fluctuations formerly experienced in the stock.

Robert Metz, a financial columnist of the New York *Times*, reports how he almost choked over a sandwich he was eating recently when he happened to glance at the stock tables and saw that Wrigley, that mainstay of widows and orphans because of its rock-ribbed stability, had plummeted 30 points the previous day, due largely to a 20,500-share block unloaded by institutional traders. Metz argues that to prevent small investors from being swamped merely because an institution's enthusiasm for a stock wanes capriciously, the stock exchanges might well consider adopting the rule of commodity exchanges and place a limit on the points a stock can move up or down in a single day.

Today Wall Street is grappling with this and other nagging

difficulties that boil down to a single overriding problem: How can the exchanges best serve the institutional block trading market and its computerized gunslingers without destroying their function as an auction market providing the most sensitive and reliable mechanism for keeping stock prices stable? The dilemma is complex. In the traditional auction market, the pricing of stocks is arrived at by thousands of traders, big and small, whose varying opinions are crystallized into a consensus usually over a period of time. In today's institutionalized market, key price decisions are being made by a handful of big-money managers whose consensus is reached often with lightning speed on the basis of herd instinct.

In 1969, when the stock market entered its biggest decline since 1929, it disclosed a serious Achilles' heel because of its institutionalized nature. Rocked by the Nixon administration's monetary squeeze, the market began to wobble in May and hurtled down for the next eighteen months. The institutional money managers, block house traders and computer whizz kid programmers were stunned.

As stocks continued to dive down and down with virtually no rebounds, the institutional gunslingers dumped carload after carload of cat and dog securities from their portfolios. And the block houses, the only channel of exit for these mass unloadings, teetered, wavered and almost collapsed under the tide. When the market had been a roaring bull, every broker and his brother had rushed in to trade blocks at big commissions from the swinging institutions. But when the chips were down and the funds stampeded for the exit, the block houses, with one or two exceptions, melted away like ice under a tropical sun.

As the decline accelerated during the spring of 1970 and the DJI Averages dropped 10 and 15 points daily, U.S. securities that had been promoted for years as a highly liquid form of investment turned out to be at the mercy of wildly erratic bids. During a span of several weeks in the spring of 1970, trades were negotiated in an atmosphere of near panic. Fund managers approached a block market maker begging him to take a dog off their hands, promising to compensate him for his certain loss by handing him a nice, easy stock, like General Electric, the next time around. Under these conditions, it was impossible to place a realistic evaluation on billions of dollars' worth of fund portfolios. Money managers went to sleep at night not knowing what their clients' stocks were worth or whether they would even be marketable the following day.

What saved the retreat from becoming a rout was that millions of Americans who had invested their discretionary dollars in mutual funds refused to panic and demand their money back. Enjoying easy credit, even while the commercial sector was being squeezed, and relieved of the necessity of using their invested savings for daily living, Americans doggedly kept their shrinking assets in the funds and saved the money managers by the skin of their teeth.

So much for the market's downslide perils, which can be severe indeed. As for the other side of the coin—the upside potential for profits—here lies perhaps the grimmest of ironies. For all the current upsurge of trading, the market may, in the words of Shakespeare, be unraveling "a tale told by an idiot, full of sound and fury, signifying nothing." Ever since the end of World War II, the market has been sold to the American people as the best place to invest to protect their savings and share in the growth of America. And this certainly was true until the mid-sixties.

However, pinched by today's galloping inflation, it is highly possible that the millions who have committed their savings and earnings to the market through mutuals and pension funds, despite bullish trading moves which may be large in magnitude, will not be protected *over the long term* adequately against the declining worth of their dollars. Despite its frequent run-ups, the market since 1965, the year when the Johnson administration gave inflation its first big push above the 3-percent-a-year level, has been highly disappointing for the long-term, in contrast to the short-term, trader-investor—for good reason. Since 1965, the growth of the nation's major bread-and-butter corporations has been at a virtual standstill. With U.S. productivity in the doldrums, the big price action on the stock exchanges has been as deceptive in terms of longer-term holdings as the aura of prosperity surrounding the rising flood of paper money.

Janos Aranyi, a financial consultant, made a computerized study of the stock price action that took place on the Big Board in 1968, the last year of the "roaring bull" market before the decline of 1969-70. He found that virtually all the major movements in stock prices that year took place in less than 10 percent of Big Board stocks and that the overwhelming majority represented the stock of firms that showed no earnings improvement whatsoever for the year. In other words, the big run-ups were not based on valid expectations of corporate growth but were triggered by stock manipulators—*i.e.,* go-go fund managers and other speculators—who ran up stocks by virtue of their massive purchasing power only to unload them on bigger fools. Nor was this surprising. There was virtually no other way to make money in the stock market in an economy that was deteriorating.

Since 1965 the return on all Big Board stocks, as measured by the NYSE composite stock index—taking into account price appreciation and dividends—has averaged about 5 percent a year, which is about the same return investors have received on government savings bonds and bank deposits—hardly enough to protect one from rampaging inflation. The future of the stock market is riddled with uncertainty. True, following the Nixon administration's establishment of the wage and price stabilization boards, the market went into one of its periodic upswings and could conceivably be flirting with 1,000 on the Dow Jones Industrial Averages before this book is published. But dangers lurk ahead. The era of a sustained bull market when one could virtually count on a steady appreciation of stock values could well be over. During the current galloping "cost push" inflation, which shows little sign of being terminated, interest rates are likely to rise to new levels, putting an ominous squeeze on corporate capital and profit margins. This is poison for a durable bull market. Moreover, faced with soaring interest costs on borrowed money, most firms will prefer to go into the equity market to obtain new funds. The accelerating number of stock offerings, by increasing the overhanging supply of stock, further dampens stock prices. It is a vicious circle. So long as serious inflation persists, it is highly questionable to picture the stock market as a *long-term* guarantor of protection against dollar erosion.

No wonder that old-timers in Wall Street are looking back nostalgically on the simple, uncomplicated days when a dollar really bought an honest weight of goods, when the market gave up good, solid profits if the dice rolled right and traders, blissfully ignorant of such new-fangled paraphernalia as computers, followed such homely nostrums as "Buy on bad news" or Jacob Schiff, the banker's, even more famous strategy, "Don't sell on Yom Kippur."

8

The Sugar Traders: "Part Economics, Part Diplomacy—and All Gamble"

What are the dollar bills in our wallets actually worth today? Several years ago a decision handed down in a court trial suggested an answer. Jerome Daly, an attorney, received a $14,000 loan from a Minnesota bank secured by a mortgage on real-estate property. In 1967 Daly fell behind on his mortgage payments and the bank foreclosed on him. Daly fought the action, and the case was brought to trial before a justice of the peace, Martin V. Mahoney. The president of the bank was called to the stand. Asked by Daly's attorney where the bank had obtained the $14,000 to lend him, he replied that it created the money by a stroke of the pen, producing credit in a bookkeeping transaction. This, the president added, was the procedure used by the Fed and banks all over the United States. It is debt —euphemistically called money, some cynics might have added —created at the whim of the banking system.

As a result of the bank president's testimony, the jury found for the defendant, deciding that the $14,000 loaned by the bank had cost it nothing but the price of ink and paper. The bank decided to appeal the decision and submitted two $1 bills to Justice of the Peace Mahoney as the fee for processing the application. The justice refused to accept the dollar bills on the grounds that they were not intrinsic money but were created out of nothing—or, more precisely, at the cost of approximately nine-tenths of one cent, which was the expense to the U.S. Treasury of printing the dollars. Justice Mahoney asked the bank to appear and show cause why his ruling should be reversed. But the bank dropped the case, giving up its $14,000 claim *rather than try to demonstrate that Federal Reserve money is worth anything more than the paper it is printed on.*

This curious case, largely unnoticed by the public, was seized upon by the eagle-eyed financial analyst C. Vern Myer, who wrote to leading U.S. Senators, members of the Treasury and other government officials asking whether they believed that American dollars were really worth anything. The attitude of the government was epitomized in a letter sent Myer by Senator Edward Brooke of the Committee on Banking and Currency. Brooke conceded that U.S. money was "in a sense" fiat money —*i.e.*, money of no intrinsic worth created by the government at will. But Brooke insisted that the worth of the dollar "was based not on some *tangible commodity,* but rather on the *confidence* of the people." To which Myer tartly inquired, if U.S. money rests simply on public confidence, what happens if the people lose confidence in their government? Perhaps this will occur, he suggested, when such large amounts of it are printed to meet the demands of deficit spending that the worth of each paper dollar will be obvious to everybody—the nine-tenths of a penny it costs to print it.

With money becoming increasingly cheap and expandable, speculators anxious to stay ahead of the game have briskly stepped up the tempo of their risk taking. Today it is not surprising that astute investors are becoming more and more enticed with one form of wagering especially—the buying and selling of commodities on the nation's future exchanges. As a sapient manager of assets puts it: "If the bombs ever start to drop, I'd sure as hell prefer to have a refrigerator stocked with meat than a truckload of dollars."

Thanks to the current surge of interest, trading on the commodity exchanges has hit the pace of growth attained by the stock market in the 1950's and 1960's. One reason for their growing allure is that the exchanges are not as tightly regulated as the stock market. While they are supervised by the Commodities Exchange Authority under the U.S. Department of Agriculture, this body has no jurisdiction over international products like sugar, cocoa or silver. It is almost as profitable to sell short on the commodities market as it used to be on the stock exchange fifty years ago, during the heyday of Wall Street plungers. (Today stock exchange regulations limit the maneuvers of short sellers.) Even in the palmy era of stock manipulation, many big-money operators preferred to play in cotton, wheat or corn. Jesse Livermore, the old wheeler-dealer who reportedly made more bear market killings than any other trader in history, once explained why he preferred to play commodities. The commodity speculator, he observed, can study conditions of the market in the assurance he knows as much about them as anyone else. He need not guard against cliques of corporate insiders. Dividends are not unexpectedly increased or passed. In the final analysis, commodity prices are governed by only one law: supply and demand. The task of the commodity trader is to get the facts about supply and demand. He doesn't have to guess about a dozen other things, as he does in stocks.

Today's permissive atmosphere permits commodity traders to deal more or less in Livermore's spirit, even though, thanks to taxes and tighter banking regulations, they cannot cut quite as handsome a caper. Moreover, traders can operate in a variety of commodities undreamed of ten years ago. To the traditional lines of corn, wheat and cotton have been added pork bellies, iced broilers and plywood. And that ultimate commodity—money—was introduced in 1969 when the New York Produce Exchange launched a futures market in some of the world's leading currencies—British pounds, German deutsche marks, Swiss and French francs, Italian lire, Japanese yen.

No commodity has taken weirder bounces for the operator trying to stay ahead of the game on and off the exchanges than the humblest, most ancient food of all—sugar. "The fortunes of empires," said Napolieon I, "have hung on the rise and fall of sugar." He wasn't exaggerating. There have been no more dramatic financial coups, quicker speculative killings or more sudden bankruptcies than those experienced with the ubiquitous sweet.

The first big fortunes were made by ancient Greek and Chinese sugar speculators. Then sugar went out of style, replaced by honey, until its usage was revived in the Middle Ages. It was rediscovered when the Crusaders on their way to the Holy Land found the cane sugar plant in Tripoli, which the natives called *zucra*. Since then bags of sugar have been worth their weight in gold. Queen Elizabeth I listed the sugar held in her royal warehouses as one of the major assets in her will.

There are two kinds of the sweet. Sugar cane is grown in sub-tropical lands around the world. The beet variety, which is chemically identical but comes from a pinkish sugar beet, is grown in more temperate climates and has a much shorter history than cane, which was harvested fifteen centuries ago. In the eighteenth century, a German chemist first succeeded in extracting sugar crystals from the long, silvery beet plant. But the process remained an oddity until the Napoleonic Wars, when Britain imposed a naval blockade on the European continent, cutting off sugar shipments from the Indies. Napoleon turned to the sugar beet and launched the industry to provide his armies and the population with a high-energy food. The first successful beet refinery in the United States was built in California in 1879, and the industry rapidly spread eastward.

The sugar trade up to the present has been a favorite boon-doggle of the Money Crowd. In 1887, an American trader, Henry Havemeyer, consolidated seventeen sugar refineries into one giant trust—the American Sugar Refining Company—and gained control over the domestic industry. Hiking the price of America's breakfasts whenever the spirit moved him, he replied blandly to his critics, "Who worries for a quarter of a cent a pound?"

In the early 1900's, while the House of Representatives was debating whether to raise the tariff on sugar, two leading Republican Congressmen, operating from a hideaway office at Moore and Schley, a Washington broker, manipulated the stock of American Sugar Refining Company, jiggling it up and down like a yo-yo on the basis of inside news leaked from committee cloakrooms and reaping a killing for themselves and their cronies. This was not the first or by any means the last instance of politicians manipulating sugar prices. They have been doing so up to the present.

One of the peculiarities of the sugar business is that it is the only U.S. industry Uncle Sam treats with such tender loving devotion. Since cane sugar has historically been grown by cheap labor in subtropical countries, the U.S. government, to keep the American grower in business, has dreamed up a system of controls and subsidies that protects everybody—everybody, that is, but the consumer.

Thanks to an intricate machinery of manipulation, not a pound of sugar can be imported into, refined or sold in the United States without the government's approval. Those permitted to sell here get a handsome premium, forcing the American housewife to pay double what she would pay in the free world market.* Domestic beet processors under the law are allocated a base quota permitting them to produce currently for 29 percent of the U.S. market; mainland cane growers are given another 10 percent, and the remainder of the American housewife's needs are allocated among a host of foreign nations.

For years, the decision as to what countries would get how much of the U.S. market pie had been in the hands of an inimitable individual, Representative Harold Cooley, Democrat of North Carolina, who chaired the House Committee on Agriculture. The quotas set by Cooley's committee were invariably written into law; everybody bowed to Cooley's will. A balding, assertive individual in his sixties, the North Carolina Democrat insisted, according to the testimony of his political opponents, that the workings of the Sugar Law were so complex other Congressmen should accept his decisions "on faith." Asked how he determined his marketing quotas for foreign countries, Cooley responded jocularly that they were "pulled from a hat." To this, Senator Thruston Morton, Cooley's colleague on the Senate Finance Committee, added, "We went through the legislation country by country. If we like a country we vote 'yea'; if we do not, we vote 'nay.' "

Cooley and company got a substantial nudge from one highly vocal quarter, the ubiquitous hordes of lobbyists who converged on Washington to push their nation's claim for a quota. "Where there is sugar, there you will find the flies," muttered one exasperated Senator who got trapped in the crush. It began in earnest after Castro seized power and Cuba, which had been the largest supplier of U.S. sugar, was banned from the market. New sources were needed immediately, and there was a vigor-

---

* Admittedly, most of the world's sugar is sold under quota and only a relatively small amount of "homeless" sugar goes into the free market.

ous scramble among nations of the Caribbean and the Far East to grab Cuba's market.

Some intriguing people turned up as lobbyists to wangle a handout from the U.S. Treasury, individuals who only recently had been working for the U.S. government. There was a former Cabinet official under President Harry Truman who bobbed up on the payroll of Mexican sugar interests. There was another high official in the Truman government who emerged as a $50,000-a-year agent for Venezuela. There are an ex-Senator from California who turned up as a lobbyist for Colombia at $200 an hour, the son of a currently powerful politician in the House of Representatives lobbying for Central American sugar interests at $70,000 annually and a former Missouri Congressman pleading for the Fiji Islands at $2,000 a month.

One resourceful American, the son of a former governor of North Carolina, appeared before the House committee on behalf of the tiny island of Mauritius. "Where the hell is Mauritius?" asked Representative W. R. Poage of Texas. None of his colleagues knew. A hurried search was undertaken and an atlas summoned, whereupon the committee solemnly recommended that Mauritius should be given a piece of the pie in view of its vital role as sugar supplier. Subsequently the lobbyist was replaced by another agent, an ex-White House aide to President Lyndon Johnson, who continued to get a bounteous handout for the largely invisible island.

Some Washington officials got mighty sticky fingers from all that treacle. This writer learned, for instance, about one aging high-ranking politician who swung important votes for sugar legislation and who carried on an affair with the attractive young female lobbyist of a Latin American country. His infuriated wife sent a detective to trail the lovebirds and found them shacked up in a sleek Manhattan hotel.

In their scramble for the honeypot, the lobbyists received kid-glove treatment from the politicos. They were given the privilege of testifying before Congressional committees, a permission denied other agents who served foreign governments. When one critical Congressman, Paul Findley of Illinois, asked a lobbyist about the size of the fee he was getting for his efforts, Cooley, who was presiding over the session, is said to have instructed the lobbyist, "Don't answer that." Then he snapped at the dissident Congressman: "It is none of your business and none of mine."

Since Cooley, whose tour of office was terminated by the voters in the 1966 election, Washington politicians have spread the largess of their blunders in a variety of ingenious ways. Uncle Sam, the benevolent padishah of the industry, in an effort to increase beet sugar production and hand out cash bonuses to farmers, has stirred up one especially sweet mess. Surveying new areas "suitable" for sugar growing, the deep thinkers at the Department of Agriculture hit upon the rocky coastline of Maine.

Historically, Maine's chief crop has been potatoes, but in recent years income from the spud has been in drastic decline, and state agriculturists, looking for a crop financed by the U.S. Treasury, seized upon the sugar beet since it has the same planting and harvesting cycle as the potato. True, beets hadn't been grown successfully in Maine for over a hundred years. The climate is hostile, the growing season perilously brief. Many out-of-state experts were convinced there wasn't sufficient sunshine in the Pine State to extract a fraction of the sugar needed to make the venture profitable.*

This did not deter politicians casting about for votes. Edmund Muskie, then governor, now Senator from Maine, spearheaded a crusade to introduce subsidized beet growing in Maine. The Johnson administration committed itself wholeheartedly to the cause.

But first a business leader had to be found who would put up a plant "on the stern and rockbound coast." A candidate stepped forward with impressive credentials—Fred Vahlsing, Jr., whose family owned a network of food processing and freezing plants. The Federal Area of Redevelopment Administration was persuaded to put up $6,000,000 toward building the plant, and the State of Maine's Industrial Authority laid out another $6,000,000. Muskie and his political confreres launched a fund-raising campaign among the natives, and another $2,200,000 was solicited through third mortgage bonds.

But the sugar interests ran into a difficulty. The Vahlsing

---

* The Maine sugar growers' association actually mailed this writer a jumbo-sized beet that had been grown experimentally to prove that big beets can be raised in Maine. He has kept it as an odd memento of broken hopes.

company operated a potato plant at the head of the Prestile, a river that twists and turns through the potato farms of a half dozen Maine communities. The Vahlsing people announced plans to put up a sugar refinery next to the potato factory and to cut costs by combining the operations.

Conservationist groups retaliated wrathfully, charging that Vahlsing's potato plant was already spewing garbage into the Prestile River at a dangerous rate and to erect a sugar factory to discharge more swill would make the Prestile unfit for man or beast. As a matter of fact, the stream was used for fishing and it enjoyed under the state Department of Parks a C rating, which meant it was just barely suitable to catch trout in.

One solution to the dilemma would have been to drop the sugar project. An alternative would be to lower the stream's rating classification so that in effect it could then officially be recognized as a cesspool and permitted to carry the utmost filth, in which case the natives would unreel fishing lines at their peril.

The politicians naturally took the second course. Heavy pressure was put by the White House on the Maine legislators to lower the rating. The Johnson administration, which at the very moment was calling for a nationwide crusade against pollution and was urging the citizenry to "make America beautiful," trained its heaviest guns on the Maine legislators to turn the Prestile officially into a sewer. Grumbled one leading state senator, irritated at the heat from the White House: "We are victimized by an arrogance that Washington usually reserves only for little states in Asia."

Bowing to the pressure, the Legislature passed the bill handily. Conservationists may have been aghast, but the farmers who stood to benefit from Washington's handout were exultant. Summed up one, "Le me tell you; they complain about trout fishing being ruined. Since the sugar crowd has moved in here, you can take a hook, put a french fry on the end and pull out dollars."

Confidently the sugar interests proceeded with their plans. The Vahlsing firm hired a German engineering outfit to put up a $23,000,000 plant along the Prestile. The engineers grappled valiantly with the granite soil; they agonizingly dug a foundation into hard rock ledge; they labored and came up with an ingeniously designed plant sewer capable of operating in subzero weather which, ironically, did not need to discharge its waste into the Prestile, so that the worst fears of the conservationists were not realized after all.

Despite these yeoman efforts, things began to sour for Maine Sugar Industries, as the Vahlsing enterprise was called. The government had handed out a quota of 33,000 acres for beet growing, but in the meantime the fortunes of the potato industry—a business Maine farmers were familiar with—had unexpectedly revived, and they were unwilling to devote more than 3,300 acres to growing beets. As a result, the crop output during the first season was highly disappointing. The next year it was scarcely any better.

Meanwhile, Maine Sugar Industries made a move into upper New York State, leasing a plant to turn out sugar from local crop allocations. This venture also misfired. The factory turned out to be defectively built. The firm was stuck in an ironic dilemma. In Maine it had a plant that worked but farmers who were unwilling to grow beets. In New York it had farmers eager to grow the sweet but a plant that didn't function properly. In two years of operations, Maine Sugar Industries went into heavy debt. However, thanks to his other enterprises which continued to enjoy solid prosperity, Vahlsing has managed to regroup his operations and remains a power in the food industry.

The travail of Maine Sugar Industries is not the first instance of a well-meaning business enterprise being booby-trapped by sugar. Throughout history a caravan of traders, punters and entrepreneurs have taken their lumps while pursuing the sweet.

There is no more histrionic instance of the perils inherent in the traffic than what befell Julio Lobo, the greatest sugar trader of modern times. The richest man in pre-Castro Cuba (Lobo never issued an earnings statement, but estimates of his fortune have ranged from $50,000,000 to $200,000,000), Lobo had a name meaning "wolf" in Spanish, and he was quintessentially the lone-wolf operator. For fifteen years after World War II, he was preeminent in the trade, the only man who stood willing on a round-the-clock basis to sell or purchase any amount of sugar offered from any part of the world. Without blinking, he put millions of dollars of his own funds on the line, buying 50,000 tons from the Germans (for $6,000,000), selling 90,000 tons to the Soviets or 100,000 tons to the Canadians at a clip.

Moving like lightning, relying on a razor-sharp trading intuition, he assumed massive risks, taking positions that seemed to defy common sense. "We all play under the same rules, and I always stand ready to take the consequences of my own bad judgment," he once told a reporter. "Nor will I whine. Business is not a kissing game."

A heavyset individual with a balding head shaped like a bullet and a jaw like Mussolini's, Lobo's mood often changed from sternness to sadness but rarely to laughter. Observed one business competitor with gruding awe, "Lobo doesn't sense a trend; he smells it." The sugar king was an ugly man when crossed. In the 1950's, he expanded his operations to the point where he became the largest single supplier of raw sugar to the United States. Not only did he have a monopoly on this trade, but he controlled 60 percent of the Puerto Rican and 30 percent of the Philippine raw going into the United States.

When Castro emerged from the mountains and threatened to overthrow the Batista government, worried U.S. refiners began hoarding supplies of the sweet, and when the revolution succeeded, they refrained from buying from Lobo, hoping to weaken Castro's economy. In addition to this buying resistance by Americans, there was a surplus supply of sugar around the world as a result of a record crop. The spot price of raw tumbled to a new low of 5.25 cents in the New York market, which set the price all over the nation. Julio Lobo found himself in a tight spot. He had sent a heavy shipment of sugar from his Philippine outlet to New York aboard the Japanese freighter *Kimikawa Maru*. But the vessel was unable to unload its cargo. No refiner would buy at Lobo's price.

Not one to be crossed lightly, he set out to accomplish what for anyone else would have been considered an act of insanity. His object was nothing less than to corner the sugar market and ram his prices down the refiners' throats. Although no one had succeeded in cornering the market for a commodity in over fifty years, Lobo ordered his agents to start buying heavily in the sugar futures market to put the price up sharply. As it began to climb, other owners of sugar mills around the world, their eyes glued to the commodity exchanges, decided to withhold their raw sugar output from the market in the hope futures prices would go even higher.

Then Lobo launched his masterstroke. He made phone calls and reserved virtually all of the space available on the charter ships that carried sugar to the United States, offering to rent them for a substantially higher price. He was now in the position of being the only major seller to the United States market, and he proceeded to tighten the noose around the refiners' necks by forcing up his price.

At first, the U.S. refiners held fast, convinced they were the victims of a gigantic bluffing operation. Then when they discovered that Lobo had actually tied up all shipping, they bought from him on a hand-to-mouth basis, certain he would have to cut bait and run. Even Lobo, they figured, would be unable to continue paying premium prices indefinitely to reserve charter ships. But they were in for a shock. Lobo kept pouring out money until he had tied up virtually the entire market in sugar, a feat considered to be impossible in the world of modern commodity trading.

The cornering of the market took only a few days, and the results were felt quickly. Pepsi-Cola, a major user of sugar, bowed and meekly paid Lobo 5.40 cents a pound for a carload they had refused to pay 5.30 cents for a few days previously. Lobo sold two more shipments at 5.60 a pound. Then twenty-four hours later, Pepsi returned for still another shipment at 5.70. Other industrial users followed suit. In two weeks, Lobo forced the price of sugar up from 5.25 to 7.58.

A revealing glimpse of Lobo's private side has been provided by his daughter, Maria Luisa:

> Father says that Napoleon was a lonely character, and so is Lobo. Napoleon built an empire, and so did Lobo. Father probably has the biggest collection of Napoleonana outside France. . . . People stumble over Josephine's chairs, and shy away from Napoleon's death mask. In my bedroom cupboard, there's a tooth straight out of Napoleon's head.

In 1945, when Lobo was sixty, he narrowly escaped being assassinated. (The assailants and their motive have never been discovered.) Late one evening, he drove home from his office with his secretary. He left her at her house and continued into a dark, deserted road. Suddenly another auto moved alongside him. There was a burst of machine-gun fire. Bullets entered Lobo's skull, tearing off a four-inch hunk and shattering his right leg and left knee. Lobo was rushed to the hospital still conscious. When the doctors told him he had to undergo brain surgery, he retorted, "Let's get it over with." Before he was wheeled into the operating room, he dictated a brief will. The doctors believed Lobo would die, but the sixty-year-old victim refused to oblige. He recovered from the brain operation. Paralyzed from his right hip and from his left knee down, he was taken to the Mayo Clinic in Rochester, where he lay on his back for hours getting his toes to wiggle, then he was shipped to a rehabilitation clinic in Manhattan where he continued his struggle to teach himself to walk.

Within six months after the shooting, he was back at his desk. He was not quite as nimble as before. Once he slipped and smashed all his toes; another time he broke his legs. But this physical deterioration resulted in only one change in his business life. Whereas previously he had worked five days a week, he now worked seven. He figured he had only a limited time to live and he had better make the most of it.

Single-mindedly he expanded his business empire. Originally a trader, he moved into the processing end of operations. For years he had had his eye on Cuban Atlantic Company, the largest sugar processor in Cuba. And in the early 1950's he began quietly accumulating a big block of the stock. Upon learning that Loeb, Rhoades, the Wall Street investment bankers, had also bought a big chunk of Cuban Atlantic stock, Lobo joined forces with them to launch a take-over.

The head of Cuban Atlantic was John Crosby, a U.S. citizen who had powerful political connections on the island, and he tried to block the attempt by warning the Cuban government that if Lobo succeeded in adding processing facilities to his trading complex, he would have a hammerlock on the island's sugar industry; and since the economy was almost entirely based on sugar, the nation would be at Lobo's mercy. The government agreed and prohibited Lobo from participating in the Loeb take-over. Lobo responded by selling his 100,000 block of stock to the Loeb group.

Shortly after taking control of Cuban Atlantic the new owners sold off one of its most desirable divisions, the Hershey properties that had once produced sugar for the well-known U.S. chocolate maker. The purchaser of record was the Chiriqui Sugar Mills, a Panamanian holding company. But word got around that Chiriqui was actually a front for Julio Lobo. Thanks to a legal stratagem, Lobo got possession of properties consisting of Cuba's biggest refinery, three processing mills, a hotel, a railroad, a golf course, a peanut oil plant and 60,000 acres of choice land. As a result, Lobo now controlled 60 percent of all the Cuban sugar processed and exported to the United States from the Caribbean and consumed east of the Mississippi River.

When Castro came to power, Lobo believed he could work with him, believing himself to be indispensable to the island's prosperity. But he was wrong. Castro turned out to be an even bigger wolf than Lobo. The Cuban dictator confiscated his holdings and forced him from the island.

Despite this expropriation, Lobo was left with sizable operations in New York and the Bahamas. And he bought property in Louisiana to extend his holdings. Then the ax fell. Always the risk taker, Lobo bet the wrong way; he zigged when he should have zagged. In 1964 he bought a heavy amount of sugar, expecting prices to go up. But world output, which had been low, unexpectedly got better; the mills worked off their inventories and prices tumbled severely.

Lobo could have averted a complete catastrophe if he had been less of a gambler. Purchasing sugar in the fall and winter of 1964 at climbing prices, he could have hedged his position by simultaneously unloading sugar on the futures market. This was normal procedure for cautious purchasers. But hedging was not for a man of Lobo's temperament. By lessening his chance of losses, he would also have limited his opportunity for profits. By the time Lobo was able to unload his sugar, prices had crashed through the floor and he was clobbered for a $5,600,000 loss.

He sought refuge in Chapter II bankruptcy proceedings to protect his remaining assets. He hoped to recoup his losses by gunning for one more big killing, like the gambler who doubles his stakes in an attempt to wipe out his debts. But the chance never came. Exhausted by anguish from the Castro expropriation and other business reverses, the heart of the wolf gave out; he died of a coronary attack.

Sugar continues to provide as emphatic a lure as it did in the days of the Crusaders and Lobo. Innumerable speculators have skyrocketed into prominence and disappeared without a trace. There is, for instance, the Florida sugar rush—a bizarre outbreak of speculativitis that took place in the early 1960's. This boondoggle was triggered, like so much else in recent sugar history, by Castro's seizure of power. Until then, Cuba had been the single biggest supplier of raw sugar to the U.S. market, contributing, in fact, one-third of all the sugar. However, when Castro moved into the Communist camp, President Dwight Eisenhower and Congress cut off Cuban sugar imports. To bolster U.S. domestic output and make up for the slack, Uncle Sam looked around for a native area where the growing of sugar could be encouraged. Florida became the cynosure of speculators.

For over thirty years Floridians had been planting cane in the lush, black mucklands surrounding Lake Okeechobee in the south central part of the state, and Florida was looked upon as having the potential makings of one of the world's richest sugar bowls. In 1962, on the gamble that the Kennedy administration would push through a new sugar act giving the Florida cane farmers the biggest quota increases in history because of the withdrawal of Cuban imports, the rush of the speculators was on with the fever of the old-time gold booms.

Former owners of Cuban mills confiscated by Castro, joining forces with U.S. businessmen and supported by farmers for a new cash crop subsidized by the U.S. Treasury, plunged $100,000,000 into the snake-infested Everglades. They bid up the muckland from $300 to $1,000 an acre, dismantled processing mills from Louisiana and Puerto Rico, hauling them for reassemblage in the Sunshine State. In 1962 seven new mills, geared for a yearly output of 500,000 tons of the sweet, were hastily thrown up around Lake Okeechobee. Overnight minuscule communities like Pahokee turned into thriving towns. Quipped one prospector, "Uncle Sam hasn't lost Cuban sugar; it has merely transplanted it to American soil." A Florida cattleman summed up the madness as he glanced at the cane sprouting up on his neighbor's farm:

It's hard to believe all this commotion was started by a little old plant that's not much more than a head high, with a stalk just two inches thick. Those mills going night and day . . . and all that worry just turns out about four tons of raw sugar an acre so we can sweeten our coffee. I used to think the cattle business was wild. But compared to cane, we cattlemen are . . . as tame as a bunch of old maids at a Church picnic.

The quality of land was the key to the gamble. Lake Okee-chobee—the name is derived from the Seminole tongue—was a 730-square-mile body of steely gray water that determined the fortunes of cane-growing ventures. Several miles south began the vast Everglades, and tucked between the lake and the swampland was the top-quality cane acreage. Cane is a tropical grass that can be destroyed by temperatures of under 30 degrees. The lake provided the warming winds protecting the stalks of young cane. Not every sugar farmer bowed to Lake Okeechobee each day upon arising. But it was constantly in everyone's thoughts. One grower told of a nightmare he had. "I dreamed a giant came down from Canada, drank the whole lake dry, then held his sides and laughed as my banker chopped me into little pieces."

Some speculators were lucky enough to get their hands on acreage near the lake and reaped a heady harvest. Several politicians close to President Kennedy who signed the legislation giving lush quotas to Florida growers made a pile of money from their knowledgeable speculations. Others were not so lucky. A mishap was experienced by one sugar firm formed by three fast-talking refugees from Cuba who induced Henry Ford II to plunge a reported $1,000,000 into building a Florida mill for it. The location was ill-advised. It was too far south of Lake Okeechobee to be sheltered by its winds. The first crop had hardly begun to ripen in 1962 when a frost suddenly struck the area. Management rushed its half-completed mill into operation in a last-minute attempt to salvage the damaged sugar. The effort was a bust.

Other ventures turned out much better. One highly successful entrant in the sugar bowl is soft-spoken, aesthetic David Keiser, a multimillionaire and patron of the arts who helped bankroll the New York Philharmonic to its present prestigiousness. The money for this originally came from the sugar fields of Cuba. Keiser's father started out as a sugar broker. During the 1890's, according to industry folklore, he received a tip to buy stock in the Cuban-American Sugar Company, a firm organized by an American who had put together a network of Cuban sugar mills. Keiser began loading up on the stock when it was priced at 5 and rode it all the way to 300—a rise sparked by the outbreak of the Spanish-American War and the resulting sugar shortage. Keiser kept his cool. As the stock ran up and up, instead of yielding to the temptation to sell, he bought more. He bought so much, in fact, he found himself the owner of the company.

His son, David, was a dreamy, artistic lad who studied to be a pianist, and sugar people didn't think he would make out when he eventually took over the helm. But the younger Keiser fooled everybody, turning out to be a resourceful, resilient businessman. When Castro seized power, he expropriated Cuban American; Keiser had to write off $20,000,000 in losses. He began a comeback in 1960 with one American property in Louisiana, acquired a second in the Florida sugar bowl. Today he operates three refineries and a raw sugar mill, and he owns 3,600 acres of land which, though it has splendid potential for industrial use, is carried on the books at substantially below its value. Keiser is an expert pianist, a friend of Leonard Bernstein and other musical luminaries, and he commutes between the art and the business worlds with no semblance of schizophrenia.

Undoubtedly the most successful long-term investor in Florida sugar is Charles S. Mott, a ninety-seven-year-old multimillionaire whose fortune is estimated at around $400,000,000 and who was one of the original founders of General Motors. He remains the single biggest shareholder, having outlived all his famous contemporaries among the industry's pioneers—Henry Ford, Walter Chrysler, Billy Durant, Alfred Sloane.

When Mott was a mere stripling of eighty-four, he recorded in his diary a dream he had about himself and a friend, Floyd Allen, who was also in his eighties. Mott and Allen attended the funeral of an acquaintance, driving to the cemetery some miles out of town. When the burial ceremony was over, Allen turned to Mott:

"C.S., how old was the deceased?"

"About eighty years old."

"How old are you?"

"I supposed you knew that I am younger than you; I am eighty-four."

"Well, C.S., it hardly seems worthwhile to go back home, does it?"

Mott was wise to come home. Thirteen years later—at ninety-seven—he is still hale, zestful and brimming with plans for the future. Continually on the lookout for "sleeper" situations, Mott first had his attention attracted to Florida sugar during the Depression of the 1930's, which hit the cane industry especially hard. U.S. Sugar Company, the leading Florida producer, went into bankruptcy. Mott moved in, snapped up the firm at a bargain and picked up the pieces. He put the production expertise he had gained in the auto industry to work in the Florida cane fields, introducing crawler-tread tractors, locomotives and railroad spurs to mechanize the hauling of the ripened cane to the factory. He built research laboratories which developed long ratooning cane varieties providing more profitable sugar yields.

Today this durable, yeasty nonagenarian owns, together with his family and foundation, 73 percent of the stock of U.S. Sugar Company. Among its assets are 100,000 acres of choice cane land right on top of Lake Okeechobee, which the company carries on its books at the $7,000,000 price it paid for it in the depths of the Depression. Knowledgeable insiders say the land today is worth at least $300,000,000.

At an age when most of his peers have long since passed to their reward, Mott continues to reconnoiter zestfully for new investment bargains like the one he stumbled on forty years ago in U.S. Sugar. He believes the biggest investment opportunities of the 1970's will be in undervalued land purchased as a hedge against spiraling inflation. A notably uxorious man, Mott has had four wives; his oldest son is in his sixties and his youngest, by his fourth wife, in his thirties.

Sugar continues to provide an enticement for a host of assorted individuals working different sides of the street. A recent notable entrant into the beet-processing end of the industry is that Eastern banking and brokerage fraternity known loosely as Wall Street.

After ignoring the business for years in favor of more glamorous areas, Wall Streeters in the mid-sixties took a sudden interest in the miles of cane and beets sprouting in the West and South and in the politicians in Washington who so assiduously nurtured the interests of the growers and processors. Investment bankers and their research staff of acquisition specialists became alive to the possibilities inherent in sugar-processing firms who were loaded with assets not reflected adequately by prevailing stock prices. The reason was that the people who headed the sugar firms were mostly agriculturists or lawyers whose conservative policies didn't take into the slightest consideration the possibilities of leveraging their assets. The sugar people had for generations concentrated on growing and selling sugar. Yet they had piled up assets in land that in many cases were heavily undervalued and were ideal for real-estate plays. Moreover, they enjoyed cash flows that made the mouth water. What could be a surer thing? The government not only paid the farmer to grow the sweet but manipulated supplies to keep prices up for the processors. Wall Streeters became enchanted with the possibilities of using sugar companies as a base for building conglomerates. Exulted one wheeler-dealer, "Sugar is beautiful collateral for getting bank credit and buying movie companies, steamship lines, or anything you want."

So the operators went to work, grabbing sugar firms via tender offers to squeeze them of their honey. One adroit take-over was managed by William White, the thirty-three-year-old scion of a Denver railroad and cattle fortune. Upon graduating Yale, White learned his financial p's and q's as an apprentice of Charles Allen, the redoubtable Wall Street broker. Absorbing all he could from the maestro, White left Wall Street to deal on his own. He began by engineering the take-over of Colorado Milling & Elevator Company, a flourishing Midwest miller. Then he cast an eye on Great Western Sugar Company, the oldest U.S. beet producer in the game. White's father had been a big stockholder in Great Western; its beet acres were contiguous to Colorado Milling and the firm seemed overripe for capture.

GW was run by Frank Kemp, a Denver septuagenarian, celebrated for being an indefatigable advocate of stronger government protection for the industry. Under his direction, GW had built enormous reserves of cash but hadn't put up a new sugar plant in almost forty years. GW had an odd capital structure. Control of the company was vested in over $20,000,000 of preferred stock carrying one vote per share, while the common represented only one-twelfth of a vote. For years, Kemp's banker friends had been warning him of the danger he ran in concentrating the bulk of voting control in only $20,000,000 worth of preferred. An outsider could grab the firm lock, stock and barrel with a relatively small outlay of money. To all such admonitions Kemp shrugged. His reluctance to restructure his capitalization proved his undoing.

To Bill White the message was irresistibly captivating. For an investment of a little over $30,000,000, he could capture control of the leader of the beet sugar industry, earning $9,000,000 annually. It was the spring of 1966. The times were not auspicious. The nation was in the midst of a credit squeeze, and the interest rates were skyrocketing. Undeterred, White launched a worldwide hunt for the necessary money to make a tender offer, and he induced several firms with cash in the till to form a syndicate and put up $37,000,000. The tender was engineered through White's firm, Colorado Milling, which offered to pay $190 a share for GW's preferred stock, then selling at $150, and to buy enough of the common to complete the deal. GW shareholders leaped at the bait. White reeled in 75 percent of the preferred and 16 percent of the common, which gave him 45-percent voting control of the company, enough for ownership. Old Frank Kemp was retired.

White, a gifted, dynamic hustler, was enthused over the prospect of using sugar processing as the base for a moneymaking empire. "I like to develop new things," he told this writer shortly after the take-over. "My whole orientation in life is somewhere out there tomorrow."

Great Western embarked on a diversification program *con brio,* erecting what some critics insisted was a veritable tower of Babel. It snapped up pizza parlors, steak houses, Christmas trees and other ventures far removed from the beetlands. And GW stock, catching White's enthusiasm, zipped from 34½ to 79 in less than twelve months.

White's boldest ploy was to plunge the sugar processor into a huge land and real-estate deal, snatching up the California City Development Company and thirty-five affiliated land firms for $30,000,000. There were questions as to the quality of some of the real estate it received. It was located in the Mojave Desert, which some people considered more suitable for cactus than people. Since water was not readily available in the eastern portion, the state ordered Great Western to offer lots located there on speculation only.

Other difficulties arose. The lots were sold on the installment plan, and although a buyer made only a 5-percent cash down payment plus one monthly payment, with the remainder due over eight years, GW reported the entire sale on its books as if it had been paid in, and its figures had little relationship to the actual cash flow. Admittedly, this was standard procedure for most land development firms, and GW was merely following the tradition. But the accounting profession, looking into the matter, began to ride herd and pressed the industry to report much more conservatively. GW, to its credit, was one of the first to revamp its accounting policy, refraining from taking land sales into income until it received 20 percent of the full purchase price. Following the restatement, the firm showed an $8,300,000 loss in a single quarter, and Wall Street reacted by sending GW stock reeling down 5⅛ points in a single day. At the present writing, GW is struggling yeomanly to regain its feet.*

Bill White's take-over of Great Western was only the opening gun in Wall Street's barrage to capture sugar firms. Shortly after the GW coup, John Loeb, Jr., launched the take-over of another major firm. In his mid-thirties, Loeb, Jr., the gifted, creative son of a Wall Street patriarch, understandably has been eager to break from the shadow of his brilliant father and try his own hand at corporate financing.

The younger Loeb got his opportunity when Holly, a venerable sugar producer, the third largest in the industry, after a decade of plodding along quietly, unnoticed by the acquisitive-minded, suddenly became the target of a take-over attempt by a

---

* In April, 1972, White resigned from Great Western United. The firm is conducting negotiations to sell off its sugar operations to a growers' association.

"go-go" Texas outfit, International Systems & Controls. It lit upon Holly, saw that its stock was dirt cheap and its assets possessed an intriguing potential for leverage. The "panicky" Holly management tried to stave off the raid by seeking a deal with a friendly partner.

At this juncture Loeb and a group of associates were approached. Holly had one redoubtable asset not shown on its balance sheet. Its newly installed president, John Bunker, was the son of Ellsworth Bunker, the U.S. ambassador to the Thieu government of South Vietnam and the highest political executive under Presidents Johnson and Nixon of U.S. policy there. Bunker the diplomat had started out as a sugar man and had risen to become president of National Sugar Company —the old Horace Havemeyer outfit—in the 1930's. During a tour in Washington, where he was a chief architect of the first sugar act, which laid down the policy of price protection for processors and quota handouts for foreigners, Bunker became so enamored of political advocacy he decided to leave the sugar game and enter the field of diplomacy full time. His son John, following his footsteps in sugar, wound up as president of Holly.

The Loeb group undertook the rescue operations of Holly. A syndicate was put together that included Dreyfus (the big mutual fund), which bought 160,000 shares. It together with Loeb and his associates purchased enough stock to snatch control of the sugar producer from the jaws of International Systems & Controls.

The Loeb group started out intrigued, it is reported, with the possibility of ultimately using the sugar company as the foundation of a diversified food empire. But the idea, if it was entertained, got no further than a glint in their eyes. A year after taking Holly over, the roof fell in. The worst weather in over a hundred years hit Holly's best growing areas; one of the earliest winters on record was followed by freakishly hot weather which ruined the contents of the beets, and Holly suffered its first red ink since the Depression. The firm's working capital dropped to the lowest level in eight years. As its troubles accumulated, financial observers began to wonder whether Ellsworth Bunker wouldn't have an easier time persuading President Thieu to accept a Viet Cong coalition government than his son John would have inducing investors to put their money into Holly.*

So the entrepreneurs, speculators and risk takers continue to be enticed and victimized by sugar. Yet not all pursuers have been ambushed. There are winners as well as losers. For all the tragedy that has been experienced in recent years, experts studying the field are convinced that brighter opportunities lie ahead for the resourceful entrepreneur.

For the first time in decades, sugar, which had been in chronic oversupply, since the cane plant grows abundantly in the tropics, seems to be entering a period of shortage. The revolutionary upheaval taking place among oppressed black people in sugar-producing countries has been exacting its toll on production. Because cane growing is toilsome drudgery and carries a low social status, large numbers of laborers in the Caribbean and other primitive areas, especially the younger workers, are turning their backs on peonage in the sugar fields and going into lines of work that pay more. In the Caribbean, for instance, those who toil in the sugar fields are so ashamed of working in front of their women folk they ask to be shipped to other islands so they can labor before strangers.

Coupled with the whittling down of excess capacity, there is developing among the peoples of the world a sharply increasing sweet tooth for sugar-based foods. America's youth, and those of other nations, have incorporated into their life-style a great fondness for sweets. The Now generation is turned off by coffee and tea but quaffs huge quantities of soda pop, cookies, candy. "You'd be amazed at the amount of marijuana that is being surreptitiously baked into brownies," remarks one expert on the drug culture, only half facetiously.

Another spur to sugar consumption has been the Food and Drug Administration's ban on cyclamates, accompanied by the growing suspicion with which the public regards all chemical substitutes. This is giving sugar producers a big psychological boost.

All in all, industry pundits suspect that the sugar business

---

* In recent months Holly has begun a brisk earnings rebound, thanks to vastly improved marketing conditions.

may be approaching a new watershed in its evolution. Over the last couple of years, prices of raw sugar have quietly moved up to a seven-year peak. Pinched by rising inflation and itching to stay ahead of the game, old-time traders are stalking the pits of the commodity exchanges with the roused instincts of the veteran hunter sensing an opportunity for new financial coups.

True, there are possibilities threatening to upset the apple cart. Castro's Cuba, after years of trying, might unexpectedly succeed in boosting the output of its sugar crop and turn a world shortage, at least temporarily, into a surplus. There is uncertainty also over the size of Russia's sugar output and whether the East European Communist bloc, along with the Soviets, might be significant sugar exporters in the years immediately ahead.

One thing is certain. The remark attributed to Napoleon, the father of the sugar beet industry, is as true today as ever: "Sugar is part economics, part diplomacy—and all gamble." Hence, the Money Crowd, which has suffered so much woe in the past trying to extract honey, had better remain wary.

9

Park Avenue Cowboys and Movie Star Bulls: How to Make a Killing in Cattle

Out on the cattle ranges where Matt Dillon and Wyatt Earp once roamed with their six-shooters, a new kind of cowboy is riding tall in the saddle. Rolling out of bed at dawn, not in a ramshackle old bunkhouse but a modern ranchland home, today's "space age" cowboy applies the latest scientific marvels —artificial insemination to mate prize bulls with calves according to instructions flashed him from high-speed computers. He sprays his pastureland from low-flying helicopters to improve the grazing characteristics and uses new chemical feeds and mineral mixtures fresh from test tubes to fatten his calves for maximum profits. Indeed, today's Matt Dillon operates on a ranch that functions more like a research laboratory than the wild pastureland where his ancestors stomped with their branding irons.

Today's ranch foreman, more often than not, has a university degree in science. The creaky old chuck wagon that used to carry food for the hands has been replaced by mobile trailers equipped with the latest cooking gadgetry. The branding iron has given way to the more humane application of a dye to the calf's earlobe to identify the owner. The cowboy functions as part nurse, part midwife, conducting pregnancy tests and carefully charting the production progress of each heifer to eliminate the culls that fail to measure up. He injects cattle with sophisticated vaccines to ward off disease and applies the latest techniques of modern medicine worked out by specialist teams at ranching headquarters.

Faced with the perils of accelerating inflation and the fading worth of the dollar, financially sophisticated people in rising numbers have been rediscovering the world's oldest refuge—the land. One especially alluring investment is ranching.

A big incentive to ranching as a gentleman's hobby is the tax advantages offered by Uncle Sam to people in the 60-percent bracket and higher. The U.S. government is intent on building up the blood and quality of the nation's herds and has provided special inducements for anybody going into the raising of cattle for breeding purposes—that is, raising them to be sold to other herds to improve their blood lines. Among other benefits, Uncle Sam has been allowing the investor to take the depreciation for cattle that he takes for other capital equipment, except that, unlike ordinary equipment which grows obsolete, cattle reproduce and perpetuate themselves.

Recently the freewheeling operations of the wealthy "hobby cowboys" have been curbed somewhat. In the course of overhauling tax exemptions, Congress in 1969 tightened up the loopholes, limiting the losses that can be charged off for tax purposes. (Previously a taxpayer was allowed to charge off up to $50,000 a year in farm losses for five straight years against nonfarm income. The new law provides that losses must be limited to $25,000 for three years out of the five and no losses be allowed for the remaining two.) Even with these and other limitations, the tax shelter provisions are still worthwhile for high-bracket individuals. Indeed the only one being exploited in the hobby ranching deal was illustrated in a cartoon run by a leading farm journal showing a cow being suckled vigorously by her calf. The cow looks up at a team of visiting Congressmen and says plaintively, "You may call this a businessman's hobby, but it's damn hard work for me."

"I'm an old cow hand" has become an increasingly popular jingle with the nation's Money Crowd. Scores of the wealthy who have at one time or other become absentee cattle kings include members of the Lehman family and partners of Salomon and Hutzler, E. Roland Harriman on Wall Street, and such music and show-business luminaries as Leonard Bernstein, Richard Rodgers, and Groucho Marx.

The actual breeding and raising of the cattle for absentee owners is arranged by several professional management teams.

By far the largest this writer has come across is Oppenheimer Industries, whose clientele reads like a who's who of finance. Board chairman is Harold "Larry" Oppenheimer, who has had a colorful career. A stepson of Jules Stein, head of Music Corporation of America and himself a graduate anthropologist from Harvard, Oppenheimer served as a brigadier general in Vietnam. (One of his key contacts with the Wall Street fraternity during the 1960's was Arthur Levitt, Jr., the son of the New York State comptroller, who served as an Oppenheimer director attracting investment money from Eastern financial circles.)

To wrest the maximum profitability for his Park Avenue cowboys, Oppenheimer runs his organization with stringent military efficiency. He has recruited a staff from former Marine Corps officers with a sprinkling of Army, Navy and Air Force brass thrown in.

Oppenheimer's marines hunt down cattle rustlers with the vigor they once employed assaulting an island in the Pacific, using jeeps, horses and helicopters for reconnaissance purposes. Says an Oppenheimer associate, "The big failures in ranching have been in execution. We are very tough. We are very expensive, too."

All kinds of wondrous technology has been introduced into the ranchlands. The biggest advance is the artificial breeding of bulls, who, thanks to their ability to sire top-quality calves that command premium prices, are bringing in a hefty share of ranching profits. Prize bulls which have developed reputations through their exceptional virility are housed in special quarters decorated with plaques denoting the prizes they have harvested in mating contests, and they are accorded the deference normally reserved for high-priced movie stars. So desirable are these ultrapotent bulls that they are frequently owned by several investors, each having a share in the bull's offspring.

With so much money on the hoof, meticulous care is taken to breed a prize bull to the finest cows available, and mates are carefully searched for all over the nation. The chore of matching a bull with a suitable love partner has been taken over by computers which keep copious statistics on the breeding characteristics of bulls from famous sires. When a prize bull is ready to mate, his characteristics are flashed to a computer installation; the electronic brain goes through thousands of statistics on heifers throughout the land and comes up with what it considers to be an ideal inamorata.

Once this is determined, the two participants don't meet. Using the techniques of artificial insemination, the sperm from the bull is frozen, packed in a vial and sent to the rancher whose heifer has been chosen for the injection. Seventy percent of all inoculations result in conception, so that there is little wasted effort. The sperm from each bull is coded by color so it will not be mixed up with another father's during shipment—a mixup that could cause mismating and heavy financial losses.

Computer breeding has become so profitable that a number of service firms have gotten into the act, and bull semen has become a highly valuable trading vehicle. Speculators seize a piece of the action by buying vials of frozen sperm from famous bulls. (Many traders consider this much better than money today.) There are men who literally measure their wealth by the vials of semen they own.

Helping to keep the trading pot boiling is a pioneer in genetic mating, American Breeders Service, which was launched as a rich man's hobby by J. Rockefeller Prentice, whose mother was a daughter of John D. Rockefeller. Flushed with its success in cattle mating, ABS has announced a research program aimed at breeding thoroughbred race horses by computer. The prospect that champion racers may soon be created by electronic brains conjures up some staggering prospects for the odds makers. There are some who even think that breeding humans by computer is just around the corner. "There is no reason at all why computer-dating services can't be converted into computer-mating services," says one earnest student of the subject.

Not surprisingly the advent of new technology, plus the burgeoning interest of investors, has opened wide the opportunity for some highly resourceful plungers to move into the ranchlands.

The big bull market of the 1960's, which fattened the genie of inflation, spawned a number of speculative ventures in cattle as a tax shelter.

One ambitious project this writer became acquainted with that went sadly awry is Black Watch Farms, which billed itself as the world's biggest breeder of purebred black Angus cattle.

Black Watch was run by H. L. Meckler, an adroit entrepreneur. Leaving the Army after World War II with a few thousand dollars in his fatigue pockets, Meckler pioneered some of the major concepts of the equipment-leasing industry and parlayed a shoestring into one of the leading firms in the field. He sold his leasing outfit, Lease Plan International, to Pepsi Company in the mid-fifties and received $54,000,000 worth of Pepsi stock; then he joined the Pepsi team. But too restless to work for anyone else, he quit, looked around for another company to build from scratch and lit upon Berman, a family-run leasing firm that was foundering in heavy debt.

Meckler took it over and gave it a "face-lifting." He changed its name to Bermec and cast about to marry Bermec to a more glamorous operation—something that would excite the imagination of the Wall Street crowd. Someone called his attention to Black Watch Farms, a breeder of pure black Angus cattle, which were peddled to investors as a tax shelter operation for which the company received a generous management fee.

The cattle farms had originally been conceived in the fertile brain of an astute practitioner, Jack Dick, one of the authentic pioneers of cattle breeding as a tax shelter mechanism, who in 1961, jobless, reportedly without a farthing in the bank, interested 100 partners in putting up close to $1,000,000 for the venture. The partnership bought a 650-acre ranch at Wappinger Falls, New York, from Everett Crosby, the brother of Bing, the crooner. Dick managed the operation until 1968, when he interested Meckler and company in buying out his controlling interest for $10,500,000 worth of Bermec stock.

The Bermec management was fascinated by what it felt were similarities in cattle raising and leasing equipment. Jack Dick's enterprise had been using a minimum of equity to gain fancy leverage. With stepped-up depreciation for tax purposes, Black Watch's cattle showed up on the books at several million dollars below their real value. Also its real estate was worth much more than what was stated.

Black Watch found it easy to attract customers. It had become the "in" thing to put money into the glamorous cattle business of the Old West. And the firm had a program to whet the most demanding appetite. Not only could barrels of cash be made, it seemed, but most of the cash needed to finance the cattle could be borrowed. In drumming up new business, the Black Watch management, following the practice of its predecessors, drove potentially big customers in the company's shiny black Cadillac to the Black Watch headquarters, showed off its nationally celebrated battery of prize bulls and the latest laboratory facilities for artificial insemination.*

The prospect was told he could sign a $100,000 note to purchase thirty-six cows for $2,500 each, plus $10,000 for a one-third interest in a bull. Black Watch would manage his herd on one of the twenty-five farms that had maintenance contracts with the company. The investor could depreciate the herd, writing off in some cases as much as $40,000 against his income the first year. He could also deduct yearly maintenance payments to Black Watch of $350 per cow. Over the long run, his herd would produce heady capital gains, went the sales argument, because the offspring of the herd would sell for $1,000 to $3,000 a head.

Not only the wealthy but people of modest means were induced to buy the program. (One newly married couple purchased five cows instead of making a down payment on a home.) And as sales rose, the price of Bermec stock jumped like a Mexican bean from $16 a share when Bermec bought Black Watch to $83 in less than twelve months.

Then things began to go sour. Meckler and his associates subsequently alleged that in making a careful study of the books, they found Mr. Dick had concealed from them the true nature of Black Watch's finances, which were in a highly shaky condition. Other ominous developments surfaced, according to details subsequently told the writer.

The American Angus Association, which set the stamp of pedigree—and therefore of value—on prize cattle, traditionally had been allowing owners to register as thoroughbreds calves born from artificially inseminated mothers only if the owner had a financial interest in the bull that was used as the father.

As a result, Black Watch personnel had to collect semen from an owner's bull wherever he might be and breed cows that were scattered over some seventy locations around the nation by shipping vials of semen to the prospective mothers. The logistics be-

* The writer was given the trip and the full treatment in preparation for a series of articles he did on Black Watch and others in the business.

came so complicated that many Black Watch animals, owing to clerical mistakes in record keeping, were bred to the wrong bulls. In one instance, a herd of spanking young heifers was shipped by mistake from the North to Florida, where the change of climate was so great it traumatized the cattle, who stood paralyzed covered with flies in the irrigation canals. On another occasion, 20,000 vials of thoroughbred sperm were shipped to the wrong depot and had to be destroyed as they deteriorated in quality.

Another blow followed. The Justice Department suddenly challenged the rule that only owners of bulls could buy and sell semen. It ordered that anyone who peddled artificial sperm had to sell it to anybody else who wished to buy. This broke down the exclusivity of cattle ownership and undermined the value of investing in a bull. Another adverse development was that a new type of breeding cattle came into fashion, and the Black Watch and other people who had bet on Angus, not foreseeing the switch, were caught with a breed that had become unstylish. Added to this, a bear market had set in on Wall Street, forcing a number of cash-needy investors to get out of their herds and sell them off, further driving down prices.

Then came a stunning letter from Black Watch to its clients. The company was filing for protection against its creditors under Chapter II of the bankruptcy code, and if its customers didn't arrange to pick up their cows, they would be considered abandoned.

Caught in the bankruptcy court were 580 cattle owners who stood to lose more than $50,000,000. Not only was an investor faced with the prospect that he might get only $15,000 on the market for a herd he paid $100,000 for, but with Black Watch apparently going out of business, he was confronted with the nightmare of having to round up his cattle and care for them himself. Until now it had never occurred to any of these absentee cowboys that their bulls might come home to pasture on Park Avenue.

At the opening of the bankruptcy hearings, over 200 lawyers and their clients trooped into the courthouse in Poughkeepsie, New York, to assay the damage. The corridors buzzed with baffled inquiries. "Why the rush to round up these heifers?" one Wall Street cowpoke asked a fellow buckaroo. "Can't they just munch the grass where they are?" "Nope, somebody has to be paid to take care of the pregnant ones."

Observed one attorney, "My clients are used to conventional bankruptcy where you close the business and take a couple of months to hammer out a deal. This is unprecedented—hordes of bulls and heifers roaming around the country—and not a damn soul is being paid to look after them."

An investor had the option of selling his animals, of course, but he'd get back only a fraction of his money. He was stuck with animals that were worth $500 a head at most, when he had envisaged getting over $1,000. One sophisticated broker told the *Wall Street Journal*, "I made a lot of money in the brokerage business. I needed a tax shelter. I heard cattle were a good investment. I don't know a damn thing about cattle. So I had my lawyer look into Black Watch. My accountant, a brilliant guy, checked it out. The Black Watch people drove me up in a black Cadillac to their farm in Dutchess County. I saw all the certified reports. Everything checked out. And look what happened." Muttered a disgruntled Fifth Avenue obstetrician over his martini, "I'll sure as hell get a write-off on my taxes—but the kind I can do without."

Only a third of Black Watch's clients had completed all their installment payments on their cattle. For the two-thirds who still owed money the news was especially gloomy. They had to continue to pay on their contracts, and if no feasible plan were developed in bankruptcy court, the judge could sell off their animals for slaughter—a procedure which would bring in only a fraction of the price earned for breeding sales. Moreover, the money from such trades wouldn't go to clients who hadn't completely paid up on their cows but would be utilized to help pay off Black Watch's creditors.

In the meantime, charges and countercharges have broken out between Black Watch's present and past managements. Bermec has filed a lawsuit against Mr. Dick, the original owner, for allegedly misrepresenting the financial condition of the venture when he sold it. Dick has fired back with a countersuit suggesting Bermec's charges are untrue and slanderous and claiming that the responsibility for the fiasco lies with current management. A leading life insurance firm is suing a top accounting firm that represented Black Watch for presenting "misleading" figures that induced it to invest heavily in an effort to rescue the cattle firm from its financial farrago. The accounting firm (naturally) is suing back.

Yet despite this tangle of suits and countersuits, some hardy spirits remain undaunted. One of the bankruptcy victims was a New York cabbie who had sunk $80,000 into the cattle venture. Since he drove a secondhand cab through the streets of Manhattan twelve hours a day for a living, it is difficult to visualize how he managed to scrape up the $80,000 for his investment. Nonetheless, when Black Watch filed under Chapter II, far from feeling stung, the cabbie looked around for a new cattle operation into which to pour more cash. No other genre possesses that inimitable mixture of cynicism and gullibility displayed by the Manhattan cabbie.

Indeed, there are a number of people in the cattle business who are not wearing frowns these days. The forced liquidation of unsound cattle deals and the dumping of cows and bulls on the market at depressed prices is bringing a wide grin to the real cattlemen beyond the Rio Grande who have not been in the business to squirrel away tax-free dollars but to raise and sell beef for the American dinner table—and these veterans couldn't be happier as they snap up herds at bargain prices.

Some ranches have been in the business since the days of the old Wild West and have made a fortune serving the nation's needs. The most successful of such operations and the one that best epitomizes a sound, in contrast to a speculative, cattle venture is the King Ranch—the largest privately owned piece of property on earth.

Started from scratch over a century ago by the King family, it is bigger than the state of Rhode Island, twice the size of the Grand Duchy of Luxembourg. It covers a territory of 1,500 square miles entirely closed in by fences. It is so vast an expanse of territory that a dozen different kinds of weather prevail on it. The ranch has been owned for four generations by the King-Kleberg family, which has held its fief against bandits, hurricanes, lawsuits, taxes and disease. Within this wire-walled kingdom, several hundred Mexican and American cowboys, wearing the garb of the early frontier—leather cuffs, spurs and high-heeled boots—and living in feudal isolation, represent in many cases (like the owners) the third and fourth generations working the ranch.

Richard King, the founder, was an Irishman born in New York City in 1824 of an impoverished couple. At nine he was apprenticed to a jeweler, but at eleven he ran off to sea as a stowaway, became a cabin boy, worked up to a pilot and, while still in his teens, rose to be a captain on the riverboats that supplied the coastal ports along the Gulf of Mexico.

In 1852 he decided to give up his career as a boatman and buy acreage and livestock, for he noticed that cattle, horses and sheep had a way of reproducing themselves and increasing their value while boats decayed or got wrecked. That same year, King rode into the wilderness below the Nueces River with his friend, Colonel Robert E. Lee, the future commander of the Confederate armies. On Lee's advice, King bought 15,500 acres of ranchland from a Spanish family at a price of $300, amounting to less than 2 cents an acre. Due to drought conditions, he was able to pick up cattle at $5 a head. And on this shoestring he found himself in business.

Captain King was a rough-and-ready chap, perfectly suited to the frontier. Tom Lea, his biographer, tells how one evening, when the captain and his young wife, Henrietta, pitched camp during a trip through Texas, a Mexican emerged from the brush and asked if he could stay overnight. King agreed and sent him out to gather firewood. When he returned and the captain bent over to kindle the fire, his wife, who was nursing her baby across from him, suddenly shouted, "Look behind you, Captain King!" The captain straightened up and, without turning around, grabbed the arms of the knife-wielding assailant. With the skill of a man used to defending against waterfront brawling, he swung him over his head, slamming him to the ground. Most men under the circumstances would have shot the assailant, but King spared his life, ordering him to get out.

The captain had a fine sense of irony. Early one morning several *vaqueros* came to him complaining they wished to live just like the *patrón* and sit around the house; the captain put out chairs for them and sat with them until noon without uttering a word. "By that time," says King's biographer, the fidgety *va-*

queros "were heartily sick of the life . . . and ready to go to work."

The captain reserved his greatest tenderness for his wife, whom he could refuse nothing. When at sixty-one he succumbed to cancer of the stomach and took whiskey to ease his pain, the doctor told him his drinking was shortening his life. He refused to let up until his wife informed the doctor, "Tell Captain King that I need him a while longer." At this the captain rose from his deathbed, rallied to live awhile longer and, despite his pain, never touched liquor again.

King's business motto was "Buy land and never sell." Pursuing this strategy, he ultimately acquired title to more than 600,000 acres of ranchland. At the time of his death in 1885 his property grazed 100,000 head of cattle and employed almost 1,000 people. It had become the biggest landholding owned by a private citizen anywhere. King feathered more than his own nest. He laid the foundations of the cattle industry in the Nueces-Rio Grande region of Texas. Says Cleveland Amory, "King's career ranks second only to Commodore Vanderbilt's as the most remarkable individual success story in American Family founding history."

Upon King's death his widow invited the ranch's thirty-one-year-old attorney, Robert Kleberg, to manage the property. And when he married her daughter Alice, the operation of the ranch passed for all practical purposes into the Kleberg family. The Klebergs were of German stock. Bob's father was a judge who had received his doctor of laws at the University of Göttingen. The family emigrated to America because it hated the militarism of its native Prussia.

Captain King's son-in-law did exceedingly well by the founder. He doubled the ranch's property to 1,000,000 acres, and he was a prime mover in bringing a railroad into southern Texas, making possible a more rapid growth in its population and industrial development.

In recent years the ranch has vastly contributed to the technology of Texas farming. In south Texas the problem of developing nutritious grass that will not wither under the blazing sun is a vexing one. At the King Ranch agronomists experimented by importing and mingling with the native grasses exotic species, notably a Rhodes grass from Africa. This seemed promising until a parasite from Japan found a foothold, attacked the Rhodes grass and destroyed it. Faced with the threatened disappearance of the entire pastureland, King agronomists searched around the clock for a way to stop the killer parasite. At the eleventh hour they discovered the existence of a wasplike insect from India that preys for its sustenance upon the Rhodes grass parasite and destroys it. Since the Indian bug was in scarce supply, King scientists patiently set out to grow a culture of it until it multiplied sufficiently to be tried on the ranch. The tiny wasp can travel only half a mile during its entire lifetime to do its job of killing, and King researchers had to drop swarms of parasite eggs, camouflaged in nodules of Rhodes grass, from low-flying planes. The first drop was made over 105,000 acres of the Encino division of the King Ranch. Thanks to this ingenious counterattack, the grass has been revitalized and is once again imparting a healthy, high-yielding range forage enabling south Texas to fatten its cattle for maximum profits.

A remarkable job of breeding a uniquely new cattle species has also been accomplished by the King Ranch. The two dominant strains in the United States ever since frontier days have been the Shorthorn and Hereford, both imported from Britain. They are suitable in temperate climates but are less than ideal for the hot ranchlands of south Texas. So King agronomists set out to create a new steer that would be at home under the Texas sun.

As early as 1915, Bob Kleberg heard about the Brahmin breed of India which was highly adaptable to tropical heat, resistant to insects and adept at foraging on pastureland similar to that of south Texas. The Brahmin had one drawback, however: Its beef was overly tough. Kleberg tackled the problem of developing a new crossbreed that would incorporate the strength of the Brahmin while providing tender beef. His research was halted when he developed cancer, but his son Bob, Jr., a student at the University of Wisconsin, left the campus, took over the direction of the ranch and carried on his father's work. After exhaustive experiments in the crossbreeding of imported Brahmins, Kleberg achieved a striking success. He came up with an animal that had never before stalked the earth:

Cherry-red, with small, delicate, white-tipped feet and packing a ton of juicy beef on the hoof, this new breed—Kleberg named it Santa Gertrudis after one of his daughters, Gertrude—was created from one extraordinary father, Monkey. Born in 1920 of Kleberg's experiments, Monkey wound up siring 150 sons, single-handedly fixing the entire breed. Monkey's descendants have been shipped to start their own herds all over the world, especially in underdeveloped countries, and a new era in the feeding of the impoverished with special high-protein beef meat is underway.

Not surprisingly, considering the mammoth extent of the ranch, the King inheritance has been the subject of continual litigation among its heirs. Rivalry began with the death of Henrietta King, the widow of Richard, the founder, who lived to the ripe age of ninety-two, serving as the grand matriarch of the clan. When she died on March 31, 1925, her funeral was richly ceremonial. Her body lay in state in a bronze casket banked with flowers in the big front room of the ranch headquarters, as cowboys from remote corners of the King spread converged on it. It took some kinenos two days of rapid riding to reach headquarters. When the home services were concluded, a cortege more than a mile long followed the coffin to the burial site. As the casket was lowered into the earth, the cowboys swung into their saddles, reined in their horses and cantered in single file around the grave, holding their hats in side salute to *la padrona,* who had worn black for her husband to the day of her death.

Several King descendants have led eccentric lives. One of them, Alice Atwood, lived to a ripe age as a recluse and, upon dying, left her millions to a Chicago cop who had befriended her. Another heir bequeathed her share of $30,000,000 to a foundation headed by a queer Trappist friar.

The ranch today remains under the stewardship of Bob Kleberg, Jr., a rugged, homespun member of the Money Crowd who is managing ranchland assets, including oil reserves, of well over $250,000,000 and who perfected the Santa Gertrudis breed. He is in his mid-seventies but still hale and active. Kleberg's goal is to hold together the ranch, all 1,400 square miles of it, in a family corporation that will long survive him.

To further this, the ownership of the ranch has been organized in a curious way. Each of the four branches of the family, which consists of some fifty heirs, has a quarter interest in the corporation, voting 15,000 shares. When the company holds its annual meeting, the entire clan gathers at the ranch headquarters, marking what is undoubtedly the most inbred stockholders' conclave in America. Kleberg presides as president and chief executive. The youngest shareholder, his grandson, attends sitting on his mother's lap.

Although Kleberg is, as noted, a septuagenarian, there is no indication he is losing his grip. He remains a stern taskmaster who has been described as having "a trace of Charles de Gaulle . . . and Captain Bligh." Unquestionably he has been giving heavy thought to who will succeed him. The betting is he will not bring in anyone from outside the family and that the new *patrón* will be someone of the blood. The King-Kleberg tribe is even more clannish than the Rothschilds.

In the meantime, Bob Kleberg runs his property with an assurance and aggressiveness as if it will last forever. Yet he is as aware as anyone of the uncertainties ahead. Asked by a reporter if he believed there would be a King Ranch in the year 2000, he replied, "Yes—if there is a world."

In the meantime, the ranch is geared to feed the masses around the world with bigger amounts and better quality protein. Demographic and social trends, especially in Asia, should provide increasingly profitable outlets. The Japanese have been changing over from their traditional rice-and-fish to a meat-eating diet, as they increasingly savor the comforts of an industrialized society. Kleberg has brought his breeding expertise to the Argentine pampas to teach the native cattlemen how to become more proficient.

At the same time, King-Kleberg is encountering growing competition from rival American ranchers who by no means intend to let it scoop up the lion's share of future cattle profits. One coveted customer being wooed by herdsmen is Soviet Russia, which has striven ever since Lenin to develop a decent beef industry to feed the people's utopia and has been frustrated by inferior cattle herds.

In the fall of 1971 that durable mediator between counter-cultures, the octogenarian industrialist Cyrus Eaton, arranged a deal whereby the Soviet commissars bought some 350 head of

Angus, Brown Swiss and Shorthorn breeding cattle from the herds of Eaton and other American businessmen to use for artificial impregnation of backward Soviet heifers.

Presumably there are no wealthy Muscovites eager to enter herd breeding as a tax shelter device, and Uncle Sam's prepotent bulls will display their talents solely in the service of Uncle Ivan to provide his children with better steaks for their vodka.

10

"Running a Conglomerate Is a Job for Management Geniuses": The Rape of Hollywood—Darling Lili *Bombs Out—* The Man Who Outwitted the Soviets

Amidst today's feverish scramble for money and gingerbread possessions, there are curious deviations in human behavior. In April, 1969, the New York *Times* carried a story under the headline THE JOHNNY APPLESEED OF MONEY VISITS COLUMBIA TO "SPREAD A LITTLE SUNSHINE." It told how H. L. Hume, a wealthy, bearded writer in his early forties, had spent four days at Columbia University handing out $3,000 in $50 and $100 bills to anybody who caught his fancy. "We pick out interesting looking cats and spread a little sunshine," Hume informed a reporter while lounging in a dorm where he was put up as a guest. At the door, a mob of students had lined up applying for Hume's largess. The writer shrugged off his philanthropy. "It's only bread." He was laying out the cash as an experiment, he explained. "Money is permission to live, you dig?" He wanted to show that this permission shouldn't depend on brains, industriousness or social standing. He was testing what he called the "amplification" factor—the phenomenon of distributing dollars quickly enough to maximize their impact on the community. "Every dollar I give out actually represents something like $50. I just throw a pebble into the well and wait for the reverberation wave." In order to speed it up, Hume insisted his beneficiaries spend their cash as rapidly as possible, but several students complained to the reporter that it was difficult to do this. One recipient disclosed, "He gave me $100 at 3:30 this morning and told me to get rid of it by 9 A.M. I bought flowers, a present for my father, a gift for my roommate. I gave a cab driver a dollar tip. But it wasn't until noon before it was all gone." Another explained how he had tried to beat the deadline by randomly handing out $10 bills in a crowded restaurant, but he was still stuck with cash and was feverishly hunting new projects to finance.

Mr. Hume, the Johnny Appleseed of folding money, in his own way stumbled upon a profound economic truth—one more and more Americans have begun to glimpse as they rise to affluence and which the rich have been aware of all along— "Money is nothing. It is merely a device to make bookkeeping more easy."

No group has lived more zealously by this credo than an aggressive new breed in Wall Street, the wheelers and dealers in corporate conglomerates. With the dollar rapidly losing its punch and a rising number of people coming to realize that it is much smarter to leverage one's assets than to conserve them, a coterie of entrepreneurs turned into big-stake gamblers, pushing debt securities around like "Chinese money," building empires on shoestrings, taking plunges fully as nerve-wracking as the capers embarked on by the Jim Fisks, Jay Goulds and Jesse Livermores of yesterday.

Abetted by the roaring bull market of the postwar years, American industry in the 1960's erupted into a peak of corporate mergers and acquisitions. But the most fertile seed bed for corporate swinging was via the phenomenon that lifted the practice of mergers to the nth degree—conglomerate building. In the simple merger, the management of one company acquired another in the same line of business to expand the scope of its operations. In assembling a conglomerate, management took over companies regardless of what businesses they were in, often not to expand its operations but to enhance the worth of its stock by showing rapidly increased earnings. Indeed, the term "conglomerate" suggests a heap of irregularly clustered particles lumped together into a heterogeneous mass (or mess).

In the 1960's, as noted, under the impact of an accelerating inflation which turned business as well as social values upside down like the logic of the mad hatter in *Alice in Wonderland*, corporate operators stepped up the practice of putting together glittering agglomerated edifices of totally unrelated activities—

electronics firms with meat packers, auto parts makers with
movie producers, insurance firms with television networks, mutual funds with real-estate developers. The acquisition-minded
embarked on their agglomerate building using a strategy of
"synergism"—a philosophy that two and two, if put together
imaginatively enough, need not add up to four but to five or
even more. The word "synergism" is said to have been coined
half-humorously by a professor who defined it as mixing coffee
with Irish whiskey; one got something he didn't bargain for.

The strategy for instant empire building was masterly in its
simplicity. A wheeler-dealer took over a company with a low
price-earnings ratio, making a play to the firm's shareholders
with a tender offer that was temptingly above the market value
of their stock. This offer was frequently made with convertible
debentures sweetened by warrants. In short, the aggressor
offered his own IOU's, planning to pay off his debts with the
cash grabbed from the till of the acquired company.

A basic method for acquiring a company was through a
pooling-of-interest method. Under this tactic of "cosmeticized
bookkeeping" the conglomerate and the acquired company simply combined their income and revenues without recording the
merger as a sale. Accordingly, the buyer, unlike in the conventional purchase agreement method of accounting, didn't have
to show the excess cost of his purchase. This technique, originally developed to describe a situation when firms of comparable size joined in matrimony, wasn't meant to apply to the
oddity of a Jonah swallowing the whale, as was the case with
many conglomerate dealers who through stock manipulation
gulped down firms many times their size.

The pooling-of-interest technique worked wonders. When a
conglomerate snapped up a company with a lower price-
earnings ratio, the combined earnings frequently jumped as if
hypoed by adrenalin. However, to show constantly rising earnings the swinger, like the heroin addict for kicks, had to take
steadily increasing dosages, devouring firm after firm and going
more heavily into debt as it leveraged itself into increasingly
higher earnings. While the snowballing debt had to be paid off
sooner or later, the corporate prestidigitators were betting that
inflation was bound to quicken and that there was little risk;
indeed, it was the smartest defense to go heavily into debt and

pick up assets since the debt would be paid off in dollars worth a fraction of the ones originally received.

Fueled by the inflationary fever that gripped the nation, a number of striking coups were pulled off by financial necromancers. James Ling, who left the Army after World War II with a few thousand dollars, put together a mammoth complex —Ling-Temco-Vought—by pushing around paper with the *brio* of a magician pulling bunnies out of a top hat. Charles Bluhdorn, a Viennese immigrant who had made a fortune in commodities dealing, began trading companies like he used to peddle corn futures, and he wound up, after eighty acquisitions, with a goliath, Gulf & Western, that dealt in sugar production, moviemaking, metals, real estate, auto parts manufacturing and sundry other things.

Sometimes the dealers got tripped up. Ben Heineman, who took over the Chicago-Northwest Railroad and diversified into a host of ventures from soup to nuts, had his comeuppance when his company, Northwest Industries, made a $1 billion tender offer for B. F. Goodrich, the nation's third-largest rubber maker. Goodrich fought tooth and nail to fend Heineman off. To increase the number of its shares and make it more difficult for him to gain control, Goodrich management hastily bought up a half interest that Gulf Oil, a synthetic rubber producer, had in Goodrich. Then, Goodrich acquired a small, privately owned trucking firm on the theory that by entering the transportation industry, it would force Northwest to apply to the ICC for permission to gobble Goodrich up, and the regulatory body would do some hard thinking before allowing a railroad to take over another transportation outfit. The final *coup de grâce* was provided by the stock market, which entered a sharp decline in mid-1969, driving Northwest stock below that of its intended target and making a take-over virtually impossible.

But the abortive attempts of Jonah to swallow the whale were overshadowed by the successes. An especially lush field plowed by the acquisition-minded was the cash-laden property and casualty insurance industry. The reason for this was the industry's curious financial structure. Property and casualty firms derive their income from two sources—underwriting premiums and the income generated by their investment portfolios. Under the regulations of most states, the firms aren't allowed to spread out in their accounting statements the expense of writing new policies, although in practice they do just this. They must expense their costs at once for the state records, thereby penalizing earnings. Moreover, while new premiums ordinarily bring in cash advances for a year or more, insurance firms cannot take these advances into earnings. The theory is that if the books of a firm were to be closed suddenly and advances refunded, its position must be shown as it exists at the moment.

Reflecting the statutory requirements, the industry has developed a combined loss-and-expense ratio to indicate how well or poorly it is doing. However, this ratio does not represent the actual state of affairs for many firms. Under this formula, they frequently show underwriting deficits (statutory losses), while in fact they are enjoying substantial earnings through their portfolio investments.

Indeed, the insurance industry provided an intriguing example of undervalued assets. While firms were required to maintain surplus cash reserves to cover new policies being written, many had accumulated through their portfolio investments "surplus surplus" reserves substantially in excess of those needed to carry on insurance operations.

Wall Street's attention was called to the industry's treasure trove of unused cash when, in 1967, one alert broker house, Carter, Berlind and Weill, did a study in depth of the business. Insurance firms by law had to sit on their massive reserves, the broker pointed out, but there was a way legally to circumvent these restrictions. The solution, it suggested, lay in setting up a holding company that did not come under the supervision of the state insurance laws and could operate the insurance business as a subsidiary owning all its stock. The subsidiary could then hand over its surplus to its unregulated parent in the form of a cash dividend. The parent could use the money as it saw fit without restriction. The end result, the broker rationalized, would be that the shareholder would be benefited by a more productive use of assets.

A number of insurance firms had tempting granaries, but their capital structure rendered them impregnable to a takeover attempt. However, at least two firms stood out because of the wide dispersion of their stock holdings. One was Great

American, with a nest egg of $100,000,000 in reserves and the other was Reliance Insurance Corporation, which was sitting on some $80,000,000 worth of cash. The market price of their stocks failed to take into account the hidden asset of their surplus-surplus, and this served to facilitate a take-over.

Not only did Carter, Berlind work out the theory of the take-over strategy, but it was prepared to be a prime mover in the actual attempt. Through its contact with key performance-oriented fund managers, it could put its hands on big blocks of stock held in these firms.

In the fall of 1967, the broker contacted Leasco, an uninhibited young conglomerate that was building an empire from a base of computer-leasing financing. Saul Steinberg, Leasco's youthful president, was in the market for acquisitions. A Carter representative approached a Leasco official and informed him that if the firm were to make a tender offer for cash-rich Reliance, he knew where some 500,000 shares, or over $10,000,000 worth of Reliance stock, could be obtained.

The offer was tempting and a little frightening. Leasco was young—in 1967, it had earned a mere $1,400,000 on $14,000,000 in sales—yet it was being asked to challenge a colossus that generated profits of $13,000,000 on $330,000,000 in revenues. Reliance's assets were more than 7 times those of Leasco's. But in this fantasy world of inflation and Chinese money, Leasco had one big advantage. Wall Street, floating on cloud nine, was appraising the worth of the Leasco minnow at much more than the insurance whale. Leasco's stock was selling at over 100 times earnings. Reliance, whose business volume was 20 times greater, was bogged down with a stock price of 30, which was below the firm's actual asset value. By using stock prices the way a conjurer manipulates mirrors to create an illusion, it was entirely feasible for a tiny computer leaser to grab a $330,000,000 insurance firm.

The operation was conducted with a secrecy worthy of the CIA plotting in a banana republic. With a delicate sense of propriety, Leasco gave a code name to Reliance, the target company—"Raquel" because, confided an insider, "it was big, beautiful and desirable like the actress Raquel Welch." Moreover, the stock accumulated by Leasco for the operation was done through a secret account number "J-10." The identity of the purchaser was not revealed until Leasco surfaced for the tender offer.

During one month alone in the spring of 1968, Leasco quietly bought over 130,000 shares of Reliance stock through Carter, and the latter's customers. It hesitated to make the final strike, fearing corporate indigestion. But pressed by the impatient holders of big blocks of Reliance stocks and their agents, it launched the tender offer and gathered Reliance into its fold with surprising ease.

Subsequently, an Emanuel Celler Congressional subcommittee that was probing into the activities of conglomerate acquisitions called the principals in for questioning. However, as was pointed out, everything had been conducted in a strictly legal fashion. There was no law in the books that prevented a broker firm from lining up the shares of its mutual fund clients to effect the take-over of an insurance company, whose cash reserves might then be diverted for whatever purpose the new owner desired.

In addition to insurance, there were other pastures that proved especially alluring to conglomerate operators. One lavish opportunity was provided by the motion picture industry, which in the mid-1960's was wide open to financial freebooting. The youth crowd, which had become the dominant audience, representing 75 percent of moviegoers, was not satisfied with the cheesecake and tinsel that had traditionally been cranked out by the studios but demanded realistic slices of life in the raw, the "now" scene, with no punches pulled.

Thanks to the development of new high-speed cameras and supersensitive color film which allowed movies to be shot at a fraction of previous budgets, shoestring independents were able to muscle into the act, shooting "socially relevant" movies in the streets of New York and elsewhere for a song, snatching audiences away from the Hollywood moguls. Such films as *Easy Rider* and *Alice's Restaurant* became smash successes. The big Hollywood studios, dispossessed of their public and unable to adapt to the tastes of youth, found themselves at sixes and sevens, clobbered by tumbling sales that left them with insufficient capital to overhaul their operations.

Into this chaos moved the conglomerate dealers, if not always with the cash at least with the fancy paper—warrants and convertibles to glue the studios together again like Humpty Dumpty. One ambitious concern which started out as a funeral parlor operator and broadened into parking lots emerged as a purveyor of cinematic art by gobbling up a major movie studio via a tender offer. Another conglomerate, which had built a spit-and-glue colossus of savings and loans, television production outlets and insurance activities, took over the destiny of another studio via an oceanful of paper convertibles. And venerable Paramount was snapped up by the aforementioned Charles Bluhdorn, the Viennese-born commodity trader who had picked up a struggling auto parts maker and eighty acquisitions later presided over Gulf & Western, a billion-dollar empire with a hundred different subsidiaries turning out everything from auto bumpers to sugar.

The take-over of Paramount was typical of the bold strategy used by the new breed. The studio was sitting on fat assets, among which was a library of movies that could have been rented to television broadcasters for over $150,000,000; yet the company was run (if that was the word for it) by a plodding group of old-timers in their seventies under whose creaky neglect Paramount's earnings had slithered and its stock had badly slumped.

Paramount's interesting condition had caught the attention of several sharp outsiders. "She was like a middle-aged matron who was pregnant with babies potentially worth far more than the old lady," summed up one financial observer. Two bright-eyed suitors bobbed up in the spring of 1965, salivating at the whiff of undervalued assets. They were Ernest Martin, a one-time Broadway producer, and Herbert Siegel, who specialized in buying ailing companies as peddlers bought old clothes. Quietly, through the companies they controlled, the duo accumulated almost 10 percent of Paramount stock and moved in for the kill. Threatened with a proxy fight, Ed Weisl, Paramount's chairman, invited them down to talk business, and they sat in on several board meetings. Weisl knew every trick of the trade. He was a major power broker in the Democratic Party, a close friend of Lyndon Johnson's and his key liaison man in New York.

When Weisl discovered that Martin and Siegel were going

for Paramount's jugular vein, he turned to a syndicate of Chicago financiers for help. A complicated legal battle broke out between the adversary groups. Round after round they struggled, with neither side able to score a knockout.

A most interested ringside spectator was Charles Bluhdorn of Gulf & Western. He watched as the fighters grew exhausted, and at a strategic moment, backed by money from the Chase Manhattan, which had bankrolled most of his previous coups, Bluhdorn approached Weisl and convinced him he was the man to run Paramount. During a marathon bargaining session lasting far into the night, Bluhdorn induced the Martin-Siegel interests to sell to him, and the Chicago financiers, left with nothing but a prayer, also yielded.

When the smoke of battle cleared, Bluhdorn discovered he had talked his way into over $250,000,000 worth of Paramount assets for an investment of a little over half that. When Bluhdorn, a volatile individual, showed up for his first board meeting as Paramount's head man, pouring out a lava of enthusiastic oratory and gesticulating like a buzz saw, the elderly, half-dozing directors suddenly recalled with fondness those previous troubleshooters Martin and Siegel. "What in the world ever became of those two nice gentlemen?" croaked one septuagenarian member.

With the acquisition of Paramount, Bluhdorn definitely left the bush leagues for the big time. Through Ed Weisl he became a guest at the White House. He was no longer in the eyes of many contemporaries a speculator but a financial statesman. In Paramount, Bluhdorn had acquired a prestigious motion picture company going back half a century to the time when Adolph Zukor, its founder, shot a four-reel film starring the one-legged Sarah Bernhardt as Queen Elizabeth and scored his first smash hit. The studio is heavy with nostalgia. It was here that Clara Bow skyrocketed to fame in the 1920's as the red-headed "It" girl; she went around the studio with seven chow dogs whose red hair matched her own. Here Gloria Swanson ruled as cinematic queen; and her whims were indeed regal. After marrying her fourth husband, the Marquis de la Coudray, in Europe, she wired Paramount executives ordering them to "Arrange an ovation" at her arrival.

Taking over the ancient company, Bluhdorn sold off its

Hollywood studio to concentrate on less expensive shooting on location, and he tightened up the operating efficiency. But despite this rigorous cost-consciousness, he couldn't help indulging in a gesture of camaraderie now and then.

One of Bluhdorn's business friends was Commonwealth United, a conglomerate put together from a gas and oil company to which was added a maker of jukeboxes and vending machines. By 1969, overextended with debt and squeezed by tight money, Commonwealth was in trouble. In June of that year, it sent out proxy material in preparation for its annual meeting, and shareholders were disturbed by what it disclosed. Almost one-third of the firm's profits reported for the previous year had been generated by a single land transaction. And this had taken place on December 31, the final day of the year. Commonwealth had purchased several thousand acres in Hawaii for $1,600,000 and the same day had turned around and sold them off for $5,400,000. The buyers were partners in a broker house that had bankrolled several of Commonwealth's previous acquisitions. These individuals hadn't turned over the full $5,000,000 in cash for the land; they had handed over a mere $540,000 and given their notes for the remainder. Nevertheless, Commonwealth had entered the entire $5,000,000 into its books as earnings.

This bookkeeping device didn't sit well with some stockholders. They filed suit claiming the land deal had been a trick to inflate the firm's earnings and push up its stock. Trading in the stock was halted. Commonwealth's debts snowballed and woes continued to accumulate like the plagues of Job. Within twelve months it went through three changes in management and teetered toward chaos.

It was with this troubled partner that Bluhdorn worked out a highly singular deal. In exchange for a package of debentures and warrants, Bluhdorn advanced Commonwealth $12,000,000 in cash and also assigned it a substantial percentage of Paramount's profit in a new picture the company planned to release in 1970. The film was *Darling Lili,* an extravaganza starring Julie Andrews. But unfortunately its fate proved to be as dreary as Commonwealth's. No sooner did it go into production than it became jinxed. Delays cropped up on location; after months of shooting, the Hollywood *Reporter* announced the picture "is now far over budget and reportedly still has some added shooting to complete it." Upon its release *Darling Lili* laid an egg at the box office. Even the gifted Julie Andrews was unequal to the task of bailing out debt-ridden Commonwealth United.*

Some irreverent folk have looked askance at the freewheeling activities of Bluhdorn and his colleagues. Snapped Lammot du Pont, Jr., the former chairman of the giant chemicals firm, "Running a conglomerate is a job for management geniuses, not for ordinary mortals like us at DuPont."

But Bluhdorn and company are undaunted by the sardonic mouthings of the old guard. Challenging incumbent management through tender offers, they believe, is a healthy development for American industry. They feel that sluggish, incompetent management has been dozing in the executive suites of too many firms, wasting the assets of stockholders; the threat of being ousted, they suggest, has lit a fire under them, causing them to clean house and become much more profitable.

In any event, Bluhdorn is a remarkable man. He came to the United States in 1942 at sixteen and went to work with a cotton broker for $15 a week; then he moved into commodities trading on his own and cleaned up a fortune. When the Commerce Department handed down a ruling cutting back on malt export quotas—a ruling detrimental to the activities of his firm—Bluhdorn rushed to Washington without any appointment, so the story goes, talked his way past the receptionist and into the office of the Assistant Secretary of Commerce, who ordered him out. But Bluhdorn induced the official to sit down and listen to him, and he wound up getting the quotas raised.

A highly emotional man who can be gentle or volcanic as the mood dictates, Bluhdorn has been called the Mad Austrian by bemused Wall Streeters. Remarks one associate concerning the impact he has at a first meeting, "Charlie stuns you for the first forty-eight minutes and horrifies you for the next forty-eight hours, but then afterwards you get to love him."

Bluhdorn has derived deep satisfaction standing the Establishment on its head. When he made his first fortune, outwit-

---

* The firm has since submitted a plan for rehabilitation that could put it on its feet again.

ting the old-time professional traders in corn and wheat, he is reported to have remarked to associates, "That will show those goddamn bluebloods."

Although he presides over a billion-dollar empire, he remains accessible, uninhibited, truly picturesque. Observed a writer, Chris Welles, who interviewed him for *Life* magazine, "Charlie's impatience throws his whole behavior out of whack. He never walks but runs, flat-footed, slightly off balance, as if he were racing down a railroad track on snowshoes, jotting down thoughts on scraps of paper as he goes."

For a time it seemed as though the ebullient operations of Bluhdorn and company would be seriously curtailed as the 1960's drew to a close. In the spring of 1969, the stock market, rocked by a tight-money squeeze as the Nixon administration applied the monetary screws, began its severe decline, and the stocks of the conglomerates were among the hardest hit. This brought the pace of accumulation to a standstill. Some of the agglomerated mastodons came apart at the seams and their founders were kicked into oblivion. Others, put together more thoughtfully and with sturdier structures, withstood the bear market and have rebounded quite smartly, thanks to the underlying strength of their parts. The temptation to exploit the leveraging of debt, while dampened, has by no means vanished, and aggressive operators will continue to strive for this over the long pull no matter how the SEC rules are written.

At the same time, other shrewd helmsmen, in their search for stable values in a fast-changing world, have been zeroing in not on corporate earnings but on undervalued physical assets. They are convinced that if inflation grows more critical, the growth of corporations will come to be measured (even in stock price ratios) not by a rise in dollar earnings as much as an appreciation in assets.

Emerging under this philosophy as a prime inflationary hedge are today's rapidly growing natural resource empires. And one of the most strikingly successful accumulators of undervalued resources is Dr. Armand Hammer.

No member of the Money Crowd better exemplifies the verve of the corporation builder whose appetite doesn't falter even when his accumulated years threaten to eject him from the arena, for Dr. Hammer is doing business at a time of life other people have vanished into retirement. Hammer is the effervescent chairman of Occidental Petroleum, a high-flying oil company that made headlines when it struck a rich deposit in Libya and whose stock became the darling of Wall Street investors. Indeed, for much of the 1960's it was one of the Street's hottest issues.

Hammer's father was a physician born in czarist Russia who emigrated to America and entered the pharmaceutical business. A middling entrepreneur, he struggled with debts until his son Armand, who was to demonstrate a genius for picking his way through the capitalist jungle, took over the firm and turned it into a money-maker.

The son had studied to be a doctor at Columbia University's College of Physicians, and even after he decided to cast in his lot with business, he continued to renew his medical license over the years. It was soon apparent, however, he would never have to hang out a doctor's shingle to keep the wolf from the door.

Revamping his father's faltering drugstore, Hammer looked for ways to expand its markets and hit on a bold idea. In the early 1920's there were few areas in the world that appeared less opportune for making a capitalist profit than Soviet Russia, whose people had just emerged from the Bolshevik Revolution and Civil War. But Hammer saw a chance to peddle merchandise in the land of the hammer and sickle.

He traveled to Russia and found that while there was a need for everything, no one had any hard cash for dealing. In those early days after the revolution, the commissars handed out business concessions to favored Westerners, and Hammer wangled a license. With the bravura of a master horse trader, he dealt in everything from soup to nuts.

In one celebrated coup, he brought in 1,000,000 tons of wheat from the United States, accepting payment in caviar and furs. He took a fling at operating an asbestos mine, imported farm tractors, and persuaded the Lenin government to grant him a monopoly for manufacturing pencils. Opening the Soviet's first pencil factory, he stayed in the business for nine years.

Not only did this singular American become rich in Stalinist Russia, he was shrewd enough to get out while his luck held.

Foreseeing that the government in a change of heart would insist eventually on making their own pencils, he sold his monopoly to the Stalin government. A lesser man might have been content in taking his profits in Russian currency, but not the astute doctor. He converted them into the one thing that had lasting value in Communist Russia—royal heirlooms. For years Hammer had been snapping up everything he could get hold of that was inscribed with the seal of the Romanov czars.

As payment for his factory, the Bolshevik government gave him its notes and permission to take his art collection home. He sold the notes at a profit in Western Europe and continued on to New York with his czarist treasures. The roly-poly little doctor—he stands only five feet five inches—opened an art gallery in Manhattan with a fanfare of publicity. He wrote a book describing his quest for the Romanov heirlooms, gaining generous press coverage. Not surprisingly the art world was intrigued with an American capitalist who had out-traded Stalin.

Events conspired to keep Hammer in the headlines. Three times he was robbed: Once a gold heirloom from the palace of the czar was stolen from his gallery; another time, the sword of a Russian grand duke; on a third occasion, an extravagantly jeweled snuffbox.

Then in the 1930's, when the maximum mileage of publicity had been extracted from his gallery and the deepening Depression dulled New Yorkers' appetite for royalty's playthings, the resourceful doctor set out on a nationwide tour with his collection. Stopping at department stores in major American cities and putting on a show that was part carnival, part Metropolitan Museum, he drew standing-room-only crowds, selling his bric-a-brac to enraptured buyers.

His nimble salesmanship caught the attention of William Randolph Hearst, the multimillionaire publisher, who, trapped in a financial squeeze, asked Hammer to sell part of his art collection for him. Hammer arranged a concessionaire deal with Gimbel's in New York through which he unloaded millions of dollars' worth of the publisher's *objets d'art* on the floor of the department store as easily as lesser men sold mops.

Then Hammer turned his talent to other fields. In the mid-1930's, the Soviet Union, which had been a major supplier of staves for U.S. whiskey barrels, suddenly cut its exports, and the domestic cooperage industry was caught in a pinch. Hammer, using contacts he had developed in his pencil-making days, and persuading the Russians to sell staves to him, went into the whiskey barrel business. Then Gimbel's, which Hammer had cut into a handsome share of his art profits, helped the doctor get into the distilling end of the field, offering to buy all the stuff he bottled. He took over an obscure brand that was sputtering in sales, changed its name to J. W. Dant and built it into the top-selling bourbon in America. Eventually Schenley bought Hammer out for $6,500,000.

One of the by-products of the whiskey-making process is a mash which makes an ideal food for cattle, and the doctor, who could find gold in a garbage dump, decided to get into the feed business. To learn more about the markets, he started raising Aberdeen cattle and in 1954 managed to sell his breeding herd for a cool $1,000,000.

During his career as a cattle breeder, Hammer struck up a friendship with Senator Albert Gore of Tennessee, a Black Angus breeder who periodically visited him to discuss business. Gore invited Hammer to John F. Kennedy's inauguration, and during the ceremonies, he remarked to the doctor that the incoming administration was worried about the outflow of government gold. Anyone who had grown wealthy horse trading with Stalin, Gore figured, should be of inestimable value as an adviser on foreign trade. Gore introduced Hammer to the Secretary of Commerce, Luther Hodges, who arranged for him to tour Europe and determine what measures could be taken to stimulate American exports and generate dollars.

Hammer polished up his sales pitch, grabbed a briefcase and embarked on the mission. Early in February, 1961, he landed in Moscow and informed the U.S. embassy he'd like an appointment with the first deputy premier, Anastas Mikoyan. During his pencil-making days, Hammer had also served as a sales agent for the Ford Motor Company in Russia, and once when he had arrived in Rostov with a shipload of tractors, he met Mikoyan, who was head of the local government. The two had posed for pictures beside the tractors.

Mikoyan, now high in the Kremlin hierarchy, hadn't forgotten Hammer, and he readily granted him an interview.

Mikoyan asked what he had been doing since he sold his pencil factory. The doctor told him about his art gallery and his whiskey business. When he came to his cattle breeding venture, the commissar pricked up his ears. Hammer happened to have with him a 350-page catalog containing descriptions of his pedigreed bulls.

Hammer left the catalog with Mikoyan. The following morning as he prepared to leave by plane for India, he received a phone call from Premier Khrushchev's office asking him to stay over for twenty-four hours; Khrushchev would like to see him.

The following morning, Hammer drove to the Kremlin in a U.S. embassy limousine. He had learned to speak Russian fluently during his years as a pencil manufacturer, and he greeted the premier in his native tongue, whereupon the interpreter was bundled off and the two sat down to have a chat alone.

Khrushchev produced the cattle catalog which Mikoyan had given him. A farmer himself, obsessed with the problem of increasing Russia's food supply, the premier told Hammer he had sat up all night looking through the brochure; the text was translated for him by his wife and daughter who knew English. The pictures of Hammer's rich-blooded beauties had impressed him deeply. He understood now, he said, why American steaks were so good. They were triple the size of Russian cattle. He was determined to fatten his people's livestock up to the American standard, and he peppered Hammer with questions about how Americans bred their prize bulls. When the interview drew to an end, Khrushchev walked over to his desk, selected a pencil engraved with a picture of the Kremlin and presented it to the American cattle raiser. Hammer had a request; he wished to visit the factory he had operated during the 1920's.

That afternoon, Khrushchev sent a car for Hammer, and he was driven out to the plant, which had been renamed the Sacco and Vanzetti Factory, after the two Italian anarchists executed in Massachusetts. The head of the plant was expecting Hammer and had arranged a banquet for him. The doctor found a half dozen of his old employees still working at the plant. Between lavish toasts of vodka, the company plunged into lively reminiscences.

This reunion of a successful American capitalist with his Communist hosts was humorously alluded to later on by Khrushchev in a speech reported in *Pravda*:

> Hammer . . . went to V. I. Lenin and said he had decided to take a concession for the manufacture of pencils. V. I. Lenin looked at him with surprise and said, "Why do you want to take a concession for the manufacture of pencils?" "Mr. Lenin," said Hammer, "you have set a goal that everybody should learn to read and write and you haven't any pencils. Therefore, I will manufacture the pencils!"

A man who could inspire the regard of both Lenin and William Randolph Hearst was someone to be reckoned with.

When he was nearing sixty, an age when lesser men are getting ready to retire, Dr. Hammer plunged into a brand-new career, opening up further opportunities to display his virtuosity. In 1956 he moved to Los Angeles, intending to relax and write his memoirs; and looking around for an investment into which to put his money, he met a friend who told him the oil industry presented an attractive opportunity. There was a struggling little outfit near home—Occidental Petroleum—that was drilling two wildcat wells. Hammer was asked to invest in the venture. He put in $50,000, and both wells struck gushers.

The little doctor, who knew nothing about the oil business, decided this was a fine field to get into more substantially. When the Oxy Pete people asked him for more money, he lent them $500,000 and took a stock option at $1.50 a share; the stock was selling over $1. Upon converting his option, Hammer wound up as the biggest stockholder, and in 1957 he became Oxy's president.

Once again his touch turned straw to gold. When Hammer was installed as president, the little oil producer had an income of $90,000 on a net worth of $125,000. Ten years later under Hammer's ministrations, Oxy Pete had burgeoned into a mammoth complex of oil, agricultural chemicals, fertilizers generating $660,000,000 annually in business volume and enjoying a net worth of $300,000,000. To his skills as horse trader Hammer had added a new tool: He had belatedly discovered the wondrous magic of leverage. His previous ventures had all been with businesses he had owned himself or with associates. Now, stumbling across Oxy Pete, he had also stumbled into the mouth-watering new world of securities promotion where the virtuoso entrepreneur could greatly magnify his holdings by titillating the imagination of dreamy-eyed security analysts and performance-minded fund managers. The Wall Street gun-slingers were constantly searching for stocks with romance. This master of financial derring-do, whose business life had packed the flamboyance of a dozen picaresque novels, was prepared to give Wall Street all the glamor it could take, and more.

Until Hammer took over, Oxy Pete, as noted, was a strug-gling wildcatter in California. Now it made headlines. The major oil deposits in the United States and abroad had for years been tied up by concessions wrested by the major oil compa-nies, and there seemed to be nowhere a struggling independent producer could gain a foothold.

Then news hit the financial world of a major oil strike in the North African country of Libya.

The giant oil firms and their satellites rushed to Libya to gobble up concessions from the aging monarch, King Idris. And into this power struggle Hammer plunged his obscure lit-tle company. The businessman who had made a fortune in Communist Russia and added millions from whiskey and cattle in the United States proved more than a match for the oil ty-coons, diplomats, influence peddlers in their maneuvering to grab the Libyan pie.

Wrote one financial correspondent, Stanley H. Brown, of the maelstrom into which Hammer had injected himself:

> On any day when the ghibli wasn't blowing sand up out of the desert, the air was redolent of buying and selling, winning and losing, bribery and the transfer of money to Swiss banks. The rival capitals of Tripoli and Benghazi offered the biggest floating bazaar and crap game anywhere.

The key factors in the struggle were governments backing the major oil firms, high-ranking cabinet ministers, military ad-venturers, lobbyists armed with secret geological documents, all plotting with the zealousness of intelligence agents engaged in a global espionage confrontation. Hammer found himself pitted against odds that were utterly congenial to him. Coming in with a two-bit company and lacking influential contacts, he emerged with the winning bid over sixteen rivals, obtaining two valuable oil concessions from the government of King Idris. He turned the trick by among other things adding as sweetener to his bid for oil an offer to put 5 percent of Oxy's Libyan profits before taxes into a vast agricultural project to turn the oasis of Kufra in the southeast portion of Libya into a fertile, crop-producing land. Kufra, it turned out, was King Idris' birthplace and the region where his father was buried. The doctor got his oil just as he had obtained his pencils from Lenin, by skillfully blending his negotiation with ingratiation.

On the occasion of the government's formally handing over the fields to Occidental Petroleum, a richly colorful observance was held. Under a splendid pavilion festooned with Libyan flags, flashing red, green and black, the king attended with his ministers, religious chiefs and top diplomats, as the band in scarlet coats played military tunes and lambs were slaughtered in a sacrificial ceremony. Amidst such pageantry, the little doctor was definitely in his element.

As the oil gushed from Hammer's Libyan wells, the price of Oxy stock soared 50 points. The exotic has always fascinated Wall Street, and there was plenty of glamor in an oil independent pioneering for riches in a country that, thanks to modern technology, was rapidly emerging from the Middle Ages.

Libya had been an Italian colony and had subsequently passed through a period of French and British rule before gaining its independence in 1951. A target for adventurers centuries before its modern colonial masters, Libya had been occupied by the Greeks, Romans, Spaniards, Turks and Venetians. Now under the impetus of the oil strike, a modern, new city of Tripoli was springing up by the side of the old. Steel and concrete office buildings, with the latest air conditioning, were rising from the rubble of stucco hovels whose residents had been moved to government-built housing projects. Girls in miniskirts with the long, flowing hair of hippie flower children walked with mothers heavily veiled in the historic garb of Moslem women. Mercedes, Jaguars and Fiats sped through winding medieval streets. In the narrow alleys of the old quarters, Arabs peddled silks and tapestries alongside gleaming new shops that featured transistor radios and other appliances for twentieth-century living.

Dr. Hammer had struck up a highly profitable bargain with King Idris. Then, without warning, the king was toppled by militant Arab Socialists. He had left Libya to take his annual cure in the mineral waters of a Turkish resort on the Sea of Marmara. A group of young army officers seized the government, and the king, with his entourage, was sent into exile in Greece. The tough new government brandished threats against foreign oil concessions and sharply raised their taxes.

Looking to hedge with investments beyond oil, the indefatigable doctor has plunged Oxy into other ventures, seeking to build it into a natural resources empire. Land and the minerals it yields, Hammer feels, will be major inflation hedges in the unpredictable, difficult years ahead. Like Charlie Mott of General Motors, Hammer apparently suspects that the big play in the next ten years will not necessarily lie in the stated cash earnings of a company but in its undervalued assets. And he's determined to exploit these to the fullest.

Accordingly, Hammer has bought up the Island Creek Coal Company to turn Oxy into the nation's third-largest coal producer with three billion tons of reserves. He has taken over Hooker Chemicals, which promptly rewarded his acumen by participating in a major new discovery of sulphur in Mexico.

Several years ago, this reporter investigated how the little doctor tried to deal himself into one of the nation's biggest ranch and farmland holdings and even though he was rebuffed came out with a tidy profit. The prize that caught Hammer's eye was the Kern County Land Company. Launched by two Kentucky financiers who grew rich during the 1849 gold rush, Kern grew over the years into a land-holding colossus, amassing almost two billion acres in California, Arizona and Mexico, equivalent to over three times the size of Rhode Island.

The value of the bulk of holdings, acquired fifty years ago, was carried in the books at what it had originally cost. In addition to these undervalued land assets, Kern since World War II added several major industrial properties, including a top auto equipment manufacturer, a producer of profitable electronic devices and a leading maker of farm machinery. Buoyed by such acquisitions, Kern's income had shot up six-fold in the last ten years, from $31,000,000 to over $180,000,000.

Intrigued by a study of Kern's balance sheets, Hammer in May, 1968, suddenly made a bid to acquire the company lock, stock and barrel. Oxy Pete announced a tender offer for 1,000,000 shares of Kern common at $83.50 a share and within several weeks reported it had received 20 percent of Kern's stock from shareholders, to become the firm's biggest stockholder. The managerial descendants of the mining tycoons who had built Kern had no stomach for being taken over by this maverick outsider. Rejecting negotiations with Hammer, they threw themselves into the arms of another, from their view, more suitable partner, Tenneco Corporation, a giant complex of natural gas, packing and chemical operations owning over $3 billion in assets.

To ward off Oxy Pete, Tenneco made a counter offer which the Kern directors immediately accepted. But Hammer was unperturbed. There was more than one way to skin a cat. As Kern's largest single stockholder, Oxy was sitting in the driver's seat even though it was unable to gain full control. Hinting it was prepared to thwart Kern's merger with Tenneco unless it was liberally compensated, Oxy asked and got $8,900,000 as its price for granting an option to Tenneco to buy the stock it held so the merger could be consumated. And Oxy received an additional $84,200,000 constituting the balance of the purchase price for its shares of the stock. This wasn't a bad day's work. For making a play for Kern and investing $75,000,000 in a tender offer, Hammer and company wound up six months later with a $93,000,000 return, which netted it a neat $18,000,000 profit.

Armand Hammer, in short, is a formidable figure in the executive suite. He has parlayed himself into several fortunes by pitting the real worth of physical assets against the inflation of paper currency. By converting Russian rubles into czarist heirlooms, moving into cattle, whiskey, oil and undervalued natural resources, he has prospered under different governments and a variety of economic conditions by realizing that the safest payoff for an investor in troubled times lies in those possessions that have an intrinsic value that can be appreciated by Marxists, capitalists and Arab sheikhs alike, even though they agree on virtually nothing else.

In the meantime, while Dr. Armand Hammer and Occidental Petroleum continue to expand their stake in natural resources, a counter trend has set in among other empire builders. The era of helter-skelter, frenetic corporate accumulation seems to have come to an end, at least temporarily, as capital for expansion becomes tighter. When conglomerate stocks received a drubbing in the recent bear market, the accountants took a hard look at the Chinese money dealings and other tactics of financial levitation indulged in by the breed and began frowning on the notion that the whole is greater than its parts. On the contrary, they are now pontificating that the whole is less than the sum of its parts. In this chastened era of the liquidity squeeze, bigness per se is no longer regarded by a growing number of corporate managements as a prime goal.

Indeed, a number of bona fide conglomerate builders have begun using the techniques of deglomeration in a reverse blueprint of their previous strategy. They have been spinning off subsidiaries and divisions (while keeping, in most instances, control or partial ownership), dressing their offspring as "new" companies through public stock offerings and, in some cases, achieving a higher stock price for their offspring than Wall Street has settled on the parent.

Bluhdorn's Gulf & Western has partially spun off its oldest company and the foundation of its sprawling operations, its auto parts business; Ling-Temco-Vought has partially split Wilson, its big meat-packing subsidiary, into four firms in public stock offerings; Northwest Industries, which gobbled up the Chicago & Northwestern Railroad during its salad days of aggrandizement, has been maneuvering to unload it into other hands. A host of others have also been shedding their offspring as gingerly as a second-story operator unloads "hot" ice.

The wheel has come full turn—that is, until the next big spin sends it off on a new splurge of leveraging via levitation.

11

The Offshore Fund Boys Sing the Bahama Blues

In January, 1970, while the writer was preparing to do an article on the Manhattan real-estate scene, his attention was drawn to the following advertisement appearing in a leading trade industry publication:

> *It'll cost you 6 cents to write us*
> *It may cost you millions if you don't.*
> *Can a multi-million dollar transaction really be initiated by mail?*
> *Absolutely.*
> *If we had time, we'd love to conduct all our business on the golf course. Or on yachts.*
> *But with $50 million monthly to invest for the USIF Real Estate fund, the world's fastest-growing buyer of income-producing property, we have to act fast.*
> *In the past 12 months we've bought more than $500 million in real estate; office buildings, shopping centers, apartment complexes and industrial centers.*
> *Your letter, with full particulars, will be handled in strictest confidence. We'll reply within a week. Most deals are closed within 30 days.*
> *Write us. If you feel sporty, use a 10¢ stamp.*

This ad had been placed by AMPROP, a subsidiary of Gramco, Ltd., and a leading member of a breed of promoters of a new investment vehicle—the offshore mutual fund. It was launched to support a nationwide buying hunt undertaken by the firm to snatch up office buildings, shopping centers, apartment houses all over America and become the largest single landlord in the United States.

The effort was directed by a company one of whose leading officials was Pierre Salinger, the jovial, cigar-smoking communications expert who had served as press secretary to President John F. Kennedy. Since leaving the hustings of the New Frontier, Salinger had risen high in the councils of the business world, becoming a top official of Gramco, soon to be named a deputy chairman. Now he was in the forefront of a promotional effort to push a heady new fashion.

The mutual fund has been the breeding ground for a host of newly made fortunes (the bulk of which has been garnered, one must hasten to add, by the managers not the investors). For the first time in history great masses of the middle classes, supported by rising wages, have found themselves with discretionary dollars available for investment. At the same time, they are being pressured by the need to protect their savings from a debasement of the dollar that is threatening to lower their living standard. The concept of the mutual fund—a vehicle in which masses of people pool their money under professional management, diversifying their exposure and presumably lessening their risk—seemed a plausible solution.

Along with their rapid expansion in the 1960's, there emerged pitfalls for the funds. Their original concept of serving as a vehicle to provide professional management for the unsophisticated who haven't the time or the expertise to invest successfully on their own became distorted by the emergence of a variation of the species, the performance fund that aimed not for the appreciation of assets through long-term investment but for quick profits through speculation. These "go-go" funds attracted huge followings as they competed with one another to reach the top spot in the performance derby. Infatuated investors followed them as avidly as rock fans pursue the hit lists.

Starring in this carnival was a new species of swingers hardly out of school and still wet behind the ears who surfaced from the junior research staffs of banks and broker houses to become fund managers, making $1,000,000 a year. Wrote Adam Smith, the financial journalist:

With individual responsibility so visible in a field where results are so easily tracked . . . the Stars were born. It seems to be the age of the Joe Namaths, and in fact, the star portfolio manager is much like a pro-quarterback; he is under continuous pressure; he must perform all the time, he is paid inordinately better than the plodding, plugging team members, and if he gets intercepted too often, he doesn't stay a star.

In the grab-a-quick-buck mood of the sixties, in addition to the prestidigitators domiciled in the United States who wheedled money from home-grown investors, a bevy of managers added still another gimmick to the strategy of leveraging assets. These were the operators of offshore mutual funds, run largely by Americans, which, headquartered in such out-of-the-way tax havens as Panama, Luxembourg and the Bahamas, catered to foreign investors and had their pie while devouring it. They put their money into American stocks, reaping a windfall from the booming bull market on Wall Street, without paying U.S. taxes or complying with the SEC regulations with regard to margin requirements that American investors endured.

To lure foreigners (they couldn't sell to Americans because they were circumventing SEC supervision), these funds hired as highly visible directors people with famous names to give them instant respectability. Former high-ranking government officials swarmed onto the payrolls, including such luminaries as Pierre Salinger, Robert Wagner, the ex-mayor of New York, "Pat" Brown, the ex-governor of California, and James Roosevelt, the ex-U.N. diplomat and son of the former President. Nor was the celebrity list confined to Americans. Such men as Reginald Maudling, deputy leader of the British Conservative Party and ex-chancellor of the exchequer, Paul Henri Spaak, former prime minister of Belgium and secretary general of NATO, offered their names in the service of the offshore fund managers.

One of the most aggressive was Gramco, Ltd., which added a new dimension to the game. Unlike most who dealt in common stocks, Gramco, through its subsidiary USIF, moved into the real-estate field, tying the concept of the mutual fund into land and property development.

History's slickest real-estate deal is supposed to have been pulled off by Peter Minuit, the Dutchman, who "bought" Manhattan from the Indians for $24 worth of wampum. In the next three centuries, this investment mushroomed into $40 billion. But this coup doesn't at all impress today's bona fide real-estate swinger. A *Wall Street Journal* reader pointed out in a letter to the editor, "For a $24 investment to grow to $40 billion in 344 years, it need only appreciate at the rate of about 6½% compounded per year. Most investors in real estate would not have anything to do with such a stagnant situation."

A wholehearted subscriber to this point of view was Gramco, Ltd., founded by Keith Barrish, twenty-eight, who when he was twenty had already gained a reputation as a financial *Wunderkind*. During a program for bright, young political trainees in Washington, he struck up ties with leading associates of President Kennedy's during the "Camelot years," and when he launched the Great American Management and Research, Ltd. (Gramco), no less than eleven of Kennedy's former entourage hopped aboard as directors. These included Kennedy's former Assistant Secretary of Commerce, his Under Secretary of Health, Education and Welfare and his ambassador to Ghana.

The most colorful alumnus was cigar-smoking Pierre Salinger, Kennedy's press secretary. Subsequently, after the other Kennedy men dropped out of the picture, Salinger continued on, becoming deputy chairman of Gramco (U.K.) Ltd. Rafael Navarro, a former political associate of Batista, the head of pre-Castro Cuba, Keith Barrish, who remained chairman, and Salinger made up the ruling triumvirate.

Gramco operated on the premise that the American economy was caught in an unending inflationary spiral and that real-estate values had nowhere to go but up. By buying shares of Gramco's USIF subsidiary, which put all its money into real estate, the shareholder was bound to grow rich with the appreciation of U.S. land values.

The idea was bold in the sense that mutual funds normally trafficked in stocks, moving in and out to buy and sell them whenever desirable, thanks to the liquidity of the securities market. Real estate was supposed to be much less liquid, for one could sell property only when a buyer was found at the right price. Hence it was deemed dangerous by the financial pundits to run a fund from which the client could demand his money at any time but which was locked in real estate from which it could not get out profitably at will.

But Gramco management shrugged off such fears. They were confident they wouldn't suffer a liquidity crisis because there would be no pressure by their clients to sell. The fund operated on leverage. It put a small down payment on a property that was valued at many times the fund's investment. It counted on collecting enough income from rents to work off the mortgage after deducting costs for maintenance of the property.

Gramco calculated that its property portfolio would yield an average 17 percent, taking into account depreciation and tax deductions. And under this umbrella, it would be easy to keep up mortgage payments no matter how tight money became.

By buying properties and paying off the mortgage via tax-free rentals (thanks to depreciation), the equity in the property would increase as the mortgage was paid off, and the net assets value of Gramco's portfolio of properties would steadily rise. Indeed, it would not be necessary to sell off any of the properties or rely on capital gains. All that was needed was a steadily appreciating asset value of the portfolio which would be translated into the rising value of shares held in Gramco so that investors were assured that at any time they wished to cash in some or all of their shares, they would receive more money than they had put in.

Because of this feature of instant liquidity, tied to the steadily appreciating values of real estate, shares in Gramco would for all intents and purposes function as a kind of new currency, much more suited to this inflation-ridden era than paper dollars, which were steadily depreciating in worth. The Gramco idea was similar in some aspects to the concept behind the issuance of the French *assignat* during the Revolution, except that *assignats* were paper money issued on the collateral of the landed estates seized from the nobility.

In addition to this largess for the investor, Gramco reserved some substantial benefits for itself. The management company took a fee from the USIF fund for its services as investment adviser. For every $1 Gramco put into a property, it obtained $3 additional through mortgages. And it charged a fee of 5 percent based on the total purchase price of each property—the $4, not the $1 it actually paid in. In addition, the Gramco management added a yearly charge of 1 percent on the net assets of the portfolio and a cut of salesmen's commissions that added up to a substantial charge before the shareholder received his cut of the pie.

At first things went very well. The fund operated out of the Bahamas beyond the jurisdiction of the U.S. tax collector and SEC supervision; and sales were made only to foreigners. In three years, the fund attracted 23,000 shareholders in Europe, Latin America and the Far East. The overwhelming majority of investors were of modest means, putting $12,000 on the average into the fund. The shares of USIF, according to its books, appreciated more than 12 percent a year. Gramco's ability to buy undervalued property with a large potential seemed uncanny. Not a single building purchased was the firm obliged to write down. (Nor did it have to since the actual worth of a property is never determined until one tries to sell it; and Gramco didn't sell any of its holdings.)

Its promotional team traveled the length and breadth of the United States buying up shopping centers, office buildings, apartment houses with the savings of 23,000 clients. With millions of other people's money to invest, the Gramco team could afford to be delightfully informal. Exempt from SEC restrictions, they would decamp on a community and insert a breezy ad in the press and trade magazines like the one previously mentioned for January, 1970.

Old-time real-estate men were flabbergasted at the manner in which Gramco was negotiating deals mounting into the millions through the mail. Ordinary mortals just didn't commit themselves to a multimillion-dollar office building or shopping center or home development this way. Rumors were rife about how real-estate brokers reading the ads would submit a selling offer on Thursday, and Gramco would snap it up and take title to the property the following Monday. Gramco went on its way, according to critical old-timers, like a child with a $100 bill in an ice-cream parlor. By 1970 the fund had become the largest single holder of real estate in the United States, the proud owner of 240 properties worth over $1 billion.

Then trouble started.

Keith Barrish and company had based their strategy (like

other fund managers) on the assumption that shareholders would not ask for their money back in significant numbers. They would watch the net asset value of their shares steadily increase. If they were pressed for cash, they could even borrow money from Gramco; the farsighted management had arranged with a group of banks to underwrite such loans. But the one thing the shareholders would never do—God forbid!—is ask for their money back. For if too many attempted to turn their shares into cash, the result would be like a run on a U.S. bank in the days before the Federal Reserve System was established.

And this is what happened. Gramco woke up one morning and found itself suffering from a massive run on its cash reserves. The events that led to this nightmare were brief and decisive. Intoxicated with its investment strategy, convinced that its portfolio would endlessly appreciate like an unterminated pregnancy, Gramco's top command allowed its operational costs to get out of hand. At the same time, the Wall Street stock market entered a sudden severe decline beginning in the middle of 1969, and the confidence of the business community became shaken. To acquire urgently needed capital, Gramco took the step of issuing stock to the public, offering 10 percent of its assets to foreign investors. The issue was gobbled up and the price of shares jumped from the initial offering of $10 to $38. However, the offering proved to be a boomerang. For in going public, the management company had to disclose its financial position to the public. It delayed the issuance of its first six months' statement, but when it was finally released, indications were that the fees it was collecting for buying new properties had tumbled substantially. Something was wrong.

The financial community stirred uneasily; redemptions mounted. Pressure on the price of Gramco shares sent them into a decline. On top of this, another offshore fund—the Cornfeld-operated IOS—tumbled into a financial crisis, and the government of West Germany placed a ban on IOS sales. Investors, whose confidence was shaken in the offshore concept, demanded their money back from Gramco.

Its stock continued to take a pounding, dropping from 38½ till finally in October, 1970, it reached 1½ a share. In the meantime, during the month of September, a tidal wave of redemptions hit the fund; shareholders demanded $40,000,000 in cash.

The situation was critical. The firm claimed to have $250,000,000 in net assets, but less than 10 percent of this was liquid.

At first, Gramco conscientiously proceeded to dole out $20,000,000 of the $40,000,000 demanded by its shareholders; but then as redemptions continued to mount and there seemed no end to the hemorrhage, Gramco announced it was "temporarily suspending" its redemptions. How long this "temporary" suspension would last, no one seemed to know. Rafael Navarro, a top Gramco official, told *Barron's* "it might take three to five years to liquidate the realty portfolio in an orderly way and distribute the proceeds to fund shareholders." In the meantime, the West German government banned Gramco's USIF subsidiary from doing any more business in the fatherland, and a group of banks, stuck with $31,000,000 loaned to Gramco for its expansive promotional program, stepped in and grabbed $11,-000,000 worth of the cash the firm had deposited with them, further squeezing its liquidity.

At this writing, Gramco's USIF subsidiary has undergone a reorganization under the direction of the Trust Corporation of the Bahamas, Ltd., which has been acting as a custodian trustee. USIF has been transformed into a closed-end fund and Arlen Reality and Development Corporation has replaced Gramco as the managing company. There are reports that Lehman Brothers has been trying to reestablish a market for USIF shares by seeking a listing on several European stock exchanges. In the meantime, pending further developments, the investors in eighty countries who put their money into the fund are waiting to salvage their investment.

Other offshore funds like Gramco mushroomed up, promising a hedge against fading dollars by basing their "currency" —*i.e.,* fund shares—on steadily rising real-estate values. And they too came a cropper.

Consider the well-publicized case of Bernie Cornfeld, whose offshore empire was the most far-ranging and ambitiously conceived of the lot.

An unprepossessing man, five feet six inches in height, portly, bald and bearded, and raised in Brooklyn white-collar poverty, a social worker and campaigner for Socialist Norman Thomas for the Presidency, Cornfeld became a larger-than-life pop hero in the current folklore of finance. Starting from scratch, he amassed in fourteen years a personal fortune of over $100,000,000 by creating a mutual fund—IOS, Ltd.—that promised to make millions of people wealthy without having to work for it. (At his zenith Cornfeld had 1,000,000 clients who handed him $2 billion of their savings.)

Cornfeld had a Socialist rationale for his efforts. "We're in the business," he told one writer, "of literally converting the proletariat to the leisured class, painlessly and without violence. It's revolutionary and goddamn exciting."

Cornfeld's share-the-wealth panacea was simple. Since World War II, the U.S. stock market had been going up, with only minor reverses, doubling its value every half dozen years. It was obvious, Cornfeld felt, that in an age of affluence we should forget such unpleasant memories as the 1929 crash. The stock market was no longer a two-way street. Like the Apollo spaceships, it had broken the laws of gravity and its only direction was to the moon. Anybody who gave Bernie his money could relax and be confident it would grow as surely as God made little apples.

Peddling from the housetops the notion that people could get something with no effort on their part, merely by hiring professional managers to do the thinking for them, Cornfeld built his fund into an international giant. Like other offshore operators, he had what he thought was a foolproof gimmick. He established his legal headquarters in the tax-free haven of the Bahamas. From here he could put money into Wall Street without being fettered by U.S. taxes and SEC regulations on margin buying and other matters. To this offshore device Cornfeld added a concept of his own. Instead of operating a fund that invested in stocks, he created a fund that invested in other funds that did the investing in stocks, thereby screwing his leverage to the highest notch. And he called his flagship operation the Fund of Funds, borrowing from the Biblical reference to Solomon as the King of Kings.

In carrying out his concept, Cornfeld gathered around him as agents and underlings some of the world's celebrated names, including James Roosevelt, the former President's oldest son, Erich Mende, the former Vice-Chancellor of West Germany, Pat Brown, the former governor of California, the sons of Ben

Gurion of Israel and of Gustaf Adolf VI, the King of Sweden and Eric Scott, the former head of the Toronto Stock Exchange.

Operating through an international network of tax havens, using a battery of brilliant lawyers to exploit every conceivable loophole, harnessing the latest developments in communications technology to tie his operation together and keep it abreast of hourly changes in stocks and of investment conditions around the world, Cornfeld seemed not only to have developed a perpetual moneymaking machine but, until he was tripped up, had ambitions for even more grandiose goals. He envisaged introducing a worldwide global credit system for IOS, Ltd., investors. He planned to buy or build an international airline to carry his card carriers wherever their hearts desired, erect a string of hotels at vacation resorts, and move into moviemaking, television and publishing. And with that Socialist compassion that constantly seeped through his capitalist façade, Cornfeld planned to build homes, hotels and vacation resorts where IOS funders, grown old and gray in the service of giving Bernie their money, could spend their last days in affluence before they passed on to greener pastures. As Bert Cantor, a former business associate and one of Cornfeld's biographers, observes, "Bernie and company hadn't got around to printing their own money yet, but were well on the way toward licking that particular problem."

From the outset, Cornfeld did a brilliant job of training his corp of salesmen. He recruited dropouts from all walks of life, unable to succeed under the traditional system, and turned their desire for survival into a fiercely aggressive drive to sell his funds. He demanded from them a limitless amount of nerve.

According to a story told by Bert Cantor, one Cornfeld "pro" who instructed sales recruits took a nervous candidate with him on a sample call at the home of a prospect. They were invited in to have dinner with the family while the salesman explained the mutual fund concept. Just before dessert, the veteran pitchman took off a shoe, unrolled his stocking, placed his naked foot on the table and picked his toenail with his fork. The trainee blanched, but the episode passed without comment by the hosts. When the dinner was over, the pro coolly signed up the family to a fund program and pocketed a check for the down payment. When they left, he told the novice he wanted to prove to him in a way he'd never forget that if he had enough confidence in himself he could get away with anything.

It was this kind of push that sent sales skyrocketing and made Cornfeld wealthy beyond his dreams.

As he soared into the stratosphere of international finance, Cornfeld's clothes and manner lost their Brooklyn touch and took on the eccentric elegance of a young-blooded snob from Belgrave Square. He got Vidal Sassoon, who dressed the hair of the Beautiful People, to take over the care of his balding pate, reshape his fading streaks of hair with magical skills, until he looked like a creature of elegance. He had the fashion king Pierre Cardin tailor suits for him in Edwardian style, and Oleg Cassini personally made up his neckwear. He bathed himself in exotic perfumes, learned to ride horseback and carry a crop with majesty. He wore cuffs of lace, jabots and top hats, and he had a house in Belgravia and in the upper East Sixties in Manhattan—and a villa in Geneva which had been built by the Emperor Napoleon for Josephine. This villa had two dozen rooms furnished in French eighteenth-century decor, and here Bernie kept a stable of mini-skirted playgirls who flopped and flounced around like pet poodles while ornately liveried footmen bowed obsequiously out of their way.

In short order, the ex-worker for New York City's welfare department had slipped with ease into a routine of all-night rock-and-roll parties, cavorting with movie stars and narcissistic young men with Prince Valiant and Beatle haircuts, as a bevy of ocelots sniffed at the champagne.

In those salad years there were rumors that Cornfeld had undertaken negotiations with that other luminary of the *bon vivants,* Hugh Hefner, to merge IOS with *Playboy* into a supercombine of nightclubs and high finance. One Cornfeld associate disclosed how he had a dream the two tycoons met to discuss a corporate marriage. "The combination of all that money and all those tits was overpowering. I woke up in a cold sweat."

And yet for all his swinging, Cornfeld remained the boy from Brooklyn, filled with the simpler graces. While the big shots around his dinner table ate caviar and helped themselves to rare vintage wines, Bernie had his footmen serve him Coca-

Cola. At first he had corned beef and hot pastrami flown to him from New York's Lower East Side; eventually he opened his own delicatessen at IOS corporate headquarters so that he could step into Second Avenue when he was tired of Mayfair.

He invited his eighty-two-year-old mother, Sophie, from Brooklyn to live with him. She moved into the top floor of Napoleon's villa with her gefilte fish, tea with lemon, and lined her walls with pictures of her son in the good old days. Proudly she showed them to visitors—the one of Bernie at thirteen on his *bar mitzvah* day; another taken when he graduated Junior High School 225; another when he signed up with the merchant marine. Below her, night and day, the mini-skirted starlets jived with long-haired male freeloaders, and rock sounds rent the air. But the stubborn old lady sat at her kitchen table, engulfed in her memories, refusing to peep into this other world. "If things get too noisy downstairs late at night," she told a reporter, "I just call downstairs and tell them to shut up."

As his mother sipped her tea, the son continued to accumulate more millions. "You've got to understand that Bernie is still like a poor boy from Brooklyn," observed one of his oldest associates. "When he was a kid he was fat, he had a bad stutter; he was extremely shy. Now he's surrounded himself with wealth and luxury, but he's still a kid. The villas, the planes, the cars, they're all things, they're toys. . . . Bernie can't say, 'I'll take one thing.' It's always, 'I'll take a dozen!' "

Cornfeld continued to take things by the dozen until trouble took him.

Several events hastened his downfall. The SEC, upon investigating IOS's affairs, slammed the door on Cornfeld's application to sell his funds to U.S. citizens. For one thing, the SEC suspected, although it was never able to nail down the evidence, that at least some of the money IOS was spiriting into the banks in the Bahamas, Switzerland and other havens was hot Mafia money and that foreign aid dollars sent by Washington to undeveloped nations were finding their way into IOS coffers. Moreover, SEC sleuths claimed to uncover evidence that the Cornfeld crowd was receiving illegal kickbacks of brokers' commissions without paying taxes to Uncle Sam. They charged that this was being done through a *femme fatale,* reminiscent of

Mata Hari, a charming, highly persuasive lady who had been born in Cuba, resided legally in the Bahamas and carried Bermuda citizenship.

In the meantime, IOS top-echelon biggies, discounting the seriousness of the SEC's prohibition on the fund's doing business in the U.S. and ignoring other signals that warned of trouble ahead, blithely continued to run up extravagant expense accounts for flashy autos, women and around-the-world frolics. The costs of the management company went out of control, soaring in a single year, 1969, from $40,000,000 to $80,000,000. At the same time, management extended itself into increasingly riskier deals, threatening to leave it badly exposed if the U.S. stock market, which had been so conveniently zooming along, were to crumble.

And sure enough, the stock market, whose steady appreciation since the end of World War II had been a major reason for Cornfeld's success, by the middle of 1969 began to wobble, and it entered a decline that was to last for eighteen months, constituting the worst bear market since the 1929 crash. This tumble, which sharply drove down the worth of the IOS portfolio, coupled with management's increasing exposure to questionable bookkeeping and its soaring expense accounts, doomed Cornfeld's tenure.

The events that led to his downfall began in April, 1970, when George von Peterffy, an associate professor at the Harvard Business School who had recently been hired, ironically enough, by IOS as a director to provide long-range planning for its operations, made a routine inquiry of the corporate treasurer as to the IOS management company's cash position. He was put off and stalled.

The professor knew his legal rights. When the SEC had refused IOS entry into the United States, the fund had established legal headquarters in Canada. Under Canadian law, a director is empowered to receive any reasonable information he requests about the finances of a corporation he serves as a director. Professor von Peterffy insisted on seeing the books; and he finally won his point.

What he discovered shocked him. IOS cash assets, which in the fall of 1969 had been $53,000,000, had by April, 1970, shrunk to a meager $5,000,000. Yet the only major expense recorded in the books for this period was $7,000,000 spent for the purchase of a mutual fund management company in Canada.

In a stormy confrontation with IOS management, Von Peterffy wrung an admission that $40,000,000 in cash had been handed out in loans to several high-ranking IOS officials. The money was lent in a series of complicated deals involving oil claims, jet plane, real-estate financing and the like, none of which, IOS spokesmen pointed out, technically violated any law.

However, the investment community was not sanguine about this offhanded bandying about of money. In the spring of 1970 the first rumors of the questionable loans to IOS officials reached the financial community, and as reports of the management company's shaky cash position mounted, the reaction was sharp. Institutions and individual shareholders began dumping their holdings. One major institution on April 8, 1970, unloaded 75,000 shares in Geneva. It received only $10 a share, a sharp decline from the $18 to which IOS had risen after a public offering the previous fall. As institutions and IOS's own salesmen, with stock options awarded as performance incentives, unleashed waves of selling, other customers around the world clamored for their cash, and redemptions rose, reaching $5,000,000 a day above sales. By the middle of April, the IOS cash redemptions had reached tidal flood proportions, and its stock continued to dive. On May 1, 1970, it fell to $3.75 on the London exchange. Brokers quipped wryly that every time a trader in IOS emerged on the floor, the stock tumbled another half point. By the end of May, it had slithered to a little over $2 in London, and in the middle of June, the London exchange suspended trading in it altogether. At the other end of the world, the Tokyo stock market was taking the greatest beating in history, and financial writers speculated that the primary cause was the massive unloading of stock by the IOS management company in a desperate effort to raise cash for its redemptions.

With IOS seemingly on the brink of bankruptcy, the panicky high command sought for a way to restore public confidence and stem the flood of redemptions. Emissaries were dispatched to the four corners of the globe to find new sources of money. One top official hopped a plane for the United States and, according to press reports, stopped off to see Charlie Bluhdorn, the chairman of Gulf & Western, to determine whether he might be interested in taking over the IOS management company and supplying urgently needed cash. Another team of executives barged in on the Banque Rothschild to find out whether, together with its London cousins, the French branch would be willing to put together an international consortium to acquire the empire. But Mr. Bluhdorn reportedly demurred and the Rothschilds were not interested.

In the meantime, as the shadows gathered, Cornfeld paced nervously up and down in his sumptuous, velvet-lined office on the second floor of his Swiss chalet, while below the latest stable of playgirls lounged in the living room, sipping champagne, playing cards and waiting for the boss to join in the frolics. Every hour or so during the death watch, observed a journalist visiting the château, Cornfeld made his appearance with the perennial glass of Coca-Cola, keeping the girls in stitches with his jokes in dialect and his bright small talk that served momentarily to break the tension. His mother sat upstairs ensconced in her memories, occasionally sallying forth in her chauffeur-driven limousine to take an airing or go to the movies.

The denouement of the scenario was inevitable. The ax was honed for the most visible scapegoat available. Cornfeld was ousted by the board of directors as chief executive officer of the firm he had founded and built to assets of over $2 billion.

After considerable maneuvering, a consortium was put together to buy Cornfeld's stockholdings and take over control of IOS. Robert I. Vesco, the chief executive officer of International Controls Corporation of Fairfield, Connecticut, who brought in $5,000,000 in badly needed cash and joined the board, becoming chairman of the finance committee, took Cornfeld out of the picture in a complex operation by buying, along with associates, Cornfeld's more than 6,000,000 preferred shares in IOS, Ltd., the parent company. Since the selling price reportedly averaged from $1 to $1.20 a share, it is apparent that Cornfeld got out for substantially less than the paper profits he had held less than a year before. In March, 1971, Vesco was elected to Cornfeld's old post of chairman.

Vesco is an enigmatic figure, as reserved as Cornfeld is extrovertive. A man who never went to college and who received factory training as an aluminum-extrusion engineer, Vesco stepped out on his own at twenty-four, selling fabricated aluminum products as a free-lance salesman for a number of small, struggling firms. Very fast with figures (he has achieved a self-taught virtuosity in accounting), Vesco waived taking commission money for his sales, accepting instead stock in the firms he represented, and in a series of intricate financial maneuvers he built up a $100,000,000 conglomerate, International Controls Corporation.

To leverage and expand his holdings, Vesco has used the Eurodollar market for some sophisticated maneuverings. He wangled a $5,000,000 placement of private nonregistered stock with a wealthy Greek shipping family. Moreover, to get urgently needed cash at a time the U.S. government had placed tight controls on domestic sources of money, he set up a subsidiary in the Netherlands Antilles, made a $25,000,000 debenture issue through it in Europe and had the U.S. parent import the cash through a system of loans for his own needs.

In jumping into the breach caused by the Cornfeld disaster, via supplying his $5,000,000 loan, which IOS subsequently repaid him, Vesco obviously sensed an intriguing challenge. However, he was faced with serious roadblocks. For one thing, the Securities and Exchange Commission, which has barred IOS from doing business in the United States, challenged Vesco's right to act as IOS chairman while he remained head of the domestically located International Controls Corporation.

Not only is the IOS banned from doing business in the United States, but the Securities and Exchange Commission in Toronto has continued its prohibition on IOS's stock being traded on the local stock exchange. Also Vesco was threatened by a suit of dissident stockholders attempting to wrest control from him.

Last year, to raise money, the once mighty IOS drastically truncated itself. It spun off the bulk of its insurance and real-estate holdings into a newly organized company called Value Capital, Ltd., and its banking assets into International Bancorp, Ltd., leaving as its sole major asset an 80-percent interest in a company that manages and sells IOS mutual funds plus some small insurance operations.

Then in April, 1972, Robert Vesco finally gave up the struggle to hold onto IOS itself. International Controls sold its 38-percent control and Vesco resigned all his posts with IOS. As a dramatic indication of how drastically Bernie Cornfeld's former billion-dollar empire had shrunk, International Controls sold its control of the erstwhile financial octopus (to four members of his management team) for a lordly $200,000 in cash and some $940,000 in notes. To such a pass had the mighty fallen. International Controls is, however, retaining a 22-percent interest in International Bancorp and a 38-percent interest in Value Capital, two of IOS's most toothsome spin-offs.

Trouble has continued to pile up for Cornfeld, Vesco's predecessor. In December, 1971, the U.S. government filed suit against Cornfeld and IOS, Ltd., charging that Cornfeld and the fund were involved in the illegal buying and selling of $37,500,000 worth of gold in 1968 during the speculative run on Uncle Sam's gold reserves that forced the United States and other nations to set up the two-tier system to insulate official Treasury transactions from free-market trades. According to the Justice Department, Cornfeld violated the 1934 law that prohibits a U.S. citizen from owning gold except for industrial or artistic purposes. The United States sued Cornfeld for double damages amounting to $75,000,000 under a law enabling it to collect such a penalty. A federal judge signed an order to attach Cornfeld's assets, but all Uncle Sam could find in Manhattan and several adjacent counties where the court had jurisdiction was $5,000 deposited in Cornfeld's name in a small Wall Street brokerage account.

In short, the woes of IOS are continuing to mount as this book is being written, and undoubtedly there are other carrion-eaters poised to swoop down on the corpse. Moreover, a number of people with well-known names who have been involved with IOS during its checkered career are presumably watching its struggle with more than casual interest. For instance, William Rogers, the current U.S. Secretary of State under President Nixon, was at one time a vice-president of Dreyfus Corporation. IOS for years was the single biggest sales outlet for the Dreyfus Fund and played a key role in its rapid growth. There is also David Kennedy, the former U.S. Secretary of the Treasury, who came into the Nixon Cabinet from the chairmanship of the

Continental Illinois Bank. This bank was a longtime financial backer of John King, a close business associate of Cornfeld's and partner in many of his ventures. The bank has also participated as a leading lender for other offshore funds, including the ill-starred Gramco. Another presumably interested observer of IOS's fortunes is Maurice Stans, until recently the U.S. Secretary of Commerce, who formerly headed the Wall Street brokerage house of Glore, Forgan Staats, which had been preparing to underwrite a public offering to launch IOS's entrance in to the market for U.S. customers until the SEC stepped in and blocked the move.

As for Cornfeld, the eager beaver from Junior High School 225 who brewed the witch's cauldron, ousted though he is from the councils of power and nursing a badly bruised ego, he isn't exactly starting all over again. He still has his homes in Switzerland, France and on Manhattan's Upper East Side, his Cadillacs and planes and many other possessions a multimillionaire can afford. The SEC has slapped him on the wrist for security violations, charging him with the illegal disbursement of broker fees and banning him for life from employment by a U.S. broker firm; but it is highly unlikely that he would go to work for anybody else after breathing the heady ozone of power.

Cornfeld failed because he overreached himself, but the social needs he sought to satisfy remain—the need of the masses of middle-income and lower-income people to protect their savings in a world economy of rampaging inflation. Cornfeld was the first to demonstrate on a really vast scale how a mutual fund, armed with the purchasing power of the masses, can swing decisive weight, for good or evil, in the financial councils of the world.

Indeed, no matter how badly or well they are run, mutual funds are continuing to attract customers just about everywhere but in Peking, where the blue-uniformed citizenry apparently haven't yet heard that every man is a king and is entitled to his own little investment plot to nurture his holdings into a blooming capitalistic harvest.

Recently, two Wharton School professors who play around with computers and issue statistical studies wrapped in the most impressive academic mystique tried to puncture what they consider to be a mass delusion. They announced that their computerized investigations reveal that the investment performance of mutual funds of all categories over the years has actually been no better than the stock market as a whole. In other words, the dons imply, professional management is a great thing for the professional managers, considering the fees they get, but the average investor is no worse off trying his own luck, using his own judgment, making his own choice of stocks.

This kind of advocacy is obviously out of harmony with the *Zeitgeist* of mass participation—group therapy, trade unionism, hippy communes and Alcoholics Anonymous. Our society has a stalwart faith that great things can be accomplished through mass involvement. So the group, that beloved fetish of modern schoolmen, will continue to participate in Wall Street stocks and get hoodwinked as a group. And, who knows, it might occasionally even make some money.

Part III

THE INHERITORS

So long as he is rich, even a barbarian is attractive.

—OVID

The audacious adventurers for wealth in the modern world of money—the self-made millionaires—constitute only one sector of the Money Crowd. Riches, like fine wine, grow more valuable with aging. The biggest fortunes are those inherited and nurtured through the generations. In addition to today's founders of fortunes there are the tribes of inheritors—those redoubtable conservers whose job it is to protect and multiply what they already have in abundance, instead of high-rolling and leveraging into the wild blue yonder on a risk and a prayer.

The inheritors, unlike the parvenus scrambling for a grubstake, have the odds on their side to begin with; they move their massive resources mostly into sure ventures; their aim is to multiply their money by playing certainties, not to make a killing via speculation.

Unlike America, where the outside corporate manager has emerged to take over the direction of the bulk of industry, family control is still quite strong in British business, where great dynasties still prevail and wield substantial power. Over 40 percent of the business heads who make up Britain's membership of the Young Presidents Association, an organization similar to the U.S. Junior Chamber of Commerce, run businesses founded by their grandfathers or fathers. In France, too, the inherited business is still strongly entrenched. French industry is reluctant to make public offerings, to bring in

*outside capital or partners for fear of losing familial control.
Its growth comes normally out of profits, and much of the
business is conducted by small family firms engaged in luxury
lines, with a few capital-intensive corporations looming dra-
matically above the herd.*

*In many instances, here and abroad, the family fortune is
all that fathers and sons have in common, for the current
generation of youth has drifted further from its forebears than
prior generations.*

*Some clans, like the Rothschilds, the Oppenheimers of
South Africa, the Rockefellers, still possess a strong family
cohesiveness; the younger generation has remained staunch to
family tradition and heritage, even though its horizons and
life-styles have been adjusted to the demands of today's turbulent world. Other clans, like the Gulbenkians and Krupps,
have suffered a serious split. In the case of the Gulbenkians,
the business dynasty seems ended with the death, in January,
1972, of Nubar, the son. In the Krupp case, the heir is alive
and hearty; nevertheless he has formerly abdicated his dynastic role.*

That is our next story.

12

Germany's Krupp Family—End of a Dynasty

Germany Yesterday

In the spring of 1970, the stock market—that traditional barometer of America's anxieties and aspirations—took a nasty tumble. Buffeted by waves of inflation that resulted in a pall of gloom not experienced since the crash of 1929, millions of dollars' worth of stock held by mutual funds, pension plans, trusts were dumped unceremoniously on the floor of the New York and American stock exchanges. As the market hurtled to a seven-year low, panic broke out. Fund managers pleaded with block house traders to take sure losses on a dog of a stock, promising to make it up to them with commission business on other stronger securities. The stock of one highly publicized "glamor" company, which had been a favorite of fund managers only a few months previously, soaring under their exuberant buying to over 100, actually tumbled to under 1 point. Summed up an expert, "Looking at this market is like staring hypnotically into the eye of a snake. One is fascinated and horrified."

The crisis had been building up for months, as the Nixon government fought desperately to stem inflation. Indeed it had been gaining momentum since the spring of the previous year, when the market, after hitting a peak on the Dow Jones Industrial Averages of close to 1,000, began to falter and then to drop relentlessly through level after level the pundits had predicted would be a bottom from which the big turnaround would be launched.

Reported the *Wall Street Journal* on April 28:

> Things are so bad that "there isn't even any gallows humor these days," says a partner of one member firm of the New York Stock Exchange. "People are too depressed to tell jokes. Newcomers to the Street have never seen such bad times. Old-timers here have, and more than a few are comparing 1970 to 1929. 'It isn't 1970 any more,' says one brokerage house official. 'It's 1928 and seven-eighths.' "

The air of tension in the trading rooms was paralleled by another crisis that exploded in the streets.

For weeks, student demonstrators had been assembling in the Wall Street area to hear antiwar speakers launch denunciations of the U.S. involvement in Vietnam. The locale for these demonstrations was the Federal Hall National Memorial building (formerly the U.S. subtreasury) at the corner of Wall and Nassau streets, a handsome old Greek temple structure that has strong historical significance for Americans. Atop the stairway stands the statue of George Washington, who took the oath of office as the first President of the United States on this spot on April 30, 1789. Across the street towers the neoclassical building housing the New York Stock Exchange, which for the dissidents represented the quintessence of the Establishment spirit.

The extremist tactics of the radical left had enraged and alienated a large section of the American community, and a countershow of force was inevitable.

On May 12, a peace gathering at the corner of Wall and Broad streets escalated into an ugly confrontation. Early that morning, 1,000 youthful demonstrators from the city's colleges and high schools had gathered at the stairs of the federal building to demand the withdrawal of American troops from Indochina. At noon, columns of construction workers, employed on jobs in downtown Manhattan, wearing overalls and yellow and orange metal hats, converged on Wall Street. The "hard hats," parading behind a phalanx of American flags, broke through the police lines, surged up the stairs and planted the flags on Washington's statue. Eluding the police, they fell upon the students, kicking them and beating them with their helmets. A broker, looking through binoculars from his office window on the thirty-second floor, saw two men dressed in gray business suits and felt hats using hand signals to direct the attack.

There were numerous incidents of violence. A Lehman Brothers partner, on his way to lunch, tried to protect a youth from being assaulted. He was seized by a "hard hat" and pushed against a telephone pole. Another bystander trying to extricate him was attacked by a worker who struck him on the skull with a pair of heavy pliers. Bleeding profusely, he was rushed to Beekman Downtown Hospital where seven stitches were sewn into his head.

Such was Wall Street, the heart of financial America, in the spring of 1970. The tension recalled the anxiety in other nations that had gone through troubled times; it seemed, to some observers, to echo certain ominous aspects of the Germany of the Weimar Republic, which during the 1920's was beset by political unrest and street violence as it fought to roll back a tidal wave of inflation.

Social instability is an offshoot of economic turmoil, and Germany had more than its share of both. As early as 1914, when World War I broke out, the German government took the nation off the gold standard and made fiat paper money the medium of exchange. This meant it no longer had a fixed, unchanging value but fluctuated according to the turns of the economy and the government's political whims. The stage was set after the war for a runaway inflation.

As the clamor for higher wages mounted and the government went deeper into debt, more and more money was distributed. Prices rose, and the cost of living jumped. Labor demanded still higher wages; manufacturers, complaining of rising costs, raised prices further, and more currency was pumped into circulation, creating even faster price rises. It was like a puppy chasing its tail.

In the early stages of the inflation, the climb of wages coupled with the tide of money flowing into people's pockets was looked upon as a sign of great prosperity. The moment of truth was not yet at hand. At first the cost of living rose moderately; then the pace accelerated. Finally, prices took off like a rocket to the moon.

As the dislocation deepened, a paradox prevailed. In the midst of poverty there was teeming plenty. While the streets of cities and towns were filled with crowds peering through the windows of grocery shops at the hams and cheeses they couldn't pay for, high-priced restaurants and nightclubs burgeoned with business. "The corks of bottles of Sekt popped into the air in the rose and emerald light of the cabarets. Expensively dressed whores paraded past tables as the band played 'Mammy.'"

In these febrile times, factions of the political left and right clashed in bloody street fights. In Prussia within a single month 461 riots erupted, 36 demonstrators died and 400 were injured. One Sunday, 18 people were clubbed to death in the streets of Hamburg, and on the following Sunday 19 more were injured in the working-class suburb of Altona.

Then, one evening in April, 1923, as several thousand citizens of Munich sat in the Buergenbraukeller beer house quaffing their brew, strong-armed forces of a militant workers' party surrounded the hall. While a detachment of men planted a machine gun at the entrance, the leader, a short, dark fanatic, strode into the hall and leaped onto a table in the rear, firing a pistol at the ceiling. As the burghers sat frozen, the intruder advanced to a platform and mounted it. "The National Socialist Revolution," announced Adolf Hitler, "has begun!"

The Nazi revolution had indeed begun, and although it was not to reach its culmination for another ten years, when Hitler took power, the seeds were sown during the 1920's as the Weimar Republic fought a losing battle against a galloping inflation that brought the economy to its knees.

During the war, the German government, as noted, had taken the mark off the gold standard. After the Armistice it met its spending needs by issuing more and more money. Today this is done in the United States through the Federal Reserve, which creates new dollars on its books whenever it is necessary to pay off on the government's debts. In the Weimar Republic the same thing was accomplished, although a little more honestly, via the printing press. For a time, as labor unions insisted on more money to keep up with the cost of living, the government was able to issue it fast enough to satisfy their appetite. But gradually the inflation got out of control, and the situation took on the elements of pure fantasy.

In 1922, when prices reached the runaway point, Isaac Marcosson, a journalist for the *Saturday Evening Post,* visited Germany and reported on the bizarre situation. Prices were no longer being raised on a monthly or even weekly but on a daily and hourly basis. One morning Marcosson left Cologne for Paris and bought a paperback to read on the train. He paid 72,000 marks. Five hours later, when he returned to buy a second copy for a friend, its price had risen to 180,000 marks. That noon Marcosson ordered a steak. The price on the menu was 80,000 marks. While he was eating it, the waiter informed him the price had risen to 100,000 marks. By the time he was ready to pay his bill, it had zoomed to 125,000.

With prices spreading out of control, the Reichsbank, printer of government currency, found it necessary to hire forty private printers to help it turn out enough money to meet people's needs. But even this wasn't enough. Fifty-six more printing plants in Berlin and twenty-eight others around the country were set up to toil day and night, pouring out currency backed by the government's promise to pay.

Still the demand was unmet. Big industrial plants, like the Krupp Works in Essen, started printing for worker payrolls their own money, which was accepted as legal tender in the community. The famine mounted. In August a large metal plant near Berlin began mimeographing IOU's signed by the company treasurer. To add to the incongruity of the situation, the printers who were turning out the money in Berlin went on strike for higher wages, complaining they didn't have enough cash for food—although they were suffocating in an ocean of paper money created via their printing presses. As one cynic observed, the best thing that could have happened would have been for them to have made the strike perpetual.

Prices continued to go up. By the summer of 1923 the money reached such stupendous figures that no one took the time any longer to print the last flock of zeros on price lists. (A 500,000-mark steak was indicated on the menu by 500.) The collapse of the mark touched off a scramble for sound foreign money. Everybody tried to get hold of American dollars in particular. In Berlin, a leading foreign journalist had some typing done; the bill was 3,000,000 marks. The typist told him, "I would be grateful if you gave me two American dollars instead. I could speculate with them." A manicurist in Cologne told an American customer that for a year it had been impossible for her to save a single mark. Her face brightened. "I'm rich because I have just bought a dollar for 30,000 marks. Now I know that whatever happens, I have a little wealth." A Munich barber suddenly blossomed into a tycoon. In a moment of aberration, an American tourist had handed him a $5 bill. It was the barber's undoing; he set himself up as a money broker, speculating in currency rates with the zest he had formerly devoted to shaving faces.

With inflation rising at the rate of 10 percent an hour, "overbuying" became a widespread phenomenon. People rushed to purchase what they did not immediately need, fearing that if they waited it would become even more expensive. Shopkeepers would have liked to have shut down, since their merchandise was more valuable than the money offered for it. But the law compelled them to stay open, and many got around it by selling goods only part time, striving during the hours they were closed to adjust their prices to the latest level the mark had plummeted to.

Everybody talked about money. There was nothing to do with it but gamble. To invest in bonds was economic suicide, for the principal (to say nothing of the interest) payable in declining marks was virtually nonexistent. Anyone who had invested 100,000 marks in government bonds ($25,000 in American money) during the war would have found himself by the summer of 1923 with exactly $2.50.

Hysteria gripped the nation. An American newsman visiting Germany met a recently retired professor of Semitic languages on a train to Bonn. The scholar told him how he had planned quitting teaching to write a work on linguistics which he had been researching for fifteen years, but his pension of 10,000 marks was totally inadequate. He had no precedent for what was happening. His family urged him to act before it was too late. He must take his savings out of the bank, they said, and spend it while the mark could still buy something. If he waited, what he could have bought yesterday would tomorrow be unattainable. The prospect panicked him; the most absurd ideas rushed into his head. Since childhood, he had craved to own a horse. Now with the whole of his fortune fast disintegrating, he realized he didn't have enough money to buy a horse but he could at least purchase a saddle. This at least he had to show for his life's savings.

Wrote a leading journalist, "Here is . . . tragedy . . . not only the tragedy of poverty or physical suffering. It is the horrible fear in the twilight of life, and this is the final word on the crime of inflation."

The journalist visited a home for the aged in Berlin:

> These old people are not beggars. They each had an income of a few hundred gold marks a year, and they came to this place with their own bits of furniture, their comfortable keepsakes, rugs, pictures and canaries. They had arranged their rooms as they liked and turned their faces to the sunset, thinking they had no more to worry about. Now they cannot understand that their gold marks have become paper marks —so nearly worthless that their income will scarcely buy a daily loaf of bread. True, they are not hungry. Their food is sent by the Government. But they have become objects of charity. Their security has been swept away . . . each day they awaken with terror in their hearts.

The savings of these people had vanished through inflation. The government had printed, in prodigious amounts, money with no relation to anything on earth except the politicians' promise to pay. Merchants who could raise their prices, workers who could demand higher wages, had adjusted to the crisis. The widow whose savings were tied up in government bonds found she could buy only a few pounds of butter. The farmer who produced the butter was sitting on a fortune. The widow with 20,000 paper marks had nothing.

Through the process of inflation, the prosperity of people on fixed incomes had been converted into the foreign bank balances of currency speculators, into the heavy gambling taking place nightly in the Berlin cabarets, into the surplus of goods hoarded in closets and cellars throughout Germany.

For the final, bitter irony was that in the midst of poverty there was feverish prosperity:

> It is a sobering experience [wrote a reporter] to leave the fine hotels, the crowded cafés and beer gardens . . . and go

into the side streets where women with babies in their arms wait in line for hours to buy a few ounces of butter. . . . Once I joined the customers in a meagerly stocked butcher shop. They were all men, well dressed and well groomed. . . . All but one bought black sausages, each a little piece, two and three inches long, carefully weighed and more carefully paid for. The one exception indulged in the luxury of buying a tiny scrap of veal, such as butchers trim off a roast for the dog, and he carried it off like a treasure.

Observed the New York *Times'* Anne O'Hare McCormack: "Germany has become a country that has lost reality; where nothing means what it would anywhere else. . . . The place is not so much a mystery as a mirage; not so much an illusion of tragedy . . . as the tragedy of an illusion." All values had been turned upside down. The worth of goods and services was wildly absurd as long as it continued to be priced in money.

Millions of people went around groping for a new standard of value. Reported another contemporary journalist:

It is an hour's train ride from Berlin to Bremen. Then a rush to a hotel. A room without a bath is 75,000 marks. . . . One tips the porter 500 marks. . . . But how can one really measure the worth of the room against the porter's services? One thinks of butter. If butter is 5,000 marks a pound, then 75,000 marks for the hotel room is 15 pounds of butter. And the tip to the porter is a little over an ounce of butter. The fare to Bremen was two pounds of butter. Now we have it! Fifteen pounds of butter for a night's lodgings, two for a five-hour train ride and one ounce for the porter to carry one's bags!

Thus it came about that the process of primitive barter was reborn. Goods in Germany became much more important than money, and the only way people trusted trading with one another was to exact payment in kind.

Germany went back to the Stone Age, before money became a measure of value. As the mark continued to plummet, the barter system was first introduced by people exchanging things privately. Soon the municipalities took up the practice of arranging loans in kind to protect lenders against depreciation.

One of the first such offerings was made by a gas and power company. The loan was expressed for a fixed tonnage of coal, divided into individual bonds, each representing a certain tonnage. Thus the lender was secured against further depreciation in the currency, although he was still liable to the risk of loss if the market price of coal fell in relation to other commodities. The coal loan was a great success; it was oversubscribed ten times.

Bartering spread through the nation. The State of Prussia arranged a loan of 50,000 tons of potash and another of 20,000 tons of wheat. Scores of companies followed with rye and wheat loans. A Westphalian power firm paid the interest on its coal bonds in the form of electric current. The federal government itself, unable to raise voluntary loans in marks, resorted to loans in goods.

Matthew Josephson, an American writer who lived in Berlin during the nightmarish winter of 1922-23, graphically recorded the conditions in his autobiography. He was earning $30 a week in American money, which virtually placed him in the millionaire class. One evening, Josephson was invited to a dinner where he met a group of German intellectuals. The gathering discussed the money crisis. "It is the most wonderful thing that could have happened to our people," declared a poet with a baby pink face fringed by shaggy white hair. "It has made Germany far better off than any other nation. Why? Because men at last have learned to live without money, the most corrosive element in modern society. I give a few lessons and accept no payment in money, but only in food—packages of rice, tins of cocoa and coffee, and so I live as free as a bird!" Another guest agreed with the poet. He earned his keep by working a few hours a day in a studio where tapestries and rugs were produced by ancient methods of handicraft. For this he received only his food and lodging. "Nevertheless," reported Josephson, "he spoke . . . like an exalted poet indifferent to his poverty," explaining his method for obtaining mental and physical discipline, in accordance with the universal spirit, the cult of Yoga.

Germany in those days burgeoned with cults of mysticism which their devotees embraced as an escape from ugly reality.

Amidst such upheaval, the mark continued to tumble. Even

before the introduction of bartering, the inflation had turned the fortunes of entire classes topsy-turvy. The depreciating worth of currency had ruined creditors because the money owed them was repaid in money that had drastically shrunk in worth. The debtor emerged as king, for the money he owed had vanished to a point at which his debt was nonexistent. The biggest borrower of all, the government, emerged as the prime beneficiary. For the state had piled up a mountain of debt in the billions of marks wrested from the labor of its people through bond issues. This debt had been incurred in sound money. Now that money had plummeted to a fraction of its previous worth, the debt had virtually been wiped out, the loans repudiated. True, the government kept coming out with self-serving statements to allay public anxiety. It exhorted all good Germans to continue to accept the paper offered them as a demonstration of their patriotism.

Some citizens refused to be fooled by this tommyrot. They had no intention of being pauperized by government IOU's. A substantial amount of capital was smuggled out of Germany in the form of manufactured goods, jewelry, foreign stocks and bonds. Other Germans managed to build fortunes by gambling on the decline of the mark.

One of the most farsighted of the speculators was Hugo Stinnes, a leading industrialist who amassed $500,000,000 during three years of inflation. A descendant of a coal and shipping family, Stinnes was one of the first Germans during the early stages of the inflation to grasp the truth that the mark was worthless when everyone else believed it still had value. Acting on this conviction, he gobbled up real values in land and goods. His technique had the simplicity of all master strokes. As the mark continued to fall, Stinnes went heavily into debt to repay at a discount tomorrow what he had borrowed yesterday. He pledged his properties for money to buy other properties and, as the mark kept declining, he repeated the process, paying back his original loans with a fraction of the money he had borrowed. When he wanted to buy he used the depreciated mark, so that his obligations liquidated themselves automatically as the mark continued to fall. When he wished to conserve money he converted his marks into dollars or British pounds.

Stinnes gambled for nothing less than the control of German

industry. At his zenith, in October, 1923, he found himself in possession of twenty coal companies, twenty-nine smelting works, four oil fields and refineries, eleven iron ore mines, three telegraph companies, sixty electric power plants, four ship-building yards, eight chemical, sugar and paper plants, four shoe factories, nine shipping companies and a complex of banks, holding companies, locomotive works, farms and timberland holdings.

Yet, as John Flynn, his biographer, points out:

> This fortune, vast . . . and sensational as it was, possessed no lasting importance. What it was worth is difficult to say. Had the whole tangle of steel and copper mines, banks, factories and hotels been reduced [from their physical value] into marks . . . billions and billions of marks . . . and converted into the currency of America or England—*it would have fetched just about enough pennies to buy an evening's bus ride!*

In those feverish days, Stinnes was "like a gambler sitting at a table piling up . . . mountains of chips . . . in a casino which was bankrupt and on fire."

The German government finally managed to stabilize its money system when the mark had fallen to one-trillionth of its former worth. It did this by undertaking a thoroughgoing reform of the currency. In August, 1924, it introduced a Reichsmark, 30 percent of which was backed by gold. Strict new taxes were imposed and a sharp curb put on credit for business expansion.

This effectively did the trick. The country embarked on an era of consolidation; and suddenly it became urgent to conserve one's liquid assets. With the stabilization of money, the winds of fortune that had been blowing Stinnes' way shifted. Matters came to a head when the leading banks refused to extend him credit not covered by goods or readily negotiable securities. Stinnes died in 1924, at the age of fifty-five, and his two sons were left with liabilities that totaled $42,000,000. They ended up where their grandfather, and founder of the family fortune, had begun—in shirtsleeves.

The collapse of the mark left ineradicable scars in the German psyche. This terrible, macabre farrago was something no citizen would ever forget. The memories provided a seedbed for the sardonic conjurings of Bertolt Brecht, the paintings of George Grosz and other artists who lived through those times.

Matthew Josephson, in his autobiography, vividly recalls the mood. One winter's evening in 1923, when the inflation was at its height, his wife and a companion walked along the Kurfürstendamm window shopping. It was bitter cold and it was snowing. "The streets fairly roared with life. There were thousands of street girls hustling for customers. Many of them, recent recruits to the harlot's trade, had no style, used no rouge, wore shapeless hats and dowdy garments of wartime ersatz material, looking more like threadbare bespectacled schoolteachers than women of pleasure. . . ."

As the writer's wife and her friend browsed among the shops, a German lad of nine or ten appeared. He was wearing neither hat nor coat. His shoes were torn. His pale, pinched face was wreathed in a sweet, idiotic smile. Hearing the American ladies speak English, he mumbled, "Money . . . money." The women turned and tried to hand him a few hundred marks. He pushed them away, repeating, "Money." The women moved on and the boy followed muttering over and over as if mesmerized, "Money."

West Germany Today

The German economy has gone through many vicissitudes since the collapse of the Weimar Republic, but the people—those who have lived through the disaster of the runaway mark and the newer generations who have been told about it—through all the oscillations of economic fortunes have never lost their fear of inflation and their phobia for paper currency. The economic collapse and recession of the 1920's brought on Hitler, and for a time Germany lived under an economy manipulated by the dictatorial wizard Dr. Hjalmar Schacht, who fixed the value of the money and did what he wanted with it by government decree.

Then at the end of World War II, Germany seemingly reached the nadir of its existence. The nation that picked its way through the bombed-out rubble of Nuremberg, Berlin and scores of other cities and towns was reduced to an even lower level than that reached during the collapse of the mark. In the earlier instance, the nation's physical plant was at least intact. The devastation was confined to a system of values; the mirrors with which the money managers created the *illusion* of prosperity had been smashed. Now, however, Germany was split into two nations, east and west, suffering the trauma of a community whose soil had become the battleground of its demolition. Yet a strange thing happened. Bonn used its defeat as the springboard for a spectacular comeback.

Cynics have it that there is one sure way to end America's adventure in Vietnam: fly a planeload of well-fed West German bankers to the leaders of North Vietnam and tell them how beneficial it can be for a nation to lose a war to the United States. When the North Vietnamese learn of the German experience, they will surrender immediately.

As punishment for being vanquished, West Germany became the recipient of a massive economic aid program financed by Uncle Sam. In the six years following hostilities, $1.2 billion worth of relief money was funneled into the devastated economy, followed by over $2 billion more in Marshall Aid funds.

Bonn rebounded with a vengeance, so much so that today, a generation after its citizens stumbled through the shambles of their cities and used cigarettes for money, West Germany enjoys the highest living standard in the world after the United States. To add further irony, this erstwhile enemy of the free world by the mid-sixties emerged as a kingpin of international finance. With the United States and Britain piling up currency deficits, it became the only major power with a currency above suspicion, and it assumed the role of lender to the world. Contributing to the paradox, this conservative country, which has historically labored under a traumatic fear of inflation, in the postwar years switched to left-wing Keynesian economics. Indeed, Dr. Karl Schiller, the economic affairs minister, sports a larger-than-life portrait of John Maynard Keynes in his office. Schiller has been an arch-advocate of big public spending, printing paper money to keep the electorate happy: Full speed ahead and damn the torpedoes!

One family that epitomizes the twists and turns of Germany's tangled fortunes, riding the crest of power, catapulting to the depths, only to recover to new heights of influence, has been the ancient, durable family of Krupp. Its armaments business has been a key leitmotiv of German history. Adolf Hitler used to tell his storm troopers to toughen themselves until they were like Krupp steel. Krupp enabled the Prussian army to vanquish Austria, Denmark and France in the nineteenth century and fabricate the Bismarck state. In World War I, Krupp turned out the dreaded Big Bertha—the largest piece of artillery assembled till then—which hurled shells into Paris from a distance of almost fifty miles. In World War II, Krupp carried on its doughty work, supplying a lethal 88-millimeter antitank gun that blasted the heaviest enemy tank armor and a host of other weapons enabling Hitler to devastate France, Belgium and Holland, invade Russia and plunge the world into a bloody nightmare.

Since the war, the Krupp empire, which provided the hardware for Hitler's battle against Communist Russia, turned tail and climbed into bed with the Soviets through a series of cosy business deals. Shifting to the production of steel and other industrial paraphernalia, rather than guns, it opened a vast new market in Russia, offering the commissars rock-bottom prices and highly generous credit terms.

In 1957, Krupp undertook to supply the Soviet Union with an urgently needed chemical plant and a synthetic fiber complex at such an attractive price that the arms maker received praise publicly from Khrushchev, then the premier. A year later, Berthold Beitz, Krupp's chief operating official, visited the Soviet Union and displayed a mood of such effusive camaraderie with the commissars that Konrad Adenauer, the West German Chancellor, publicly rebuked him for pursuing a policy that was "sabotaging" Germany's national interests. Retorted Herr Beitz blithely, "What could be more logical than to shake hands with a customer who buys $12.5 million worth of goods from you?"

Not only has Krupp provided the Soviets with key industrial products as dispassionately as it once built the tanks that ravaged Russia for Hitler, but the firm in the 1960's wangled contracts to strengthen the Communist dictatorship of Rumania with mining machinery, the Politburo of Poland with a plant to turn out a raw material for making polyester fibers, and it has built five chemical factories in other Soviet satellites.

However, Krupp in its eagerness to serve its eastern brethren finally tripped itself up. Privately owned and tightly controlled by a family that refused to go public and disclose its financial affairs to outsiders, Krupp ran out of money to finance its ambitious *Drang nach Osten* policy and toppled into debt of $700,000,000 with some 260 West German banks. In 1966, German money grew tight, the economy turned down and the banks balked at extending any more credit to Krupp. Moreover, they threatened to call in their loans unless Alfried Krupp, the head of the house, accepted humiliating conditions: He would have to hand over supervisory powers to a board of bankers acting as a watchdog over him and turn the family regnum into a company owned by the public, which previous generations of Krupps had stubbornly refused to do. It was the bankers' contention that the family dynasty was no longer capable of running an enterprise that comprised 100 plants turning out over 2,000 products, ranging from tankers to meat and artificial teeth.

Alfried Krupp reluctantly acceded. The business of operating one of the world's most complicated industrial entities as a feudal fief was drawing to an end. The firm had virtually run out of its liquid assets.

Yet even as his debts mounted and his cash flow grew slimmer, Alfried kept procrastinating until a new development proved decisive. The Supreme Court of Taxes in Bonn suddenly reversed a decision, taking away from the Krupp family an exemption it had enjoyed successively under Kaiser Wilhelm, the Weimar Republic and Hitler. It had been allowed to hand down its business intact to a single heir-successor without dividing the property, in what amounted to a German version of the British rule of primogeniture. Now the Supreme Court abruptly canceled the exemption. Also it ruled that family-owned corporations would henceforth have to pay taxes on sales made between their various subsidiaries—a provision from which publicly held firms were exempt. Under this decree, Krupp would have to pay $15,000,000 more in annual taxes. In short, the German government was nudging Krupp by every device it could muster to surrender its private status.

On January 31, 1968, the Krupp family finally yielded its tenure, going public. By this time, Alfried Krupp had become philosophically resigned to adversity, having suffered a series of clobberings that would have finished off a less durable fellow. During the war, the Krupp Works was bombed over 150 times by Allied war planes. The bulk of its facilities was reduced to rubble; the remainder was dismantled by Soviet troops, who lugged all portable machinery to Russia. Upon the Nazi defeat, Krupp was clapped into prison by Allied occupation authorities for his role in building Hitler's war machine. He was sentenced to twelve years.

However, Krupp was lucky in one respect. The man appointed to be the high commissioner during the American occupation of West Germany was John J. McCloy. He was a leading member of what Ferdinand Lundberg calls the Finpols class. McCloy responded wholeheartedly to Krupp's no-nonsense pragmatism, his pursuit of profits regardless of the political environment. He trimmed the twelve-year sentence imposed by the Nuremberg Court to five and released Krupp in 1950.

Because the Krupp Works was not so much a business as an institution, it was altogether fitting that Alfried sit down to negotiate the terms of the reassumption of his enterprise, not as a private party, but a sovereign power. The spectacle of the jailers, the United States, Great Britain, France, sitting down to negotiate terms with the ex-convict had an exhilarating effect on Krupp's teutonic blood. Gradually the old arrogance returned. Krupp was no longer harkening to the terms of a parole board; he was barking out orders. Although his erstwhile captors offered to hand back his business, subject only to relatively minor restrictions, throwing in his 300-room estate at Villa Hugel and all other personal properties to boot, Krupp wasn't at all happy. He pointed out that 370 art treasures had been stolen from the Villa Hugel during the war and the occupation, and he insisted the Allies put their top agents on the case and restore every work to him. The British, who took on the chore, pulled their ace detectives off other assignments and managed to recover most of the heirlooms. When the terms of the treaty restoring the Krupp regnum were finally hammered out, Krupp didn't even bother to be present at the signing ceremony

with the occupying powers. He sent one of his underlings to
affix the Krupp signature and took off on a skiing vacation in
Switzerland.

Krupp had been convicted at Nuremberg as a war criminal
not only for supplying armaments that enabled Hitler to
launch the war but for employing slave labor from the Nazi-
conquered nations to work his munitions plants. By some
subtle ethical distinction that permitted Albert Speer, Hitler's
Armaments Minister, to be jailed for twenty years, Krupp, the
manufacturer of war weaponry, spent, as noted, only five years
in prison; and this didn't go down well with Europeans who
had so recently been the recipients of Krupp high explosives.
There was an uproar in the British Parliament; the French and
Dutch press seethed at this speedy rehabilitation of a man who
had used their countrymen as slave laborers.

The Krupp family studiously turned to the task of cosmeti-
cizing its image. No job is too formidable for a smart public
relations firm, not even the task of imparting to a family of munitions makers the aura of benign fraternity before a world it
had tried so hard to annihilate. The plastic surgery performed
on the Krupp image succeeded brilliantly. A public relations
team of forty expert manipulators of the mass mind planted a
series of persuasive articles in the world press describing the
new, "regenerated Krupp." Heel-clicking, monocles, all the paraphernalia associated with old-fashioned Prussianism were
abolished from the Krupp offices. Berthold Beitz took to calling
his foreman by their first names, in jovial American style. So
eager was Krupp to erase his association with munitions making that the big department store in Essen run by the firm
wasn't allowed to peddle water pistols, toy soldiers or any other
war games to children.

This drive to launder the Krupp name was given a heady
boost by Uncle Sam. The Eisenhower administration accommodatingly handed over to the Bonn government (on the
grounds they were its rightful property) the original
Nuremberg trial documents that had convicted Krupp detail-
ing the extent of the war crimes for which he had been convicted. These documents rapidly became mysteriously unavailable in West Germany. The Bonn government, as well as the

Krupp family, found it most expedient to bury the past by obliterating whatever research materials German scholars would need to reconstruct it.

Under the terms worked out by the occupying powers as a result of a special law passed by the Bundesreich, it was popularly supposed that Krupp had been permitted to repossess his business only on condition he quit making armaments. However, technically speaking, there was no ironclad, really enforceable prohibition against his making military weapons again *if* the German government called upon him to do so as his patriotic duty. A second provision of the treaty required Krupp to divest himself of a substantial part of his heavy steel production, but only if he could find a German buyer at a price acceptable to him. Under this invitation to procrastinate, Krupp never complied with this provision, arguing that he could not find anyone willing to pay a fair price. The Krupp Works is still making heavy steel products.

In rebuilding his postwar empire, Krupp displayed the evenhanded impartiality that was a hallmark of his ancestors. He took a plane around the world seeking out as new allies former enemies as well as friends. He wooed Cyrus Eaton, Jr., whose father was the leading capitalist spokesman for a rapprochement with the Soviet Union, and spent hours with him in a helicopter circling over the Arctic exploring the possibility of exploiting mineral resources beneath the frozen wastes.

On the other hand, he emplaned for the Bahamas to confer with Axel Wenner-Gren, the enigmatic Swedish financier who had been an associate of his father's and grandfather's and during World War I had served as custodian of the Krupp family's foreign assets to keep them out of Allied hands, subsequently collaborating with the Krupps in rearming Hitler's Germany.

Alfried held several meetings with Wenner-Gren in his Bahamanian retreat plotting a strategy for jointly carving out world markets. Then Krupp flew to Argentina to bring Buenos Aires millionaires into the scheme. He even took a plane to the unlikely country of Ireland. A report had reached him that geologists of the impoverished republic had unexpectedly discovered vast resources of minerals under its stony soil, and Krupp wanted to check the rumors for himself and if possible grab a slice of the action.

Despite his business hustle, Krupp found time to get entrapped in a marital alliance that smudged the family's scutcheon and saddled his staff of public relations manipulators with overtime work. When he left prison he was a single man; he had been divorced from Anneliese Bahr, daughter of a Hamburg businessman, who had irritated Alfried's relatives and the other *Herrenvolk* because she was a divorcee. Now he got involved in another *déclassé* relationship. His new romance, Vera Hossenfeldt, was, as the French put it, an *intrigante*, who had three former husbands, had worked as a saleswoman in a Los Angeles department store, and had been a showgirl who had swung with the crowd at Las Vegas. Alfred was forty when he met Vera. They were married secretly in Berchtesgaden; the mayor who performed the ceremony was heavily tipped to keep his mouth shut; the couple made a quick exit in a high-powered Porsche. After their honeymoon, the Krupps refrained from moving into the lavish Villa Hugel; because they longed for "modesty" they chose a smaller house on the grounds of the estate with only fifteen rooms, a dozen servants and a stable of racing horses.

However, Vera was hardly the sort to remain confined to the drab, conventional role of a Krupp *Hausfrau*. The couple separated. Vera, who was an American citizen, thanks to one of her previous marriages, left for Las Vegas and points west. Along the way, she bounced into the American press, named as the co-respondent in an adultery case.

A divorce by Krupp became imperative. But Vera had played her cards carefully. Her lawyer had launched an intensive investigation into Krupp's finances and came up with the gamey tidbit that the current descendant of German patriots had withdrawn over $250,000,000 from the fatherland and stashed it into Swiss, Argentine and Bahamian banks, presumably in case of an adverse turn in the German economy or his own private affairs. Wielding this knowledge as a threat, Vera filed suit for divorce, asking for a lump settlement of $5,000,000 and an annual alimony of $250,000. Since Krupp managed to have the case settled quietly out of court, how much he paid to get rid of the jaunty *frau* has not been disclosed.

One item, however, managed to creep into the press. To keep the ebullient Vera from bobbing up again in a lurid spotlight, Alfried bought her a 520-acre ranch west of Las Vegas for $1,000,000, suggesting it would be an ideal place for her to settle down and live quietly in.

Vera accepted the ranch and lived there for several years until, growing restless, she offered it to the United States government for $1,000,000 to be used as a national park. Uncle Sam demurred, but Howard Hughes, briefly emerging from his pervasive isolation, snapped up the ranch for his own use.

Less than a year after Vera sold out to Hughes, Alfried Krupp's tangled career came suddenly to an end. He had yielded under pressure to turning the Krupp Works into a public enterprise. But he did not live to see the outcome of the venture. He died on August 30, 1967, in the midst of negotiations. The cause of his death was not disclosed officially. The Krupps have managed to keep their personal affairs as secret as those of a medieval royal family. But unofficial sources indicate that Krupp died of bronchial cancer. He was a chain smoker of American cigarettes. When physicians examined him, the cancer was so widespread, according to reports, it was too late to treat it. The news was kept not only from the public but from other members of the family. To avoid attracting attention, one of the world's most powerful men was put to die in a little hut on his estate, attended by a nurse.

The funeral was simple yet magisterial. According to family tradition, the body was placed in a plain, uncovered coffin in the great hall of the ancestral home, while uniformed retainers stood guard in great plumed hats. At the head of the corpse, Alfried's faithful business steward Herr Beitz "unconsciously crossed his own hands as Alfried's were crossed; and wept."

Two months after Alfried's death, in October, 1967, Vera Hossenfeldt Krupp, who had injected so much spice and tragedy into Alfried's life, passed away in a Los Angeles hospital. Much as she had tried to run away, she followed him.

The ghost of Krupp emerged to taunt Germany from beyond the sepulcher. The ultimate quip, at the community's expense, was yet to be disclosed. In January, 1968, the Krupp Works formally became a joint stock corporation and its books were open to outside scrutiny. What they revealed was a shocker. Thanks to its freewheeling dealings with the Soviets and other East European satellites, the firm was so broke it wouldn't be able to pay income taxes to the German government for the next four years at least.

However, this state of virtual pauperdom did not affect Alfried Krupp's descendants. Their life-style would not have to be crimped at all. Three months before his death, Alfried had hastily drawn up a will under which his only son, Arndt, currently in his thirties, would be able to skim off 2,000,000 marks ($500,000) a year for life from the firm's cash flow before any other claims—stockholders', creditors'—could be satisfied.

This annual stipend extracted from the Krupp Works was destined to support the Epicurean tastes of a Krupp heir who cared nothing about the family business and had no intention of sacrificing a moment from his sumptuous capers on the Riviera.

Born in 1938 to Alfried's first wife, Anneliese Bahr, Arndt Friedrich Alfried von Bohlen und Halbach experienced the divorce of his parents when he was four. He was closely attached to his mother and as a child traveled extensively with her. "A limp, dainty, almost beautiful man," in the words of biographer William Manchester, Arndt's chief hobby for years has been to design pieces of costume jewelry and present them to his mother.

He has adopted a life-style that only a Krupp fortune could subsidize. In addition to the 300-room Villa Hugel and chalets around the world, he maintains an estate in the interior of Brazil—a country he is especially fond of—which covers over forty square miles, featuring a private airstrip for his jet-set guests, a park landscaped after the gardens of Versailles and prize racing stables. It takes almost 200 servants to run the establishment. Arndt has a personal jet plane big enough to carry his Rolls-Royce in the luggage department.

This jaunty *bon vivant,* so unlike his tight-lipped, Calvinistic-minded ancestors, has indulged in some fancy high jinks. During a joust with the wine cups in a cabaret in Nice, Arndt lost a $40,000, fourteen-carat solitaire ring and merely shrugged. He has danced the cotillion with Princess Soraya, the former Queen of Iran, and has escorted Gina Lollobrigida to a variety of night spots. Once when he prepared to go on a holiday in Paris, Krupp agents interviewed 100 *fräuleins* to select a suitable playmate.

Recently Arndt has turned aside to savor the experience of marriage. In February, 1969, the thirty-one-year-old heir exchanged vows with Henriette von Auerspan, an Austrian princess. The wedding was an ostentatious affair held in an eighty-room Krupp castle nestling in the mountains outside of Salzburg, which was originally built by the Austrian Archduke Francis Ferdinand, whose assassination launched World War I.

Snow fell heavily for several days before the event, and 200 servants toiled around the clock cleaning the roads that led to the castle. Further snow delayed the wedding reception for three-quarters of an hour. According to newspaper accounts, the princess, who is six inches taller and five years older than the groom, wore a crown of artificial flowers that gave a jocund touch of spring to the wintry proceedings. Hosting the affair was the ubiquitous Berthold Beitz, the ex-manager of the Krupp Works, who still had a lucrative pipeline into family councils. "I am so happy the boy is finally married," Beitz beamed. "He needs a strong hand." And Anneliese Bahr, the groom's mother, chirped, "Hetty is such a modest girl!"

Modesty (and plainness) seem to be a major attribute of Krupp women, those directly of the blood as well as those who marry into the family. The most celebrated Krupp on the distaff side was Arndt's great-grandmother, the redoubtable Bertha (after whom the kaiser named the artillery gun that bombarded Paris).

Bertha's homeliness was evident even when she was a baby. But her grandfather prophesied that, thanks to her inheritance, she would be besieged by an army of suitors by the time she was twenty. Since Bertha was the sole heir—there were no male descendants—the job of getting her a proper husband to run the Krupp juggernaut (which meant the German defense industry) concerned the highest echelons of state. Kaiser Wilhelm II personally directed the quest.

He astonished everyone by selecting Gustave von Bohlen und Halbach, an obscure diplomatic hack who was an attaché in the Prussian embassy to the Vatican. The prospective bridgroom was sixteen years older than Bertha, several inches shorter and wore a corset to hide a pot belly. He was, from the kaiser's viewpoint, sufficiently mediocre to remain subservient even though he acquired the estate of one of the world's richest women.

The wedding ceremony was not so much a marriage as an industrial merger. The kaiser, who was present along with the top officials of the army, navy and the state, bestowed his blessing in the spirit of a chairman of the board addressing a stockholders' meeting. "My dear daughter, may you succeed in continuing the production and standards of quality your ancestors achieved, providing the German Fatherland with military weapons of an efficiency exceeding those of any other nation." The kaiser added that while a bride normally assumes her husband's name, in this case, by state decree and to "insure the continuity of the dynasty" the groom would take his wife's name.

In short, by the use of every conceivable stratagem, as well as a display of durability tougher than the steel it poured from its furnaces, the Krupp dynasty has persisted over four centuries, surviving wars, changes of government, economic upheavals only to rebound to new heights of influence.

But now it has suddenly bumped up against an obstacle even Krupp resourcefulness cannot handle in the person of Arndt, the current heir, who—*mirabile dictu!*—refuses to interest himself in the family business, who is unimpressed with the Krupps' formidable history (although he doesn't scorn the family money) and who, in his own sybaritic way, possesses a highly penetrating insight into the true worth of family dynasties under what Spinoza called *sub specie aeternitatis*. Echoing the ruminations of Shakespeare's Henry IV, "Uneasy lies the head that wears a crown," the current heir is well aware of the misery that the family in pursuing the Krupp mystique has inflicted not only on others but time and again on itself. Recently Arndt told newsmen, "I am not like my father, who sacrificed his whole life for something, not knowing whether it is really worth it. . . . My father has worked more than he has lived. I'm not like him, and I'm not about to be."

Which is about as devastating a commentary as an heir can pronounce on his patrimony.

In the meantime, the Krupp Works, Arndt's financial base of support, has been undergoing an impressive rehabilitation under outside professional management. After the firm was turned into a limited liability company in 1968, Gunter Vogelsang, a successful steel executive, was named managing director and launched a thoroughgoing streamlining of operations. He sold off several of the firm's unprofitable properties, including a hotel, a truck manufacturing division and the Krupp department store in downtown Essen. In the second year of Vogelsang's stewardship, Krupp turned the corner and showed a profit of 63,000,000 marks ($19,500,000). By 1971 the firm had paid off virtually all of its bank debt.

However, a power struggle broke out between Vogelsang and his predecessor, Berthold Beitz, who in 1968 when the family ownership was dissolved left the firm to take up guidance of the Krupp foundation. In 1970 Beitz returned as chairman of Krupp's supervisory board, which acts as a watchdog over the firm's operating executives. In this post, he frequently clashed with Vogelsang. The quarrel broke into the open when Vogelsang, at the beginning of 1972, announced he was retiring at the year's end, giving up an annual salary of 1,000,000 marks.

Insiders say the clash between the men is basically one of temperament. Beitz is flamboyant, intuitive; Vogelsang, an unspectacular but indefatigable hustler. According to some rumors, Beitz became jealous over his successor's achievement in turning around so quickly a company that, under his own management, had been pushed to the verge of bankruptcy. Others speculate that with the house of Krupp streamlined for action, Beitz feels his brand of salesmanship is needed to launch the firm on a new phase of international expansion and that Vogelsang is unsuited to this task. While Krupp is much healthier now, it is also much smaller. Once the giant of the German economy, it now ranks only tenth or so in size among West German corporations. Whether Beitz's ambition will drive Krupp once again into a fanfaronade via a *Drang nach Osten* policy and into a risky expansion of its commitments remains to be seen.

In any event, for the time being at least, the financial base and wellspring of Arndt von Bohlen und Holbach seems secure. The Krupp Works will continue to be run by professionals while Arndt continues his researches into the good life.

Indeed, Arndt Krupp is part and parcel of a society and an

era. He is living in a world where more and more of his contemporaries are striving for the fleshpots.

As a result, West Germany has been trapped in what to Germans is the most traumatic of predicaments—virulent inflation.
West German labor, which for over a decade has been in short
supply amidst a giant industrial boom that has forced the government to import foreign workers to help run the economy,
has lately been flexing its muscles and exerting to the utmost
the leverage empowered by its strategic position.

Beginning in 1969, German workers, spearheaded by the
younger ones insisting on a larger hunk of good living, plunged
the *Reich* into an orgy of strikes that paralyzed industry and
brought about wage increases averaging 14 percent. Prices
promptly began to zoom as industry passed on the increases to
consumers, and the nation, which since the war had been
enjoying a remarkably stable economy with the cost of living
rising only about 1½ percent a year, experienced a sudden rise
in the index to between 4 and 5 percent.

The impact was sobering. Germans, motivated by fears dis-
quietingly similar to those of the 1920's, although the current
situation was not nearly as serious, withdrew their savings en
masse and embarked on a mammoth buying binge in the belief
that goods and services would become even more expensive if
they waited.

Today, the Willy Brandt government, and particularly Karl
Schiller, the finance minister who is the leading exponent of
public spending "to elect and elect"—is confronted with a dangerous dilemma. The Bonn government has twice revalued the
mark; the nation has gone through a recession since Nixon
floated the dollar. Yet the pace of inflation continues unabated.
Like other Western politicos, postwar Bonn governments have
chosen to print money and risk the consequences of a deteriorating currency rather than face mass unemployment and a revolt of the voters.

Karl Schiller, the architect of the Social Democrats' Keynesian program who, because of the aggressive role he has played
managing the economy, has been dubbed Karl der Grosse after
that other dictator Charlemagne, has his work cut out for him.
The West German mark, once the strongest in Europe, has

been growing significantly weaker. While no one believes the Germans will be reduced again to buying goods with cigarettes or, going back to Weimar times, be forced to come up with a wheelbarrow of paper marks to buy a single smoke, Karl der Grosse and his countrymen should be the last to forget that the treacherousness of paper marks has done more to undermine the German capitalist society than the teachings of Karl Marx, with Rosa Luxemburg thrown in.

Be that as it may, Arndt Friedrich Alfried von Bohlen und Halbach and his less wealthy countrymen are grabbing for more and more of that seductive folding money before the coming of Walpurgisnacht.

13

The Comeback of the Rothschilds
in the Computer Age

In the 1920's, a gang of criminals taught the financial world a lesson it never forgot. It robbed the bank of the government of Portugal of $100,000,000, shaking up the tiny nation, setting off a revolt of the army, bringing about the ultimate installation of Dr. Antonio Salazar as dictator.

The scheme of the swindlers was ingenious. Unlike the usual counterfeiters who print fake money, this gang issued real money, managing to get hold of the plates and paper on which the Portuguese government engraved its official escudos. (The money was printed by a British firm under contract to Portugal.) The gang produced a flood of perfectly legal notes and thanks to its freewheeling spending caused a sharp improvement in the lagging Portuguese economy. The financial press exultantly reported that "there was suddenly lots of money around. Loans were easier to get. There were more jobs, more buildings going up."

The gang was caught finally and its ringleader, Alves Reis, was sent to jail. But a legal complication arose. The Bank of Portugal, which had unwittingly accepted millions of the gangster notes for deposit, sued the printing firm which had let itself be duped by the criminals. The printer, in defense, retorted that the bank had not suffered any loss since its official money was only paper currency not convertible into gold, and hence it had merely exchanged one series of paper notes for another. An ex-director of the bank conceded under questioning in court that the bank had gone off the gold standard in 1891 and that it had been functioning ever since as a moneymaking machine serving the needs of the state.

The case was appealed and landed in 1931 in the British House of Lords. (The printing firm, as noted, was English.) The British were in the throes of the Great Depression and had just gone off the gold standard. Citizens no longer could present pound notes at the Bank of England and expect to receive the equivalent in gold sovereigns.

During the trial the lawyer for Alves Reis, the ringleader, argued that his client had not been a counterfeiter but an "inflationist" who had in his own fashion been carrying out the policies of the government of Portugal; and the London *Economist* commented wryly that the criminals, whatever their motives, had indeed done the Portuguese economy a favor in the best tradition of John Maynard Keynes.

Others felt the same way. A Portuguese author wrote a bestselling novel about the bank swindle in which he imagined Alves Reis being elected Prime Minister by a grateful people. When Reis is called a crook in the Chamber of Deputies by his political opponents, he retorts: "I will answer . . . I will not lie . . . Alves Reis is the only one who brought this country to prosperity . . . what did you have before I came: a decadent hungry nation without industry or trade . . . and now I've given you homes, bread . . . they say my notes are false? What about the Government's? Could anyone in 1925 exchange 20 *escudos* in paper for 20 in gold? What I did was create credit. . . . I didn't steal from anyone. . . . All this money was created and spent without expense to the taxpayer." Whereupon, wrote the novelist, Alves Reis was lifted to the shoulders of the cheering deputies and triumphantly carried out of the chamber.*

For centuries a debate has raged as to whether inflation-minded governments that issue floods of paper money are benefactors of their nation; but rarely has the case been put in so striking a perspective as by the gang who went to jail for doing what virtually every government has been doing ever since the long nose of the modern politician smelled out his first vote.

---

* *The Man Who Stole Portugal,* by Murray T. Bloom, offers a graphic account of the Reis swindle.

This is a practice the Nixon government has been striving to restrain, for without some fixed, universal value of exchange which is independent of the political manipulations of government, how can one measure the worth of a pound of butter against a train ride to Bremen, as the German people learned to their anguish in the crash of the mark? The same need was responsible 170 years ago for the rise of the world's leading banking dynasty—the Rothschilds. They were fortunate that in a world buffeted by wars and money crises, they possessed the one unchanging article of value—gold—and this proved more powerful than armies and kings. As Jews, the Rothschilds were hounded and persecuted, but their strategic control of the world's most precious metal enabled them to rise above their adversity.

The foundation of the family's fortune was laid at the time of the Napoleonic Wars during which the British, seizing an opportunity to drive the French emperor from the Spanish peninsula, sent an army to Portugal under Wellington. A vexing problem was how to get gold to the duke to pay off his troops. Lisbon was almost 1,000 miles from the nearest English port, and the sea was infested with enemy privateers. In his impatience for funds, Wellington dunned the government, threatening to quit. Finally he resorted to issuing his own paper money as if he were a sovereign government. A million pounds was handed out. The problem with this scrip was that it ultimately had to be backed by gold. Governments as a rule didn't yet dare to create money out of nothing and force their citizens to accept it.* Wellington's soldiers could use his paper money to buy supplies locally, but the merchant who accepted it had to transmit it to bankers who discounted it and sent it on and on to an ultimate purchaser, who had to turn it into gold for his eventual remuneration. Trading was a tedious process.

Thanks to the war, which had paralyzed the European economy, gold was almost as scarce as water in the desert. Its export was forbidden by governments; and smugglers combed the world for it.

One of the most assiduous hunters was Nathan Rothschild,

---

* Exceptions were the governments of Louis XV and the French Revolutionary Tribunal. It is no coincidence that the French today are obsessive gold hoarders.

who came from a family of moneylenders in the Frankfurt ghetto. His father, Meyer, had sent him to London to keep his eyes open for gold. In the course of browsing around old metal dealers, curio shops and junkyards, Nathan developed valuable contacts and he got wind of important news. The East India Company, he learned, was bringing in a large shipment of gold bars which was to be sold at auction. Nathan showed up punctually and knocked down the entire shipload with his bid. The British government learned of the transaction and sent an emissary to Nathan offering to buy the gold from him. Moreover, it invited Nathan to supervise the complex undertaking of sending it to the irascible Wellington in Portugal.

It was a staggering problem. Nathan and his seven brothers, knowing no language but the Yiddish of the ghetto, organized themselves into an underground network spanning the continent. They passed through hostile armies, using false names, fake passports and clever disguises. The two youngest brothers acted as anchor men, one in the Pyrenees, the other on the Channel coast. A third brother stationed himself in Paris.

The penalties for smuggling were severe. Capture by the French police meant the guillotine. The brothers overlooked nothing, greasing the palms of officials all the way from the mountains to the English Channel. The prefect of police on the Channel coast was lavishly bribed and blossomed forth into such a luxurious style of living that he aroused the suspicions of his boss in Paris. Fortunately the secret was kept. Under Nathan's supervision from London, hundreds of thousands of pounds in gold, English guineas, Dutch gulden, French Napoleon-d'or were spirited southward to feed Wellington's army. Upon retreating from his march into Russia, Napoleon was astonished to find that Wellington had wriggled out of the trap set for him in the peninsula and was moving into France with well-fed, high-spirited troops. In saving Wellington, the Rothschild brothers had unwittingly organized the world's first international bank clearing system.

After the Battle of Waterloo, the Rothschild fortunes skyrocketed. The family spanned Europe with railroads, financed Britain's purchase of the Suez Canal, paid the tab for oil explorations in Russia and the Sahara Desert, financed the czars, backed Cecil Rhodes' diamond enterprises. Rothschild loans helped France carve out an empire in Africa, financed the Hapsburg monarchs, rescued the King of Naples and the Papal States from bankruptcy.

For generations, the Rothschilds continued to retain their Yiddish accents and alien manners, but their wealth brought them acceptance in the highest echelons of society. Byron and Thackeray celebrated them in verse and prose. Ingres painted portraits of Rothschild wives and daughters. Rossini composed tunes for their soirees. Balzac and Browning were frequent guests at their dinner table.

The outbreak of World War I brought a sharp setback to the family's fortunes. And World War II intensified the decline. Hitler destroyed the German house. The French Rothschilds were hard hit when the Nazis occupied Paris. They were forced to sell their securities in a falling market, and the Germans confiscated the family's extensive art collection.

The British branch has also felt the impact of war and social change. Hit by onerous taxes as an aftermath of World War I, it was forced to give up country estates, which were turned into public parks. In the 1930's Baron Lionel's town house, where his ancestor met with Disraeli to arrange the financing of the Suez Canal, was shut down. To raise funds, the second Lord Rothschild was compelled to sell his valuable collection of birds to the New York Museum of Natural History. Another Rothschild property, the estate in Kensington, is now owned by the Soviet embassy.

Even more doleful were the experiences of the Austrian house. When the Nazis took Vienna, storm troopers swooped down on the princely estate of Baron Louis de Rothschild, who leisurely finished his dinner, took a last puff at his cigarette and went off to jail.

The Nazis offered to free the baron but at a stiff price. They demanded all the assets of the Austrian house. Goering asked personally for $200,000 in cash. One coveted prize was Vitkovitz, the largest iron and steel works in Central Europe which, although located in Czechoslovakia, was owned by Baron Louis. The French Rothschilds, who negotiated with the Nazis for their cousin's release, held a trump card. Vitkovitz, unbeknownst to the Nazis, had secretly become British property. When the Naxi take-over of Austria seemed imminent, Baron

Louis, in a series of intricate maneuvers, had reorganized Vitkovitz as a subsidiary of Alliance Insurance Company, a British firm, so that the $20,000,000 property was placed technically under the protection of the British flag, although Baron Louis retained ownership of it. At the time the Nazis were not yet at war with Britain and they did not dare to confiscate the steelworks.

In the bargaining to obtain Baron Louis' release, Vitkovitz became the chief bait. The Rothschilds agreed to surrender control, but only after Baron Louis had crossed safely into Switzerland. The Germans accepted. They were prepared to buy Vitkovitz for 3,000,000 pounds sterling. But before the contract could be signed, war broke out with Britain and trade was halted. Vitkovitz remained in Rothschild hands under British protection. Hitler had been outwitted. Baron Louis, who had slipped from the reach of the German armies, came to the United States and lived the rest of his life quietly on a Vermont farm.

Today, despite two world wars, the confiscation of family holdings and heavy inheritance taxes, the fortunes of the Rothschilds are on the rebound. Under the direction of Baron Guy de Rothschild, the French branch of the tribe has been overhauling its operations to survive in today's world of the Common Market, conglomerates and multinational corporations. Baron Guy is seeking to change the Rothschild image. Historically, the family has served elitist clients—kings, statesmen and wealthy industrialists. Today, in an age of rising wages and mass prosperity, the Rothschilds are wooing the man in the street. Symbolizing the change is Rothschild's rehabilitation of the family's austere old sandstone bank at 21 Rue la Fitte, which never bothered to publicize itself with so much as a nameplate on the door. Baron Guy has razed the building and put up in its place a spanking new edifice of glass and concrete. The bank's name has been changed from Monsieurs des Rothschilds Frères to simply Banque Rothschild S.A. Computers have replaced the scratchy quill pens which the family, defying the advent of modern technology, had used until quite recently.

In December, 1967, the Rothschilds opened a bank for small depositors, and a network of branches is planned throughout France. Amounts as little as $200 are accepted.

Another step in the rejuvenation of its fortunes has been the banding together of the two main family branches, the French and British Rothschilds (historically aloof from one another) in a series of joint ventures. Alert in an age of spreading inflation to the opportunities for a play in assets rather than depending on earnings in francs and pounds, the Rothschilds have been moving aggressively into a number of natural resources operations.

In addition, the French Rothschilds have financed the biggest privately owned uranium firm in France. In May, 1968, the French branch organized a syndicate to make one of the first direct loans by Western capitalists to a Communist-bloc nation, advancing $50,000,000 to Hungary.

The British Rothschilds, for their part, have launched a consortium to move into Newfoundland and exploit the minerals, timber and hydropower of a 50,000-square-mile area; and together with their French cousins, they are engaged in a billion-dollar project to dam up Hamilton Falls and build the world's largest hydroelectric plant. Moreover, the British Rothschilds are making a substantial investment in Asia in partnership with Nomura Securities Company of Japan and Merrill, Lynch, the U.S. broker. The syndicate plans to invest in growth industries in Japan and Australia, whose economic potential the Rothschilds feel is substantial.

One area into which the Rothschilds are moving with bold plans is the development of strategic metals. To this end, Guy de Rothschild has joined with the Kaiser Aluminum Company to form Société le Nickel, a production and marketing organization designed to challenge the giant International Nickel Company of Canada, Ltd. (Inco), which had been exercising a virtual monopoly over this critical material in steel making. The Rothschild-Kaiser combine operates a subsidiary which mines nickel in New Caledonia, an island east of Australia, and another subsidiary located in North America to market its products halfway around the world. Société le Nickel has become the second-largest producer, providing a rising threat to Inco.

In teaming up with Kaiser Aluminum, the offspring of the shrewd old industrialist Henry Kaiser, Baron Guy de Rothschild has thrown in his lot with one of the world's leading complexes husbanding natural resource deposits as prime assets. The Kaiser companies are past masters at ferreting out valuable deposits of minerals from the bowels of the earth and overcoming the obstacles of jungle, mountain and bad weather to market them anywhere in the world.

Rothschild's new partner was responsible for one of the most daring mineral explorations in history. In 1952 a cattleman, Lang Hancock, while flying a plane over Australia's Hamersley mountain range, was forced by a low cloud formation to steer through a gorge. He noticed, glancing at the cliffs around him, extensive rust-colored outcroppings. Realizing he may have stumbled on an important iron ore discovery, Hancock contacted Rio Tinto, a worldwide mining concern, which proposed to Kaiser to join forces in investigating the region. Kaiser assigned Tom Price, its raw materials expert, to the project. Price reported that the Hamersley Range looked as if it might contain one of the largest iron deposits in the free world, totaling close to 5 billion tons of prime-quality ore, so rich it could be shoveled out of the ground and heaved, without any further processing, into a blast furnace.

As a result, Kaiser entered into a partnership with Rio Tinto —Kaiser acquiring a 40-percent interest and the remainder assumed by Rio, which subsequently joined with Consolidated Zinc to form the Australian corporation of Conzinc Rio Tinto.

In December, 1964, after two years of negotiations, the Kaiser-Rio Tinto combine signed the largest iron ore contract ever written, to supply seven of Japan's major steel firms with 65,500,000 tons for a period of sixteen years. The first shipment was guaranteed to be delivered within nineteen months. And to meet the terms, the Kaiser combine had to turn the semiwilderness of northern Australia into a thriving mining complex virtually overnight.

This took some doing. For the Hamersley Range is in a remote part of Australia, geologically as primitive as it had been in pre-Cambrian times. Despite the obstacles, the Kaiser complex dredged and constructed in record time Dampier, a deepwater port 180 miles away on King Bay. Dampier was chosen as the port of export since it offered excellent protection from the violent storms and heavy tides that frequently hit the coast. A railroad was built from the mine site to Dampier, over rough mountain terrain, heavy enough to withstand the hauling of

crushed ore loaded in 100-ton cars pulled by 2,750-horsepower
diesel locomotives.

In August, 1966, eighteen months after the signing of the
contract, the first shipment of ore was delivered to Japan. By
the end of 1967, close to 6,000,000 tons of iron ore had been
shipped. Supplied with a massive new source of iron ore, the
Japanese steel industry, previously starved for raw materials,
plunged into a major expansion that has been a key factor in
boosting the Nipponese into an industrial superpower.

Such is the character of the trouble-shooting combine that
has joined Baron Guy de Rothschild's organization to process
and market strategically located nickel. In a world riven by
shaky currencies and turbulent social change, Rothschild and
Kaiser are convinced that the unfluctuating assets wrung from
rock, forest and soil will become increasingly valuable commodities of exchange.

Like the Kaisers, Baron Guy is exploring new opportunities
to serve the needs of today's fast-exploding technology. He has
entered the management consultant field by joining forces with
an aggressive young firm started by John Diebold, a *Wunderkind* of the American business scene who in the 1950's, while
still in his twenties, wrote the first definitive book on automation and what it portended for society. (It was Diebold who
coined the word "automation" in its modern sense.)

Diebold previously had been an adviser on computer
technology to the Olivettis of Italy and to the Swedish tycoon
Axel Leonard Wenner-Gren, who began as a factory worker
and wound up with one of the word's biggest fortunes. When
Diebold met him in the early 1950's, Wenner-Gren had taken a
fancy to the fast-growing phenomenon of computers and
wanted advice on how to profit from them. The industrialist
owned a computer manufacturing plant in California that was
losing money. Diebold stepped in and cut down the losses. His
reputation reached Rothschild, who made a bid for his services.

Diebold conveys what it meant to him to link up with the
Rothschilds by telling about a French economics professor who
used to demonstrate in his classes the meaning of credit with
the following anecdote. A man applied to a Rothschild for a
large loan. He was turned down, but Rothschild offered to walk
with him arm-in-arm across the crowded floor of the Paris

bourse. "That, gentlemen," exclaimed the professor, "is *credit!*"

Baron Guy, scion of history's proudest banking dynasty, offered the young American a partnership because the Rothschilds are fascinated with the potential of computers. Diebold has written, "[Man] himself has created machines which increasingly are able to . . . outthink . . . him. Already in existence are heuristic [goal-oriented] computers which solve problems without being told how—by trial and error processes which no longer can be differentiated meaningfully from what we know as human learning."

In an age of developing symbiosis—*i.e.,* the marriage of man with the machine—the Rothschilds, who once sent messages by carrier pigeons and maintained until not so very long ago in their London bank footmen dressed in the garb of the eighteenth century, are acutely aware of the seminal importance of the black box and are determined to stay abreast of its technology.

In peacetime—let alone wartime—the Rothschilds are exposed to hazards that stem from their wealth and notoriety. Since people are continually trying to grab a hunk of their money, Rothschilds have been the targets of robberies, extortions, gun downs. In the fall of 1969, a foreign legionnaire tried to extort 2,000,000 francs ($360,000) from Baron Guy. The gunman entered the apartment of Baron David, Guy's twenty-seven-year-old son, near the Bois de Boulogne, introducing himself as an official from the Interior Ministry and handing the young man some papers. As David began reading, the intruder pulled a revolver, demanding 2,000,000 francs. David telephoned his father, who realized from his voice something was wrong. He phoned the police and rushed with them to his son's apartment. In the meantime, Baron David sat with a pistol in his gut while the gunman launched into a harangue on social injustice. The police waited outside as Baron Guy and his chauffeur entered the apartment with a valise stuffed with cash. The gunman took the money, ordered Baron Guy and his chauffeur at gunpoint to enter his auto and drove off. The police rescued them after a chase that would have done justice to a Hitchcock movie.

So far as genealogy is concerned, the Rothschilds have been

notorious for their insistence on family inbreeding. In the nineteenth century, fifty-nine marriages took place in the family, half of which were between Rothschild cousins and all within the faith.

The tribe's stubborn adherence to the Jewish faith is attested to by a celebrated painting in the study of Jacob's house in London showing Lionel, Nathan's son, entering the House of Commons in the nineteenth century to take the oath of office as a Member of Parliament. On three occasions Nathan had been elected to the seat; each time he refused to remove his hat for the swearing-in ceremony, which was conducted according to Gentile tradition. He insisted on taking the oath with his hat on his head, according to Jewish custom. Three times the house refused to seat him. But Lionel won his fight against prejudice. When he was elected overwhelmingly a fourth time, Parliament yielded and allowed him to be sworn in as a Jew.

In recent years, the Rothschilds have relaxed their clannishness. Gentiles have been taken into the business in top positions and even into the family by marriage. Baron Guy, for instance, has displayed a typically Gallic lack of inhibition by divorcing his first wife and marrying a Catholic. He had to give up his role as the leader of the Jewish community in France, one of his cousins taking over.

In addition to the insistence through the generations on inbreeding, other eccentric qualities have been passed down over the years. One of the most eccentric—and redoubtable—of the clan was unquestionably Nathan, the founder of the British branch who shipped gold to Wellington. Suspicious to the point of paranoia, Nathan in his final years displayed a terror of assassination and kept a loaded pistol under his pillow. Once two strangers paid a visit. As they reached into their pockets to extract something, Nathan seized a book and hurled it at them, following with a heavy vase and an inkstand. Only when his servants pinned them to the floor did Nathan learn they were bankers who had come to pay their respects to him but were so awed at finding themselves face-to-face with "the great Rothschild" they were unable to speak and were reaching into their pockets for their cards when the banker unleashed his barrage.

Nathan was a very rough man to tangle with. Once the Bank of England, which he had helped save from bankruptcy in the panic of 1825, drew his wrath. He had sent a draft on his personal stationery to be cashed for a sizable amount of money. But the Old Lady of Threadneedle Street demurred, saying it cashed only its own bills, not those of private individuals.

Rothschild ordered his agents to purchase as many Bank of England currency notes as they could lay their hands on. Then one morning, when the bank opened for business, Rothschild strode up to the teller with a heavy stachel. He took out a 5-pound note and asked the clerk to hand him its equivalent in gold sovereigns. He examined each piece carefully before putting it away. Then he drew out a second 5-pound note and went through the same procedure. At this point, nine of Rothschild's clerks appeared with bags and carefully began changing notes for gold. The operation went on all day until closing time, at which point the Bank of England's gold reserves had been reduced by 200,000 pounds.

The next morning, when Rothschild and his clerks showed up with their satchels to repeat the operation, the manager asked why he was harassing the bank. "You told me you were not prepared to change my bills," replied Rothschild. "If you have no confidence in mine, I am free to express a doubt about yours. I shall demand gold for every one of your notes and I'll keep your tellers changing them for the next two months." A meeting of the bank's directors was hastily called and a formal apology was sent to Rothschild, assuring him that the Bank of England would henceforth be happy to cash his bills anytime.

There has been a feeling among geneticists that family inbreeding leads to genetical deterioration. The case of royal families is cited. But the Rothschilds' practice has had highly gratifying results. Far from being narrowly constricted in their abilities, the current generation of Rothschilds is displaying a remarkable variety and breadth of talents. A number of modern Rothschilds are achieving distinction outside the banking field. Baron Philippe, a cousin of Baron Guy's, is a man of impressive literary parts. He is the official translator into French of the playwright Christopher Fry's *The Lady's Not for Burning*. With his wife, Pauline, he has translated the Elizabethan poets into French. Philippine, the couple's daughter, has won kudos as an actress, and a niece, Nicole, is a successful film producer.

Lord Victor Rothschild, head of the London family, has achieved a reputation as a biologist and has taught at Cambridge. (He has lectured over the BBC, shocking the prudes with his graphic discussions of sex.) Lord Victor's daughter was the youngest girl ever to enter Cambridge (at fifteen). A cousin, Edmond, is an authority on gardening. Leopold de Rothschild is an accomplished concert pianist.

Baron Philippe, Christophe Fry's translator, has another fascinating hobby. He owns the vineyards of Mouton, which turn out wines for top connoisseurs. He lives at Mouton with his American-born wife, the Baroness Pauline, who was a hat designer for Hattie Carnegie before she met and married the baron after the death of his first wife.

On the grounds of the chateau where the wine is tended, the Rothschilds maintain a richly stocked museum. Several years ago, the baron told a journalist how he came to build it:

> Mouton has been in my family possession for more than one hundred and eleven years, but none of my ancestors lived here. My grandfather, Baron James, never touched red wine. My father visited Mouton only twice in his lifetime. But unlike my family—unlike most Frenchmen—I happen to love living in the country. . . . It happens that I inherited a number of works of art capable of forming the nucleus of a collection. The earlier Rothschilds made loans . . . to many German princes who, when they couldn't repay their debts with money, repaid them with precious family possessions . . . notably, with beautiful objects in vermeil for which the courts of Germany were renowned. My family's taste has been for such things ever since. . . . It is only now, it seems to me, in the setting that we have been able to give them at Mouton, that they have reacquired their true personalities and feel themselves at home.

In addition to *objets d'art,* the Rothschilds have accumulated a celebrated collection of wines for the museum. "Working on the collection," recalls the Baroness Pauline, "we discovered that people have been drinking wine since the beginning of recorded time. No important talk with the gods, no victory, no treaty, no civilized business luncheon has ever been complete without a libation. We have been struck by the recurrence of the phrase 'they drank together!' "

In collecting specimens of rare vintages, the baroness and her husband delved avidly into the historical conditions that led men first to quaff out of stone jars, then metal, porcelain and glass goblets. The couple discovered all kinds of fascinating details—for instance, that the Greeks sipped their wine with three parts water in a bowl similar to one in the Mouton collection; that the emperor Nero shelled out the equivalent of 17,000,000 French francs for a cup made of murra (a material that has long since disappeared) because of the incomparable flavor it imparted to the wine. They came across in the works of Horace, the Latin poet, an observation that the Sabine wine of his time was thought to have an improved taste if drunk from a Greek amphora—exactly like the specimen the Rothschilds had discovered for their collection. In the course of writing catalog notes on a Sassanian bowl, one of the glories of the display, the couple took a trip to Iran to study the drinking habits of the early Iranian tribes.

The former designer for Hattie Carnegie and her husband can indulge to the utmost in whatever hobbies they desire. While nobody outside the family knows the precise worth of the Rothschild fortune—estimates run to well over a billion—it is substantial. The family has come a long way since Meyer Amschel Rothschild first peddled coins in the Frankfurt ghetto. There is an anecdote telling how Meyer first came to the attention of Prince William, the powerful ruler of Hesse, and was appointed his financial counselor, thus taking his first big step toward wealth. Meyer was summoned one day to the palace by a business associate of the prince's and admitted into a chamber where William was absorbed in a game of chess. The little moneylender stood timidly behind him watching the game. Prince William turned around, saw Meyer and asked, "Do you play chess?" "Yes," replied Rothschild, "and if Your Highness will make the move I suggest, you will win the game in the next three plays." The suggestion was a masterstroke. The prince won and the Rothschilds have been making the right moves ever since.

14

King of Diamonds: Harry Oppenheimer
of South Africa

One day in 1867 a South African farmer paying a visit to a friend noticed that the son of the household was playing marbles with a stone that had an unusual sparkle. When the farmer expressed admiration, his host handed it to him as a gift. He hadn't the slightest notion what he was giving away. The farmer showed the stone to a minerals expert in Capetown who pronounced it a diamond. The farmer sold it for 500 pounds.

Two years later an African witch doctor visited the farmer and showed him another stone with the same kind of sparkle. Fully on the alert, the farmer offered the witch doctor everything he owned—his house, a dozen oxen, several hundred sheep—for the stone. He sold it to a dealer for 11,000 pounds. It was resold to a British nobleman, who named it the Star of Africa. It was a brilliant of the finest purity, weighing 83 carats. These diamonds, discovered by a child at play and a native witch doctor, were destined to revolutionize the history of South Africa.

Word of the discoveries spread rapidly over the veld and people streamed in from every ship and train to dig along a seventy-five-mile stretch of river in the Orange Free State for the glittering stones that could make them wealthy beyond dreams.

Today South Africa is the world's number-one producer of diamonds, and most of this sprawling industry which for generations was split by factional struggles has been gathered into the hands of a single family that runs it monolithically and with the utmost profitability.

This is the Oppenheimer family, which, in addition to controlling the output of diamonds, operates a processing combine that turns out one-sixth of the world's supply of gold and also has extensive interests in uranium, timberland, breweries, plastics, fertilizers and real estate. The Oppenheimer complex, the Anglo-American Group, exerts the greatest single influence on the mining economy of South Africa; its assets total over $3 billion. Its diamond-processing arm, De Beers Consolidated Mines, Ltd., which, together with affiliated South African producers, controls over 80 percent of the world output, merchandises its gems through a so-called Central Selling Organization in an ingenious and arbitrary manner. It has a small, select list of dealers to whom it chooses to sell and invites the lucky ones once a month to a sales meeting held in London. (Everybody else must get his diamonds as they trickle down through the outlets of cutters and wholesalers at a much higher price.) The organization does not sell its clients individual stones; it puts a random assortment of sizes, shapes and value into a canvas bag and hands it to the would-be purchaser, who must accept or reject the lot. The Oppenheimer interests defend the procedure as a safeguard to keep a buyer from gaining a monopoly of stones of a single size and manipulating the market for these. After the meeting is concluded, the dealers transmit their selections through the regular trade channels.

The world's number-one center for diamond cutting is Antwerp, Belgium. Next largest is Tel Aviv. Many cutters and dealers are Jews who, fleeing Hitler, have learned the value of turning their life's savings into easily carried, readily concealed precious jewels. They are a picturesque lot. Hassidic Jews with patriarchal beards, some of whom were Talmudic scholars, now go about carrying millions of dollars in gems in their pockets. The dealers are a close-knit fraternity; a number are related by intermarriage. In Manhattan's Diamond Club, the headquarters of U.S. dealing, millions of dollars in jewelry are traded daily on a personal word and a handshake. When a deal is struck it is closed (by non-Jews as well as Jews) with a traditional gesture. The seller wishes the purchaser "*mazel* and *broche*," which is Hebrew for "good luck and the blessings of

God." Once these words are uttered, they have the effect of an ironclad contract.

Diamonds don't have as long a history as might be imagined. They first became popular in the seventeenth century when an Italian stonecutter peddled for a high prices a gem which had been so formed by nature that the light entering it was reflected back directly through the same facets, providing a remarkably dazzling fire. The first big market for the brilliants was in France under the Bourbon kings, where the first popular stone is reported to have been cut at the direction of Cardinal Mazarin. "Popular" is a loosely used term. Only the very rich could afford diamonds, and the mistresses of Louis XV, notably Madame du Barry, were the chief customers keeping the diamond-cutting industry in Paris prosperous almost single-handedly with their patronage.

Since the Bourbons, diamonds have been a favorite medium of investment as well as show. In our own times, especially since the mid-sixties, when inflation picked up speed, diamonds have come increasingly into favor, and the value of the best-quality gems has risen substantially more than the Dow Jones Industrial Averages. In the opinion of many people, particularly Europeans, whose antecedents have been pauperized by the overturn of governments, diamonds are much safer than money in the bank and will have value when ermine coats wear out and Mercedes cars become junk. They are a tempting medium for illegal operations. A daring citizen in a country where controls have been clamped down on currency exports—as in Great Britain after World War II—can convert $1,000,000 worth of cash into gems that can fit into a pack of cigarettes and move undetected across the border.

In point of fact, there are heavy risks as well as benefits to diamond investments. The gems have been known to fluctuate notoriously in price. Dealers who buy at wholesale and have the patience to wait have the best chance for capital appreciation. But even the professionals can be stung. To cite a recent example: Mrs. Harriet Annenberg Ames, the sister of the U.S. ambassador to Britain, Walter Annenberg, recently sold a diamond because the insurance on it was too expensive. (It was insured for $30,000 annually, and since she wore it only twenty times or so in a year, it cost her $1,500 for each display.) The diamond had previously been peddled to Mrs. Ames by Winston, the jeweler. Now, only a year later, Mrs. Ames unloaded it on Cartier for twice what she paid Winston. Cartier then managed to sell it to Richard Burton for his wife, Elizabeth Taylor, a one-woman mass consumption market for the jewelry industry. What Burton paid for the stone has not been disclosed, but it wasn't, as the Welsh say, for a mere run of one's teeth.

In recent years there has been a significant change in the world's supply-and-demand equation for diamonds. Historically, the only nations, apart from South Africa and the Congo (now called the Republic of Zaïre), producing them in any appreciable amount were Brazil and India. But some years ago the Soviet Union discovered a diamond field in Siberia of all places. Ironically the Soviets, for a time, joined up with Harry Oppenheimer to sell its diamonds through his monopolistic capitalist organization and take a healthy cut of the profits. But after a squabble over the division of the spoils, the Soviets withdrew.

When Mao Tse-tung seized power in China, the government confiscated from the wealthy Chinese all the diamonds it could lay its hands on, to obtain urgently needed foreign currency, the Reds sold their booty through Hong Kong merchants who were secretly invited to come to Canton and who, upon buying the gems, resold them through regular diamond channels.

Recent reports hint that for the last ten years the Chinese Reds have been mining diamonds in commercial quantities from a deposit in the basin of the Yuan Kiang River in western Hunan. Whatever the final outlet of the baubles, it is a safe bet none of them have found their way into the hands of the unisexed-garbed mass of Chinese womenfolk.

For years synthetic gems have been competing with natural ones in industrial markets. Indeed, some time ago scientists at Union Carbide came up with a flame-fusion method for creating artificial diamonds by passing a fine aluminum oxide powder through an oxygen-hydrogen flame that congealed it into rounded, hard crystals, replacing natural hard gems, at much lower cost, in bearings and other industrial products. General Electric scientists have also succeeded in turning out synthetic diamonds of gem quality of up to one carat in weight. But so far no one has found a way to make artificial larger-sized diamonds that equal the natural ones ablaze in milady's tiara or ring.

What's more, the natural diamond promises to broaden its stake in the industrial market. Recently an extraordinary gem was dug up in the Premier Mine of South Africa which, because it has a unique transparency that covers an important area of the infrared spectrum and possesses a quality of unusual conductivity, promises to serve as a key component in a wide range of electronic uses. Acting as the "heat sink" in miniature microwave generators, the diamond is being experimented with as a key component of Bell's new picture-telephone system which was inaugurated in Pittsburgh and which in the coming years could be a fixture in homes and offices around the world. Moreover, the stone is making possible microwave burglar alarm systems of remarkable sensitivity, as well as computerized radar to help the docking of the world's biggest steamships and oil tankers without injury. And the diamond is being studied for use in the detection of military aircraft, armored vehicles and for use in weather satellites. Officials of the Premier Mine claim that they can produce enough of the gems to supply the probable needs of the electronics industry for the immediate future.

The market for natural diamonds, in short, is steadily growing, and the Oppenheimer family remains unchallenged in its monopoly of their production. The founder of the fortune, Sir Ernest, was the son of a German-Jewish cigar maker, born in 1880 near Frankfurt-am-Main. In his teens he became an apprentice to a jeweler, was taught to grade and sort crude diamonds and became a skillful judge of their value.

In 1902, when he was twenty-two, he was sent to South Africa as a buyer for his firm. Before he was thirty he struck out on his own. The times were propitious. South Africa was loaded with vast mineral resources. Most seekers of diamonds and gold in the veld were one-shot prospectors bent on a lucky strike. Oppenheimer, on the other hand, had the shrewdness of the empire builder who harnessed the labor of others to put together properties. With the backing of influential partners, he took over De Beers, the firm Cecil Rhodes, South Africa's leading statesman and explorer, had founded to produce diamonds. Oppenheimer invested in the Rand Gold Fields and bought out numerous smaller competitors. With ruthless efficiency he obliterated independent producers, not only in South and West Africa, but as far away as the Belgian Congo and Portuguese Angola.

Oppenheimer's philosophy was forthright. He was out to create a worldwide monopoly that would police and control the output of diamonds to keep their prices high. "No one would want a diamond if it could be bought in a five and dime store," he pointed out. Before Oppenheimer achieved his dictatorship, diamond prices had been very sensitive to changing markets. By the time of his death and the transmission of the business to his son, Harry, in 1967 the Oppenheimer control was complete. Its effectiveness may be judged by the fact that a decade ago a share of De Beer's common sold at $15 on the London and Johannesburg stock exchanges. By early 1969 it had soared tenfold.

Recently Sir Ernest's son, Harry, who is the current head of the empire and who is fully aware of the investment role diamonds are playing for those fortunate enough to possess them in a world buffeted by inflation, justified the tight grip De Beers exerts on the market in this fashion. Control is necessary, he argues, "not because production is excessive or demand is falling, but simply because wide fluctuations in prices which have, rightly or wrongly, been accepted as normal in the case of most raw materials would be destructive of public confidence in the case of a pure luxury such as gem diamonds of which large stocks are held in the form of jewelry by the general public." Why? Because, in Oppenheimer's view, people buy jewelry not only for show but as a long-term hedge against the uncertainties of political and economic changes in society.

Early in 1972 the West Coast Commodity Exchange, always on the hunt for a promotional gimmick, announced with a great deal of fanfare that it was launching the world's first experiment in trading diamond futures. But the plan in the opinion of industry experts is highly impractical. Diamonds are totally unlike other commodities, for their price is arrived at through a subtle psychological process similar to the way prices of rare paintings are arrived at. So far there has been little enthusiasm for trading futures in the brilliants.

To return to the Oppenheimer family, Sir Ernest, the

founder of the empire, was, oddly, despite his reputation for aggressiveness, personally a shy man. Standing only five feet and a half inch, he was quite un-Napoleonic in his demeanor. Not until he reached seventy was he reluctantly prevailed upon to hold a press interview. He deftly handled all the questions a roomful of reporters shot at him. But when the newsmen left, he fainted. His assistants rushed over and quickly revived him. That evening his wife told a visitor that the excitement and bad air—the room had been full of cigarette smoke—had gotten to Sir Ernest. "After all, he's an old man."

Sir Ernest's son, Harry, who took over the helm in 1957 at his father's death, is a much more outgoing individual. Currently in his mid-sixties, he is, as one reporter observes, "a gentle-looking and disarming man. With his dapper mustache and twinkling eyes, he could be a debonair French boulevardier." He is also under average height, like his father. Unlike Sir Ernest, however, who had only a grade school education and went to work in his teens, Harry was sent to an exclusive school in England and went on to Oxford, receiving honors in politics, economics and philosophy.

Harry was elaborately deferential to his father. During the final years of Sir Ernest's life, the son moved into a sumptuous residence in Capetown with a lavishly designed courtyard and pathways made of the dust of gold drillings that glittered so spectacularly in the sunlight they seemed, as one visitor put it, "paved with gold." Harry called his estate Little Brenthurst, not because he was in any way modest, but because his father had named his own mansion Brenthurst, and Harry never forgot he was the junior Oppenheimer.

The transference of power was under macabre circumstances. One morning in December, 1957, Harry was having breakfast with his father; they were exchanging small talk when the older man suddenly slumped over with a heart attack. He was seventy-seven. Harry took over the one-hundred or so companies his father had put together and since has added fifty more.

Emerging from the shadow of the senior Oppenheimer, Harry is exhibiting a tough, independent mind. His business approach is scarcely a carbon copy of Sir Ernest's. He doesn't have the latter's zest for gold exploration and is content to rely on the output of the company's older mines. But when the subject of uranium is mentioned, a gleam comes in his eye. "There is a speculative element in uranium which we accept."

Like his father, who was mayor of Kimberley and sat in the South African Parliament, Harry has also tried his hand at politics. He has served for nine years in the House of Assembly as a member of the United Party in opposition to the government and acting as its chief specialist in financial affairs. Harry finds himself in a peculiar position. He is a liberal in his social outlook by South African standards, objecting vigorously to apartheid and the exploitation of native blacks. Not only is it morally intolerable but bad business, he is convinced, for South Africa to be ostracized by the rest of the world. A highly educated, well-traveled man who spends almost as much time in London as in South Africa, Oppenheimer has been a growing source of embarrassment to his government; and in return he has been regarded with increasing suspicion by it. But the Establishment politicians haven't dared go beyond veiled threats, so essential are Oppenheimer's industrial interests to the health of the economy.

In taking over from his father, Harry Oppenheimer displayed the latter's zest for vigorous living, and then some. In the 1950's, when he was especially active in politics as a member of the House, he commuted constantly between his business headquarters in Johannesburg and Capetown, the site of Parliament, 800 miles to the south. He would spend half the week in Capetown, plane to Johannesburg for the weekend to take care of financial matters, and often stop over on his way back to Capetown to talk to members of his constituency at Kimberley and frequently make an additional trip to his stud farm at Mauritzfontein to see how his thoroughbreds were doing.

In Johannesburg Harry built a residence which was a showpiece of the city. It boasted an unusually splendid collection of old Chinese porcelain and rare nineteenth-century engravings graced with the seal of the Dutch East India Company, which discovered Capetown. Harry modestly disclaims any expertise in art. "I don't really collect from an historical point of view. I don't really collect at all in the true sense of the word—I just buy something now and then if it has beauty."

Since he spent half of his time in Capetown during the legislative season, Oppenheimer bought and remodeled a gracious old house in the Malay section of town. His friends raised their eyebrows at the choice of a site that was located in a run-down native section. But the Oppenheimer residence is a picturesque one, built of pink stucco, fronting on a hilly street; in the rear it opens into a stately courtyard rimmed with yew trees; in the center there is a baroquely sculptured swimming pool. The grounds are enclosed by a wall over which the dome of a native mosque just peeps.

As a member of the United Party, Oppenheimer developed a reputation as a speaker for his lucid, witty attacks on the ruling Nationalist Party. Annually when the government's Minister of Finance delivered his presentation of the budget, Oppenheimer while he served in the House was chosen to give the rebuttal address, pointing out the inconsistencies of the government's program.

Ironically, this heir to one of the world's great fortunes won distinction attacking the Establishment, not presiding as a pillar of it. While the House proceedings were bilingual—the Nationalists spoke in Afrikaans and the United Party replied in English—Oppenheimer was one of the few members of his party who had undertaken the task of learning Afrikaans when he entered politics; he spoke the language fluently, which was a source of envy to his colleagues who had to wait for the translation before they knew what was going on.

The occasion of an Oppenheimer attack on the government budget caused a social, as well as political, stir, and he packed the galleries. Harry's wife would invite a circle of friends down to Capetown to accompany her to the House when Oppenheimer was slated to speak. The night before the session, the party would gather in the cool, spacious courtyard for drinks and a discussion of politics as the muezzin of the Moslem mosque chanted prayers to Allah and the wails of the faithful drifted into the courtyard.

The following morning the guests, dressed in formal attire—the women with picture hats and white gloves, the men in ties and tails—started out for the House in their black limousines. It was like going to a gala opening of the opera. They were ushered to a special box reserved for the family as the gallery rapidly filled with the city's fashionable elite.

An Oppenheimer speech was notable for gentle but pervasive

sarcasm and withering analysis. One of his characteristic addresses took place at a time when the government launched a highly publicized program to combat inflation, which was putting a serious strain on the economy. The Minister of Finance, it happened, like Pooh-Bah in *The Mikado*, held several other portfolios as well.

Oppenheimer spoke quietly, extemporaneously. The government was playing both ends against the middle, he said. The Finance Minister, on the one hand, claimed the government had rolled back inflation, and on the other hand, it asked for increased powers from the legislature to fight rising prices:

> Now, these clear contradictions which underlie this budget require a good deal of fundamental thinking. Fundamental thinking, even for someone as quick-witted as the Minister, takes a good deal of time, and the Minister is a busy man. He has not only to cope with Finance but also with External Affairs, and he has, in addition, to cope with his self-imposed portfolio of propaganda which probably occupies the greater part of his time. I must say that I wish the Minister would give up this self-imposed portfolio of propaganda . . . because, while he has very great capabilities for work, in this field he is extraordinarily incompetent. . . . There is surely no one who devotes more attention to the press than the Minister of Finance, but there is surely no one who succeeds in getting a worse press for himself, or for South Africa, than he does.

When Oppenheimer concluded the ladies in their big hats and white gloves stood up and left. The spectacle was over; few bothered to notice who the next speaker was. Off went the women to their mint juleps and croquet and the men to the commodities and stock exchange.

For years Oppenheimer remained a leading member of the United Party. But as time went on and South Africa's social problems became less susceptible to a facile solution, the United Party's liberalism became increasingly tenuous. On the issue of dealing with the blacks, in particular, the party grew excessively timid and adopted a platform that was a virtual echo of the government attitude.

Oppenheimer parted ways with the party on the apartheid issue and joined the one political party in South Africa that stood for complete racial integration of blacks into the white society—the newly formed Progressive Party. He is acutely aware of the anomaly of a nation of 15,000,000 Bantus (Africans) and 2,000,000 coloreds (of mixed racial ancestry) who are ruled repressively by an elite of 4,000,000 whites, 2,200,000 of whom are Afrikaners (descendants of Dutch settlers) and who wield the key power.

In recent years Oppenheimer has become increasingly blunt in his warnings to the nation. Speaking at a rally of the Progressive Party, he declared he was "sick and tired of hearing how sound South Africa's economy is. . . . I don't think that the economy of a country which deliberately sets out . . . not to make proper use of 80 percent of its potential working population can be described as sound."

In black-run countries to the north of South Africa, where the Oppenheimer business interests are influential, he has been providing a generous infusion of capital to bolster their economies. In Zambia Oppenheimer's companies have built schools and hospitals providing free medical care for black workers. He has persuaded white unions to accept blacks and give them the opportunity for better paying jobs. Oppenheimer is fond of quoting from the Book of Job, "Iron is taken out of the earth, and brass is molten out of the stone . . . and it hath the dust of gold . . . but where shall wisdom be found, and where is the place of understanding?"

If Oppenheimer presents a strange paradox—that of an aggressive, old-fashioned monopolist in his business practices who espouses liberal politics—so too does the government he has been attacking. While maintaining a rigid policy of apartheid at home, Prime Minister Balthazar Vorster's government, seeking to break out of its political and economic isolation, has launched a foreign aid program, sending money and technical help to the independent black nations around it. It is exporting to Nairobi the ultimate in housewife conveniences—canned foods. It has sent machinery to Ghana to upgrade its mining industry. It is helping Malagasy build a viable tourist trade.

President Nixon's severance of the dollar from the gold standard was a shock to South Africa's ruling whites, since their nation is the world's leading gold producer. However, its mines are continuing to sell gold steadily to the free market, and the price of gold mining shares (Kaffirs) has remained generally firm. While Washington is striving to demonetize gold in the international sphere, this could take some doing as far as the rest of the world is concerned.

In any event, South Africa has other irons in the fire. The country has been blessed with enormous reserves of cheap uranium deposits, and for years it has been adding to its stores by separating the uranium from gold shavings in its mines.

In 1969 Prime Minister Vorster announced that South African scientists had perfected a way of taking this cheap uranium and enriching it to make it competitive as a nuclear fuel for the international utilities industry. Not only will South Africa's entrance with a low-cost process into this multibillion-dollar field substantially bolster its economy, but there is an ominous implication in Vorster's announcement. Hitherto the technology for the enrichment of uranium, which is essential not only for nuclear fuels but for making atomic weapons, has been monopolized by the United States and the Soviet Union because of the massive plants and vast outlay of money required. South Africa's new process may substantially cut the expenditures and could be practical for adoption by nations with only modest economies. If, in fact, it proves out, it could mean that scores of smaller nations will be able to make their own atomic war weapons—a possibility that is giving Washington and the Muscovites fits.

So far as is known, South Africa has brought the process only up to the pilot plant stage of development. No one outside of the government knows when or whether it will become feasible on a large scale commercially and, if so, whether the government will make the technology available to other nations.

In any event, it may be appropriate to cite a favorite motto of South Africa's leading industrialist—and maverick son—Sir Harry Oppenheimer. It is the family credo, adopted by Sir Ernest when he was knighted by Queen Elizabeth: *"Spero Optima"* ("I hope for the best").

15

Senjitsu—the New Japanese Blitzkrieg: Morita and Ibuka of Sony

On August 5, 1945, a U.S. pilot looked down from his B-29 aircraft, the *Enola Gay*, at the mist, smoke and fire that were spreading like a huge umbrella beneath him and muttered sardonically, "Jesus Christ, if people knew what we were doing we could have sold tickets for $100,000!"

That may very well have been the understatement of the century. Below the *Enola Gay* the air was belching forth a thick vapor of smoke. Water like huge beads of sweat tumbled from the column of dirt and flame spouting miles into the sky above Hiroshima. Children asked their mothers, "Why is it nighttime in the morning?"

But amidst the devastation caused by the world's first atomic bombing, a miracle of the utmost irony occurred. A Jesuit priest who ran a missionary in Hiroshima, regaining consciousness after being stunned by the nuclear explosion, staggered inside the mission house to see what he could salvage. Only one thing stood unharmed in the shambles of his study—a papier-mâché attaché case that lay under his desk in the position he had placed it before the bombing. With 100,000 people destroyed, 60,000 buildings reduced to rubble, this papier-mâché case survived without a scratch. It was crammed with money—several thousand yens' worth—belonging to the Society of Jesus.

The survival of this packet of money was a harbinger of things to come. It symbolized the inimitable resiliency of the

Japanese economy—its ability to survive a nuclear holocaust and transform itself into one of the mightiest powers on earth.

Japan emerged stunned. Almost 2,000,000 of her people were dead, over 500,000 as a result of civilian bombings. Tokyo's population was lopped in half. Osaka, Japan's second-largest city, shrank to one-third. Kobe and Nagoya were in shambles. Japan's industry was at a standstill, and her wealth was reduced to the products of her farmland. The peasantry found itself possessors of the bulk of the GNP. Although the farmer grew less food than previously because the proper fertilizers were unavailable, he was reaping profits greater than he ever thought possible by selling in the black market. The currency was deteriorating so rapidly that he preferred to take his urban customers' kimonos and family heirlooms rather than their paper money.

As the currency continued to tumble, the bank and postal savings which millions of Japanese had painstakingly accumulated in prewar years became virtually valueless. A family that before the war had lived adequately on a salary of 100 yen a month no longer could exist on 20,000 yen. In the cities people scrounged for eatable scraps. Those who found a strip of cultivable soil strove to grow food by planting seeds in slits of ground that peeped from the wreckage of their houses or digging gardens out of the rocky slope of hills. City dwellers walked miles into the countryside offering farmers shoes and typewriters for a sweet potato.

The war's end brought other hardships. During the final months of combat it was impossible to keep clean, and this was damaging to Japanese morale, since the people worshiped physical cleanliness. Soap couldn't be obtained anywhere. Public baths were shut because of the lack of heating facilities. The lovely kimonos of thousands of women had gone up in the flames of gutted houses, and they were forced to wear coarse trousers.*

Yet all this is history. Rising from this catastrophe, the islands have become the world's third-largest industrial power

* For a more detailed study of the ordeal of the Japanese wartime economy and its political consequences reference is made to a book co-authored by the present writer: *Shoriki, Miracle Man of Japan*, Edward Uhlan and Dana L. Thomas, 1957.

(after the United States and the Soviet Union). Japan is the biggest shipbuilder, the second-largest manufacturer of television sets, the third-largest maker of steel and autos.

And, as in the case with Germany, Japan's wartime defeat provided the sinews for its renaissance. Its devastation forced it to sweep clean the decks and start anew with modern plants and the most up-to-date technology. Protected by U.S. military power, Japan has had to devote only a minor portion of her resources to defense needs and has been able to commit the lion's share of its budget to civilian uses. A striking example of the advantages reaped from military defeat is Japan's top steel company, Nippon Steel, which pours more tonnage of molten steel than any other producer on earth. Explains Shigeo Nagano, Nippon's chairman: "So long as we had to start from nothing, we wanted the most modern plant. We selected the cream of the world's technology. We learned from America, Germany, Austria and the Soviet Union and adapted their methods in our own way."

Japanese industrialists have honed to a fine art the tactic of finding a technological loophole in Western industrial practice and rushing in with a more efficient process—usually by buying from other countries patents lying on their shelves or being used only on a limited scale. In this way, Japan seized upon a technology for making steel more cheaply than ever before by using oxygen furnaces that were first developed by Austrians but neglected by Western industrialists. While burning steel in a bath of oxygen speeds up the operation and greatly lowers costs over the conventional open-hearth method, for U.S. steelmen to have immediately converted to it would have meant scrapping their huge investments in open-hearth furnaces accumulated over decades. But the Japanese industry, starting from scratch, latched onto the process. Today more than 80 percent of Japan's steel is turned out in oxygen furnaces, and these products have been beating their U.S. competition to a frazzle, forcing Americans to build oxygen furnaces in self-defense.

Confronted with a postwar money shortage, Japanese industry had to resort to borrowing heavily from government-supervised banks. Currently it receives four-fifths of its financing via bank loans—a huge proportion compared to U.S.

industry, which derives much more of its capital from common stock. The Japanese don't mind in the least being heavily in debt. This means they don't have to cater to shareholders, as in equity arrangements, and they can keep their dividend payouts as low as possible.

One competitive edge Japanese industry has over the American is the lavish subsidization it gets from the government. Nipponese industry is organized into virtual cartels, with the government acquiescing in the carving out of markets and the regulation of prices—something that would bring the U.S. Justice Department down on American industry in a hurry. The Nipponese government has been financing studies of foreign markets for native firms to enter, providing cheap loans for export business and levying the smallest corporate income taxes for any highly industrialized country. Premier Eisaku Sato wears a second hat as the head of the Japanese export council, and he has been making no bones about harnessing the government behind a national export *Putsch*.

Japan's wartime defeat yielded one especially important dividend. Until the American occupation, the Japanese economy had been concentrated in the grip of a few tremendously rich *zaibatsu* clans—Mitsubishi, Sumitomo, Mitsui—whose money and influence had been handed down intact through the generations. For example, Hachiro Mitsui, who launched the family fortune by introducing a chain of mail order stores in seventeenth-century Japan (a remarkable innovation for the times), drew up before his death a constitution to perpetuate his wealth. This agreement, which was honored by succeeding generations through World War II, established categories for each of his sons and their families and allotted to each a percentage of the inheritance. Each son managed a branch of the business, but the profits belonged to the clan as a whole, which at a formal meeting determined what portion of it each family unit should receive. On coming of age, a Mitsui heir was required to take the following oath:

> In obedience to the precepts of our father and in order
> to strengthen the everlasting foundation of our House and
> to expand the enterprise bequeathed by our forefathers, I
> solemnly vow in the presence of the August spirits of our

ancestors, that as a member of the House of Mitsui I will serve
and follow the regulations handed down in the Constitution
of our House, and that I will not wantonly seek to alter them.

The MacArthur occupation eliminated these family heads of
industry who had held their position through hereditary privilege and were in many cases highly incompetent. In their place
expertly trained managers took over, qualified solely by their
superior performance capabilities.

Japanese industry is blessed with a cooperative, cheerful
labor force willing to accept low pay and toil with an esprit de
corps unknown in any other industrialized nation. Militant
trade unions, nationwide strikes are much less prevalent than
elsewhere. Also capital investment in industry has been subsidized by the Japanese masses to an extraordinary extent. In an
average year the Japanese people save over 19 percent of their
income, three times the rate of U.S. savings in a good year. This
huge sum is fed via the banks into the Japanese business complex. While it is true that in recent years under the impetus of
Japan's export boom wages have risen from abnormally low levels (in 1969 they passed Italy's wage scale and France's in 1970
and today average about 95 cents an hour), productivity has
kept pace remarkably with wage rises. Unlike U.S. unions, Japanese workers have not placed obstacles against the introduction of new technology designed to increase production efficien-
cies.

One reason is there is virtually no job insecurity. If a job is
eliminated, employers exercise great flexibility in shifting
workers to another job. Company spirit is unusual. A recent
newspaper poll disclosed that almost 70 percent of Japanese
business managers claimed their companies were more important to them than their wives and children. The corporation
has also become the ego center, the matrix and the fountain-
head of life for millions of Japanese workers. Traditionally
family- and group-oriented, many Japanese have transferred
their emotional allegiance to their business unit without reser-
vation. It is not unusual for a worker to refer to his firm as
"my" company, using the same Japanese letter "my" that is employed with reference to his relatives. At Nippon Steel, Sony
and other big industrial combines the help gathers each morn-

ing to sing a company song before taking up posts on the assembly lines. Workers going off one shift are given *banzais* by other workers waiting to go on. When a Japanese executive leaves on a business trip abroad, frequently the entire staff, from the lowliest clerk up, will gather at the airport and give him the kind of send-off college cheerleaders provide their football team as it takes the field.

Corporate managements treat their employees in a fatherly way, strange to the West. Some of the psychology used is quaint, indeed. One major corporation has encouraged its workers to let out their frustrations by placing a wooden effigy of the boss in the auditorium. Any employee with a grudge can pick up a sword and strike "the boss" to his heart's content. If that doesn't help, he is sent to the company psychiatrist.

In short, rising from the shambles of war, Japan has become an industrial superpower. It is employing the technology and promotional strategies developed by the Western world harnessed to the peculiarly Oriental characteristics of patience and self-sacrifice, foreign to the comfort-loving Occident. Western technology coupled to the Oriental spirit of endurance has made Japan a uniquely formidable competitor.

The flood of Japanese exports inundating foreign markets has aroused hostility and fear. Explodes one U.S. trade official, "The Japanese are still fighting the war, only now instead of a shooting war, it is an economic one. Their immediate intention is to try to dominate the Pacific and then perhaps the world." Like their military predecessors who during World War II rolled over China, Indochina and other neighboring countries in a tidal wave, briefcase-carrying Japanese businessmen have moved indefatigably into foreign countries using the same "human-sea" tactics, called *senjitsu* by the old Japanese generals.

Until the mid-fifties the Japanese bought more than they sold in the United States. By the time President Nixon made his speech in August, 1971, declaring a 10 percent surcharge on imports and pressuring Japan to revalue the yen, the situation had completely reversed itself. The losers of the war had gained an impressive commercial foothold in America and were expanding their bridgehead, taking over entire markets. The West Coast was being inundated with steel products undercutting the goods of Pittsburgh steel makers and Oakland-based

Kaiser Steel Company. In California, Toyotas and Datsuns had seized over 30 percent of the new car market from the Detroit auto makers. Honda and Yamaha motorcycles bobbed up everywhere on American highways. Mitsui traders had infiltrated the grain floor in Chicago and the cotton pits of Memphis and New York, slugging it out with American traders. Japanese-controlled banks had mushroomed up on the West Coast and, according to one California finance executive, "are a heavy presence in our banking circles." Sony transistor radios and television sets had been installed in homes from coast to coast. Sony-built video tape recorders guided U.S. astronauts on their trips to the moon.

Japan has come a long way, but troublesome problems remain. Despite their material prosperity, the Japanese are suffering from a deep-seated malaise of the spirit. While the majority of people reject the right-wingers who want to restore Japan's former military-imperialistic values, most Japanese feel a strong nostalgia for many aspects of the past; and no new ethical value system has been developed to fill this emptiness. "We are seeking a new vision for the future," remarks one political leader, "but no consensus has been reached on what the new national purpose should be, or even what the alternatives are."

Japan is suffering the tensions of a society caught between its traditional culture and the mystique of modern technology. The contrasts between the old style of life and the new are showing up in the entire spectrum of society—in the cities where next to gleaming skyscrapers of steel and glass the Japanese are still building huts of unpainted wood; in the behavior of the nation's leading industrialists who after a day spent with computers put on their ancient ceremonial gowns and devote themselves to Buddhist prayers.

Max Ways, a journalist who visited the industrial center of Kawasaki, writes of this "intertwining" of the old with the new, of the "morning glory by the machine-shop door; the willows above the congested street, the elegant kimonos for sale in tawdry shops, the sea breeze that stirs the polluted air, and, everywhere, the sense of dignity amid bustle, of a clinging continuity that defies change."

Throughout the fabric of the present linger indissoluble traces of the past. In this modern age of restless mobility there persists the deep-seated reluctance of the Japanese to parting with relatives and friends, the need to dally awhile longer before saying *sayonara*. At Tokyo's airport there is a room with one wall entirely of glass, which affords a final glance at the departing loved one; it is punctuated by holes through which a mouth may speak a last farewell before the traveler boards the plane.

This ambivalent mixture of the past and the present is strikingly exemplified by the career of two leading Japanese businessmen who have helped thrust postwar Japan into the very forefront of the world's technology. One is Akio Morita, a wealthy inheritor descended from a family of brewers who have been making sake from the rice fields outside Nagoya for fourteen generations. His name means "prosperous rice fields." The other is Masaru Ibuka, who comes from an ancient Samurai family in the mountain shrine village of Nikko. They joined forces in 1947—Morita with the family money, Ibuka with his engineering brains—to start a little electronics firm in a bombed-out Tokyo department store and built it into one of the world's leading empires, Sony, known in 160 nations for its pioneering of transistorized portable radios, television sets and tape recorders that have enriched the lives of people everywhere.

Sony has established itself by characteristically Japanese means—taking over the basic inventions of others that have been lying on the shelf because no one foresaw a practical use for them. Ibuka, Sony's chairman, calls the strategy "finding unnoticed utility in others' inventions, seasoning them with original ideas of our own and making them into marketable products. We do," adds Ibuka, "what others don't."

In deciding what to manufacture, Sony proceeds not like most American firms launching elaborate consumer surveys to find what the public currently wishes but trusting its own judgment as to what the man in the street will be desiring tomorrow. "People can't tell what they will want three to five years from now," points out Morita, Sony's president and the Mr. Outside or promotion-minded partner of the team. "That's where we're doing the thinking and that's where we have to be the experts."

Unlike American firms which set a budget for technical research and stay within its limits, Sony operates informally, playing by ear. It spends what it takes to do the job. It employs a high ratio of graduate engineers, some 2,000 out of a work force of over 12,000 employees. Most of its top-echelon executives are young, in their mid-forties. Sony's technical reputation is very high in the electronics world. Prestigious IBM turned to it for advice when it wished in 1965 to start making magnetic tape for its computers. The Japanese firm provided the blueprints and supervised the building of a production plant for IBM.

Sony is the quintessential international company. Over 50 percent of its sales comes from exports to 160 nations, half of this from the United States. Such a ratio of exports is high even for a Japanese firm. Most Nipponese companies—even the most aggressive—derive no more than 25 percent of their business abroad.

To promote what perhaps is the most widely sold brand name in the world, Sony has departed from Japanese tradition. Other manufacturers limit themselves to producing their goods and leave it to the huge, influential Japanese trade companies to do their marketing for them. Sony has built its own hand-picked sales force to sell its television sets, transistorized radios and tape recorders to dealers from America to South Africa. Its methods are subtle. Its advertising in the United States does not imply, let alone divulge, that Sony is a Japanese company. The majority of Americans who own its transistor radios and television sets are under the impression they are put out by an American firm. Not long ago, Sony did research among U.S. dealers asking whether they handled Japanese radios. Most answered they didn't. The next question was, "Have you handled Sony radios?" The majority replied yes.

The financial community is a little more knowledgeable than the average consumer, and it has learned to know and respect Sony's achievements. Sony was the first Japanese firm to offer its common stock for sale to Americans back in 1963, through the instrument of U.S. American depository receipts. Each ADR when issued was worth ten shares of Sony and was deposited with an agent of Morgan Guaranty in Tokyo. Morgan pays the dividends to American stockholders in dollars. Currently Americans own 35 percent of Sony stock, and they have done very well in the last eight years.

The company was originally conceived by Masaru Ibuka, an electrical engineer who worked on infrared detection devices and a telephone scrambler for the Japanese military during World War II. In 1947 Ibuka took over a gutted and boarded-up Tokyo department store that had been wrecked by American war planes and opened his first factory with a team of fifty employees. The conditions were highly primitive. When it rained the workers had to shield their machines with umbrellas, so leaky was the roof. The plant was located in a slum area where the poor hung out their smelly wash on lines. "The only thing we really hated," Ibuka reminisces, "was passing under washed diapers to reach our main entrance."

Fumbling around for some article to produce that would win consumer acceptance, Ibuka hit on turning out a shortwave converter for radio sets, which would allow the Nipponese to listen to broadcasts outside their country. Isolated for years by the war and still living in semi-ruins, the Japanese were hungry for news from abroad. A leading newspaper published a story about Ibuka's device, and Tokyo citizens rushed to Ibuka's plant, lining up for a chance to listen to the "miracle" radio.

This newspaper article was read by, among others, Akio Morita, who had been an expert in electronics research for the Japanese Navy and was looking for a postwar business into which to invest his energy and his money. Morita, as noted, came from a wealthy family of sake brewers. He had studied physics and received a degree at Osaka Imperial University before doing a stint with the Japanese Navy.

For fourteen generations the oldest son had taken over the Morita sake business, and Akio, who was the eldest of the current generation, was expected to do the same. But Morita persuaded his father to let the second son manage the family firm, and he threw in his lot with Ibuka in the ramshackle electronics plant, providing not only brains but the necessary financing for the firm to survive and expand. Today Morita remains the largest stockholder of Sony.

With the money provided by Morita, Sony was launched on its way. The big breakthrough occurred with the firm's development of the first Japanese tape recorder. Ibuka first became acquainted with the concept of a recorder when he saw an American machine borrowed from the U.S. occupation army. It seemed to him an excellent product for the infant company to make because of his own background in sound recording.

In 1950 Ibuka completed a version that sold for nearly $500 and weighed almost 40 pounds. Because of a shortage of materials the firm used for its tapes paper made from rice.

But Ibuka was in for a shock. There was no rush to buy his recorder. Only a few were sold as novelties. A Tokyo restaurant, for example, bought one to record its patrons and play back their voices as a promotional gimmick. Otherwise buyers were apathetic.

Looking for an angle, Morita loaded a secondhand Datsun truck with his product and went around Japan visiting schools, giving demonstrations of the recorder as an educational device for teaching classes. And his pitch struck paydirt. The schoolteachers responded by inundating him with orders for 50,000 recorders. Sony had begun to roll.

Seeking a new product to exploit and following the strategy of licensing inventions that others considered risky, turning them into a successful consumer package, Ibuka visited the United States in 1952. He found that Western Electric engineers had achieved a major breakthrough by developing transistors—tiny electronic circuits which, doing the same job as the much larger vacuum tubes, made possible the creation of smaller-sized equipment for more sophisticated uses.

This new technology of microelectronics was an offshoot of the space age. The need to lighten the weight of satellites designed to reach the moon and to develop more efficient guided missiles had spurred the U.S. aerospace industry to find a way to miniaturize electronic systems; and Western Electric had found the solution. But while transistors were useful for spacecraft and military programs, electronics experts did not foresee any immediate commercial consumer use for them.

Masaru Ibuka, however, had an idea. Why not use the transistor to replace the vacuum tube in consumer radios and turn out small sets which could be carried anywhere within range of a transmitter—into the kitchen, the backyard, the beach or the countryside.

Ibuka discussed his concept with Western Electric engineers, who discouraged him. It wouldn't work, they said. The technology for making transistors had too many bugs. Currently 95 of every 100 transistors coming off the assembly line were defective and had to be thrown away. The cost of commercial production would be prohibitive. To eke out profits, a manufacturer would have to charge $6 for a transistor alone. Complete vacuum tube radios were selling in the States for as little as $6.95. The economics of the situation made it impossible to mass-produce a transistorized radio.

But Ibuka was a stubborn man. Everywhere he went in America, he saw the enormous popularity of radios. He was convinced that advances in technology would eliminate the defects in production, bringing down the costs substantially. Ibuka wangled a license from Western Electric to make transistors, and he returned home to perfect the technology, managing to cut the faulty percentage turned out on the assembly line from 95 to 2 percent and shaving the costs from $6 to eventually under 10 cents.

As a result, Sony came out with the first pocket-sized transistor radio, which had an overwhelming response in the United States and around the world.

Continuing with its red-hot concept of producing "personalized easy-to-carry consumer products," Sony plunged into a technology that made possible even smaller-sized products—integrated circuits.

The methodology was highly complex. Diagrams of electronic circuits had to be reduced to a quarter of a millionth of their original size. These were photoetched onto a sliver of silicon; the pattern of the circuits, impressed on the wafer, was then put through gas-diffusion furnaces; electronic currents were forced through the windows and holes formed by the photoetching, so that the silicon was charged electrically to perform all the functions of a larger circuit.

The production technology was one of the most intricate ever to be tackled. Most of the manufacturing had to be done in a microcosmic area invisible to the human eye. Sony engineers toiled to develop improved camera work, better photoetching processes and gas-diffusion furnaces. And they achieved what a few years previouly would have been considered the product of a science fiction writer's fantasies: integrated circuits that incorporated entire electronic circuits—transistors, diodes and resistors—on a single chip of silicon smaller than a dime. Thanks to its wizardry, Sony has been able to turn out a three-ounce radio that can be affixed to the end of a key chain; it has produced a tape recorder the size of a pack of cigarettes.

In 1959 the firm introduced the world's first transistorized portable black-and-white television set, a nine-inch screen model, and it followed with a four-inch screen. (Sony has experimented with making a one-inch TV screen just to prove it can be done.)

Subsequently, Sony carried its miniaturization skills still further into the field of portable color television sets. The problem keeping others from making them was the necessity of developing a tube that would flash color pictures bright enough to be seen wherever the set was carried—into the broad daylight, to the street or the beach. RCA and other manufacturers had been experimenting with one type of tube, and they were having serious trouble with it. Sony took another route.

Pursuing its strategy of seizing on unused and long-forgotten inventions and turning them into successful commercial packages, Sony obtained a license for a tube invented years before by Dr. Ernest O. Lawrence, winner of the Nobel Prize. By one of the grim twists of history, Lawrence had been a leading developer of the atomic bomb that ravaged Hiroshima. Sony engineers took Lawrence's device and perfected it into a microcolor tube that guided electrons to the colored phosphors with such intense concentration as to produce pictures much more brilliant than previously achieved. In 1960 Sony took the wraps off the world's first transistorized color television set, operated with batteries and small and light enough to be carried anywhere indoors and out. In such a fashion one of the inventors of the A-bomb made recompense to the Japanese people.

Currently Sony is up to its ears in technology to exploit what looms as the biggest entertainment device since television—the home videotape recorder. It has developed a machine that using a cassette of prerecorded tape, which can be slipped on as simply as a record on a phonograph, will play through a television set any program the user chooses to record.

Sony has come a long way. Starting in a bombed-out department store on an investment of $537, it has grown into an industrial complex generating over $400,000,000 in sales from 160 nations. Quips Morita, Sony has scored its huge success by "thinking small."

As befitting its new international position and worldwide appeal, the firm changed its name in 1958 from Tokyo Tsushin Kogyo (Tokyo Telecommunications Company) to Sony. The name was thought up by Morita from the Latin *sonus,* meaning "sound." "It's easy to remember and pronounced the same all over the world."

Needless to say, Sony scarcely lives up to the image of the conventional Japanese industrial company. Ibuka and Morita are looked upon as mavericks by other Japanese businessmen. The Sony factory has a breezy informality that shocks the tradition-minded Nipponese. Ibuka and Morita mingle freely with their workers, wearing the same blue cotton smocks.

Morita confesses that he has become heavily Americanized. Now fifty, trim-waisted and silvery-haired, he has flown the Pacific over sixty times, commuting from Tokyo to New York. He brought back from one trip a nickelodeon that stands in the library of his Tokyo home, along with a batch of nickels that he inserts to play American hit tunes.

In 1960 Morita moved with his wife and three children to New York to set up a Sony sales force in the States. He took a Fifth Avenue apartment, sent his children to American schools and to a summer camp in Maine, joined a golf club and became a member of a local parents-teachers association. He remained in the States for fifteen months, traveling around the country and studying consumer psychology. "I didn't realize how big the United States is until I drove my own car here," he reminisces.

With Japanese labor costs rising and the government forced to revalue the yen and accept greater competition in its foreign markets, while being pressed to allow a greater flow of foreign capital into the country, Japan has reached a critical turning point in her affairs. Morita is a strong advocate of opening up Japan to American investments. With typical Japanese pragmatism, he argues, "If we allow more U.S. investment, we will not need a security treaty. Of course, the Americans will protect us then. Everybody protects his own property."

Faced with rougher competition, Morita urges his country-men to adopt more of the business strategy that has made the West so powerful an industrial force. He has roundly criticized the Japanese industrial establishment for its backward prac-tices. Several years ago he wrote a book indicting native mana-gerial policies and aroused the ire of his countrymen.

"There are too many 'Japanese factors' in Japanese compa-nies," Morita complained in another piece written for Colum-bia University's business journal, "employment for lifetime, promotion by seniority, plenty of fringe benefits, difficulty in discharging an employee. In short, a Japanese company looks like a social-security organization." Ibuka agrees. "Historically, we Japanese have been conditioned to follow, according to the lord-and-retainer system. We have never been brought up to think of our own goals or targets. We lack target creation in Japan."

The fact is, concludes Morita, Japanese business is still heav-ily encrusted in thousands of years of national tradition and psychology. Individual initiative is looked down upon. Every-body works for the advancement of the group. Workers who join a company remain until they are automatically retired with a pension in their mid-fifties. Job and monetary advancement on the basis of performance is virtually nonex-istent. Salary increases are automatic.

While some workers are given nominal promotions, their corporate career for the most part is determined by the record they achieved in school before entering the firm. A graduate from a prestigious university with a top-notch academic record will go much further in a Japanese corporation than a graduate with a poorer record, no matter how well he subsequently per-forms on his job.

Ibuka and Morita, running a firm in the forefront of technol-ogy, were forced to scrap much of this Japanese tradition if they were to continue to grow. In the mid-sixties, Sony shook the Es-tablishment by running an ad in Japanese newspapers inviting young workers in other firms to apply for a job overseas with Sony. (Luring a worker away from another company was an unheard-of practice.) The ad promoted the unthinkable. "The seniority system and the emphasis on scholastic background is preventing young, capable men and women from fulfilling their capabilities and aspirations," it declared. It called for all who "are not satisfied with being buried in an organization" to join forces with Sony, a firm that has eliminated all school records from its personnel files, encouraging promotion strictly on job performance.

And yet even Morita and Ibuka, for all their dynamism and emancipation from the past, have not been willing, or able, to break entirely from it. Radical as their innovations have been, some basic features of Japanese corporate life have been retained; a skillful compromise between the avant-garde and the orthodox has been effected.

Like other Japanese corporations, Sony provides its quota of social benefits—dormitories, day nurseries for working mothers, a high school for its teen-age employees. Women between the ages of fifteen and twenty-four comprise almost half the Sony work force. (Other firms also have a heavy proportion of female labor.) The girls apply for a job with Sony through a national competitive examination. They are alert, quick-witted and manually dextrous; many come to Sony directly from family farms. Within a week after joining the firm, they have assimilated an on-the-job training program and taken their places on the assembly line to turn out integrated circuits. The production job has been broken down into extremely simple components that make quick learning easy.

Sony operates a high school, as noted, and runs its plant in two shifts. Half its teen-age employees work mornings and attend school afternoons; the other half go to school mornings and work afternoons. The girls live in company dormitories, four to a room, sleeping in double-decker beds. When they graduate from high school, they are entitled to move into private homes built by the company—ten girls to a house. Here they practice housekeeping until they get married, usually in their mid-twenties. After giving birth to babies, they continue to work at the firm. Sony runs a nursery where the young mothers can deposit their children for a small fee.

In short, Sony, for all its "Americanization," provides basic paternalistic benefits that are endemic in the Japanese system. The firm is a curious mixture of the traditional and the innovative in a nation that is experiencing the same conflicting pressures on a larger scale.

From his office window, Masaru Ibuka can see, on days when the air is clear, the majestic summit and slopes of ancient, enigmatic Mount Fuji. In the foreground is Sony's ultramodern integrated-circuit assembly plant. Every hour Japan's newest and fastest express train, the Mikari, roars by at 130 miles an hour, carrying the modern descendants of this ancient country and culture from city to city at an unprecedented speed.

Ibuka, a thoughtful man of sixty-three, standing five feet nine, keeps a golf putter in a rack by his desk. He practices by daily swinging on the carpet. He has cut his golf handicap substantially by having his swing photographed via a Sony video tape recorder and analyzing his mistakes as they are played back to him. Having improved his own game this way, he is doing a land-office business selling the recorder to Japanese golf clubs. Ibuka and Morita are especially enthusiastic about the potential benefits of their video tape recorders for educational and medical uses.

Recently the Japanese economy, whose aggressive exuberance is so aptly exemplified by Sony, has run into stormy seas. Since August, 1971, when the Nixon administration staged a revolt against Japan's penetration of U.S. markets and forced Japan to revalue her currency upward by 16.9 percent, the Nipponese have been stripped of their hubris and compelled to work even harder to sustain their foreign markets. Japan has unquestionably suffered a severe psychological blow from what the newspapers called the *doru shokku*—the "dollar shock"—brought on by Nixon's economic onslaught. The country had gone for six straight years without a recession, and the people had adopted the attitude that the boom would go on indefinitely.

However, after the initial shock wore off, Japanese economists made a realistic evaluation, predicting that the results of Nixon's blitzkrieg wouldn't be all that devastating. True, the prices of Nippon's exports were higher now; but even before Nixon got tough, the Japanese were not competing solely on a price basis on a growing number of goods. Sony, Toyota and other resourceful firms had done such an excellent job of establishing quality brands with a worldwide reputation that a 10-percent rise in price did not significantly threaten them.

As for laid-off workers, the Japanese ethos would take care of that. Since the nation follows, as noted, the practice of employment for life, "laying off" employees because of declining business hasn't meant firing them. They are sent home to wait for a pick up, meanwhile receiving full pay. Explains an official of a textile firm forced to "discharge" its workers because of poor business, "As long as our company survives, we aren't going to tell our employees, who haven't done anything wrong like stealing company money, 'You're fired!' "

While the Japanese economy remains essentially stable, there are, to be sure, manifestations of uneasiness. Not long after President Nixon took the dollar off the gold standard there was one curious reaction. In the fall of 1971, the U.S. fish industry reported that the Japanese had suddenly begun to buy up shrimp in huge unprecedented quantities on the world market. While the Nipponese have always been avid fish eaters, this unexpected rise in demand, which was four times what had been projected, baffled most outside observers. Some professed to see a relationship between it and Nixon's new economic policies. The Japanese were holding vast sums of dollars which were no longer convertible into gold, reasoned these experts, and nervous Japanese were anxious to convert them into something of unquestioned value that could be quickly reconverted into yen. Since shrimp is to the Japanese what apple pie is to Americans, it was the safest temporary medium into which to put shaky dollars.

If this is true, President Nixon, while he may have bruised the Japanese ego, has been paid back in spades. By placing a higher monetary value on the lowly shrimp than on dollar bills, the Japanese could be setting a portentous precedent.

16

Portraits in Autos and Oil: Agnelli of Fiat, Italy's Richest Citizen—Nubar Gulbenkian, Prince of Bohemia

Agnelli of Fiat, Italy's Richest Citizen

Strolling daily along the Via Vittorio Veneto, Rome's Fifth Avenue, is a mélange of people representing the social spectrum of modern Italy. There are the young male hustlers who have arrived from the hinterlands, winning the favors of wealthy old men, sleeping with elderly dowagers, scavenging for bits of gossip with which to blackmail the reigning powers in the climb to the top. There are the aging survivors of the Mussolini regime, former petty functionaries and provincial officials who once swaggered about in their jackboots and now sit in a sidewalk café sipping Cinzano and dozing over memories of yesterday's glory. There are the hordes of young women who flock to Rome, flaunting themselves to catch the eye of a Fellini or a Rossellini and be lifted overnight into film stardom, only to end up more likely as not as the whore of an elderly banker. Walking along the Via Veneto are prima donnas of the opera, nursemaids wheeling the babies of wealthy Roman matrons, pimps and heroin pushers, the *paparazzi* poised with their cameras to snap an international celebrity, men of uncertain years, dressed in mod fashions, who look for an easy living tumbling with either sex.

This is urban Italy, the best and worst of it, engulfed in an age of technology and tawdriness, of social awareness combined with deep feelings of insecurity and self-incrimination. Despite its troubles and a current economic recession, Italy since the war has undergone a lively rise in its standard of living. A little over a decade ago refrigerators were a rarity. Today they are everywhere. Two-fifths of the population own washing machines. Millions drive autos.

True, there still exists a serious gulf between living standards in the north and the south, where Italians continue to struggle in poverty. The nation is plagued with a chronic outflow of capital by wealthy and middle-class Italians who are worried about the cloudy political climate. The Christian Democrats, who have ruled Italy for most of the postwar period, holding a majority in Parliament with the help of the Socialists, have beaten off a serious onslaught by the neo-Fascists in the 1972 election, and the continued rule by the moderate center and left of center is being increasingly threatened.

Italy's economic difficulties are complicated, as noted, by the periodic flight of investment capital and by the cavalier attitude of the people toward the payment of taxes. In a typical year, 8,000,000 Italians don't even bother to make out tax returns. And even when they do, it's a farce. One of Italy's top film directors, who gets $500,000 a picture, reported for 1970 that he earned the princely sum of $8,000. A leading actress who made her fortune from Italian movies informed the tax collectors that she recently became a Swiss citizen and did not feel obligated to pay a lira to the country of her birth.

Not only in Italy but in most of Western Europe tax evasion is not considered a criminal offense. If a tax dodger is caught red-handed, he is merely slapped on the wrist with a civil fine. No Italian within memory has gone to jail for tax fraud. Explains a government official, "We don't accept limitations of personal liberty in connection with taxes." Only in democratic United States and Britain, those lordly sanctuaries of civil liberties, does the government see fit to use its maximum police powers and the full weight of its criminal system to collect taxes.

Italy's industrialists, like its film directors, painters and architects, tend to be prima donnas. Like the stage of the Milan opera house, the industrial scene is dominated by temperamental virtuoso soloists.

The greatest of these on the business scene, and the nation's richest citizen, is Giovanni Agnelli, who lives with the *beau geste* of a Renaissance doge. Widely regarded as the Henry Ford of Italy and a major architect of *il boom* which the nation has enjoyed for much of the postwar era, Agnelli owns Fiat, the giant concern which makes 80 percent of Italy's autos. A dark, handsome man of fifty-one, he exudes for his countrymen the charisma John F. Kennedy had for Americans.

The family fortune was founded by his grandfather, also named Giovanni, a Piedmontese soldier who left the army in 1899 to start an auto factory with three partners, winding up eventually as the sole owner. His son entered the business but died in a plane crash when Giovanni, the grandson, was fourteen.

The current Giovanni—he calls himself Gianni, for short—served in Mussolini's army on the Russian front during World War II and after Italy's surrender joined a detachment that fought with the Americans that liberated Rome. After the war, he took up the life-style of the Riviera playboy, making the rounds with Ali Khan and Porfirio Rubirosa, the Dominican diplomat-swinger.

But this cavorting came suddenly to an end. Early one morning in 1952, while whizzing to Monte Carlo after an all-night party, Agnelli rammed his car into a truck. He spent three months in a hospital and came out with a permanently damaged right leg and a limp.

He settled down, married a Neapolitan beauty, Princess Marella Caraciolo-Castagneto, whose mother, like Gianni's, was an American. And he entered the family business.

As auto firms go, Fiat has an ancient history. It was launched four years before Henry Ford started making his own cars, on a shoestring capitalization of about $150,000. It struggled through a number of lean years and was kept alive by a timely loan from the house of Morgan. However, in the 1930's Fiat found a home, becoming a favorite of Mussolini's and supplying engines for the fighter planes and torpedo boats of Il Duce's war machine. For the civilian market, it built a hugely popular small car, dubbed the little mouse by Italians, which was a forerunner in concept of Germany's Volkswagen.

During World War II Allied bombings virtually demolished the Fiat factories. After the overthrow of Mussolini, the Communist-dominated auto workers' union forced Agnelli's resignation as active head of his business because of his role as Mussolini's armaments maker. However, Agnelli's second-in-command, Vittorio Valletta, was allowed to stay, and as caretaker he managed to salvage the business for Agnelli's heirs.

Valletta was a subtle, astute individual who had been a professor of finance noted for his liberal views and enjoying influential contacts in leftist circles, thanks to which he avoided being axed from Fiat along with his boss. For the next twenty years he served as head man, mollifying the unions while remaining staunchly loyal to the Agnelli family, using much the strategy Berthold Beitz, the number-two man at Krupp, adopted in guiding the fortunes of that erstwhile armaments maker through the perilous postwar period, zigging and zagging to avoid the reprisals of the postwar society.

Indeed, like Beitz, who made dramatic overtures to the Soviet Union and its satellites, Valletta arranged an agreement to build a multimillion-dollar auto factory for the Russians at Togliattigrad, a locality named after the leader of Italy's Communist Party, Palmiro Togliatti. According to business colleagues, Valletta displayed the subtlety of a Mazarin. He figured that if enough Russians had their own autos they would assume the psychology of property owners, not have-nots, and they would be less desirous of overthrowing the capitalist system in the West.

Valletta held onto the helm while Gianni, the founder's grandson, entered the business and learned the ropes; and in 1966, his mission completed, he retired in his seventies, turning over the post of chairman and chief executive officer to Gianni.

Agnelli had learned his lessons well. After an extensive study by a management consultant firm imported from the United States, Fiat's organizational structure was modernized. Its centralization of authority was deemphasized to allow for quicker action by delegating more power to its subsidiaries.

From 1966 through 1970, Agnelli increased Fiat's sales by over $1 billion (from $1.6 to $2.7 billion). A year after he took the helm, Fiat passed its arch-rival, Volkswagen, in the number of autos it produced.

With the aim of becoming global in scope, thereby providing a hedge against Italy's uncertain political and economic climate, Agnelli in 1968 reached across the border in a bid to take over one of France's major auto makers, Citroën. It was owned by the tire-making Michelins, who were looking for more effective management. President Charles de Gaulle, fearing a threat to France's economic sovereignty if Agnelli acquired direct control, raised objections. Accordingly Agnelli and the Michelins worked out an arrangement whereby a company was set up to control Citroën, 51 percent owned by the Michelins, 49 percent by Fiat. In this way, De Gaulle's sensibilities were soothed and Agnelli, who is a close friend of the Michelins', acquired a valuable subsidiary.

As in the United States, the auto industry is a key barometer of Italy's economic growth. (The Italians are fanatical car buyers.) And Fiat is a colossus. It is the world's third-largest auto maker, after GM and Ford, operating production or sales facilities in over 140 countries. As a financial analyst has observed, "Fiat is more than a company. It is a city state." It employs over 170,000 workers. Two-fifths of the over 1,000,000 residents of Turin are supported one way or another by Fiat wages. And these are high by European standards. Indeed, in the last three years they have climbed more than 50 percent and are the top wages offered anywhere in Europe but Sweden.

Agnelli's interests embrace more than autos. Istituto Finanziaro Industriale is the holding company for the family investments—Gianni has nine brothers and sisters—and it controls over $1 billion worth of the Italian economy. Besides Fiat, the Agnellis own Cinzano vermouth, *La Stampa,* one of Italy's leading newspapers whose editorial position is slightly left of center, and hold sizable interests in shipping, chemicals, cement and real-estate properties throughout the nation.

There are no limits to Italian snobbery. Although their personal fortune amounts to $500,000,000 or more, the Agnellis are looked down upon by the hidebound conservative aristocracy of Turin as mere parvenus—newly rich. After all, they have had their wealth for only sixty years.

This hasn't bothered Agnelli one whit. His manner of living is a mixture of the old and the new. His private life has all the splendor of a sixteenth-century Florentine potentate. But his business life is that of the modern industrialist-technocrat. "I'm afraid of losing time," he confesses. "I want to get everything done in a hurry."

He is restless, perpetually on the go. Frequently he'll stride from a business conference in Turin, hop his private helicopter and go off to the Alps for a couple of hours' run on skis before attending his next meeting. (Despite his damaged leg, which is in braces, he is an expert skier.) A speed addict, he drives a Ferrari that can do 160 miles an hour, and he has no hesitation about opening up the throttle, placing his game leg on a specially built prop. Once during a vacation on the Mediterranean, he went aloft in his helicopter and while circling the sea at a low level impulsively jumped out of the door, injured leg and all, for a swim, to the consternation of his pilot, who yelled, "I've lost Mr. Agnelli."

Agnelli has tabbed his younger brother Umberto to succeed him as top man at Fiat when he is ready to call it a day, but obviously this is still a long way off.

"Agnelli's sense of hurry is what makes him tick," a friend observes. He behaves as if the eleventh hour is striking not only for him but for Italy. Improvements in the economy have a long way to go, Agnelli realizes. He is dissatisfied with conditions in the south, where the government's attempts to raise the standard of living by encouraging the inflow of capital have, by and large, failed. He is dissatisfied with the physical deterioration of Rome and other cities; he believes that the government must greatly expand its programs for housing, education and medical care, reform the law code and meet the job demands of Italy's restless youth reasonably fast or the nation will turn either Communist or Fascist.

Currently Italy, like most of Western Europe, is going through the wringer of strikes, inflation, deterioration of the physical environment; and, with the flamboyancy and histrionic fervor that is so characteristically Italian, it is experiencing a series of political crises that have left it in a highly unsettled condition.

The nation's facilities have been overtaxed by the migration of rural workers into the already overcrowded cities. Venice is finding it increasingly hard to breathe, thanks to the industrial pollution that has settled over it. Rome, plagued by overpopulation, is mired in $2.5 billion worth of municipal debt. The slums are getting filthier and the housing shortage even more acute as the peasants from Sicily and other parts of the south trek into the northern urban centers seeking higher-paying jobs. The Italian postal and telephone services are even worse than those in the United States. Bankers in Rome complain they have to wait hours to get the closing stock price quotations from the Milan exchange.

Italy has been tortured by an epidemic of strikes. Blue-collar unrest is high even by today's standards elsewhere. With inflation pushing prices beyond the reach of many, labor unions are forcing wage settlements of 20 percent and over. Virtually every day there is a wildcat strike in some part of Italy.

The ground workers at the Milan Airport go on strike so frequently and unexpectedly that a traveler has to check daily before heading out to the airport to see whether the planes are running. When Coca-Cola, Inc., recently tried to liquidate its plant in Rome because it was losing money, the workers seized it and held it for days before allowing management to enter with its accountants to look over its books and conduct the sale.

One strike that proved immensely popular to just about everyone, however, took place when the personnel walked out of the nation's tax-collecting offices, postponing the mailing of assessment notices for several months.

An especially punishing labor dispute occurred in 1971 at Gianni Agnelli's Fiat facilities, which boast one of the most progressive workers' programs in the nation. The wages and fringe benefits are so generous by Italian standards that crowds of rural workers from the south have been pouring into Fiat seeking jobs, placing a heavy burden on the company's housing facilities. The southern workers, many of whom are Sicilian and characterized by a fierce clannishness and militancy, spearheaded a strike that cost Fiat over 15,000,000 man-hours of labor and 400,000 cars of lost production before it was settled.

The Italian political situation has become dangerously unstable. The coalition between the Christian Democrats and the Socialists, which has ruled Italy since the end of the war, broke up in 1970, and until December, 1971, Italy was governed by a minority caretaker administration, while the politicians strove to put together a majority coalition. Eventually, after much wrangling and delay, a new president was elected, but the problem of effective leadership remains and casts a pall over the economy.

Spurred by skyrocketing prices, there has been a growing drain on the currency as nervous Italians smuggle capital out of Italy. This reached epidemic proportions in 1969 when $2.5 billion worth of currency took flight. Much of it was carried or sent across the border into the Swiss canton of Ticino, whose chief city, Lugano, with a population of only 20,000 citizens, suddenly blossomed forth with thirty new banks, to become the nation's third-largest financial center after Zurich and Geneva.

Shaken by inflation, strikes and the deterioration in the political situation, Italians carried their money to Lugano in overnight sleeping trains from Rome, past lax customs officials who, while they went through luggage, didn't bother to search passengers personally. In some cases, a judicious tip to a porter smoothed the way. Other Italians motored from Milan across the border to Chiasso, twenty-five miles to the north, a Swiss town with a population of less than 10,000 which suddenly sprouted up with sixteen banks primed to convert jittery Italian money into solid Swiss francs.

The Italian government, alarmed by the flight of the lira, intervened in February, 1970, to stop the smuggling. The Bank of Italy announced that henceforth every lira note brought into the country from abroad and previously accepted by an Italian commercial bank now had to be processed directly by its own central office in Rome. Because this promised a huge work backlog and long delays, since the central bank didn't have the staff to cope speedily with the huge amount of notes expected to be presented, it cooled off the desire of Swiss bankers to accept smuggled lire for conversion into Swiss francs. They were reluctant to wait interminably to get paid by the Bank of Italy. This emergency measure slowed down the drain on the lira, to be sure, but the message was clear. The Italians have little trust in their currency and will abandon it again, by one device or another, if conditions don't improve.

Lay people are not the only ones who are worried about money. In the summer of 1971, when foreign holders of dollars, disturbed by inflation in the United States and the sliding value of Uncle Sam's scrip, began a run on Yankee greenbacks to turn them into gold, a major citadel of faith, the Vatican, displayed disbelief in America's folding money. It presented to the U.S. Treasury $2,000,000 it had been holding in its clerical coffers, demanding payment in gold. Previously there had been currency dealings between the pope's representatives and Uncle Sam, but on such occasions, the Vatican had sold gold to collect dollars. Now the Holy See apparently glimpsed the handwriting on the wall.

There is no indication that the Vatican is ready to convert the gold into lire any more than dollars. For the problems that afflict America have turned up in an even more acute form in Italy. The nation is passing through its most serious crisis since the fall of Mussolini. If it comes through safely without turning to a new dictator in jackboots, it will be because of industrial leaders like Gianni Agnelli, who are striving to demonstrate that capitalism, whatever its shortcomings, remains the best hope for the people and that soaring prices, strikes and political wrangling are better than the structured calm of slave labor camps.

Nubar Gulbenkian, Prince of Bohemia

The push by the world's most powerful nations to secure strategic natural resources in a fast-changing political and economic climate has been escalated by a recent development in the battle for oil. In the spring of 1971, the increasingly militant oil-producing nations of the Middle East and North Africa gave the Western world its comeuppance, sending tremors of anxiety into places as far away as Japan. Acting together as a bloc, and threatening the shutdown of supplies and the confiscation of properties, the native oil producers extracted from the foreign combines an unprecedented $15-billion increase in government taxes. Libya broke the traditional fifty-fifty profit-sharing relationship, raising the government's percentage to 55 percent of the take. And the only thing the oil companies received in return was a hope of five years of peace, the life of the agreement—that is, if the Arabs don't choose to interrupt it unilaterally with still other decrees, including the nationalization of their oil properties when they feel strong enough to do so. (Since the signing of the contract, the Soviet Union has moved onto the scene, arranging an agreement with Libya to help her process her oil resources, a development that doesn't bode good for the West.)

This ominous shift in power is worrisome for Britain, which depends on the Middle East for over 80 percent of her oil needs, and for the rest of Europe, as well as Japan. The global demand for oil over the next ten years alone will exceed the entire need for it since the first major field was discovered in Titus, Pennsylvania, over a century ago.

In recent years the Western nations have been speeding up their search for deposits in Alaska and the Canadian Arctic, launching operations in the North Sea, where rigs able to drill through more than 500 feet of ocean and withstand the pressure of 60-foot waves, are hunting for urgently needed reserves. In the meantime money is being pumped into the capital-hungry industry through, among other stratagems, tax-sheltered funds that attract wealthy investors. While for years there have been numerous small funds associated with independent wild-catters serving this function, only recently has a major oil company stepped into the picture. This is Continental Oil, which in conjunction with Morgan Stanley & Company has launched a fund to raise $75,000,000 through the sale of limited partnerships.

The recent victory of the Arab producers, which has accelerated the push to find other sources, contrasts sharply with the situation in former days when gunboat diplomacy was supreme, the British Navy really ruled the waves, and assorted sheikhs and pashas stepped smartly to attention, saluting the foreign oil companies when they demanded oil concessions from the barrel of a rifle.

One exceedingly wealthy oil family whose fortune was founded during the palmy days of oil exploration in the Middle East and which has kept the news headlines boiling during much of the twentieth century with its financial and social intrigues is the Gulbenkians, father and son. The elder Gulbenkian laid the groundwork for the family fortune in 1914 when he succeeded in negotiating one of the biggest petroleum deals in history, a contract between the Anglo-Persian Company and the Royal Dutch Shell Group, out of which Gulbenkian, as middle man, received a whopping 5-percent cut on royalties from every ounce of oil drilled in the Middle East.

Calouste Gulbenkian, an Armenian, was born at Scutari on the Bosporus. When Calouste was seven, his father handed him a Turkish 5-shilling note and told him to invest it in an old coin. When the kid came home with a wad of Turkish delight candy instead, the father gave him a tongue lashing. "If you're going to use your money this way, you'll end up in the gutter." Calouste never forgot this advice. He lived by it until his death some seventy-nine years and half a billion dollars later.

Gulbenkian sprang from a well-to-do banking family which had originally made its money as merchants in the old Turkish Empire. It had influential contacts with the monarchy, and Calouste as a young man joined the council of ministers of the government. Here he received invaluable training in the art, literally, of keeping his head. Every business transaction was sealed with a bribe, or baksheesh, as it was called. The credo was "The hand you dare not bite, kiss." The test was merciless. Calouste and his associates periodically dined with the royal family, who paid them the supreme compliment of handing them food from the royal plate. It was an insult not to eat the plate clean. And for good reason. This was a device used by the sultan, called by his enemies Abdul the Damned, to protect himself from being poisoned. It was an easy matter to slip a fatal dose into a highly spiced Turkish dish. Government intelligence agents watched to see whether the food was eaten as a test of a subject's loyalty.

Calouste got into the oil business as a result of a fortuitous situation. At the beginning of the twentieth century Great Britain and Germany in their struggle for political hegemony vigorously sought new sources of oil, the key fuel for their military machines. The German government received reports from its mineralogists that valuable findings were waiting to be tapped in Turkey. The kaiser, acting deviously, decided to build a railroad from Berlin to Baghdad and, through a rail subsidiary controlled by the Deutsche Bank, sign up not only the rights of way for the railroad but concessions to the mineral rights of territory twenty kilometers along both sides of the tracks.

But the Turkish government, getting wind of Germany's intentions and eager to commandeer whatever oil might be found for the sultan, decided to undertake its own investigations. It couldn't trust a foreigner to do the job, so it turned to one of its own subjects, Gulbenkian, who had recently made a tour of the Russian oil industry and written a series of highly publicized articles on his observations. Gulbenkian carried out the sultan's assignment and prepared a report affirming the possibility of oil being present in Mesopotamia. As a result, the Turkish government refused to grant the Germans mineral concessions.

Henceforth, Gulbenkian became deeply involved as a broker in the maneuverings of the European powers to capture concessions. He functioned as an indispensable middleman in deals all over the world. He was an individual of considerable influence and of mystery, possessing no assets of his own but his brains and, some insiders hinted, the power to disclose embarrassing secrets that, if leaked to the press, would compromise governments and highly placed individuals. This gave him tremendous leverage.

Gulbenkian's biggest coup came just before the outbreak of World War I. The international situation was deteriorating rapidly, as Germany and Britain appeared headed on a course toward armed conflict. Winston Churchill, who had been appointed First Lord of the Admiralty in 1911, was locked with his political opponents in a stiff debate on how best to equip the British fleet. Churchill argued for building a squadron of battleships speedier than anything the Germans could muster by equipping them with not traditional coal power but the new "wonder" energy, oil. However, an influential block of politicians felt that from the standpoint of national security it was a lot safer to rely on coal, which Britain mined in her own backyard, than on oil, which she would have to get from foreign suppliers.

Churchill was also worried about Britain's dependency on foreign oil, and he decided on the strategy of organizing a British company to acquire oil concessions in regions where British influence was strong. At his direction, the Anglo-Persian Company was formed under the control of the British government, which became a part owner. The company immediately launched a campaign to obtain concessions from the Turkish government. Other powers were also vying for these concessions, and the Turks had a delightful time playing off the rival suitors against each other.

Calouste Gulbenkian stepped in to mediate an agreement between the contesting groups and take a healthy cut as middleman. Complex negotiations were held during which the bargainers agreed to set up a consortium representing British interests and a rival Royal Dutch Group to work the major oil fields of the Middle East. The consortium decided that Gulbenkian, as his fee for hammering out the arrangement, should receive a shilling-a-ton royalty for all the oil drilled by the company. But Gulbenkian, the wariest of men, objected. He didn't want to be paid in British shillings, he said, because they were no guarantee against a depreciation of the British pound that could be caused by an outbreak of inflation. The issue was debated back and forth, and finally Gulbenkian suggested he would have to be paid directly in the oil itself, the value of which he could convert in any manner he chose.

The upshot was that Gulbenkian received 2½ percent from the British interests, another 2½ percent from the Royal Dutch Group—5 percent in *toto* of the royalties on all the oil to be dug out of the Middle East—for the remainder of his life. This deal, which won for the elder Gulbenkian the sobriquet of Mr. Five Percent, turned out to be one of the most profitable investments of all time.

In 1965 Nubar, pressed by reporters as to just how much money the Gulbenkians had drawn from their investment, disclosed that for the past ten years alone they had been receiving between 5,000,000 and 6,000,000 pounds a year.

The elder Gulbenkian was a highly eccentric fellow. His early experiences amidst the intrigues of the Turkish court left deep scars. At the zenith of his wealth he built a lavish $50,000,000 residence in Paris behind a 30-foot barricade, supported by a team of watchdogs, a network of burglar alarms and a force of security guards.

He trusted no one, not even his family. The house was a beehive of intelligence agents who spied on his wife and children and reported to him what each was doing when he was away. A tyrant in the grand Oriental manner, he ordered rare gourmet dishes for himself, letting his family and other guests sit with their mouths watering while he dined.

Sometimes, however, his son participated in these gastronomical delights. The junior Gulbenkian recalls how when he was a boy his father's friend Cesar Ritz, the hotel magnate whom Gulbenkian had helped get started in business, used to boast that the Ritz would serve any food asked for no matter how difficult it was to procure. Once a wealthy, exacting American asked the chef d'hôte for a helping of elephant's feet. Undaunted, Ritz requisitioned an elephant from the Jardin des Plantes, had its four feet roasted and served up in the most piquant sauce. A portion of the repast was reserved for Gulbenkian's table. Nubar remembers how he was given a mouthful. "It tasted like something between sponge and flannelette."

The elder Gulbenkian lived like a caliph in a wondrous *Arabian Nights'* tale until the ripe age of eighty-six. He resisted the notion of death, virtually to the end, insisting he would live to be one hundred and six, which was the age at which one of his grandfathers died. For years he refused to draw up a will and arrange for the disbursement of his gargantuan fortune. There were many anxieties, not the least of which was the possibility that some claimant heir could bob up as a result of his numerous left-handed dalliances, and his lawyers kept asking the old man whether to his knowledge any such descendants lurked in the wings. Happily none made an appearance. In his final years, to avoid high death duties Gulbenkian retired to Portugal, where taxes were suitably low, and here he died.

The senior Gulbenkian's end was an anticlimax. Not expecting to go anywhere after his earthly journey, despite his $500,000,000 travel ticket, he had given instructions to be cremated. However, Portugal is a Catholic country and there are no crematoriums available. Moreover, Gulbenkian had heard how a retired Indian maharajah had been put to the flame in Portugal, but the oven did not work properly and the result was a horrible fiasco.

So at Gulbenkian's request his body was flown to Zurich, where it was as easy to find a good fire as a good banker. Unfortunately, it was an extremely hot day, the body had to wait an unseemly time at the airport due to the delay in getting a plane, and Mr. Five Percent almost decomposed prematurely.

Nubar carried on his father's tradition of opulence. Unscarred by the Byzantine intrigues of the Turkish court, raised in London and thoroughly Westernized, he was less neurotic and more frankly uninhibited than his father had ever been. Indeed, he was the very paradigm of the hedonist. He kept a retinue of courtiers and hangers-on, who followed him for the show he put on and for the pennies he flung to the cleverer of the court jesters. Once Nubar was asked what his number-one hobby was outside of women, wine and food. *"Pantaraxia,"* he replied. (Nubar had the Greek of a gentleman as well as the appetite of a pasha.) This meant "keeping people on their toes."

Nubar was to the world of sexuality what Heifetz is to the violin. His father once told him that, upon the recommendation of his physician, to keep in shape, he took a seventeen-year-old mistress and changed her every year for a new one until he reached the age of eighty. The Middle Easterner has a talent for this sort of thing. Gulbenkian was following the tradition of the Arabian harems, where several girls just emerging from puberty were always kept handy to rejuvenate the powers of an aging pasha.

The younger Gulbenkian carried on his father's credo with filial zeal. When he was a student at Oxford, a classmate observed, "Nubar is so tough that every day he tires out three stockholders, three horses and three women."

Nubar was not only well heeled and well tailored but well educated. He went to Harrow, received honors in French, entered Kings College in Cambridge, graduated with a first-class degree in civil engineering when he was only nineteen, received two honor degrees at Trinity College, entered his father's oil business and proved to be as sharp and clever as his progenitor in the world of money.

Portly, with the appearance of an opulent Falstaff, a sort of upper-class crony of Prince Hal, and as he entered his fifties, appearing more and more like a stand-in for King Edward VII, no mean *bon vivant* himself, Nubar wore a monocle, sported a lavish, lovingly husbanded aristocratic beard, rinsed in blue toilet water, tweezed his eyebrows and carried a fresh orchid in his lapel every day.

Charlesworth and Company, the florist, made a career of supplying Gulbenkian with these orchids. Packed with their stems wrapped in plastic bags, lined with damp moss to keep them fresh, they were sent to Gulbenkian in Istanbul, the Mediterranean, Moscow, the Riviera—wherever he happened to be at play. And in its finest hour, Charlesworth outdid itself by breeding, to Gulbenkian's specifications, two unique species of orchids of yellow and dark-blue hues.

The dark-blue flower became a favorite of Gulbenkian's and

attracted much comment in the press. Once asked by a reporter how it was bred, Nubar, a man of rare humor, replied without batting an eye that there was only one place on earth where blue orchids can be grown and that is an acre of land fifty miles from the holy city of Lhasa atop the Northern Himalayas. The bloom must be transported in a caravan of yaks (yaks only), since the effluvium of these animals exudes a special chemical that coupled with the scarcity of pure oxygen at that dizzy altitude keeps the orchids in their pristine shade of dark blue until they reach the lowlands of India, from whence they are whisked onto a plane and flown directly to the Gulbenkian home in London. The news writer swallowed the story and reported it as a "scoop."

"Born," like Scaramouch, "with the gift of laughter and a sense that the world is mad," Gulbenkian upstaged with his bacchanalia all the pain, sorrow and suffering that is the lot of common humanity. He married three times, in between his endless liaisons. His first wife was a Spanish beauty, the daughter of a businessman; his second was an ex-musical stage star; his third marriage, which lasted the longest, fourteen years, was to the heiress of a French champagne fortune. During his third alliance, he reminisced philosophically about his earlier consorts. "I've had good wives, as wives go." And he added with a twinkle, "As wives go, two of them went."

Gulbenkian loved Rolls-Royces as passionately as women. He owned one valuable model that he lent to King George V for use in a state ceremony. He lent another to King Edward VII during a naval review, and a third to Queen Elizabeth for her tour in Nigeria.

While the senior Gulbenkian lived, there was acrimonious quarreling between father and son. Indeed, the hostility and competitiveness between them would have made a fertile textbook for psychoanalysts. The two Gulbenkians belonged to different generations and had been raised in different backgrounds. Their conflict was an earlier manifestation of today's massive generation gap between sires and their offspring. Recalling his father, Nubar said in later years, "He could not bear waste. Where we disagreed was on what one could define as extravagance. He chose to invest in art. I preferred to invest in life. I have only one."

The simmering feud finally erupted over a remarkably trivial incident when Nubar was forty-four and his father was seventy-one. The son shared offices with the older man, and one day, overloaded with work, Nubar decided he didn't have time to go out to lunch, and he ordered in a meal consisting of chicken in tarragon jelly and asparagus tips, which came to $2.22 and which Gulbenkian billed to the firm.

Several weeks later the senior Gulbenkian, who would stoop to pick up a penny in the gutter, noticed this entry of $2.22, and he flew into a rage at such "extravagance." He summoned Nubar and tongue-lashed him for having the gall to charge his lunch to the business instead of paying for it out of his own pocket. Nubar, explaining he had taken his meal at his desk to be able to do more work for the firm, heatedly upbraided his father and strode from the room.

This was the most extravagant $2.22 old Calouste ever tried to collect. Humiliated and outraged by years of paternal despotism, Nubar really let the old man have it. He filed a $10,000,000 suit against Gulbenkian senior, charging that his sire had prevented him from achieving financial independence by withholding from him money that was due him for his contributions to the business.

Old Calouste, during a career of sixty years in the business, had amassed thousands upon thousands of documents relating to his complex business maneuverings. Nubar, like the Mikado in Gilbert and Sullivan, now conceived of a punishment that most exquisitely fitted the crime. He persuaded the judge to issue a subpoena forcing his father to bring every single one of his documents—all 987,000 of them—into court for legal inspection. Collecting and trucking this mountain of records turned into a nightmarish operation.

For three days the legal battle raged in the courtroom, making sizzling headlines as one tidbit after another was disclosed about the Gulbenkians' business dealings. Then suddenly the son withdrew his suit. He had made his point. His father agreed to a financial settlement, and he paid in addition the court costs and lawyers' fees which amounted to over $80,000. This was a pretty expensive hassle over a chicken lunch. But the older Gulbenkian for once in his life did not begrudge a penny of the cost. He was a man who reveled in wily tactics.

When Nubar subpoenaed close to 1,000,000 documents, Calouste had turned to his legal advisers with pride in his eye. "Isn't my son clever to have thought of this idea? He's a chip off the old block."

Nubar Gulbenkian was a witty man who had an elephantine ego. He not only welcomed notoriety and drummed up an audience for his posturings in this life, but he insisted on knowing what reviews his performance would get after he faded into the wings. The London *Times*, like other important newspapers, prepares obituary articles on celebrities sometimes years before their death and files them away for last-minute updating at the arrival of the Grim Reaper. Gulbenkian knew that the *Times* had written his obituary, and he was bursting with curiosity to know whether the editors had drafted a good or a bad notice. For years he pestered them to let him see it, insisting he wished to correct any factual errors cropping into the text. The editors retorted that his request was unheard of, and they were perfectly willing to take the risk of errors. Gulbenkian tried to soften up the editor in chief, Sir William Haley, and got nowhere.

Happening to meet the chairman of the *Times*, Gavin Astor, at a business luncheon, in a burst of mellow camaraderie over a glass of wine, Gulbenkian once more pleaded to be allowed to see his obituary. "It's against our principles," Astor told him, "but give Haley a good lunch and see if you can get any change out of him." Gulbenkian replied he had already invited Haley not only to a sumptuous lunch but to an elegant dinner and had failed to budge him one inch. Astor responded by asking Gulbenkian to be his dinner guest at the *Times* offices, and he provided a repast to delight the most fastidious gourmet—filet steaks, fried sole, a white wine and vintage claret, a rare cheese, a vintage brandy, topped off with Havana cigars. But that's all Gulbenkian got.

In January, 1972, the press notice was finally released. Gulbenkian died of a heart attack at the age of seventy-five on the French Riviera. He had received his first heart seizure three years before and had been confined to a wheelchair ever since. He passed on without ever finding out what the editors thought about his performance as a *bon vivant* who had an incomparable flair for self-dramatization in surroundings of physical splendor more extravagant than those ever dreamed up in the theater by the fertile imagination of Max Reinhardt.

With the passing of Nubar Gulbenkian the galaxy of oil multimillionaires has become noticeably less sparkling. True, J. Paul Getty and H. L. Hunt are still around in their eighties to make a headline or two. But Gulbenkian was one of the last of what Lucius Beebe, the chronicler of high society, called the really big spenders, who lived in the spirit of the Renaissance, with the zest of Frans Hals' *Laughing Cavalier*, and who flung money about as if it were meant to be thrown from the platform of speeding trains.

17

The Rockefellers and the Fords: How to Succeed in Business by Really Trying

The Rockefellers

No family is more committed to hedging against paper money and the hazards of an invidious inflation than the Rockenfellers of Sagendorf, Germany, more popularly known as the Rockefellers. Hand in hand with their forays into the philanthropic service of humanity, they have nursed their private interests with tender loving care.

At the end of World War II, foreseeing that in a period of mounting inflation the purchasing power of the family billions would not be adequately protected in conventional investments, the Rockefellers plunged their money into a number of bold ventures which, in addition to enriching themselves, helped thrust America into the forefront of space technology. Laurance Rockefeller, who had been handling the family investments through the Rockefeller Brothers Fund, astutely foresaw the need for automation in the stock market, and he put money into Scantlin Electronics, a small engineering firm which was experimenting with a device for flashing stock prices coming off the Big Board ticker tape onto television desk screens for brokers, bankers and fund managers. The idea caught on, and today automation promises to revolutionize the structure of stock trading.

Convinced that industrial utilities in their hunger for new sources of energy would seize upon nuclear fuel as a substitute for coal and oil to generate electricity, the Rockefellers financed a struggling young firm to explore uranium deposits. Subsequently it merged into another company, and the new combine, United Nuclear Corporation, thanks to its holdings of invaluable uranium deposits, is in a strategic position to become a key global supplier of utilities. The potential for atomic power generation is immense in terms of economics and efficiency, and as time passes the Rockefeller judgment is looking better and better.

Discussing the family's uncanny instinct for backing winners, Laurance Rockefeller explained, "We invest in a company before it's ready for the underwriters. Sometimes it's only an idea for a business among some technical men. This increases our risk and also the opportunity for profit."

Following this strategy, the Rockefellers financed Eddie Rickenbacker in his launching of Eastern Air Lines and reaped a harvest when the airline became a big money-maker. Similarly Laurance Rockefeller came across Jim McDonnell when he was running a small mechanics shop toying with the revolutionary new concept of applying jet propulsion as navigating power for airplanes. With Rockefeller money, McDonnell went into jet plane production and expanded his research to make a major contribution to the designing of the first capsule putting Americans into space. In the meantime, the Rockefellers sold their investment consisting of 20 percent of the common stock of McDonnell Aircraft for a handsome profit.

Laurance Rockefeller has financed other businesses when they were a gleam in the founder's eye. He took Reaction Motors under his wing when it was experimenting with liquefied rockets and badly needed cash to survive. Reaction Motors went on to develop the rocket-powered engines for the Bell XSI airplane, which was the world's first craft to reach supersonic speeds. Rockefeller backed Itek in its development of information handling and data retrieval systems, and it became one of the stellar contributors to the communications revolution.

In addition to investing in high technology, the Rockefellers have fallen back on a classic hedge against the declining worth of the dollar—real estate. With land values, apartments and commercial buildings nearly tripling in many parts of the nation since World War II, the Rockefellers are utilizing a new investment medium especially suited to today's economy—the mortgage investment trust.

Chase Manhattan, the family-controlled bank, has launched a trust which is a resourceful exploiter of tight-money conditions. When the pressure is on banks to reduce loans during a money squeeze, the first to feel the pinch is the building industry. With banks moving out, the way is opened for the mortgage trusts to move in and offer construction and development loans at highly profitable interests rates.

The trusts are organized as tax shelter operations. Unincorporated and managed by trustees representing transferrable shares of beneficial interest if they distribute at least 90 percent of their net income to shareholders, they are exempt for this amount from paying corporate income taxes, so their earnings are doubled.

The Rockefellers formed their mortgage trust with a $100,000,000 public stock offering through Chase, its affiliate. Chase not only receives a generous fee for managing the trust and originating loan business for it, but the Rockefellers have gotten into a field with intriguing potential, since the nation urgently needs housing and the real-estate industry requires more efficient and larger-scale financing.

The Rockefeller interests are not confined to the United States but are global in scope. Their international role has engendered controversy and stirred up criticism. It has become highly fashionable for crusading journalists to take pot shots at the family. Some imply it is a moot question whether Rockefeller investments follow the American flag or whether the flag follows them.

For example, it is charged by some polemicists that Chase Manhattan, through a branch bank in Saigon, has lent heavy sums of money to South Vietnamese businessmen and has a financial stake in the survival of a non-Communist government there. Moreover, they insist that other Rockefeller investments around the world depend upon an aggressive American posture. Sponsors of the devil theory place significance in the circumstance that a number of highly placed officials carrying out U. S. foreign policy have been associated with the Rockefellers. John Foster Dulles, the chief architect of the U. S. policy of cold war confrontation with the Communist world, was, before becoming Eisenhower's Secretary of State, a former executive head of the Rockefeller Foundation. Allen Dulles, his brother and head of the CIA during much of the cold war period, had previously been associated with the law firm of Sullivan and Cromwell, legal representatives of the Rockefeller brothers. Dean Rusk, the hawkish Secretary of State under President Johnson, had formerly been a head of the Rockefeller Foundation, and so on.

That the Rockefellers swing a lot of weight is obvious. Yet despite the ratiocination of the demonologists, the Rockefeller power has obvious limits. Family influence was unable to put brother Nelson in the White House in two tries for the Presidency, although multimillionaire Joe Kennedy was able to turn the trick for his kin.

The Rockefeller brothers, point out sympathetic biographers, were raised on the philosophy espoused by their mother, Abby, that the family fortune is a gift from the Almighty and they are duty bound to improve the social lot of their fellow men. Certainly the fourth generation is displaying lively enthusiasm for this credo. Michael Rockefeller, Nelson's son, spent the adult years of his short life as an archeologist exploring the tribal artifacts of Pacific Islanders until he died in New Guinea at the age of twenty-three, reportedly at the hands of cannibals. Laurance Rockefeller, Jr., upon graduating college joined Vista to work with the blacks in East Harlem. Steven Rockefeller, another of Nelson's sons, has been a minister in Chicago.

Other young Rockefellers have broken from the mold of the rich, young do-nothing. John D. Rockefeller IV, who is in his early thirties, has entered politics and gotten elected secretary of state for West Virginia. A tall, friendly man with ample charisma and a wife who is a daughter of Senator Charles Percy of Illinois, John, in the view of political observers, is the family's most promising hope for capturing the Presidency someday.

Another young Rockefeller staking out a distinctive career is Rodman, Nelson's oldest boy, who is an economist and head of the International Basic Economy Corporation, a family-operated philanthropic organization. Dr. Lucy Hamlin, Laurance's daughter, is a physician who interned at Manhattan Harlem Hospital and has specialized in psychotherapy. Abby O'Neill, John D., Jr.'s granddaughter, is a expert in Colonial

American history. And Mary Strawbridge, Nelson's daughter, is a specialist in primitive art.

The Rockefeller family—it originated in Germany in the seventeenth century—has been extremely sensitive about the controversial reputation of John D., Sr., the founder of its fortune. The most fiercely attacked capitalist at the turn of the century, John D.'s memory continues to keep the family on the defensive. "I never studied American history," confides Dr. Lucy Hamlin. "I didn't want to sit in a class and risk hearing my great-grandfather described as a robber baron." And Nelson, the governor of New York, in an economics honors thesis he wrote during his days at Dartmouth stoutly defended his grandfather's memory. Rebutting historians who have charged that Rockefeller practiced illegal rebates with railroad shippers to monopolize the industry, young Nelson insisted, "Those competitors who did not wish to join him could go on just as before. They were not forced to sell out under threats of being crushed nor were any of them coerced into selling. As Mr. Rockefeller himself says, 'We left them to the mercy of time.' "

There is little question that John D. was an aggressive fellow who drove a hard bargain—or, equally, that in the later stages of his life he gave away millions for medical, scientific and educational purposes. While tax considerations obviously played a role in the setting up of the Rockefeller Foundation, it had been planned a decade before the advent of federal income and corporate taxes, so that the project was more than merely a tax shelter mechanism.

John D., Sr., is not the only controversial member of the tribe. The Rockefellers have had a healthy share of eccentrics whose behavior raised the eyebrows of their contemporaries. There was, for instance, Edith Rockefeller, the second-oldest daughter of John D., Sr., who in 1895 married Harold Fowler McCormick, son of the inventor of the cotton reaper.

Mrs. McCormick believed in reincarnation. Upon all within earshot she fixed her gaze like the Ancient Mariner's and vowed that she had lived a previous life in ancient Egypt as the teenage wife of the pharaoh Tutankhamen. In a day when women's liberation was only a gleam in the eyes of suffragettes, Edith Rockefeller, according to the historian Cleveland Amory, studied psychoanalysis as a pupil of Carl Jung in Switzerland and treated close to 100 patients on her own, not for the fees—she was already one of America's richest dowagers—but for the satisfaction and sheer fascination of it.

Her marriage was an unhappy one. After twenty years of spousehood, her husband became infatuated with a Polish singer many years younger, and he divorced Edith to marry her. Before doing so, he took the precaution of secretly entering a hospital and having an eminent surgeon, Dr. Lespinasse, transplant the glands of a younger man in him. The glands had belonged to a virile blacksmith, and a jaunty stanza was passed around the salons of the *haute mondaine:*

> Under the spreading chestnut tree,
> The village smithy stands;
> The smith a gloomy man is he,
> McCormick has his glands.

Edith Rockefeller lived into the 1930's and died under somber conditions. Due to ill-advised investments, she suffered severe losses in the 1929 stock market crash and the subsequent Depression. Her family moved in to assume her debts. She died of a painful illness, the nature of which was never publicly disclosed, after reportedly trying to cure herself by psychoanalysis.

Several of Edith's descendants kept the gossip columnists busy. Fowler, her son, married a divorcee who before entering the hallowed clan had been the lover of an Indian guide in the Canadian Rockies. Mrs. McCormick's youngest daughter, Mathilde, ran off as a teen-ager with a Swiss riding master pushing forty. Another daughter, Muriel, a girl given to fantasies, insisted on going through a wedding ceremony with the ghost of a young army officer killed years before in World War I.

The Rockefellers, like other baronial families, have secured for themselves a healthy share of God's little acres. They own 3,500 of them in the Pontico Hills above the Hudson—a landholding seven times larger than Central Park in Manhattan. John D., Sr., began building his Babylonian residence in his middle fifties. To beautify the grounds, hundreds of trees were uprooted from all over the world—willows from England, larch from the Scottish highlands, orange trees from France; their

roots wrapped in balls of earth and transplanted to the Rockefeller fief. Magnificent Japanese gardens were re-created with
rivulets that cascaded into tiers of falls, and an island was placed
like a jewel in a sparkling artificial pond below an exquisitely
designed Japanese teahouse.

One thing that has outlived the muckraking, the controversy,
and continues to speak out loud and clear is, of course, the
Rockefeller money. The family has borne its fortune like the
Golden Fleece through the treacherous tides of inheritance, income and real-estate taxes. As to its present size, experts who
have studied the matter believe that by 1911, when the
Standard Oil Trust was dismantled by government order, John
D., Sr., had accumulated about $800,000,000 for his endeavors.
During World War I, when income taxes were first imposed
and the statistics opened to outside scrutiny, the evidence is
that old John had become the nation's first bona fide billionaire. By the 1920's the fortune had grown to an estimated $2.5
billion. Yet when John D. died in 1937, just before his ninety-
eighth birthday, he left a taxable estate that amounted to a pid-
dling $25,000,000. All the rest had been distributed to his de-
scendants.

John D., Jr., to whom the bulk of the money was transmitted, had to work hard for his first million. His father
kept him for years on a relative pittance. In 1913 the son began
to collect Chinese porcelain as a hobby. Two years later he had
a golden chance to buy a celebrated collection put together by
J. P. Morgan III, who asked $1,000,000 for it. Young Rockefeller
couldn't scratch up the cash. He pleaded with his father to give
him the money and was turned down. Rockefeller, Jr., persisted, writing the old man, "I've never squandered money on
horses, yachts, automobiles or other foolish extravagances. The
fondness for these porcelains is my only hobby—the only thing
in which I care to spend money." John shrewdly pointed out it
was not only a hobby but an excellent investment; for if he sold
the collection in the future, he would obtain a substantially appreciated price for it. That did the trick. Once the porcelain
deal was presented to John, Sr., like an investment in oil, he
handed over the money.

In another eight years young John could have spent
$1,000,000 of his own as pin money. By then his father had

transferred the bulk of his wealth to him. In 1923 Rockefeller, Jr., paid the highest income tax by an American—over $7,000,000. By the time of his death, he had sluiced the bulk of his fortune into tax-exempt channels. Most of it went into trust funds set up for his heirs. Of the $150,000,000 that remained, half went to the Rockefeller Foundation; the rest went to his widow. Since World War II, the fortune has appreciated considerably. Fueled by the postwar economic boom and the roaring bull stock market, experts figure it has virtually doubled from $2.5 to around $4 billion.

However, the claimants to the family till have also been multiplying rapidly. John D., Sr., had a son and daughter. These brought six Rockefellers into the world. Their offspring consist of twenty-three cousins, in their twenties and thirties, a number of whom are married and have children of their own. But it is the current heads of the tribe, the third-generation Rockefeller brothers, who are bearing the brunt of the battle to multiply the family wealth.

The most controversial of the brothers, after perhaps Nelson, the politician, is David, chairman of Chase Manhattan, the family-controlled bank. A soft-spoken, moon-faced man in his late fifties, David has been both vigorously criticized and lauded for his banking policies.

There was the occasion, for instance, when Representative Wright Patman, chairman of the House Banking Committee, summoned Chase to ask it about what seemed uninhibited financing it provided corporate operators in their overly generous campaigns to put together conglomerate empires.

Chase has also been involved in an odd little episode in the Bahamas, that sunny archipelago of islands that served as a seventeenth-century haven for pirates and smugglers. The islands' chief modern industries are tourism and casino gambling, and one of the leading beneficiaries is Resorts International, Inc., which runs a $15,000,000, 500-room hotel on Paradise Island, across the bay from Nassau. One of the officials had a brother who reportedly was involved in underworld gambling.

In 1969, catching the infectious fever of the conglomerate builder, Resorts International launched a dramatic attempt to expand into a new area. For some months it had been eyeing Pan American World Airways with the possibility of acquiring it. The idea had a plausible logic. The airline was bulging with rich assets; it carried the tourists who swarmed into the Bahama casinos. What could be more natural than to marry the airline operations to the roulette wheel?

Nevertheless, when Resorts International surfaced for this try at a take-over, the financial world was shocked. The figures underscored its audacity. In 1967 Resorts International had a mere $518,000 worth of profits on $19,000,000 of revenues. Pan Am had earnings of $60,000,000, on sales of close to $1 billion. Wrote a leading financial paper, "The idea that a midget like Resorts International has dreams of taking over one of the world's largest stockholder-airlines seems ludicrous."

But the notion wasn't as preposterous as it seemed to outsiders. For Resorts International, thanks to two key deals it had put together, was on the verge of getting its hands on 3,300,000 shares of Pan Am stock, which would turn it into the biggest single stockholder of the airline, with 9.7 percent. Armed with this block, it could make a tender offer to Pan Am shareholders that had an excellent chance of being accepted.

The manner in which Resorts acquired this position in Pan Am was intriguing—if one accepts the version told by Charles Bluhdorn, the Austrian-born magnate who built Gulf & Western into a billion-dollar conglomerate. According to Bluhdorn, in December, 1969, he was vacationing in the Bahamas when he mentioned to his friend Crosby, the Resorts president, that Gulf & Western had bought 1,800,000 shares of Pan Am, comprising 5 percent of the total shares outstanding. Immediately Crosby came up with an "irresistible" offer—to purchase 900,000 shares Bluhdorn owned with an option for the rest.

Shortly thereafter, Resorts learned from a Beverly Hills broker that the Chase Manhattan Bank of New York owned another 1,500,000 shares of Pan Am stock, worth $40,000,000, that it might be willing to sell. This stock came from a series of workers' pension funds which had been entrusted to Chase for investment purposes.

Crosby contacted the Chase officials in charge of investing these funds and invited them to fly down to Paradise Island to look over his operations. The Chase boys came and, after sufficiently soaking in the Bahama sunshine, agreed to sell the casino operator their Pan Am stock. Oddly, Chase didn't bother to demand cash from Resorts. It was content to accept a complex package of financing which largely amounted to IOU's. As a result, Resorts International stood to come up with 3,300,000 shares—9.7-percent ownership—of Pan Am, for a layout of $16,000,000 in cash and notes.

When Chase accepted the deal to help the casino operator snatch Pan American, even the Crosby-Bluhdorn crowd was flabbergasted. A friend of Bluhdorn remarked to a financial writer: "Who would believe that David Rockefeller would permit his trust department to sell Pan Am stock to this little company? . . . I tell you, people were so amazed."

Chase's role in the transaction was also embarrassing to the bank's stockholders. At the annual meeting which took place shortly afterward, one shareholder asked Chase management, "Are we going into partnership with a gambling casino, with charter flights for stockholders?" At this point, according to the minutes, David Rockefeller referred the stockholders to statements he had made earlier that the deal had been okayed by the bank's investment committee which believed the terms were very attractive.

Other sources weren't as pleased. The idea of a shoestring outsider trying to take over one of the nation's major airlines threw Washington into an uproar. Legislation was introduced into Congress to give the Civil Aeronautics Board power to block any nonairline concern from grabbing more than 5 percent of the stock of an airline or an amount sufficient to support a take-over. When news of the Pan Am deal was made public, trading was halted on the Amex in Resorts International stock.

The SEC launched an investigation. It was curious to know, among other things, why Chase so accommodatingly agreed to sell its pension trust stock not for cash but for terms that amounted to a loan, including debtor's warrants. Resorts International, for its part, bowed to a consent judgment on the SEC complaint. In the wake of the hullaballoo from Washington, it announced it was cutting its Pan Am purchase to half—4.8 percent—of the projected total, and it publicly disavowed any intention of trying to take over the airline. Moreover, to remove all suspicion of corruption associated with its operations, the firm removed one casino official whose brother was reported to be involved with the Mafia. A Washington law firm, consisting of former crime busters in the Justice Department, was hired to set up a security system that would block infiltration into the casino by the underworld. A company spokesman later boasted that "aside from the Atomic Energy Commission, Resorts International is perhaps the world's most security conscious organization."

It may very well be that David Rockefeller was not personally involved in the decision to help Resorts International buy Pan Am and was highly irritated by the judgment of some Chase officials when it was brought to his attention, even though the deal could, under certain circumstances, have resulted in a handsome appreciation for the pension funds of its clients.

While Chase, along with other banks, has undoubtedly made misjudgments, David Rockefeller is displaying strong financial leadership in one area of vital importance. This is his aggressive espousal of the one-bank holding company concept. While it obviously means more profits for Chase, there is more to it than merely self-interest. America is suffering from a severe drought of liquidity, and matters are going to get worse in Rockefeller's opinion. By the end of the century the U.S. population may be over the 300,000,000 level, and an explosive demand for goods and services will necessitate greatly expanded sources of financing. In the meantime, American industry, faced with increasing competition from abroad, is going to have to modernize its facilities or lose the race for global markets. The continued burgeoning of technology will result in a rising demand not only for research but for the financing of an array of increasingly sophisticated and costly working tools. The need for mass housing will necessitate larger-scale financing than can be provided through conventional mortgage banking outlets.

In short, the nation is going to need virtually a quantum expansion of capital liquidity. And yet the outlook for this has been bleak. The chief reason, argues Rockefeller, is that the banking industry, which is the nation's major provider of capital, has not been allowed to grow with the rest of the economy but has been kept in a straitjacket of government regulations designed to promote safety for depositors, but carried to a self-defeating degree. There are fewer banks today than in the 1930's, although the GNP is up exponentially.

In appearances before Congress as well as in speeches and articles in the press, Rockefeller has been an articulate spokesman for a solution—namely, for Congress to pass legislation permitting banks to reorganize themselves into holding companies with the authority to diversify into a wide spectrum of financial activities, subject only to the requirement that such activities will not present a danger to their depositors.

Rockefeller argued that banks, which largely serve local or regional areas, be permitted to affiliate with mortgage-lending companies, national in scope, to provide funds for housing and other real estate on a coast-to-coast basis. He advocated that banks also be allowed to enter equipment-leasing activities. Under the present shortage of capital, many businesses prefer to rent their equipment rather than buy it. Rockefeller pointed out that the need for commercial aircraft, computer equipment, software services and other electronic paraphernalia to keep the communications revolution going will require much vaster sums than are presently available through ordinary leasing firms.

The efforts of Rockefeller and other advocates have borne fruit. Congress has passed legislation permitting the formation of one-bank holding companies, and Rockefeller has reorganized Chase into the new-type vehicle.

In short, the Rockefeller clan promises to be around a long time providing funds and entrepreneurial know-how as long as the nation values initiative, boldness and ingenuity.

The Fords

As economists never tire of pointing out, oil is the lifeblood of our modern economy. One of Uncle Sam's major problems is the growing energy shortage and the fact that he is dependent for over 20 percent of his needs (this may rise to over 60 percent by the mid-eighties) on foreign sources that at any time can be shut off by political upheaval.

In recent years a major development took place that promised to change this. Oil was struck in America's backyard—Alaska—with indications that the ultimate reserves of the find might double the nation's total current supply. The problem was how to ship the oil deposits found in the Prudhoe fields, northwest of Baffin Bay, to the lower forty-eight states at an economically feasible cost.

To tackle the problem, Humble Oil, the Standard Oil of New Jersey subsidiary, in the summer of 1969 launched a program bent on realizing the age-old dream of navigators to send a vessel through the ice fields of the Northwest Passage and open up a shortcut route for commercial shipping.

In making the experiment, Humble outfitted a tanker, the SS *Manhattan,* with extrapowerful engines and a bow strengthened with specially thick steel designed to plow through Arctic icebergs. A critical piece of equipment was a complex radar system which mapped the polar ice pack, warned of dangerous floes ahead and enabled the tanker to accomplish man's first successful commercial trip through the Northwest Passage.*

Key components for this system were made by the Ford Motor Company, a firm which is better known for turning out products no more esoteric than Falcon and Thunderbird autos. Actually Ford, through its Philco Division, is engaged in ventures that would impress the most exacting science fiction buff. In addition to radar components for Arctic exploration, Ford has been working with the U.S. Space Agency developing a network of ground systems to support interplanetary spacecraft communications in preparation for the day when passengers will be whisked from the earth to the moon as routinely as they now travel from New York to Boston.

For all its manifold, far-flung activities, the Ford Motor Company, more than any other major firm in the United States, continues to be the story of a single private family. Henry Ford II, the grandson of the founder, in the words of one associate, is "the last of the corporate dictators." Like his grandfather before him, he runs the Ford empire with an iron grip. The current chairman definitely belongs in the category of those descendants who, far from wasting their patrimony, have enlarged it.

He saved the Ford Motor empire from going into bank-

---

* Subsequently this plan was abandoned in favor of building an overland pipeline from Prudhoe Bay to Valdez on the Gulf of Alaska, from which tankers would carry the oil to the West Coast of the United States. Environmentalist groups are fighting the project.

ruptcy. When he left the Navy during World War II to take the helm, the company had been run to the ground through incredible mismanagement. There was no viable accounting system; no audit had been conducted for over twenty-five years. Most of the talented executives had quit under the autocratic regime of Harry Bennett, old Henry's chief operating official. The company's costs were out of proportion to the rest of the industry's. Ford was without a serious research program, and administrative and liaison controls were virtually nonexistent. After the war it was found, for instance, that although the company had stopped making the Ford tri-motor plane some years previously, one department was continuing to manufacture propellers for the plane, unaware of its demise.

Under Henry Ford II, the company has made a noteworthy comeback. Young Henry took a firm that was losing $10,-000,000 a month and turned it into a money-maker, pushing it into the number-two spot in the industry. Ford got rid of deadwood personnel, firing over 1,000 executives. He sold old Henry's rubber plantation in Brazil, as well as his soybean, lumber and mineral properties, which had exerted a serious drain on company earnings.

Henry II's leadership has acted like a shot of adrenalin. He turned around a firm that had been heavily in the red into one earning over $500,000,000 annually. The team of executives he picked to run the day-to-day operations became celebrated on its own. Bob McNamara rose to be president of Ford and went on to become U.S. Secretary of Defense. "Tex" Thornton subsequently founded Litton Industries, a leader in the electronics field.

Today the house that Henry built is doing over $15 billion in sales all over the world. In 1970 it flung the gauntlet down against the tidal wave of small-car imports—the Toyotas, Datsuns and Volkswagens—by unveiling the Pinto, the lowest-priced and smallest four-passenger car to be assembled in the United States. Exploiting the multinational character of their operations to cut costs to the bone, Ford engineers used for the Pinto an engine produced by Ford of Britain and a manual transmission system put out by Ford of Germany.

The company follows an enlightened labor policy; 19 percent of its work force is made up of minority groups. And unlike in previous years, it is maintaining extensive research to stay ahead of events. In 1971 Ford was balked in an attempt to acquire an interest in a leading Japanese auto maker, Toyo Kgoyo Company. There are reports that the headstrong personalities of Henry Ford and Kohei Matsuda, head of the Japanese firm, were at loggerheads. Toyo is the leading manufacturer of an automobile powered by the so-called Wankel rotary engine, developed by German interests and which in the opinion of many engineers will be more adaptable than the conventional piston engine to the antipollution equipment Washington insists the Detroit car makers must adopt in the coming years. Ford, according to some reports, was primarily interested in Toyo in order to obtain the engine. However, with the collapse of the Toyo talks, Ford turned around and bought the license to the Wankel engine directly from the two West German firms who hold the rights to it so as not to be outflanked by advancing technology. Moreover, several years ago Ford engineers invented a sodium sulphur battery, and they are experimenting with a lighter, more efficient electric motor to make possible a standard electric automobile, if the disgust with pollution reaches the point where millions of Americans eventually welcome electrically driven cars—although the firm believes the time is far off.

Alert for new opportunities outside the auto field, Ford has launched a land development company to exploit promising opportunities in real estate. It has acquired over 2,360 acres (part of which was owned by Henry, Sr., including the location of his birthplace and boyhood home), to develop a multimillion-dollar community involving a commercial town center and a residential complex. When the huge project is completed within the next ten or fifteen years, it will be the largest new town development in the state of Michigan.

In short, the Ford Motor Company, like its autos, is rolling along. However, the canny sense Henry has displayed in his business has faltered from time to time in his personal investments. As noted elsewhere, he was enticed by Cuban refugees into plunging $1,000,000 into a sugar enterprise located in a part of Florida that was highly hazardous for cane growing because of the threat of freezes. Ford's investment got chilled when a premature frost destroyed the cane harvest the first year of operations. More recently he has reportedly put money into a casino gambling and tourist complex in the Caribbean that may turn out to be more profitable than the sugar deal but would probably have caused his stolid, conservative grandfather to twitch in his grave.

Unlike Henry, Sr., who had the frugality of an eremite bred into him, Henry II loves the fleshpots, and he has grown quite portly from the infusion of fine wines. Observes a friend, "I think there's a lot of peasant in him"; and another, "I always think of him as Henry the Eighth."

Away from the tensions of the executive suite, Ford's appetite for frolicking is said to be quite keen. When his spirits are high, the cognoscenti allege, he tends to throw his weight around literally as well as figuratively. Stories, especially about his younger days, have bobbed up in the press how during a night of festivities at a chi-chi social club, Ford hurled a pie at the portrait of the august founder and was never allowed to set foot there since; or how, on another convivial occasion, Ford jumped with the members of a jazz band fully clothed into a swimming pool and exhorted the jazz men to continue their melody-making.

Whether or not such tales are pure journalistic fantasies belonging to the fictional apocrypha that crop up around all "hot copy" personalities, the consensus is that Ford has definitely loosened up in recent years. With his first wife, the Catholic Anne McDonnell, Henry led a relatively austere life. But under the breezy influence of his second spouse, the charming Cristina Vettore Austin, Ford has become a notable member of the international jet set. He was forty-two when he first met the red-headed Cristina, the divorced wife of a British navy officer, at Maxim's in Paris. They hit it off immediately. In 1964 Ford and his first wife were divorced. In 1965 he married Cristina and got excommunicated from the Catholic Church, which he had joined upon his marriage to Anne.

A leading business associate of Ford's (relates a Detroit newsman, William Serrin) told how he sat in the boss' office talking with him when he happened to remark to Ford he was on a salad diet to trim his waistline. Besides taking off weight, he confided, the salad intake substantially increased his sexual prowess. Afterward they went to lunch. A waiter asked Ford what he wanted. He glanced over the menu and mumbled, "Salad."

Social watchers have been captivated not only by Ford's social life but also by that of his offspring. One daughter, Anne, married Giancarlo Uzielli, a member of the Rothschild clan, and the couple is living quietly away from the spotlight. However, the other daughter, Charlotte, has had a stormier career. In 1965, when she was twenty-four, she married Stavros Niarchos, the Greek shipping magnate and brother-in-law of Onassis, after a spirited courtship during which Niarchos pursued the Ford family in his yacht, the *Creole,* through the Mediterranean. Charlotte and her father were aboard their own boat, the *Santa Maria,* and society writers speculated whether papa gave the captain orders to steam full speed ahead because Ford was nettled at the thought of acquiring a son-in-law eight years older than he was. In addition to being Charlotte's senior by over thirty years, Niarchos had been divorced from two wives and was currently married to a third. Despite such obstacles, most fathers less wealthy than Ford would have been impressed with a suitor who was pursuing his daughter in the world's largest yacht, decorated with Renoirs and Van Goghs, and who handed out gold cigarette boxes to friends as though they were sticks of gum.

Niarchos finally caught up with the *Santa Maria,* and Ford yielded. The couple had to wait until Niarchos' divorce from his third wife, Eugenia, came through in Juarez, Mexico. Then matters got cracking. Charlotte flew with Niarchos' attorney to Juarez. Niarchos came in on another plane from Canada. The wedding party took over a motel in Juarez. A local judge was summoned to marry the couple, whereupon they hopped a Ford company plane for the Bahamas, where a Boeing 707, which had been chartered by the groom for $40,000, was waiting to fly them to Zurich. From there, the bride and groom transferred to Niarchos' personal Lear jet for the final leg of the voyage to St. Moritz. Here they went into honeymoon seclusion in a hotel. Niarchos owned a chalet in the mountains nearby, but to go there would have been rather awkward since his newly divorced wife, Eugenia, was vacationing there with their children. Charlotte's marriage to Niarchos ended in divorce after the birth of a daughter.

Now fifty-four, earning almost $3,000,000 a year in dividends plus another $500,000 in salary and bonuses, Henry may very well be the last of his tribe to hold his business in such tight personal control. While his son Edsel Ford II, in his early twenties, will probably succeed him at the helm, 60 percent of Ford stock is owned by the public, and it is unlikely he will be able to play the benevolent despot like his father.* Outside professional management is bound to wield increasing power. Henry II is undoubtedly the last of the mold. Indeed, prosperity is taking a swipe at Henry, Sr., in more ways than one. Not only is his business drifting increasingly from the family moorings, but the Ford Foundation has taken a direction which if Henry I were around to witness it would curdle his blood.

No work of old Henry's has evolved in a manner so out of harmony with his philosophy as the Ford Foundation. As noted elsewhere, Henry, Sr., to avoid punishing taxes, hastily set up the foundation into which the bulk of his millions was sluiced tax free. This shelter, over which the family has no direct control (the foundation owns 90 percent of Ford Company stock), has $3 billion assets, dispenses over $200,000,000 in annual largess and is by far the largest private foundation in existence. Moreover, it is having an impact on American society that cannot be measured by its financial muscle alone.

It is up to its ears subsidizing such controversial programs as fighting black ghetto poverty, pushing civil rights, rehabilitating migrant farm workers. The foundation has ladled out money to militant activist groups, financing all manner of stratagems in the arsenal of radical politics. Retorts McGeorge Bundy, the head of the Ford Foundation, when accused of lending financial aid and comfort to black revolutionists: "Do you want us to crawl in a hole and go back to building libraries?" Under Bundy, the foundation has given substantial sums to CORE to spread the gospel of Black Power. It supported the CORE registration drive in Cleveland, resulting in the election of Carl Stokes as the first black mayor of a major American city. On a somewhat lower key, it has financed a wide spectrum of

* Under the 1969 tax law the Ford Foundation must reduce its holdings of Class A nonvoting stock in Ford by 1979, and Ford has begun arranging for the sale of this stock.

black artists and performing groups, including the Negro Ensemble Theatre in New York.

McGeorge Bundy, like Henry Ford II, in whose family name these programs are being financed, is the wealthy inheritor of a textile and banking fortune, with even better social credentials than Henry's. On his father's side he descends from the prestigious Lowells of New England, one of whom, Abbott Lawrence Lowell, played a leading role in sending the Italian anarchists Sacco and Vanzetti to the electric chair.

Bundy's career displays a striking illustration of how to have one's cake and eat it. A bona fide liberal, he became friendly with John F. Kennedy, moved into the White House as the President's Special Assistant for National Security and continued in that position with President Johnson, turning into one of the most unrelenting hawks of the Vietnam War.

Midway in the Johnson administration, Bundy left the White House and emerged as head of the Ford Foundation, shedding the image of the tough hard-liner for the bleeding-heart liberal again. Bundy masterminded the original plan for decentralizing the New York City school system and financed the Ocean Hill-Brownsville project that triggered a major confrontation of black militant groups with white schoolteachers. Remarked one teaching official during the heat of the crisis, "I have a pretty negative attitude toward the high-type foundation planner who is willing to destroy somebody else's children for a Utopian plan which feeds his own ego and doesn't affect his own elitist position."

Bundy faces this criticism with the aplomb that only the scion of a rich old New England family can muster. No one is more aware than he of the irony that an inheritor of a fortune wrested from child labor in the textile mills should be handing out millions to reform the social system. "It is not a very New Englander thing to be doing," he chuckles.

Bundy is merely one example of a curious syndrome that has cropped up in a somewhat less striking fashion in Henry Ford II and other rich inheritors who crave acceptance from the elitist sociologists, economists and other social engineers who have placed their stamp so pervasively on modern society's system of values. Henry Ford II is considerably more liberal than his grandfather. He has an enlightened labor relations program at

Ford, is an advocate of slum rehabilitation and other programs that have become *de rigueur* for the progressive-minded captain of industry.

If this process of transmogrification continues, future Fords, to elude the depredations of social change, may even bob up leading the charge of the sans-culottes.

18

Big Brother and the Gentleman Dunner: J. Paul Getty, Hugh Hefner & Company Plan for Tomorrow

In the early part of the seventeenth century a strange aberration gripped an entire nation. Holland was swept by a mania for buying tulips. Exchanges sprang up in Amsterdam, Rotterdam and Haarlem to deal with bulbs. Prices boomed; one rare species called *Semper Augustus*, which previously had been worth a few pennies, skyrocketed to 5,300 florins ($2,120). The price for an *Admiral Liefken* went to 4,400 florins ($1,700).

The craze infected all classes. A farmer sold his 38-acre farm together with 100 head of cattle for a single specimen of the *Semper Augustus,* convinced its price would continue to soar and he would make a killing. A Haarlem merchant gave half his savings for another rare tulip root. Peddlers, sailors, charwomen from The Hague to Zuider Zee converted their possessions into florins and bought tulips right and left. The Dutch government was convinced the nation had stumbled on the key to perpetual prosperity. The rich all over the world would continue to send to Holland for tulips at fancier and fancier prices, it believed; ultimately the wealth of the entire planet would be drawn, as if by a magnate, to the shores of the Zuider Zee, and poverty would be extinguished in Holland forever.

For a time all went well. Foreigners indeed were as bewitched as Hollanders, and the money for tulips poured in. Triggered by burgeoning prosperity, the prices of necessities, homes and farms rose astronomically. Belief in tulips became an article of national faith, and an intricate code was drawn up to regulate the business. Special functionaries were appointed exclusively to administer the trade. Public notaries changed their titles to tulip notaries and became the most important officials in town.

In the small villages and rural communities which had no trading exchange, the chief tavern was commandeered and landowners and businessmen, dressed in their richest finery, gathered to trade in tulips. Banquets were held to celebrate the biggest transactions of the week. The feasts were attended by hundreds of people, and large vases of tulips in full bloom were placed in the hall as reverently as the ancient Greeks decorated their banquet chambers with statues of pagan gods.

Then suddenly it all ended. The big landowners, who were the growers of the tulips, decided to call it a day. They had kept prices up by quietly rationing the marketing of the bulbs, promoting the notion among the gullible that certain tulip varieties were valuable because they were in short supply or, in some cases, absolutely unique.

Having reaped a financial harvest, the syndicate went short and came to the market with a tremendous supply of new tulips, including many "rare" species the public thought no longer existed. As the news swept the country, panic hit the trading marts. Holders of "rare" tulips who had sold their homes, farms, and businesses for them hunted hysterically for buyers; but the takers vanished into thin air. Within two weeks, a tulip that had brought the equivalent of $900 in American money was going for $100; four weeks later it went for $12. Several months afterward, the seller was lucky if he got 12 cents.

Anger swept the land as men accused their neighbors of egging them into a trap. A few people with foresight, who had reaped fortunes by selling their bulbs while prices were still going up, quietly sent their wealth out of the country, converting it into British pounds, French francs, German real estate. Others who for a brief moment had been catapulted from poverty into wealth were hurled back into obscurity. Rich merchants became street beggars.

Amidst the panic, holders of worthless tulips held public meetings to discuss what to do. They turned to the government for help, sending delegations to the Provisional Council at The

Hague, hoping that this august body would come forward with a solution. To have achieved one would have taken the wisdom of an army of Solomons. Many Hollanders who had bought tulips at peak prices had made contracts to sell them in the expectation of still higher prices. But with the sudden collapse, none of the buyers were willing to live up to the contracts. A few Hollanders who had unloaded their bulbs in time had walked away with all the marbles, while everyone else was left destitute. The question was should the profiteers be allowed to keep their winnings or should they be forced to redistribute them with their neighbors?

The council held meetings, debating the question week after week, and after three months declared it could not arrive at a solution unless it had more information. So another committee of investigation was set up—a favorite device of governments— and it stalled for time, hoping the population would cool off.

The fact was that finding a solution was beyond the collective wisdom of the politicians. The public was left to lick its wounds and pay the price of its fatuousness. Those who had made a financial killing were allowed to keep their profits; those unfortunate enough to be stuck with valueless bulbs had to endure their bankruptcy as stoically as possible.

The debacle of the tulips underlines man's greatest dilemma. What is the true worth of things? Throughout history man has been on the hunt for the most elusive element in life—outside of life itself—a fixed, unchanging measure of value against which he can ensure the security and perpetuity of his material possessions. Like Goethe's Faust who, indulging in round after round of frustrating, unsatisfying pleasures, looks for the one moment in time of such transcendent happiness it would move him to exclaim, *"Verweile doch, du bist so schön* ("Linger awhile, thou art so beautiful"), so man, in his pilgrimage, has been hunting constantly for the bedrock of eternal value underlying all transient treasures.

The futility of this search was understood by one of the world's richest and most powerful men, who saw through the glass not darkly but with bitter clarity. He was Maximilian I, the fifteenth-century Holy Roman Emperor, who during the last four years of his rule over the mightiest imperium on earth insisted on being accompanied wherever he went by a plain oak coffin as a continual reminder of his mortality. He gave strict instructions that upon his death his head be shaved, his teeth extracted, pounded into powder and burned in the chapel of his palace; that his body be covered in silk, dumped into a sack of lime and exposed to the populace to remind it of the vanity of riches. And he ordered his corpse to be placed under the altar of his chapel so that the priest who said the mass would daily trample over his head and his heart.

One manifestation of this transiency of the human regnum is, as we have noted, the brevity of man's money. It has deteriorated at times almost as rapidly as sand through an hourglass. In Rome of the early emperors the chief measure of wealth was the denarius, a coin of virtually the purest silver. By the time the empire was in an advanced stage of disintegration, the silver denarius had been debased to a piece of copper. During the Middle Ages, in his search for the everlasting, man devoted a great deal of his ingenuity toward creating what he considered to be the ultimate standard of value—gold. A group of alchemists appeared who claimed they had discovered a way to make the precious metal, and they were feted by kings, ministers and the general population with an adulation normally reserved for saints.

The alchemists used various tricks to display their magic. They would coat a piece of gold with quicksilver and exhibit it as inferior metal. Then, adding a little aquafortis, which washed the quicksilver off, they would show how the dross metal had been transformed into gold. Or they would hide gold in a crucible with a false bottom, fill it with quicksilver, place it over a fire; and lo, out of the misty heat popped the miraculous lump of gold. It is significant that many of these alchemists were mystics who, in addition to "making gold," claimed they had discovered the Philosopher's Stone, the possession of which led to life everlasting. For the hunt for gold and the search for immortality were merely different manifestations of man's drive for security in a changing, frightening world.

The hunt went on. In feudal times merchants in their search for the most practical barometer of value fixed on salt, a rare delicacy, as a superior measure of exchange. Stores of salt were guarded by townspeople in fortresses as zealously as gold is hoarded in Fort Knox.

Then when trade was opened with Asia, pepper became the rage. The King of Portugal had a monopoly of the business, and constantly in need of cash, he sold the rights to his cargoes while still at sea in return for advances of money. The value of pepper was set by the supply of imports and the prices administered by the merchant syndicates who bought it en route to Europe. Speculation was heavy; pepper was as much a bellwether of the trading exchanges as big steel was in the 1920's and Xerox in the 1960's; and a breed of market forecasters mushroomed up who made a career predicting the course of pepper prices as zealously as "head-and-shoulder" technicians chart stocks in Wall Street today.

With the discovery of the New World and the mineral resources of Mexico, gold—real gold, not the fake metal of the alchemists—was seized upon as the long-sought Philosopher's Stone; and while it was not expected to assure eternal life as in the medievalists' dream, it guaranteed influence, indestructibility on this tiny island of mortality.

So satisfactorily did gold function as a measure of exchange that the nations of Europe hoped in the middle of the nineteenth century to adopt it formally as a standard of trade. A conference was called in 1865, but it was thwarted by France, which insisted on maintaining its own standard of a bimetallism that was fixed by a gold-and-silver ratio. For the better part of the century the French house of Rothschild had been harvesting huge profits by engaging in constant arbitrage operations, playing gold and silver prices off against each other, and these Rothschilds, who were most influential in French monetary councils, prevented the conference from scrapping the bimetal standard and pulling the game from under them.

In the twentieth century nations have fixed on paper money as the Philosopher's Stone. And just as millions in today's lay society have lost their faith in eternity, so the modern Philosopher's Stone is a debased, highly tarnished version of the original, eroded by the acids of skepticism.

Paper money is hardly a new phenomenon. It was introduced into Europe during the thirteenth century when the first paper mill was built at the foot of the French Pyrenees. Until then the secret of making paper had been monopolized by the Chinese and the Arabs. Once the mystery was penetrated and the

making." And everywhere it is exploding in the face of its creator.

In this search for the utopia of unchanging value—oddly enough, the Greek word *utopia* means "nowhere"—contemporary man is entrapped in a world so caught up in change as to make the hunt more frustrating than ever. The wide-sweeping revolution in social institutions is having an incalculable impact upon *Homo sapiens*.

Swept up, among other things, are the traditional hierarchies of social status. With historical foundations in general under assault, it is not surprising that those pillars of the Establishment, the first families of wealth, should be under especially heavy attack.

Traditionally, the Very Rich have been the prime cavaliers of pleasurable living. But in today's crazy quilt pattern of values, the cavalier rich have, in the best Hegelian fashion, been spawning their dialectical opposite—a growing species of young Roundheads with a Puritan humorlessness and a zest for the message.

Sons and daughters of the rich have been displaying a virulence for breaking from tradition that has no counterpart in previous youth rebellions. Even the "lost generation" of the 1920's, which renounced Babbittry with a vengeance, did not turn against every aspect of man's yesterdays. F. Scott Fitzgerald felt there was one thing at least his generation had salvaged from the Wasteland. "We possess together the incommunicable past."

But today's youth have dislodged the past from its hold on posterity. Existentialists, they have annihilated the spectrum of time and foreshortened the universe of experience. The pride of previous generations of heirs in their inheritance was grounded in a sense of time, a feeling for roots, a reverence for property. This has been shattered in today's youth uprising.

The generation gap is indeed nowhere more piquantly exemplified than by the Very Rich. Wealthy young inheritors have been displaying a magnificent contempt for their lineage (while not necessarily renouncing the very handy by-product of the money).

One can pick up almost any newspaper to cite examples. In London recently the press reported that Lady Kathleen Reynolds, the nineteen-year-old daughter of one of Britain's ranking bluebloods, the Duke of Newcastle, a girl who had married and left a London subway guard, was subsequently sentenced by a British judge to two years' probation for giving her new boyfriend a map indicating the layout of the estate of the duchess, her stepmother, disclosing how he could enter and burglarize it.

A number of the opulent younger generation have been leading radical agitators. One militant—at least during her student days—was Josephine Drexel Biddle Duke, a descendant of James Duke, the founder of the tobacco fortune, who amidst a series of confrontations with the power structure led a demonstration through police lines to greet the then Secretary of State Dean Rusk with a shower of garbage and debris when he arrived in New York to deliver an address on the Vietnam War. A dignitary whose limousine was hit by a bag of blood was the State Department's chief of protocol, Angier Biddle Duke, who happened to be Josephine's uncle.

Then there is Diana Oughton, the bluest of bluebloods. One of her great-grandfathers, William Boyce, founded the Boy Scouts of America. Her father was a multimillionaire banker and owner of real estate. Diana was brought up in the horsey society tradition to the nth degree. She was sent to a fashionable finishing school, attending classes with the daughter of Laurance Rockefeller. Even in such a galaxy, she stood out for her family wealth. Her classmates nicknamed her Miss Moneybags.

Gravitating, after graduating Bryn Mawr, into radical politics, she joined the extreme leftist faction, the Weathermen, who were dedicated to the overthrowal of the U.S. power structure by a Maoist-style people's revolution; and she went underground to train in a guerrilla cadre for street warfare.

One Friday morning in March, 1970, Diana and a fellow Weatherman entered the basement of a townhouse at 18 West Eleventh Street in Manhattan and began fiddling with a mess of batteries and detonating caps to make bombs presumably for guerrilla action. Some wires erroneously got crossed, and the house was blown up. Two days later detectives picking their way through the wreckage found the tip of a finger that belonged to Diana's right hand. She was twenty-eight when she died.

Diana's burial took place in the family plot in Dwight, Illinois, where her ancestors lie. When it was over, a neighbor who had known of the parents' anguish over their daughter's activities remarked to the editor of the town newspaper, "It must be a relief, in a way. At least they now know where their daughter is."

The Weathermen, that iconoclastic wing of the student movement that espoused Jacobean terrorism, displayed a pattern of behavior that will fascinate psychologists and sociologists for years to come. They numbered during the peak of their influence only several hundred members, the vast majority of whom were sons and daughters of America's richest families. Indeed, the Weathermen joked that the number-one qualification for membership was that one's father must be earning at least $50,000 a year.

One radical youth leader whose father was a top U.S. utilities magnate and who regularly received a handsome allowance from his indulgent sire remarked about this incongruity: "If (the old man) wants to finance the revolution, that's okay with me." The lad summed up his social program graphically: "Kill all rich people. Break up their cars and apartments." When reminded that his parents were prime candidates, he replied, "Yeah. Bring the revolution home. Kill your parents, that's where it's really at." And still the allowance checks kept coming.

This virulent reaction of the children of the rich has been discussed, debated, rationalized by a variety of pundits. Nicholas von Hoffman, a journalist and student of American high society, believes that the well-heeled Weathermen were not true revolutionaries at all but were merely carrying their patrimonial arrogance into another sphere. "A rich man can afford moral sensibility; he's got the resources to buy a social conscience. . . . In the case of our rich revolutionaries . . . they're young people who grew up accustomed to . . . having their own way." Hoffman and others of his mind believe that the living in communes of filth, the flaunting of bad manners, the uncompromising iconoclasm resulted not from the psychology of the genuine sans-culotte but the laziness and insolence of spoiled children who have been reared to expect servants to make their beds and pick up after them.

In short, with America and Europe shaken to its roots by a welter of conflicting values and large numbers of people, especially the young, questioning the basic assumption on which the society has been run, the future shape of the economy, as well as the political and social organization of the Judaic-Christian world, is hanging in the balance. The savants are being forced to project their judgments not on the basis of historical experience which evolves along rationally predicated lines but on the assumption that past guidelines are no longer reliable for the future and that an increasing factor of randomness could vitiate all attempts at prophecy.

With regard to the financial scene, the tribe of money managers, investment counselors, entrepreneurs are trying valiantly to get a fix on tomorrow. Naturally enough, those who have made millions on their judgment in the past are the most insistent on continuing their proven strategies.

An example is J. Paul Getty, who turned a $15,000,000 estate left by his father into more than $1 billion and who made a good part of this money during the Depression, snatching up undervalued assets at bargain prices. He bought shares in the Tidewater Oil Company in 1932, for instance, for $2.50 a share; and by 1966, each was worth over $300. Getty, who has reached eighty, is protecting his fortune by, among other things, continuing to invest heavily in the stock of his own oil imperium. "I know that goes against the principles of good business; that you should be diversified; that you shouldn't own 80% of one company, you should own 1% of eighty companies."

However, Getty has always pursued a lone-wolf strategy. Oil, he believes, as one of man's key natural resources represents an increasingly attractive investment hedge as the world's expanding population continues to be squeezed by growing needs for energy.

Getty remains one of the few entrepreneurs still committed to the principle that business management by personal owners is more effective than by professional outsiders. He figures that the man who has his own money in a venture is better qualified to make it successful than the most highly trained business graduate turned out by Harvard.

Getty at eighty still looks zestfully forward to the battle. And battle for him is a literal analogy since he believes that the art of the successful business entrepreneur is closely akin to that of the successful general. In either case, he thinks, an effective campaign cannot be conducted by committees but only by a supreme commander.

At the other end of the multimillionaire spectrum is Hugh Hefner, the publisher of *Playboy*, almost forty years Getty's junior, who has made a fortune by astutely gauging the young man's market and who is constantly trying to project trends so that he can stay ahead of this mercurial field, fathoming its wants, its prejudices, its life-style.

Hefner, who is said to be an introspective, restless individual who holes himself up in a forty-eight-room mansion in Chicago bristling with videotape, stereophonic players, movie screens and other electronic ganglia, and who rises in the afternoon, working until late the following morning, has heard the pundits say he has gotten out of touch with the times. Since the first nudie appeared in *Playboy*, sex has erupted on the stage, screen and in pornographic publications with a frankness that makes *Playboy* look like a Sunday school manual. Moreover, the vociferous rejection by current youth of materialistic possessions as the trappings of the Establishment would seem to challenge *Playboy*'s exultant message of hedonism.

But Hefner stands stoutly by his evangelical campaign for the materialistic life, convinced that in the days ahead all the beards in Barbary and communal vegetable growing in Cambridge, Massachusetts, won't wash away man's yen for pagan pleasures, his craving for sunshine in the Bahamas, scuba diving and bunny playgirls.

"The solution to the world's problems," he told a reporter recently "is to . . . give everybody the Good Life." Obviously Hefner hopes that hedonism will be afforded high priority by the social engineers, the Women's Liberationists, the Gay Power population in the years ahead.

The course of events over the next decade, to say nothing of the longer term, is difficult to prognosticate because of several major imponderables. Never before has society experienced a situation where the average man is so successfully asserting his rights, organized as he is into highly effective power blocks that are demanding a redistribution of the world's wealth. The free market play of business and financial forces have never before been tested under such conditions. Never before did mankind have the power to annihilate itself. As more and more nations learn how to make nuclear weapons in cheap abundance, atomic war threatens summarily to end the human experiment and render the financial consultant, the Wall Street chartist, along with the doctor and the minister, obsolete.

Barring an Armageddon, however, the prognosis for tomorrow must project new variations in the struggle for economic power and the shift in the ownership of capital if it is to find an effective haven for private wealth. Already the financially sophisticated are enlarging their grubstake in natural resources empires, putting their money into venture capital operations that hopefully will outpace the debasement of the dollar and exploiting the possibilities of one-stop shopping centers of financial services, for as problems of capital grow more acute in the 1970's, the management of funds will take precedence over the emphasis on production and merchandising, traditionally the major concerns of American industry. The astute investor will exploit the growing business possibilities in environmental control as the nation becomes increasingly worried about pollution. More money will be put into the rapidly spreading communications and transportation revolutions—i.e., into satellite communications in the air and container ships on the seas. Knowledgeable investors will plunge rising sums into new forms of energy; already big money is going into the leasing of nuclear equipment for the utilities industry in the conviction that atomic energy will ultimately become the major generator of electricity.

The future will experience a vast burgeoning of computerized data banks and information-retrieval services, along with, unfortunately, a growing invasion of personal privacy by electronic surveillance.

With a new dimension of social awareness increasingly entering into business relationships, more money will be spent in venture capital operations to help members of minority groups get started in their own businesses and get a larger slice of the capitalist pie. Currently there are less than thirty black-owned banks in America, having total assets of less than $200,000,000, which is less than 2 percent of the assets of one white-owned institution, the Bank of America. There are less than 50 bona fide black millionaires, none of whose fortunes approach a fraction of the wealth accumulated by white Americans. The black fortunes have been made in a very narrow spectrum of businesses—banking, insurance, funeral homes and the black press.

The prospects are that considerably more venture capital money will be forthcoming to lift minority citizens into the position of capitalists in these and other fields. Blacks will not enjoy any real substance of economic power until there are 15,000 millionaires, not just 50, observes Theodore I. Cross, a lawyer and editor of the *Bankers Magazine*:

> In America full economic equality means black men holding stock options and leading syndicates financed on Wall Street executing dramatic takeovers of major corporations. . . . Equality means black people negotiating sale and leasebacks, major mergers, spinoffs and split-ups. Indeed, equality requires a few black people having misunderstandings with their government and breaking anti-trust laws as well as traffic laws.

Not only the black people of the United States but the have-nots around the world will need more money, if not in the form of handouts, which are becoming increasingly unpopular with the taxpapers of the donor country, then through private capital ventures, to lift their economies by the bootstrap and provide higher living standards for the people.

Foreign capital is eagerly awaiting investment in the oil fields of Libya and Nigeria. The only limiting factor is the fear of prohibitive taxes and possible expropriation of property. Niger, which is loaded with uranium deposits, and the resources-rich Congo (recently renamed the Republic of Zaire) are other African markets providing tempting investment opportunities when the political situation stabilizes.

The underdeveloped economies of Latin America will undoubtedly obtain more venture capital from enlightened outside investors in the years ahead. Brazil presents a particularly fascinating opportunity. The nation has historically been fantastically rich in natural resources. At the end of the nineteenth century the Manaus jungles in the northwestern portion of the country provided rubber trees that turned Brazil into a major supplier for the industrial world. Huge fortunes in rubber were hacked out of the steaming jungle, and Brazilians became rich overnight. But then British industrial agents slipped into the jungle, secretly absconded with seedlings of rubber trees, grew them experimentally in Kew Gardens outside of London and shipped them to Malaya to launch a competitive rubber industry that virtually knocked Brazil out of the market.

Despite such industrial sabotage and exploitation by foreign businessmen, a handful of Brazilians managed to become tremendously wealthy in recent decades. Reportedly the wealthiest of them, perhaps the richest in all of Latin America, is Francisco Matarazzo, Jr., who resides in São Paulo, Brazil's chief industrial city. His father, an immigrant from Italy, started out as a peddler of lard, and before he passed on in his eighties, he had accumulated an empire in food, chemicals and textiles consisting of over 300 companies which produce over 1 percent of the nation's entire gross national product. Francisco, one of fourteen children, currently heads this huge vertical complex and is zestfully carrying on his father's strategy of keeping a firm grip on a large chunk of the nation's food and textile supplies.

Not only is an oligarchy of the rich continuing to flourish under Brazil's present military regime but the industrial sector has become an alluring target for outside capital. Brazil represents one of the world's fastest-growing auto markets, and Volkswagen and Mercedes-Benz, as well as the Detroit auto makers, have been pouring heavy sums into plants and equipment.

In recent years West German capital has been moving in with especial velocity. Volkswagen has been investing more money in Brazil than anywhere else overseas. This dramatic influx of deutsche marks into a Latin American country plagued with an unstable currency and inflation seems rather surprising. But German investors rationalize that the money is going into property not into the Brazilian cruzeiro. "Once you put money into buildings and equipment, you aren't so concerned with devaluations," explains a Volkswagen spokesman. "The property keeps its real value."

Looming over the future of Latin America, the United States and, indeed, the entire world is a phenomenon that in recent years has been serving as a major leitmotiv of economies with increasingly ominous overtones. That is the implications of inflation and a relentlessly deteriorating currency, which is the other side of the coin of debased cultural and moral values that have gripped modern societies.

The problem is an exceedingly complex one. Enlightened people agree that there must be some redistribution of national wealth to allow people below the subsistence level to survive. Yet how do we redistribute wealth to meet the demands of some political pressure groups who insist that everyone be guaranteed not only survival but a steadily increasing share of the easy life whether or not he makes any contribution to it? *

The perplexity of a society driven by well-intentioned social goals to force-feed the economy at any price is illustrated most vividly by what has been happening recently in Argentina. Not so long ago the Argentine peso was one of the strongest currencies in South America. But the soaring cost of living, abetted by escalating prices and sharply climbing wages wrested by the powerful labor unions, has thrust the nation into a surrealistic nightmare. To check the debasement of the peso, the government imposed a ceiling on wage increases. Labor unions objected and riots broke out. In the middle of May, 1969, students at the University of Corrientes in Córdoba staged a demonstration to protest the rise of food prices in cafeterias. Labor leaders, angered by the government's freeze on wages, called out workers to join the students, and a full-scale riot erupted. For five hours, from noon to five o'clock in the afternoon, on May 30, the city of Córdoba was in the hands of the mob. The army had to move in with heavy force to restore order.

The government yielded. Bowing to the threat of further violence, it repealed the wage freeze. A succession of civilian governments had previously failed to solve Argentina's inflation and the army had taken over. It was under the administration of El Presidente Lieutenant General Alejandro A. Lanusse, Army Chief of Staff, that the wage ceiling was repealed.

* The writer does not necessarily suggest that the world return to gold as a panacea. He realizes that flexibility must be permitted to allow an economy reasonable expansion. The key is *restraint*. In the absence of gold what do we use as a reliable control mechanism for restraint? The writer is pointing out problems, not offering solutions. The solutions have eluded man for the last 5,000 years.

With the wraps taken off and the economy left to the "good judgment" and "sense of restraint" of labor and business, the economy promptly went to pieces. From January to August, 1971, the government devalued the peso no less than five times. On each occasion, the Minister of Finance assured the people that there wouldn't be another "massive devaluation." The government accompanied the last devaluation of 6.4 percent with an imposition of a 90-percent surtax on 120 foreign imports in an effort to alleviate the nation's serious balance of payments deficit and check the run of foreign investors on its dwindling reserves. Throughout 1971 the peso lost 4 percent of its purchasing power *each month,* winding up in December with a value 50 percent lower than the previous January. Ten thousand dollars' worth of life savings, deposited in an Argentine bank, shrank to $5,000 in the course of those eerie twelve months.

Convinced that runaway inflation had become a way of life and that the peso would be devalued continually, the Argentines turned to IOU's on a truly macabre scale. Half of all purchases were made on credit. To cope with the customer's lack of cash worth anything, merchants began accepting "flying checks"—that is, checks the customer made out that floated to the merchandiser, who in turn floated it to pay for his own supplies, and so on down the line. None of these checks was meant to see the inside of a bank.

Each time the peso was devalued, workers received hefty wage increases to allow them to pay off a portion of their debts. But these pay increases only served to trigger a new round of price increases, plunging the workers still deeper into the red. Quipped a credit officer: "If all these so-called flying checks could . . . take wing, they would blot out the skies over Buenos Aires; day would turn into night."

In short, credit, that formidable instrument of capitalist expansion used to jack up the living standard of Americans from Maine to San Diego, has been pushed to its ultimate in inflation-ridden Argentina.

The one unpardonable blasphemy is defaulting on monthly debt payments. Writes H. J. Maidenberg, the New York *Times* correspondent in Buenos Aires: "A new 'terrorist' organization has taken to the streets recently. Although they are not rightist

or leftist bomb throwers . . . their impact is far more profound than that of the anti-Government guerrillas."

This new cadre refers to itself as the Gentlemen. Its members
dress impeccably in silk top hats, tails, white ties and gloves.
They are "Gentlemen Dunners," and they belong to the Eagle
Eye, an organization of bill collectors which was formed in
1970 and which has proved to be the most formidable bill collection agency the nation has ever had.

The Gentlemen Dunners, appearing suddenly at a home or
shop or office in broad daylight in their top hats and tails, send
a wave of panic through the community without opening their
mouths. For credit has become the survival raft of the citizenry.
Once an Argentine's credit standing is impugned, all he owns
collapses. His home, his clothes, his auto and television set, his
children's education—all have been bought by hiking checks
and piling on debt. Small wonder that the mere appearance of
the Gentleman Dunner at the front porch is enough to trigger
terror.

This Eagle Eye organization is an advance way-station on the
galloping road of inflation. The symbolism is exquisitely apt.
Like the destructive force of inflation which comes garbed in its
early stages in the aura of smiling prosperity, the collector of
the final installment for the debauch comes dressed not as
Death, not as the Destroyer, but as a smiling, impeccably tailored gentleman.

Over the centuries man has tried gold, silver, spices, paper
money as the ultimate measure of value, and now in today's dis-
oriented world—the world of the Gentleman Dunner—he is
being sorely tempted to seize on a new, and perhaps the ultimate, currency, not in yen, dollars, marks, but the currency of
Big Brother, the *patrón* of the managed society who solves all
problems by manipulating them according to dictatorial
decree.

The perils of money debasement are usually seen only as
that. But the issue is far more than an economic problem. The
philosophers and economists of managed money argue that
citizens shouldn't be forced to rely on an intrinsic measure
of value, such as gold, since this value is barbarous and obsolete for current needs. The worth of money, say these advocates, can be safely entrusted to government politicians and

banking officials, who can be depended on in their wisdom, enlightenment and selfless efficiency to preserve the value of your money and mine by controlling and rationing its issue and budgeting the goals for which it will be spent.

There are those, however, who are wary of entrusting their possessions to Big Brother no matter how wise and benevolent he may appear to be. They point out that money is a passport to freedom. Only with money can an individual choose his work, his leisure, his place of living, his entire life-style. Only with money can he travel and live anywhere on earth in whatever society he desires.

When a government decides what the life savings of a citizen shall be worth, thanks to its power to manipulate and debase the currency, it has taken a long step toward the elimination of individual freedom. The government that can no longer give people an honest weight has to resort to manipulating the people into accepting whatever weight it offers. Indeed, a citizen will no longer even ask for an honest accounting if he has been propagandized into believing that two and two equal five.

One is reminded of Winston Smith in George Orwell's nightmarish novel of the ultimate totalitarian society. Smith is the last angry man, the final citizen with a spark of freedom, however feebly enkindled, the last with the courage to dissent, to question, to rebel against Big Brother, who in his infinite wisdom has decided by decree what value to give the currency of thought as well as coin.

But, alas, Winston's rebellion is doomed. He is unable to stand up against the collective wisdom of the social engineers. After being beaten, drugged, cajoled, terrified into acknowledging the supreme authority of the state, he not only accepts its counterfeit currency of propaganda, its paper money of lies, he comes to *love* it for its trickery and fraud. This is the ultimate triumph of the social planners. It is their finest hour.

> He gazed up at the enormous face. Forty years it had taken him to learn what kind of smile was hidden beneath the dark mustache. O cruel, needless misunderstanding! O stubborn, self-willed exile from the loving breast! Two gin-scented tears trickled down the sides of his nose. But it was all right, every-

thing was all right, the struggle was finished. He had won the victory over himself. He loved Big Brother.

Big Brother may indeed be hovering in the wings of tomorrow. If so, he will be far more terrible than the Brobdingnagians of past societies. Despite their faults, the wealthy oligarchs, for the most part, were a less frightening folk. Whatever the future may bring to a world that threatens to disintegrate into spiritual barbarism, one has to regard with a certain affection the archmagnificoes of the human race, those accumulators of elephantine wealth and gargantuan spenders from the legendary Croesus to the very much flesh-and-blood Nubar Gulbenkian.

They have livened the annals with their gaudy capers, their grandiose ambitions to burst the shard of mortality and frolic for a time on the heights of Mount Olympus.

The adventurers in sugar and cattle, the dealers in art and gold, the pursuers of *Admiral Liefkin* tulips, pepper from the Indies, and alchemist's gold, all seek the transcendent hour in the eternal realm of Nowhere. That is the irony. To rephrase Abraham Lincoln, God must really love those who want to be rich; he's made so many of them.

Reference Notes

Chapter 1—For anecdotal material about early American society the writer is indebted to Cleveland Amory's valuable studies *Who Killed Society* (Harper, 1960), *The Last Resorts* (Harper, 1952), *The Proper Bostonians* (Dutton, 1947). Other sources referred to have been Dixon Wecter's *The Saga of American Society* (Scribner, 1937), *The Passing of the Idle Rich* by Frederick Townsend Martin (Doubleday, Page, 1911), *The Right People*, by Stephen Birmingham (Little, Brown, 1968). A provocative study of current American wealth is *The Rich and the Super-Rich*, by Ferdinand Lundberg (Lyle Stuart, 1968). Quotes from Mary Quant and Alexander Plunket Greene come from *The Beautiful People*, by Marylin Bender (Coward-McCann, 1967).

Chapter 2—The quotation of Myers on inflation comes from *Myers' Finance Review* (October 14, 1971), published in Zurich, Switzerland.

Chapter 3—Material on the Salik Bank is based partially on the writer's own researches. For further data, reference is made to "Sterling Bears to Goldbugs," by Dana L. Thomas, *Barron's National Business and Financial Weekly* (November 27, 1967) and "Solid Gold," also by Thomas, *Barron's* (November 8, 1971); also referred to is an interview with Dr. Erdman by Ray Vicker in the *Wall Street Journal* of October 8, 9, 1970. Other references include the 1970 annual report of Western Bancorporation and a letter to Congressman Patman from William A. Burckett, chairman, Security National Bank of Monterey County, California, October 1, 1970.

Chapter 4—Chief source materials for Marguerite Guggenheim's career are Miss Guggenheim's autobiographies, *Confessions of an Art Addict* (Macmillan, 1960) and *Out of This Century: The Informal Memoirs of Peggy Guggenheim* (Dial Press, 1946). Quotation on bidding practices at Sotheby's and Christie's comes from Duncan-Norton-Taylor, *Fortune* (September, 1966).

Chapter 5—Quotation on the "uselessness" of gold is taken from *Gold Today*, by Joachim Joesten (McKay Co., 1954).

Chapter 6—Excellent sources for Monte Carlo history include *The Big Wheel: Monte Carlo's Opulent Century*, by George W. Herald and Edward D. Radin (Morrow, 1963); *Der Zauberer von Homburg und Monte Carlo*, by Conte Egon Caesar Corti (H. Scheffler, 1951); *Revelations of Monte Carlo Roulette*, by J. Cousins Lawrence (T. F. Unwin, 1919). Reference to Ford casino group appears in the *Wall Street Journal* (August 17, September 25, 29, 1970).

Chapter 7—One good source of biographical data on institutional fund managers is *The Money Managers*, edited by Gilbert Edmund Kaplan and Chris Welles (Random House, 1969). For additional material on use of computers in stock market trading, refer to Dana L. Thomas, *Barron's* (August 30, September 6, 1971; March 24, 1969; August 14, 28, 1967; June 28, 1965; June 22, 1964).

Chapter 8—An important source for the abuses of sugar lobbying is Paul Findley, U.S. Congressman from Illinois. (See Findley's, "Sugar, A Sticky Mess," *Reader's Digest* [June, 1965].) For other data on the sugar industry, refer to Dana L. Thomas, *Barron's* (October 12, 19, 1970; April 15, 1968; September 27, 1965; August 20, 1962; July 4, 1960). Additional references to Maine Sugar Industries' operations include the *Congressional Record*, June 16, 1969; February 10, 16, April 14, 1970; also the General Accounting Office Examination into Federal Government Participation in Establishing and Financing a Sugar Processing Plant in Aristook County, Maine.

Chapter 9—A major historical source for the King-Kleberg families is *The King Ranch*, by Tom Lea (Little, Brown, 1957). For further data on tax shelter ranching, refer to Dana L. Thomas, *Barron's* (August 5, 19, 1968; October 6, 1969).

Chapter 10—Perceptive studies of Bludhorn have been made by Chris Welles, *Life* magazine (March 10, 1967); William S. Rukeyser, *Fortune* (March, 1968); *Business Week* (July 5, 1969). Good sources for biographical data on Dr. Hammer include Stanley H. Brown,

Fortune (July, 1968); *New Yorker* (December 1, 1962); *Newsweek* (May 29, 1967).

Chapter 11—Gramco subsidiary ad appeared in the *National Real Estate Investor* (January, 1970). Two recent informative books on Cornfeld are *The Bernie Cornfeld Story,* by Bert Cantor (Lyle Stuart, 1970) and *Do You Sincerely Want to Be Rich?* by Charles Raw, Bruce Page and Godfrey Hodgson (King Press, 1971).

Chapter 12—The writer has drawn from numerous contemporary newspaper and magazine accounts to describe the impact of the collapse of the mark. An excellent autobiography by an American living in Berlin is *Life Among the Surrealists,* by Matthew Josephson (Holt, Rinehart and Winston, 1962). Sources on the Krupp family include *The Arms of Krupp,* by William Manchester (Little, Brown, 1968); *The Incredible Krupps,* by Norbert Muhlen (Holt, 1959); *Krupp: Gesichte Einer Unternehemerfamilie,* by Ernest Schroder (Musterschmidt-Verlag, 1957).

Chapter 13—For an account of the Reis swindle refer to *The Man Who Stole Portugal,* by Murray T. Bloom (Scribner, 1966).

Chapter 14—For other data on diamond trading, see Dana L. Thomas, *Barron's* (April 19, 1965); *Men of Wealth,* by John T. Flynn (Simon & Schuster, 1941); *Forbes* (February 1, 1970); *Green's Commodity Market Comments* (February 23, 1972). For more about Harry Oppenheimer's social views, refer to interview in *U.S. News and World Report* (November 13, 1961). A provocative glimpse into Oppenheimer's private life has been provided by Emily Hahn in the *New Yorker* (September 29, 1956).

Chapter 15—A source used for the postwar reorganization of Japan's economy is *Shoriki, Miracle Man of Japan,* by Edward H. Uhlan and Dana L. Thomas (Exposition, 1957). Good studies of Ibuka and Morita have appeared in *Fortune* (July, 1964); *Business Week* (May 25, 1968); as well as the *New York Times Magazine* (September 10, 1967), latter by Jerrold Schecter.

Chapter 16—The best source on Nubar Gulbenkian is his autobiography *Portrait in Oil* (Simon & Schuster, 1965). Some recent good biographical sources on Agnelli include *Fortune* (August, 1971) and *Time* (January, 1969).

Chapter 17—Sources on Chase's involvement in the attempted Pan Am take-over include the writer's own researches, as well as reports in the financial press. For more on merger financing, refer to the hearings of the House antitrust subcommittee, July 31–August 21, 1969. A source for Henry Ford II's corporate philosophy is *The Human Environment and Business,* by Henry Ford (Weybright and Talley, 1970). Useful books on the Ford family include *Ford: An Unconventional Biography of the Men and Their Times,* by Booton Herndon (Weybright and Talley, 1969). A fine journalistic profile has been provided by William Serrin in the *New York Times Magazine* (October 19, 1969).

Chapter 18—The best account of the tulip swindle appears in *Extraordinary Popular Delusions and the Madness of Crowds,* by Charles Mackay (L. C. Page & Co., 1932). For reference to Miss Duke and the radical students see among other sources the *New York Times Magazine* (February 9, 1969). Neighbor's remark after Diana's burial comes from *Diana, The Making of a Terrorist,* by Thomas Powers (Houghton Mifflin, 1971). Quotation on the uncontrollability of money is taken from *Money and Man,* by Elgin Groseclose (Frederick Ungar, 1961). Quote on Big Brother comes from *1984,* by George Orwell.

Index